Communications in Computer and Information Science 2389

Rationale

The CCIS series is devoted to the publication of proceedings of computer science conferences. Its aim is to efficiently disseminate original research results in informatics in printed and electronic form. While the focus is on publication of peer-reviewed full papers presenting mature work, inclusion of reviewed short papers reporting on work in progress is welcome, too. Besides globally relevant meetings with internationally representative program committees guaranteeing a strict peer-reviewing and paper selection process, conferences run by societies or of high regional or national relevance are also considered for publication.

Topics

The topical scope of CCIS spans the entire spectrum of informatics ranging from foundational topics in the theory of computing to information and communications science and technology and a broad variety of interdisciplinary application fields.

Information for Volume Editors and Authors

Publication in CCIS is free of charge. No royalties are paid, however, we offer registered conference participants temporary free access to the online version of the conference proceedings on SpringerLink (http://link.springer.com) by means of an http referrer from the conference website and/or a number of complimentary printed copies, as specified in the official acceptance email of the event.

CCIS proceedings can be published in time for distribution at conferences or as post-proceedings, and delivered in the form of printed books and/or electronically as USBs and/or e-content licenses for accessing proceedings at SpringerLink. Furthermore, CCIS proceedings are included in the CCIS electronic book series hosted in the SpringerLink digital library at http://link.springer.com/bookseries/7899. Conferences publishing in CCIS are allowed to use Online Conference Service (OCS) for managing the whole proceedings lifecycle (from submission and reviewing to preparing for publication) free of charge.

Publication process

The language of publication is exclusively English. Authors publishing in CCIS have to sign the Springer CCIS copyright transfer form, however, they are free to use their material published in CCIS for substantially changed, more elaborate subsequent publications elsewhere. For the preparation of the camera-ready papers/files, authors have to strictly adhere to the Springer CCIS Authors' Instructions and are strongly encouraged to use the CCIS LaTeX style files or templates.

Abstracting/Indexing

CCIS is abstracted/indexed in DBLP, Google Scholar, EI-Compendex, Mathematical Reviews, SCImago, Scopus. CCIS volumes are also submitted for the inclusion in ISI Proceedings.

How to start

To start the evaluation of your proposal for inclusion in the CCIS series, please send an e-mail to ccis@springer.com

Arun Sharma · Ritu Rani
Editors

Artificial Intelligence and Speech Technology

6th International Conference, AIST 2024
Delhi, India, November 13–14, 2024
Proceedings, Part I

Springer

Editors
Arun Sharma
Indira Gandhi Delhi Technical University for Women
Delhi, India

Ritu Rani
Bhagwan Parshuram Institute of Technology
Delhi, India

ISSN 1865-0929 ISSN 1865-0937 (electronic)
Communications in Computer and Information Science
ISBN 978-3-031-91330-3 ISBN 978-3-031-91331-0 (eBook)
https://doi.org/10.1007/978-3-031-91331-0

This Springer imprint is published by the registered company Springer Nature Switzerland AG
The registered company address is: Gewerbestrasse 11, 6330 Cham, Switzerland

Preface

The field of artificial intelligence (AI) has experienced remarkable progress and groundbreaking innovations, making earlier versions pale in comparison. These advancements have greatly enhanced the capabilities of machine learning, natural language processing (NLP), and deep learning, enabling transformative developments in specialized areas, particularly speech technology. AI is widely utilized in various aspects of speech-related solutions, including speech analysis, representation and modeling, spoken language recognition and understanding, affective speech detection, synthesis and interpretation, the creation of speech interfaces, human factors engineering, emotion recognition in speech, and audio-visual speech processing, among other applications.

This volume contains papers presented during the Sixth International Conference on Artificial Intelligence and Speech Technology (AIST 2024), organized by the Indira Gandhi Delhi Technical University for Women (IGDTUW), India, and held during November 13–14, 2024. Like the previous five editions of the conference (AIST 2019, AIST 2020, AIST 2021, AIST 2022 and AIST 2023), this sixth edition of AIST was a great success, with the participation of experts and authors from countries including Japan, Australia, France, Germany, Hungary, Czech Republic, Myanmar, Uzbekistan, Austria, Vietnam and others.

The Technical Program Committee of AIST 2024 is extremely grateful to the authors who showed an overwhelming response to the call for papers, with over 398 papers received. All submitted papers went through a double-blind peer review process, with each paper being reviewed by 3–4 experts, and finally 55 papers were accepted for publication in the Springer CCIS series. We are thankful to the reviewers for their efforts in assessing the high-quality papers. We are sincerely thankful to the Department of Science and Technology, Government of India, for their support in establishing the Centre of Excellence in AI at IGDTUW, under whose banner AIST 2024 was organized. We are also thankful to ANRF, DST for their support for AIST 2024.

The conference was distinguished by the esteemed presence of delegates representing various industries, academia and renowned institutes. We were honored to welcome Lalit Kumar Awasthi, Vice Chancellor, Sardar Patel University, Mandi, N. Venkata Subramaniam, Quantum India Leader, IBM, Bjöern Schuller, Imperial College London, UK, Samiya Khan, University of Greenwich, UK, Subramaniam Ganesan, Oakland University, USA and Omid Mahdi Ebadati, Kharazmi University, Iran. Monica Mehrotra, JMI, Devendra Kumar, NSUT, Arun Solanki, GBU, S. S. Agrawal emeritus Scientist CSIR and several others graced the occasion as Keynote Speakers or Session Chairs. We would like to extend special thanks and sincere gratitude to the Hon'ble Vice Chancellor, IGDTUW Ranjana Jha for her continued support and guidance. A total of 55 papers were presented by authors hailing from India and various other countries, utilizing both online and offline modalities during the conference. The papers were strategically organized into 7 distinct tracks, each aligning with the specific theme of the respective track. Notably, each track was overseen by appointed session chairs and co-session chairs, ensuring a systematic and focused approach to the proceedings. To recognize outstanding contributions, a Best Paper Award was conferred in each track, acknowledging and celebrating excellence in research and presentation.

We are sure that this colloquy of researchers and experts from academia and industry greatly benefited researchers, students, and faculty. Young scientists and researchers will find the contents of the proceedings helpful to set roadmaps for their future endeavors.

November 2024

Arun Sharma
Ritu Rani

Organization

General Chair

Ranjana Jha	IGDTUW, India

Technical Program Committee Chair

S. S. Agrawal	CSIR, India

Conference Secretary and Convener

Arun Sharma	IGDTUW, India

Organizing Co-chairs

Syed Zulkarnain Idris	Universiti Malaysia Perlis, Malaysia
Ritu Rani	Bhagwan Parshuram Institute of Technology, India

Guest of Honour

L. Venkata Subramaniam	IBM Research, India

Chief Guest

Lalit K. Awasthi	Sardar Patel University, India

Technical Program Committee Co-chairs

Odette Scharenborg	DUT, Netherlands
Chandra Sekhar	IISC Bengaluru, India
Milan Stehlík	Johannes Kepler University Linz, Austria

Shakir Ali	Imam University, Saudi Arabia
Kirti Tyagi	Inha University, Uzbekistan

Publication Chair

Jasdeep Kaur Dhanoa	IGDTUW, India

Publication Co-chair

Deepak Kumar Sharma	IGDTUW, India

Keynote Speakers

Yudong Zhang	University of Leicester, UK
Priyankoo Sarmah	IIT Guwahati, India
Sardar M. N. Islam	Victoria University, Australia
Helmy Bin Abd Wahab	Universiti Tun Hussein Onn Malaysia, Malaysia
Meena Jha	Central Queensland University, Sydney Campus, Australia

Technical Program Committee

Yudong Zhang	University of Leicester, UK
Sardar M. N. Islam	Victoria University, Australia
Meena Jha	Central Queensland University, Sydney Campus, Australia
Nick Campbell	Trinity College Dublin, Ireland
P. C. Ching	Chinese University of Hong Kong, China
Hiroya Fujisaki	Tokyo University, Japan
R. K. Singh	IGDTUW, India
Bin Ma	Institute for Infocomm Research, Singapore
Hsin-Min Wang	Academia Sinica, Taiwan
Ashish Seth	Inha University, Tashkent
Mirna Adriani	UI, Indonesia
Syed A. Hossain	ULAB, Bangladesh
Laurent Besacier	Naver Labs Europe, France
Vinod Shukla	Amity University Dubai, UAE
Ravinder Kumar	Shri Vishwakarma Skill University, India

Sunita Arora	CDAC, India
Ashwani Kumar	IGDTUW, India
Anu Khosla	SAG DRDO, India
S. K. Shrivastava	DRDO, India
S. K. Jain	CFSL, India
Anuj Sharma	Panjab University, India
Deepak Garg	Bennett University, India
Mani Madhukar	IBM India Pvt. Ltd., India
Pramod Yadav	NIT Srinagar, India
Kamini Malhotra	SAG, DRDO, India
Ankush Jain	NSUT, India
Rajesh Kumar	Thapar University, India
Rajesh Tyagi	SRM University NCR, India
Shrddha Sagar	Galgotias University, India
Arun Kumar	IIIT Delhi, India
P. K. Saxena	PSA, PMO, India
Sunil Tyagi	IHQ MOD (Navy), India
Shakir Ali	Imam University, Saudi Arabia
P. K. Dass	IIT Guwahati, India
Omar Farooq	AMU, India
Arun Kumar	Jubail University, Saudi Arabia
Anup Girdhar	Sedulity Solutions, India
Vishal Bhatnagar	NSUT, India
Geeta Sharma	Mewar University, India
Sakriani Sakti	NAIST, Japan
Jianhua Tao	Chinese Academy of Sciences, China
Chiu-yu Tseng	Academia Sinica, Taiwan
Alexey Karpov	SPIIRAS, Russia
Sebastian Stüker	KIT, Germany
Eric Castelli	MICA, Vietnam
Etienne Barnard	NWU, South Africa
Claudia Soria	ILC-CNR, Italy
Lori Lamel	LIMSI, France
Emmanuel Dupoux	EHESS-ENS, France
P. S. Grover	GGSIP University, India
Ashish Khanna	MAIT, India
Sangeeta Arora	AKTU, India
Selvamani K.	Anna University, India
Senthil P.	SRM University Chennai, India
Sanjay Singla	Chandigarh University, India
Purushottam Sharma	Amity University Noida, India
Gagan Tiwari	Chandigarh University, India

Laxmi Ahuja	AUUP, India
Adesh Pandey	KIET, India
Gianluca Valentino	University of Malta, Malta
Nisheeth Joshi	Banasthali University, India
Pratishtha Mathur	Sikkim Manipal University, India
Pradeep Sharma	MANNU, India
Mona Bharadwaj	IBM (I) Pvt. Ltd., India
Khundmir Syed	IBM (I) Pvt. Ltd., India
Kranti Athalye	IBM (I) Pvt. Ltd., India
Shikha Maheshwari	IBM (I) Pvt. Ltd., India
Ruchika Gupta	IBM (I) Pvt. Ltd., India
Vipin Tyagi	JUIT, India
Somnath Chandra	DEITY, India
O. P. Sangwan	GJU Hisar, India
Sandeep Chauhan	Bank of America, India
Vijai Kumar	Ciena India, India
Mayank Singh	JSS, Noida, India
Mamta Mittal	Delhi Skill and Entrepreneurship University, India
Sushil Yadav	Delhi Skill and Entrepreneurship University, India
D. P. Mohapatra	NIT Rourkela, India
P. K. Behera	Utkal University, India
Ajay Rana	Amity University, India
Vineet Kansal	AKTU, India
Amit Prakash Singh	GGSIP University, India
P. K. Yadav	NIT Jammu, India
Kumkum Garg	IIT Roorkee, India
Durga Toshniwal	IIT Roorkee, India
Rajesh Bhatia	PEC University, India
Bindu Narayan	Independent Consultant, USA
Pooja	NIET, India
Sanjeev Sofat	PEC University, India
Suneet Gupta	Bennett University, India
Anubha Gupta	IIIT Delhi, India
Anand Nayyar	Duy Tan University, Vietnam
Kanwalinderjeet Gagneja	Florida State University, USA
Mansaf Alam	Jamia Millia Islamia, India
Monika Mehrotra	Jamia Millia Islamia, India
Iftekhar Raza Khan	Jamia Hamdard University, India
Sourabh Bharti	Munster Technological University, Ireland
Aruna Bhatt	DTU, India
Neha Bansal	British Council, India
Neha Gupta	VIPS, India

Arun Garg	Ramanujan College, India
Garima Jaiswal	Bennet University, India
Rashmi Gandhi	Amity University, India
Chandra Prakash	NIT, India

Local Organizing Committee

Preeti Chauhan	IGDTUW, India
Nonita Sharma	IGDTUW, India
Shalini Arora	IGDTUW, India
Ranu Gadi	IGDTUW, India
N. R. Chauhan	IGDTUW, India
A. K. Mohapatra	IGDTUW, India
Khyati Ahlawat	IGDTUW, India
Mohona Ghosh	IGDTUW, India
Bhawna Narwal	IGDTUW, India
Vibha	IGDTUW, India
Najme Zehra Naqvi	IGDTUW, India
Karuna Kadian	IGDTUW, India
Bhawna Jain	IGDTUW, India
Vijay Kumar Yadav	IGDTUW, India
Rahul Sachdeva	IGDTUW Anveshan Foundation, India
Shreshtha Singh	IGDTUW, India
Deepti Aggarwal	IGDTUW, India
Manushree Gupta	IGDTUW, India
Monalisa	IGDTUW, India

Sponsers

Department of Science and Technology, Government of India

IGDTUW-Anveshan Foundation, India

AI Club, IGDTUW, India

About University

Indira Gandhi Delhi Technical University for Women (IGDTUW) was established by the Govt. of Delhi in May 2013, as a non-affiliating teaching and Research University at Delhi. The aim of the University is to facilitate and promote studies, Research, Technology, Innovation, Incubation and extension work in emerging areas of professional education among women, with focus on Engineering, Technology, Applied Sciences, Architecture and Management with the objective to achieve excellence in these and related fields.

Glimpse of University Awards and Accolades (In the recent past)

NAAC Ranking - It is a matter of immense pride that IGDTUW has been awarded NAAC "A+" Grade in the First Assessment Cycle.

World Times Higher Education Impact Rankings

- IGDTUW made India Proud by being Ranked in the band 101-200 by the prestigious 'Times Higher Education World Impact Rankings for Sustainable Development Goals (SDG-4) i.e. Quality Education
- IGDTUW made India Proud by being Ranked in the band 101-200 by the prestigious 'Times Higher Education World Impact Rankings for Sustainable Development Goal (SDG-5) i.e. Gender Equality

ISO Certification - IGDTUW has become an ISO 9001-2015 Certified University, marking a significant milestone in its journey towards excellence and commitment to quality education.

THE Awards Asia - IGDTUW left a notable mark in the 'THE Awards Asia' in 2022 and 2024, by being shortlisted among the top 8 universities globally in the category of 'Outstanding Support to the Students'.

World's Universities with Real Impact (WURI) Ranking

- It is a matter of immense pride that IGDTUW secured 40th position in the overall "World's Universities with Real Impact (WURI) Ranking" as the Innovative Universities for 2023".
- The University also bagged 8th position in the special category "Entrepreneurial Spirit" of WURI ranking, 2023.

University of the Year Award by FICCI

- IGDTUW has been conferred with the prestigious "FICCI University of the Year Award 2021" (1 to 10 Years Category) for its continuous commitment towards Quality Education
- IGDTUW has been conferred with the prestigious FICCI University of the Year Award 2022 (For Best Placements).

Sushma Swaraj Stree Shakti Samman Award

IGDTUW received Sushma Swaraj Stree Shakti Samman owing to its vision and outstanding commitment.

Lifetime Organization Membership Granted to IGDTUW by IETE

IGDTUW has been granted "Lifetime Organization Membership" by the very reputed organization "The Institution of Electronics & Telecommunication Engineers (IETE)" on 13th September 2022

CSR Top University Innovation Award:

IGDTUW has been conferred with the "CSR Top University in Innovation Award" on 23rd April 2023 for demonstrating excellent contribution to Innovation and Entrepreneurship.

NPTEL Rating

It is a matter of immense pride that IGDTUW has been ranked as the Highest 'AAA' Rating for the NPTEL & Swayam Course.

Plastic Free Campus

IGDTUW has been awarded the Certificate of Appreciation by the Municipal Corporation of Delhi (MCD-Delhi) for "Zero Waste and Zero Plastic Campus" on 23rd April 2023 for efforts towards Environment and Conservation.

Brief About Centre of Excellence – Artificial Intelligence

IGDTUW has established "Centre of Excellence in Artificial Intelligence (CoE-AI)" with the support of the CURIE-AI (Consolidation of University Research for Innovation & Excellence in Women Universities-Artificial Intelligence), an initiative of Department of Science and Technology (DST), GOI under the magnanimous leadership of Dr. (Mrs.) Amita Dev, Honourable Vice Chancellor IGDTUW.

The Centre possesses the state-of-the-art world-renowned NVIDIA DGXA100 SERVER, state-of-the-art AR/VR Lab, E-Studio for recording high quality online video lectures along with other advanced computing facilities featuring the latest software availability and competent manpower available to assist the students in their research work. The Centre fosters self-directed and peer-to-peer learning, promoting continuous education for students. Its mission is to educate both students and faculty about the ever-evolving capabilities of AI, enabling them to pursue their chosen courses and careers.

To achieve this goal, the CoE-AI organizes Summer Internships, workshops, and Faculty Development Programs. Workshops and Internships play a pivotal role in enhancing student's capabilities, enabling them to contribute to various research projects and create innovative prototypes. Furthermore, the Centre offers mentoring support to students, assisting them in the writing high-quality research papers that can be published in prestigious International Conferences and Journals.

The Centre engages students and young researchers in discussions about the evolving relationship between humans and machines. In view of this, various upskilling Sessions are organized time and again via the renowned speakers from reputable Institutions (IIT/NIT/IIITs) and industries to share their expertise and help students stay relevant in the ever-changing technology landscape.

The Centre actively encourages interdisciplinary collaboration in AI research, emphasizing the study of AI social implications. Hence, the Centre hosts the Prestigious International Conferences like Artificial Intelligence and Speech Technology (AIST), International Committee for the Coordination and Standardization of Speech Databases and Assessment Techniques (Oriental-COCOSDA). These conferences provide a platform for experts, researchers, and practitioners to share their latest findings, innovations, and insights in the various domains like Computer Vision, Machine Learning, Deep Learning, Natural Language Processing, Speech Technology etc. This facilitates the dissemination of knowledge and the exchange of ideas.

The Centre remains upfront in fostering collaboration with industrial experts and academicians to stay at the forefront of AI innovation. A number of prestigious collaborations has been established in the academic, research and Industrial front. Centre of Excellence in Artificial Intelligence stands as a beacon of innovation and knowledge dissemination. Through its multifaceted initiatives, it not only equips students and faculty with the latest technologies but also promotes research, collaboration, and international recognition. Its contributions extend beyond the confines of academia, making a lasting impact on the ever-evolving landscape of AI, ultimately shaping the future of this transformative field.

Contents – Part I

Contents – Part II

Analysis Using Hybrid Technologies with Artificial Intelligence

Exploring New Horizons in Computer Vision Research

About the editors

Dr. Arun Sharma completed his PhD Degree in Computer Science from Thapar University, Patiala India in 2009. Prior to this, he did M. Tech. (CSE) from Punjabi University, Patiala in 1997. He has a teaching experience of more than 28 years.

Currently, he is working as Professor - IT and Dean (Academic Affairs) at Indira Gandhi Delhi Technical University for Women (IGDTUW), Delhi. He is also having the additional responsibilities as Managing Director – IGDTUW Anveshan Foundation, an Incubation Centre at IGDTUW. He has also been involved as Coordinator in establishing the Centre of Excellence – Artificial Intelligence with a financial grant of approx. INR 80 million from DST, Govt. of India. He has been the Dean – Examination Affairs (2020-23), Founder Head of the Department – AI and Data Sciences (2020-22) and served as Head – Department of IT (2018-21), Head-Department of CSE (2022-23) and Dy. Dean – Examination Affairs (2025-18), Convener-BoS (2016-20), Admission Nodal Officer JAC during 2020-23 at IGDTUW.

His areas of interests include Machine Learning, Software Engineering, Soft Computing and Big Data. Under his guidance, 16 students have completed their PhD degree. He has published more than 200 papers in SCOPUS/SCI/SCIE indexed international journals and conferences. He is also the author of two books. He is a Senior Member-IEEE and Life Member- CSI.

Dr. Ritu Rani is working as an Assistant Professor in Bhagwan Parshuram Institute of Technology, Delhi affiliated to Guru Gobind Singh Indraprastha University, Delhi. She has worked as Research Associate-III in Center of Excellence- Artificial Intelligence, DST CURIE-AI funded Project at Indira Gandhi Delhi Technical University for Women, Delhi for nearly 3 years. She has more than 10 years of teaching and research experience. She received her Undergraduate Degree (B. Tech in ECE) with distinction from Kurukshetra University in 2010, received her Post graduate degree (M. Tech in ECE) with distinction from Deenbandhu Chhotu Ram University of Science and Technology, Murthal in 2013 and Doctorate Degree (PhD Electronics and Communication Engineering) in 2021 from Guru Gobind Singh Indraprastha University, Delhi. She has published nearly 65 research papers in various renowned International Conferences (IEEE/Springer)/SCI indexed journals/Scopus Indexed journal/UGC listed journals/ESCI Journals. She has published 3 Indian Patents and two of them are granted as well. She has served as an editor for the 4th Artificial Intelligence and Speech Technology 2022 Conference proceedings for IEEE and 5th Artificial Intelligence and Speech Technology 2023 Conference proceedings for Springer. Her research domain includes Image processing, Computer vision, Machine learning, object detection.

Trends and Applications in Speech Processing

Speech Emotion Classification with Acoustic Features Using 1D CNN and LSTM Networks

Yesha Vyas(✉), Shofiya Bootwala, and Neha Soni

Sardar Vallabhbhai Patel Institute of Technology, Vasad 388306, Gujarat, India
{21ce2,21ce14,nehasoni.comp}@svitvasad.ac.in

Abstract. Speech emotion recognition, with its wide range of applications in robotics, customer service, and HCI (human-computer interaction), is being continuously improved using new models, features, and feature extraction mechanisms. This study proposes 3 deep learning models: 1D CNN, 1D CNN combined with LSTM, and 1D CNN combined with BiLSTM, these models exhibit remarkable performance on a merged dataset comprising RAVDESS, TESS, CREMA-D, and SAVEE emotional speech corpora. Furthermore, they demonstrate strong performance when evaluated on individual databases. For reference, experiments using conventional machine learning algorithms, such as SVM, logistic regression, and ensemble methods are also performed on the datasets. The proposed deep learning models leverage a fusion of acoustic features including MFCC, RMSE, and ZCR, for training. Augmentation techniques like noise addition and pitch scaling were employed to enhance the models' robustness. Notably, the proposed 1D CNN model achieves an impressive accuracy of 96% on the combined datasets, outperforming prior studies on merged datasets.

Keywords: Speech emotion recognition · Human computer interaction · Convolutional neural networks · Long-Short Term Memory · Emotion recognition

1 Introduction

Despite the abundance of available communication channels, speech continues to be the most important mode of communication. With its ability to provide both language and paralinguistic clues, it remains the most widely used method of human connection. Human interactions are shaped by the emotions that are deeply ingrained in speech and play a crucial part in everyday communication. Recognizing the subtle emotional undertones in speech is essential to understanding people's mental states and drawing significant conclusions from conversation.

The significance of emotions in speech has led to expanding research in speech emotion recognition (SER), which seeks to identify the underlying emotions conveyed through speakers' speech. In human-computer interaction (HCI) systems,

A. Sharma and R. Rani (Eds.): AIST 2024, CCIS 2389, pp. 3–16, 2025.
https://doi.org/10.1007/978-3-031-91331-0_1

where emotions play a pivotal role [5], SER emerges as a crucial technology. SER has far-reaching applications across various domains, including education, healthcare, business, psychiatry, etc. For instance, it finds utility in market research endeavors aimed at evaluating consumer responses to products, advertisements, or branding messages, as well as in assessing the emotional reactions of individuals in therapeutic or psychological settings.

Despite extensive research, speech emotion recognition (SER) remains challenging due to inherent subjectivity of emotions. The perception of emotions can vary significantly between individuals, resulting in divergent interpretations of the same speech signals. Moreover, speech encompasses many features [31], further complicating the task of determining which features yield optimal results.

A speech emotion recognition system comprises three key stages: preprocessing of speech data, affective feature extraction, and classification of emotions [8]. Data preprocessing involves essential tasks such as normalization and data augmentation. The extraction of crucial speech features containing emotional information includes energy, formant frequency, Linear Prediction Cepstrum Coefficients, pitch, Mel-frequency cepstrum coefficients (MFCC), and modulation spectral features (MSFs) [13,31]. Subsequently, feature vectors are concatenated and fed into classifiers, which are typically classifiers such as Support Vector Machine (SVM), Hidden Markov Model (HMM), and K-Nearest Neighbors (KNN) [34]. Additionally, recurrent neural networks (RNN) [14] and various other deep learning techniques are also popular choices for classification tasks in SER systems.

2 Literature Survey

The research in SER is rich with studies exploring conventional ML approaches with more recent advancements using deep learning techniques. SVM is the most cited conventional ML approach in the SER domain [18]. Gao et al. [7] computed prosodic and spectral features including MFCC, pitch, intensity, ZCR, and LSP to represent the emotive components of speech, subsequently, these features were then used to classify emotions using a linear kernel SVM classifier. The authors identified that varying frame durations and overlaps exert distinct impacts on the outcomes. Consequently, they utilized depth-first search algorithm to determine the optimal parameters. Sinith et al. [30] used MFCC, pitch, and energy as input features and a Support Vector Machine (SVM) classifier. They achieved an accuracy of 75% on the EmoDB dataset [3]. The authors in [26] achieved a higher classification accuracy of 89.80% on the same database [3] by employing frequency, energy, and MFCC features from short-time wavelet signals as input for the same SVM classifier. Furthermore, experiments were performed by Yang et al. [36] to compare TWINsSVM and SSVM (Standard Support Vector Machines). They observed that the former shows more accurate results. Notably, achieving speaker-independent SER is vital as it enhances the model's ability to generalize. Shegokar et al. [28] introduced speaker-independent features derived from continuous wavelet transform and prosodic coefficients.

Liqin Fu et al. [9], on the other hand, adopted a model-centric strategy for speaker-independent SER, utilizing a combined system of Hidden Markov Models (HMM) and SVM. Yu [32] used pitch, energy, and spectrum features, including first formants, LPCC, and MFCC, they observed that Hidden Markov Models (HMM) outperformed other classification algorithms such as k-nearest Neighbors (kNN) and Linear Discriminant Analysis (LDA). Wu et al. [35] combined 3 different classifiers "GMM, SVM, and MLP" using a Meta Decision Tree (MDT) to gauge confidence in recognizing emotions based on arousal and valence dimensions. They used semantic labels and sound-related information as features. Despite having few emotion labels to work with, their method boosted the effectiveness of each classifier by supporting the idea of MDT. FWang et al. [33] explored the use of harmony features to detect emotions in speech. They found that certain differences in harmony features are key in spotting emotional tones. They proposed the use of Fourier parameter (FP) features, which were much better at recognizing emotions compared to using MFCC features. These FP features improved recognition rates by significant margins on databases including the German EMODB [3], Chinese CASIA, and Chinese EESDB.

Deep learning is a widely recognized and popular research domain within machine learning. Naturally, it was used in SER applications, and the results were comparable and even outperformed the traditional machine-learning approaches. Han et al. [11] utilized neural networks for extracting features from raw data, their proposed approach learned affective information from low-level features and led to a 20% relative improvement in accuracy over the approaches of that time. Convolutional Neural Networks (CNNs) are widely used in computer vision and tasks with sequential data, while Recurrent Neural Networks (RNNs) are adept at working with sequential data. Interestingly, in SER, both CNNs and RNNs have demonstrated promising performance [16,19]. Lee et al. [32] proposed an RNN-based SER framework that accounted for long contextual effects in emotional speech as well as the uncertainty of emotion classes. These experiments were performed on the IEMOCAP database [4]. Lim et al. [17] integrated CNNs and RNNs, leveraging the strengths of both architectures. Notably, their approach eschewed traditional hand-crafted features, yet outperformed conventional classification methods prevalent at the time. Zhang et al. [37] proposed a method that demonstrated impressive performance across four datasets including EMO-DB [3], RML, eNTERFACE05, and BAUM-1s. Initially, they extracted 3 channels of log Mel-spectrograms, this was then fed as input to a CNN. High-level features were then learned using a pre-trained AlexNet DCNN model and aggregated through a discriminant temporal pyramid matching (DTPM) strategy. Finally, emotion classification was carried out using a linear SVM. This study emphasized the discovery that leveraging a pre-trained DCNN model, initially designed for image applications, yields satisfactory results in extracting affective speech features.

Recent works in SER have extended research boundaries by proposing innovative approaches and feature representations. Mehmet Bilal [8] proposed the use of a hybrid feature vector where acoustic features including RMS, MFCC, and ZCR were combined with deep features. The ReliefF algorithm was then utilized to filter more relevant features from the hybrid feature vector. Finally, an SVM was used for classifying emotions. The authors in [2] employed various features such as MFCC, log mel-scaled spectrogram, ZCR, chromagram, and RMS as inputs to an ensemble model. This ensemble model combined the predicting ability of 3 different architectures. The first was a 1D CNN followed by Fully Connected Networks (FCN). In the other two, LSTM-FCN and GRU-FCN layers were applied following the CNN layer, respectively. To improve generalization, they used data augmentation techniques which included adding white Gaussian noise, pitch shifting, and stretching. Notably, their approach achieved a very high weighted average accuracy of 99.46% on the TESS dataset. Accuracy remained strong for other datasets as well, reaching 95.42%, 95.62% 93.22%, and 90.47% on EmoDB, RAVDESS, SAVEE, and CREMA-D respectively. These results highlight the effectiveness of the ensemble models in handling diverse tasks. An SER approach inspired from human perception of the analysis of sound was proposed in [29]. The authors claimed that CQT-MSF when used with a 2D CNN provided a time-shift invariant and deformation-insensitive representation of SER. It was discovered through experiments on Berlin EmoDB and RAVDESS databases that CQT-MSF outperformed the mel-scale-based spectrogram and its modulation features. Recently, Rudd et al. [25] explored the effect of the harmonic and percussive components of Mel spectrograms in classifying emotions. They proposed an algorithm for decomposing acoustic features to leverage the mel spectrogram. It resulted in 2D images which were then used to learn deep features using a pre-trained CNN-VGG16 model. Finally, a multi-layer perceptron (MLP) classifier was used to predict the emotion label. Their work achieved an accuracy of 92.79% on EmoDB [3].

3 Proposed Method

3.1 SER Workflow

RAVDESS, TESS, SAVEE, and CREMA-D speech datasets were merged to create a larger, comprehensive speech dataset for our experiments. We focused on classifying seven emotions: sadness, anger, disgust, fear, happiness, neutral, and surprise. Only data corresponding to these emotions were extracted from the individual datasets. The combined dataset was then augmented using techniques such as pitch shifting, noise addition, and a combination of both. To address the imbalance in the number of data points across emotions, particularly, for the surprise emotion, further augmentation was applied to the surprise label. This process resulted in a balanced dataset composed of both original and augmented speech audio. A Python package, libROSA, is used to extract features from the speech signal. The features extracted are Mel-Frequency Cepstral Coefficients (MFCCs), Root Mean Square Energy (RMSE), and Zero Crossing Rate (ZCR). This varied set of acoustic features for each speech signal forms the feature dataset. The CNN-1d model and the LSTM model are trained using these features. Prior work utilizing CNN-1d and LSTM for speech emotion recognition served as the basis for the baseline model that was employed [2]. After testing the accuracy of the model on the testing dataset, the models are fine tuned by adding layers and changing the hyperparameters like learning rate, batch size, etc. The workflow of the proposed SER system can be seen in Fig. 1. The paper's subsequent sections go into greater detail about each step of the procedure.

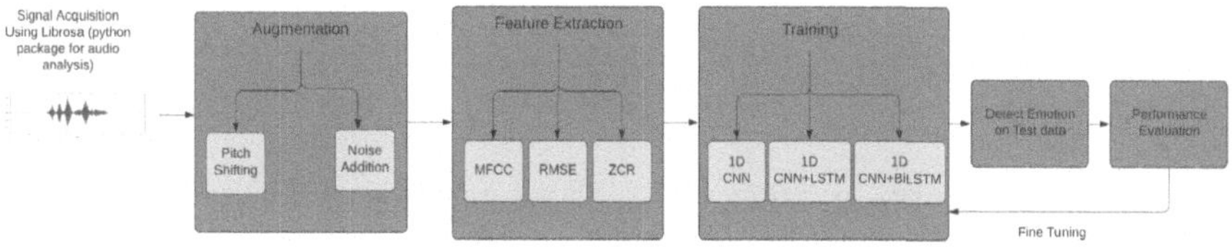

Fig. 1. Generic workflow of the SER system

3.2 Data Augmentation

Data augmentation is used in audio data tasks to solve data scarcity, avoid over-fitting, and make the model more robust [15]. It involves creating modified versions of the existing data by applying various transformations. In audio data, these transformations can be applied to either signals or spectrograms. In [12], by using the warping technique to transform spectrograms, CNN's performance improved. Without increasing the training epochs, these improvements achieved by transforming data, highlight the significance of its use in training neural networks for speech. Building on the data augmentation techniques used in [6], we made minor alterations to speech signals by adding noise and pitch shifting.

To add noise to the training data, we generate random samples with 0 mean and 1 standard deviation. Random samples were scaled by a fixed factor and added to the audio signal. Pitch shifting involves changing the frequency of the speech signal to create an augmented speech signal. We changed the frequency of each audio signal in the training data by a random number to create new data. A combination of noise addition and pitch scaling was also applied to the training data to create augmented speech signals.

3.3 Feature Extraction

To understand the emotional cues in speech, we decompose the signal into its fundamental components by extracting acoustic features. These features are then combined in various ways to identify the most effective configuration for recognizing emotions in speech. In this work, we utilize the popular libROSA library [20] to extract a set of acoustic features from speech samples belonging to different emotional categories. Among the plethora of acoustic features, ZCR, RMS, and MFCC are some of the most promising features to classify emotions from audio, we have utilized this feature set in our experiments. These features are then normalized about their mean for use in subsequent tasks.

Mel-Frequency Cepstral Coefficients (MFCCs) represent a compressed version of the power spectrum on the mel scale, closely resembling human auditory perception [22]. Typically, the first 13 MFCCs are extracted, capturing the most significant spectral information. The feature extraction process of MFCC coefficients can be seen in Fig. 2.

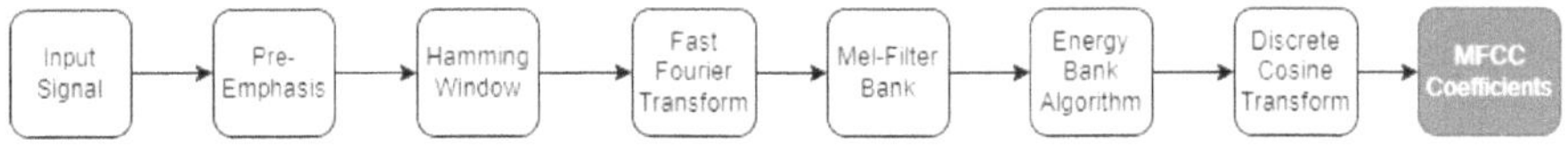

Fig. 2. MFCC feature extraction process

Root Mean Square (RMS) Energy. reflects the overall loudness of the speech signal, calculated as the square root of average squared amplitudes within a short time window. The equation to calculate RMS is mentioned in Eq. 1.

$$RMS = \sqrt{\frac{1}{n}\sum_{i} x_i^2} \tag{1}$$

Zero-Crossing Rate (ZCR). indicates the rate at which the speech signal cuts across the zero amplitude line, reflecting the signal's rapidity of change.

3.4 Classification Methods

Ensembles: The basic idea behind ensemble algorithms is to build a predictive model by integrating many models [24]. Our research explored the effectiveness of ensemble methods for emotion classification using the tools provided by the scikit-learn library's ensemble module.

We employed three ensemble techniques in our approach. First, bagging was used with SVMs as base learners, leveraging their success in sentiment analysis. We further explored Histogram Gradient Boosting, a bagging variant that uses histograms for efficient training. Second, we applied stacking, a two-stage method where base learners (KNN, SVM, bagging classifiers, logistic regression) were trained at Level 0. Their predictions formed a new dataset, used to train a meta-model (SVM at Level 1), combining base learner outputs for enhanced accuracy. Lastly, we implemented voting ensemble classification, combining predictions from KNN, decision trees, SVMs, bagging classifiers, and logistic regression. The optimal configuration was a layered ensemble with a histogram gradient classifier, SVM, KNN, and a decision tree, improving emotion classification accuracy.

1D CNN: One of our proposed models is a 1D CNN model. The normalized acoustic features are stored in an array, creating a vector, which will be our input features. The size of the feature vector is 2376. The model consists of convolutional, max-pooling, batch normalization (BN), and hidden layers. As for the learning rate, it is initialized as 0.00012500, it is then modified using the ReduceLROnPlateau callback function in Tensorflow with a minimum learning rate value being 0.00001. The model is trained for 50 epochs with a batch size of 64, the complete 1D CNN model can be seen in Table 1.

Table 1. 1D CNN proposed architecture

Layer	Architecture with hyperparameters
	Input Size = (35026, 2376)
1, 4	Conv1D, neurons = 512, kernel size = 5, activation function = ReLU, strides = 1
2, 3, 5, 6	Batch Normalization, Max Pooling (pool size = 5, strides = 2)
7	Conv1D, neurons = 256, kernel size = 5, activation function = ReLU, strides = 1
8, 9, 11, 12	Batch Normalization, Max Pooling (pool size = 5, strides = 2)
10	Conv1D, neurons = 256, kernel size = 3, activation function = ReLU, strides = 1
13	Conv1D, neurons = 128, kernel size = 3, activation function = ReLU, strides = 1
14, 15	Batch Normalization, Max Pooling (pool size = 3, strides = 2)
16, 17, 18	Flatten, Dense (neurons = 512, activation function = ReLU), Batch Normalization
19	Dense (neurons = 7, activation function = softmax)
	epochs = 50, batch size = 64, loss function = Categorical Cross Entropy, optimizer = Adam

1D CNN + LSTM: The 1D CNN combined with LSTM, extends the previous 1D CNN architecture by incorporating LSTM layers after the final convolutional layer. The first LSTM layer comprises 256 nodes, followed by another LSTM layer with 128 nodes, culminating in fully connected layers. This model achieves an accuracy of 95.65% on the merged database and demonstrates superior generalization compared to the proposed 1D CNN model. The LSTM layer will be used in the architecture seen in Table 2 for the CNN + LSTM model. The 1D CNN + LSTM model has the same combination of hyperparameters as the 1D CNN model.

1D CNN + BiLSTM: Bidirectional LSTM (BiLSTM) is recognized for its ability to capture information from both past and future contexts concurrently, making it advantageous for tasks like speech-emotion recognition. We combined 1D CNN with BiLSTM, replacing the LSTM layers in the 1D CNN

+ LSTM model with bidirectional LSTM layers, keeping the hyperparameters same. Despite its potential, the 1D CNN + BiLSTM model achieves a slightly lower accuracy of 91.41%. Both variants have the same architectures, the only difference in 1D CNN + BiLSTM is that BiLSTM layers replace the LSTM layers of the 1D CNN + LSTM model. The BiLSTM layer will be used in the architecture seen in Table 2 for the CNN + BiLSTM model.

Table 2. 1D CNN+(LSTM/ BiLSTM) proposed architecture

Layer	Architecture with hyperparameters
	Input Size = (35026, 2376)
1, 4	Conv1D, neurons = 512, kernel size = 5, activation function = ReLU, strides = 1
2, 3, 5, 6	Batch Normalization, Max Pooling (pool size = 5, strides = 2)
7	Conv1D, neurons = 256, kernel size = 5, activation function = ReLU, strides = 1
8, 9, 11, 12	Batch Normalization, Max Pooling (pool size = 5, strides = 2)
10	Conv1D, neurons = 256, kernel size = 3, activation function = ReLU, strides = 1
13	Conv1D, neurons = 128, kernel size = 3, activation function = ReLU, strides = 1
14, 15	Batch Normalization, Max Pooling (pool size = 3, strides = 2)
16	LSTM/BiLSTM, neurons = 256
17	LSTM/BiLSTM, neurons = 128
18, 19, 20	Flatten, Dense (neurons = 512, activation function = ReLU), Batch Normalization
21	Dense (neurons = 7, activation function = softmax)
	epochs = 50, batch size = 64, loss function = Categorical Cross Entropy, optimizer = Adam

4 Experimental Results and Analysis

To establish a baseline performance for speech emotion recognition, we evaluated a range of classical machine learning algorithms on four publicly available emotional speech databases: RAVDESS, TESS, SAVEE, and Crema-D. Each dataset was preprocessed using 20 MFCC features. We explored various aforementioned algorithms including SVM, Logistic Regression, and ensemble methods like Bagging, HistGradientBoosting, Stacking, and Voting.

Our evaluation of traditional machine learning algorithms revealed ensemble methods achieved the highest accuracy across most datasets among traditional Machine learning models. Notably, the voting ensemble achieved impressive results on TESS (98.93%) and RAVDESS (65.60%), demonstrating its effectiveness in classifying emotional speech. While SVM emerged as the best performing algorithm on the SAVEE dataset (68.69% accuracy), the stacking ensemble yielded the most favorable outcome on CREMA-D (47.31% accuracy). Table 3 states the observed performance of classifying emotions using SVM, Logistic Regression, and aforementioned ensemble methods on TESS, RAVDESS, SAVEE, and CREMA-D databases.

Table 3. Accuracy (%), Precision (%), Recall (%), and F1 Score (%) with MFCCs as input features on traditional machine learning models across different datasets

Dataset	Model	Accuracy	Precision	Recall	F1 Score
TESS	Logistic Regression	94.04	94.06	94.31	94.15
	SVM	98.80	99.08	99.13	99.10
	Bagging	98.66	98.60	98.73	98.66
	Stacking	98.80	98.76	98.86	98.81
	Voting	98.93	98.44	98.60	98.50
RAVDESS	Logistic Regression	50.43	48.49	47.12	47.20
	SVM	61.70	61.50	59.20	59.30
	Bagging	64.70	64.30	62.50	62.70
	Stacking	64.13	64.40	61.90	62.30
	Voting	65.60	60.50	58.40	57.80
SAVEE	Logistic Regression	65.21	62.17	62.25	62.00
	SVM	68.69	64.53	64.91	64.10
	Bagging	65.21	60.41	60.68	60.13
	Stacking	66.08	64.68	62.12	60.05
	Voting	63.47	60.67	59.12	58.50
CREMA-D	Logistic Regression	43.61	42.57	43.25	42.30
	SVM	44.09	43.00	44.00	43.00
	Bagging	46.41	45.60	46.27	45.59
	Stacking	47.31	47.17	47.34	46.18
	Voting	42.54	41.00	43.00	41.00

To improve model generalizability, a combined dataset of RAVDESS, TESS, SAVEE, and CREMA-D was utilized, which included a broader range of emotions. Augmentation techniques were also applied to this dataset, the resulting augmented dataset was then utilized to train and evaluate our proposed deep learning models. We proposed three novel architectures: a 1D convolutional neural network (Conv1D) model, a combined Conv1D-LSTM model, and a combined Conv1D-BiLSTM model. These models utilized ZCR, RMS, and MFCCs as input

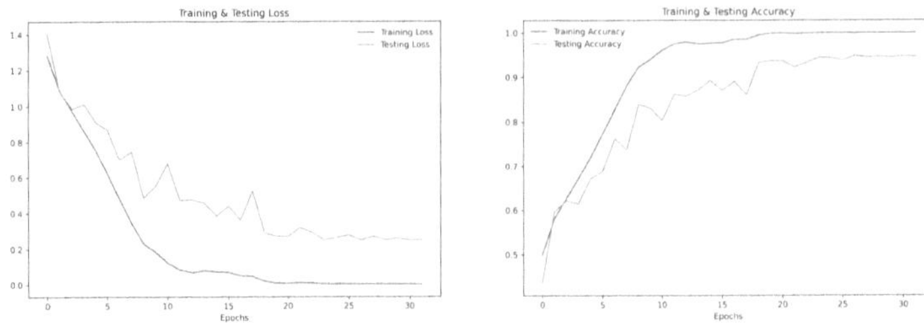

(a)

Fig. 3. (a) Loss and accuracy during training and validation of the combined dataset using CNN

features. The performance of the proposed models on the merged dataset can be observed in Table 4. Figures 3, 4, and 5 depict the loss and accuracy variations with respect to epochs of the proposed deep learning architectures.

Table 4. Accuracy (%), Precision (%), Recall (%), and F1 Score (%) of Combined Dataset Using Proposed Deep Learning Models

Model	Accuracy	Precision	Recall	F1 Score
CNN 1D	96.03	96.20	95.96	96.07
CNN + LSTM	95.65	95.85	95.53	95.68
CNN + Bi LSTM	91.41	91.69	91.28	91.48

Additionally, the best-performing Conv1D model was tested on the individual datasets (RAVDESS, TESS, SAVEE, Crema-D), this evaluation yielded impressive results as seen in Table 5, with the proposed model significantly outperforming all classical approaches, including previously established best performers.

Table 5. Accuracy (%), Precision (%), Recall (%), and F1 Score (%) of Individual Datasets Using the Proposed 1D CNN Model

Datasets	Accuracy	Precision	Recall	F1 Score
TESS	100.00	100.00	100.00	100.00
SAVEE	90.88	92.06	89.84	90.92
CREMA-D	94.83	94.98	94.76	94.89
RAVDESS	91.15	91.51	90.80	91.15

Notably, these deep learning models surpassed even some state-of-the-art (SOTA) models from recent research. This substantial improvement in accuracy across diverse datasets underscores the effectiveness of our proposed deep-learning architectures for SER tasks. We have compared our proposed work with

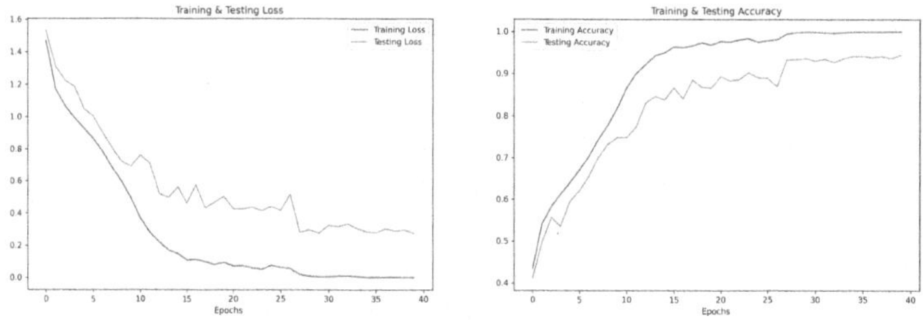

(a)

Fig. 4. (a) loss and accuracy during training and validation of the combined dataset using CNN+LSTM

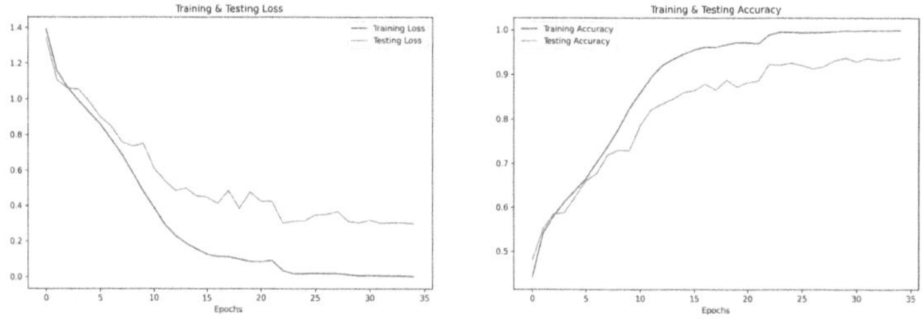

(a)

Fig. 5. (a) loss and accuracy during training and validation of the combined dataset using CNN+BiLSTM

recent literature in Table 6. Note that in Table 6, T refers to the TESS dataset, S refers to the SAVEE dataset, C refers to the CREMA-D dataset and R refers to the RAVDESS dataset.

Table 6. Comparison of this work with recent papers that combine different datasets for SER

Paper	Datasets	Features	Algorithm	Accuracy (%)
[21]	T+S+C+R	Spectral + prosodic	D-CNN	90.27
[1]	T+S	MFCC	CNN+LSTM	84.35
[10]	R+T+S	MFCC+Mel+Chroma+ZCR+RMS	CNN+LSTM	92.73
[23]	T+S+C+R	MFCC+ZCR+Chromagram+Mel Spectrogram+RMS	Meta-learning and CNN+LSTM	90.94
[23]	R+T+S	MFCC+ZCR+Chromagram+Mel Spectrogram+RMS	Meta-Learning and CNN+LSTM	97.37
[29]	R+S+T	MFCC	LSTM + Attention + CNN-2D	90.19
[27]	R+S+T	MFCC	Random Forest	86.3
Proposed	T+S+C+R	MFCC+RMSE+ZCR	CNN 1D	96.03
Proposed	T+S+C+R	MFCC+RMSE+ZCR	CNN + LSTM	95.65
Proposed	T+S+C+R	MFCC+RMSE+ZCR	CNN + Bi LSTM	91.41

5 Conclusion and Future Scope

This paper thoroughly investigates speech emotion recognition, proposing 3 deep learning architectures: CNN 1D, CNN 1D + LSTM, and CNN 1D + BiLSTM. Additionally, traditional ML models such as SVM, logistic regression, and ensembles are analyzed for comparison. Among the proposed models, the CNN 1D model exhibits superior performance, with an accuracy of 96.02% on the merged dataset of RAVDESS, TESS, SAVEE, and CREMA-D, with accuracies of 91.14% on RAVDESS, 99.99% on TESS, 92.45% on SAVEE, and 94.83% on CREMA-D individually.

Additional exploration in the domain could involve the utilization of diverse feature combinations and augmentation techniques. It must be noted that the majority of emotional speech data consists of actor-performed dialogues, and acted speech, real speech differs greatly from acted speech, the models trained on the scripted speech may fail to perform with the same accuracy on speech used in real-life conversations. With a dataset of speech signals gathered from commonplace situations, the model's robustness would be increased by utilizing real emotional speech. Another relevant area to be worked on is addressing cultural differences in SER. The only dataset in the current research that accounts for diversity is CREMA-D.

Application of deep learning models like CNN and LSTM to SER tasks has significantly advanced the domain, this hints at a promising future of easily recognizing complex human emotions from speech. In the future, we hope to develop a model that works well with real-world emotional speech, with consideration of various cultural aspects of the speech.

References

1. Adnan, M.N., Ema, R., Galib, S., Kabir, S., Hazra, S.K.: Emotion recognition of human speech using deep learning method and MFCC features. Radioelectron. Comput. Syst. **2022**, 161–172 (2023)
2. Ahmed, M.R., Islam, S., Muzahidul Islam, A., Shatabda, S.: An ensemble 1D-CNN-LSTM-GRU model with data augmentation for speech emotion recognition. Expert Syst. Appl. **218**, 119633 (2023)
3. Burkhardt, F., Paeschke, A., Rolfes, M., Sendlmeier, W., Weiss, B.: A database of German emotional speech. In: 9th European Conference on Speech Communication and Technology, vol. 5, pp. 1517–1520 (2005)
4. Busso, C., et al.: IEMOCAP: interactive emotional dyadic motion capture database. Lang. Resour. Eval. **42**, 335–359 (2008)
5. Chen, M., Zhou, P., Fortino, G.: Emotion communication system. IEEE Access **5**, 326–337 (2017)
6. Choudhary, R., Meena, G., Mohbey, K.: Speech emotion based sentiment recognition using deep neural networks. In: Journal of Physics: Conference Series, vol. 2236, p. 012003 (2022)
7. Dahake, P.P., Shaw, K., Malathi, P.: Speaker dependent speech emotion recognition using MFCC and Support Vector Machine. In: 2016 International Conference on Automatic Control and Dynamic Optimization Techniques (ICACDOT), pp. 1080–1084 (2016)

8. Er, M.B.: A novel approach for classification of speech emotions based on deep and acoustic features. IEEE Access **8**, 221640–221653 (2020)
9. Fu, L., Mao, X., Chen, L.: Speaker independent emotion recognition based on SVM/HMMS fusion system. In: 2008 International Conference on Audio, Language and Image Processing, pp. 61–65 (2008)
10. Gupta, M., Patel, T., Mankad, S.H., Vyas, T.: Detecting emotions from human speech: role of gender information. In: 2022 IEEE Region 10 Symposium (TENSYMP), pp. 1–6 (2022)
11. Han, K., Yu, D., Tashev, I.: Speech emotion recognition using deep neural network and extreme learning machine. In: Interspeech 2014 (2014)
12. Jaitly, N., Hinton, G.E.: Vocal Tract Length Perturbation (VTLP) improves speech recognition (2013)
13. Jing, S., Mao, X., Chen, L.: Prominence features: effective emotional features for speech emotion recognition. Digit. Signal Process. **72**, 216–231 (2018)
14. Kerkeni, L., Serrestou, Y., Mbarki, M., Raoof, K., Mahjoub, M.A., Cleder, C.: Automatic speech emotion recognition using machine learning. In: Cano, A. (ed.) Social Media and Machine Learning. IntechOpen, Rijeka (2019). Section: 2
15. Ko, T., Peddinti, V., Povey, D., Khudanpur, S.: Audio augmentation for speech recognition, p. 3589 (2015)
16. Lee, J., Tashev, I.: High-level feature representation using recurrent neural network for speech emotion recognition. In: Interspeech 2015. ISCA - International Speech Communication Association (2015)
17. Lim, W., Jang, D., Lee, T.: Speech emotion recognition using convolutional and Recurrent Neural Networks. In: 2016 Asia-Pacific Signal and Information Processing Association Annual Summit and Conference (APSIPA), pp. 1–4 (2016)
18. de Lope, J., Graña, M.: An ongoing review of speech emotion recognition. Neurocomputing **528**, 1–11 (2023)
19. Mao, Q., Dong, M., Huang, Z., Zhan, Y.: Learning salient features for speech emotion recognition using convolutional neural networks. IEEE Trans. Multimed. **16**(8), 2203–2213 (2014)
20. McFee, B.: librosa/librosa: 0.10.1. Zenodo (2023)
21. Mohanty, A., Cherukuri, R.C., Prusty, A.R.: Improvement of speech emotion recognition by deep convolutional neural network and speech features. In: Kumar, S., Sharma, H., Balachandran, K., Kim, J.H., Bansal, J.C. (eds.) Third Congress on Intelligent Systems, pp. 117–129. Springer, Singapore (2023)
22. Muda, L., Begam, M., Elamvazuthi, I.: Voice recognition algorithms using Mel Frequency Cepstral Coefficient (MFCC) and Dynamic Time Warping (DTW) techniques. J. Comput. **2**(3) (2010)
23. Ottoni, L., Ottoni, A., Cerqueira, J.: A deep learning approach for speech emotion recognition optimization using meta-learning. Electronics **12**, 4859 (2023)
24. Rokach, L.: Ensemble-based classifiers. Artif. Intell. Rev. **33**(1), 1–39 (2010)
25. Rudd, D.H., Huo, H., Xu, G.: Leveraged Mel spectrograms using harmonic and percussive components in speech emotion recognition. In: Gama, J., Li, T., Yu, Y., Chen, E., Zheng, Y., Teng, F. (eds.) Advances in Knowledge Discovery and Data Mining, pp. 392–404. Springer, Cham (2022)
26. Seehapoch, T., Wongthanavasu, S.: Speech emotion recognition using Support Vector Machines. In: 2013 5th International Conference on Knowledge and Smart Technology (KST), pp. 86–91 (2013)
27. Shah, N., Sood, K., Arora, J.: Speech emotion recognition for psychotherapy: an analysis of traditional machine learning and deep learning techniques, pp. 0718–0723 (2023)

28. Shegokar, P., Sircar, P.: Continuous wavelet transform based speech emotion recognition. In: 2016 10th International Conference on Signal Processing and Communication Systems (ICSPCS), pp. 1–8 (2016)
29. Singh, J., Saheer, L.B., Faust, O.: Speech emotion recognition using attention model. Int. J. Environ. Res. Public Health **20**(6) (2023)
30. Sinith, M.S., Aswathi, E., Deepa, T.M., Shameema, C.P., Rajan, S.: Emotion recognition from audio signals using Support Vector Machine. In: 2015 IEEE Recent Advances in Intelligent Computational Systems (RAICS), pp. 139–144 (2015)
31. Swain, M., Routray, A., Kabisatpathy, P.: Databases, features and classifiers for speech emotion recognition: a review. Int. J. Speech Technol. **21**(1), 93–120 (2018)
32. Yu, W.: Research and implementation of emotional feature classification and recognition in speech signal. In: 2008 International Symposium on Intelligent Information Technology Application Workshops, pp. 471–474 (2008). Journal Abbreviation: 2008 International Symposium on Intelligent Information Technology Application Workshops
33. Wang, K., An, N., Li, B.N., Zhang, Y., Li, L.: Speech emotion recognition using Fourier parameters. IEEE Trans. Affect. Comput. **6**(1), 69–75 (2015)
34. Wani, T.M., Gunawan, T.S., Qadri, S., Kartiwi, M., Ambikairajah, E.: A comprehensive review of speech emotion recognition systems. IEEE Access **9**, 47795–47814 (2021)
35. Chung-Hsien, W., Liang, W.-B.: Emotion recognition of affective speech based on multiple classifiers using acoustic-prosodic information and semantic labels. Trans. Affect. Comput. **2**, 10–21 (2011)
36. Yang, C., Ji, L., Liu, G.: Study to speech emotion recognition based on TWINsSVM. In: 2009 Fifth International Conference on Natural Computation, vol. 2, pp. 312–316 (2009)
37. Zhang, S., Zhang, S., Huang, T., Gao, W.: Speech emotion recognition using deep convolutional neural network and discriminant temporal pyramid matching. IEEE Trans. Multimed. **20**(6), 1576–1590 (2018)

Analysis of Online Hate Speech Detection for Multilingual and Multimodal Data Using Artificial Intelligence

Navya(✉), Anjum, Neha Rani, and Riya Singh

Indira Gandhi Delhi Technical University for Women, New Delhi, India
rajputnavya.official@gmail.com, anjum@igdtuw.ac.in

Abstract. Online hate speech (OHS) on social networking sites such as Facebook, Instagram, Twitter(now X), WhatsApp, Reddit, etc. has emerged as a growing concern due to its negative psychological and emotional effects on the people and society. This issue is amplified by the enhancement of voices, misinformation, anonymity, and the lack of accountability on social media, where users may not face immediate or tangible consequences for their words. Recognising the detrimental impact of OHS on individual well-being, there is growing interest in developing effective mechanisms for its detection and mitigation. This study presents a comprehensive survey of existing literature on OHS detection for multimodal and multilingual data available on social networking sites. The analysis involves examining available datasets and reviewing 23 most recent research papers published between year 2020 and 2024. The surveyed papers are categorised based on the datasets and approaches used such as traditional machine learning, deep learning algorithms, and other approaches like rule-based and hybrid methods are also explored.

Keywords: social media · hate speech · dataset · techniques · multilingual · multimodal · online hate speech (OHS)

1 Introduction

In contemporary times, social media has seamlessly woven itself into the fabric of everyday life, enabling users to connect and engage globally. Networking sites like Instagram, Facebook (FB), WhatsApp, & X continue to see growing user bases, with 5040 million media members reported in January 2024 [1]. Social media enables users to share their opinions openly, but it often contains misinformation, rumors, trolling, defamation, aggression, abuse, death threats, harassment, cyberbullying, and hate speech targeting individuals or groups based on gender, religion, nationality, race, ethnicity, caste, social status, region, color, age, or society [2]. Example: 1. "Let's kill all jews, they are dirty shit". 2. "I hate muslims, fuck allah". 3. "They said bhraman, i say nange bhikmange". 4. "All muslims are terrorists". 5. "Wipe out Palestine from the world map". These examples shows

A. Sharma and R. Rani (Eds.): AIST 2024, CCIS 2389, pp. 17–26, 2025.
https://doi.org/10.1007/978-3-031-91331-0_2

OHS towards a particular group or religion. The anonymity provided by these platforms exacerbates the issue, as users often use fake accounts to conceal their identities while committing such acts. Hate speech extends beyond text and can also manifest as audio, video, or images.

1.1 Motivation

Detecting as well as eliminating OHS from social networking sites is both crucial and demanding today. It contaminates online communities, infringes upon human rights, and leads to tangible harm, including physical violence, psychological distress, discrimination, anxiety and depression among individuals, both through direct and indirect means. It can escalate to violence, mob lynching, geopolitical tensions between nations, often fueled by religious, political, or regional animosities. A significant challenge in detecting hate speech is its presence in multimodal and multilingual formats, often mixed with vernacular and colloquial language. This paper provides a succinct systematic review of the literature on the detection of hate speech in multi-modal as well as multi-lingual contexts using AI techniques. Our primary contributions to the review are in the following manner:

1. We have examined the modern approaches to detect OHS and performed a comparative study among diverse methods.
2. We have contrasted various models for detecting hate speech in both multilingual and multimodal contexts.

1.2 Methodology

In this paper, we have examined multilingual and multimodal hate speech detection. We began with a systematic literature search using targeted keywords such as "hateful", "offensive", "abusive", "toxic", "aggressive", "cyberbullying", "cyberstalking", "exclusion", "harassment", "trolling", across databases like Google Scholar, IEEE Xplore, ACM Digital Library, Research Gate, & ScienceDirect. This led us to select 23 recent papers in 2020–24 as shown in Fig. 1, providing a comprehensive overview of the field. We examined various OHS datasets from these papers and different social networking sites, gaining insights into certain complexities of detection. Our analysis focused on multimodal datasets (audios, textual, videos & pictorial) and methods (ML, DL, others), simplifying the literature review process. We rigorously evaluated the detection models using metrics like F1-score, recall, accuracy, precision, & AUC-ROC curve to assess their performance across different scenarios.

1.3 Approaches Utilized for Hate Speech Detection

1. **Machine Learning:** Machine Learning (ML) is a subset of AI which entails creating algorithms that learn from data to autonomously make predictions or decisions. Rather than relying solely on programmed instructions, ML

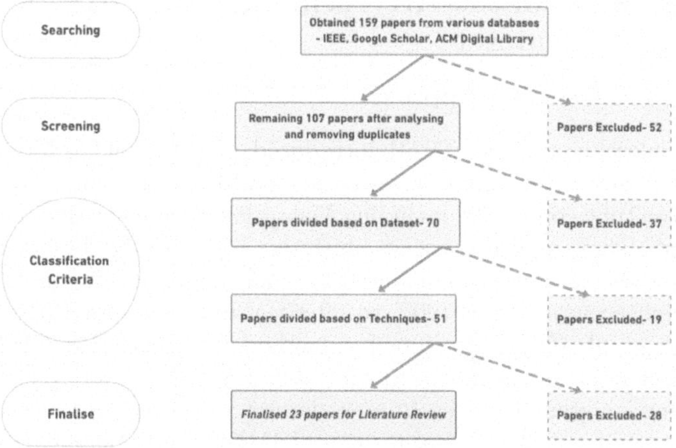

Fig. 1. Retrieval of papers based on datasets and techniques.

algorithms use statistical methods to learn from data and optimize its performance progressively. The main categories of ML include Supervised, Unsupervised, and Reinforcement learning.

2. **Deep Learning:** Deep Learning (DL), a branch of ML which employs deep neural networks to process several data formats like text, picture, & audio. Inspired by the human brain's organization, these networks can manage large datasets and make intricate decisions or predictions. DL has significantly influenced progress in areas such as image and speech recognition, computer vision (CV), natural language processing (NLP), fraud detection, robotics & self-driving vehicles.
3. **Other Approaches:** In addition to ML and DL, various other approaches are used in hate speech detection, often to complement these techniques. Rule-based detection employs predefined rules or patterns, from basic keyword matching to sophisticated linguistic rules. Lexicon-based analysis uses dictionaries of offensive terms to identify hate speech. Network analysis examines user relationships and interactions to identify potential hate speech spreaders or communities. Crowdsourcing and human moderation involve using human judgment and annotations to label hate speech instances for training and validating automated systems. A Hybrid-approach integrates multiple methods, leveraging their strengths to enhance detection accuracy.

The paper's subsequent sections are structured as follows: Sect. 2 delves into the Latest state-of-the-art techniques for OHS detection in Textual dataset, while Sect. 3 focuses on Image dataset. Section 4 covers the Latest state-of-the-art techniques for OHS detection in Audio dataset, and Sect. 5 does so for Video dataset. Section 6 explores the Latest state-of-the-art techniques for OHS detection in Multi-modal dataset, followed by the Conclusion in Sect. 7, Limitations are in Sect. 8, Future Work is in Sect. 9 & References at the end.

2 Latest State-of-the-Art Techniques for OHS Detection in Textual Dataset

2.1 Machine Learning Approach

Vimala Balakrishnan et al. (2023) introduced a methodology for identifying offensive hate speech in Tamil [3], using a Tamil-English (code-mixed) dataset of 43,919 YouTube comments, including Malayalam, Kannada, and Tamil mixed with English. They applied K-means clustering to group the dataset into offensive and non-offensive clusters, followed by undersampling. Ensemble classifiers achieved high accuracy rates (90% to 99.87%) and F1 scores (91% to 100%). Mohsan Ali et al. (2023) developed a method for identifying OHS in Urdu using ML techniques [4], achieving 81.87% accuracy with support-vector-machine (SVM) using unigram features from a dataset of 14,732 instances including Urdu tweets and translated sentiment and IMDB data. Henna Paakki et al. (2024) introduced a technique for OHS detection in English using aggression and trolling datasets, balanced with SMOTE [5]. They utilized natural language inference (NLI)-based tagging for feature extraction, optimizing Random-Forest (RF), K-nearest-neighbour (KNN), Logistic-Regression (LR), & XGBoost models with Random and Bayesian-Search. Their top-performing model achieved macro F1-scores of 0.90 & 0.92 on aggression and trolling datasets, respectively.

2.2 Deep Learning Approach

Angana Chakraborty et al. (2024) developed a method to identify hostile content in Hindi using a dataset of 8,192 data points in Devanagari script [6]. They employed DL frameworks, including PyTorch & Hugging Face transformers, and achieved a macro F1 score 97.21% with their Indic-BERT+Emoji model. Deepawali Sharma et al. (2024) introduced the THAR dataset for identifying anti-religion hate speech in Hindi-English, comprising 11,549 YouTube comments [7]. They employed the multilingual representations for Indian languages (MuRIL) model, achieving a macro-average F1 score 0.78. Sanjay Kumar (2024) [8] addressed negative stances in multilingual dataset (low resource) by translating nine datasets into English and using bi-directional encoder representations from transformers (BERT) & convolutional-neural-networks (CNN) architectures, achieving the best F1 scores for all datasets except German and English.

2.3 Other Approaches

Abhishek Chopra et al. (2023) developed a method to detect OHS in Hindi and Hindi-English code-mixed text, using a translated Hinglish dataset with 11,835 tweets (training) and a dataset containing Devanagiri script with 4,665 posts (testing) [9]. Employing MuRIL for tweet embeddings and principal-component-analysis (PCA) for dimensionality reduction, their Tabnet model achieved 90% accuracy. Sheth et al. (2024) introduced CATCH for cross-platform hate speech detection, using data from GAB, Reddit, X, and YouTube (58,338 posts) [10].

CATCH outperformed other models with accuracies of 0.71 on Reddit and 0.70 on YouTube datasets. Soham Poddar et al. (2024) introduced MuLX-QA for multi-tag hate speech classification utilizing RoBERTa, achieving T-F1 scores of 56.51% on HateXplain and 45.14% on CAVES [11].

3 Latest State-of-the-Art Techniques for OHS Detection in Image Dataset

3.1 Machine Learning Approach

Aruna Bhat et al. (2023) tackled hate speech moderation on social media by developing a multimodal framework that integrates visual and textual cues, using ML models like LR, SVM, and Decision Tree (DT) for classification [12]. Their model, tested on datasets like MMHS150K and a crafted collection of 12,140 hateful memes, achieved 68.32% accuracy and a 73% AUROC on MMHS150K, and an AUROC of 0.83 on social network sites' data. Nitish Babu M et al. (2023) introduced a method using Genetic Programming (GP) for the detection of Hate images, focusing on datasets covering age, ethnicity, and religion [13]. Their GP approach, employing a unique mutation strategy, trained Naive Bayes (NB), RF, and DT models, achieving a 97% accuracy rate, outperforming traditional ML models.

3.2 Deep Learning Approach

Bagas Prakoso Putra et al. (2022) emphasized identifying OHS via image analysis using convolutional algorithms & DL techniques. [14]. Their dataset verified, consisted of 1,223 data entries from X, comprising 578 non-hate & 645 hate speech instances. By employing Optical-Character-Recognition (OCR) & data-preprocessing techniques, their refined CNN model attained a 95% precision rate. Ajay Nayak et al. (2022) focused on detecting OHS within memes, using a Facebook dataset of 9,000 hateful memes [15]. They employed ML models such as visual-geometric-group (VGG16), BERT, residual-neural-network (ResNet), gated-recurrent-unit (GRU), and multi-layer perceptron, highlighting the importance of early detection and multimodal approaches for improved accuracy.

3.3 Others Approaches

Greeshma Arya et al. (2024) emphasized a crucial need to autonomously detect and categorize hate memes that combines images and texts. [16]. They applied Contrastive-Language-Image-Pre-Training (CLIP) model and prompt design training on FB Hate Meme Data. Methodologically, they employed CLIP for feature extraction and classification, refined through prompt engineering and contrastive training, achieving an accuracy of 87.42%.

4 Latest State-of-the-Art Techniques for OHS Detection in Audio Dataset

4.1 Machine Learning Approach

Michael Ibanez et al. (2021) introduced an audio-based hate speech detection approach for TikTok reels, utilizing the TikTok API to collect over 4,746 videos [17]. They extracted features like Chroma values, Spectral Centroid, and MFCCs. Their optimized RF model achieved an accuracy of up to 78.5%, surpassing the 50% benchmark. Mahesh Kumar Nandwana et al. (2024) employed WavLM for OHS detection in audio datasets, integrating a balanced human-annotated set containing 9,795 utterances and an extensive dataset comprising 5,37,311 utterances [18]. Multi-task learning notably enhanced performance of keyword detection, F1 score enhancements spanning from 6.3% to 11.5% and weighted average precision enhancements from 9.4% to 23.8%.

4.2 Deep Learning Approach

Midia Yousefi et al. (2021) introduced an audio-based toxic language classifier using acoustical features, with a dataset of 113,252 and 25,660 of toxic & non-toxic utterances respectively from brief online gaming audio clips [19]. They utilized a Self-Attentive CNN model, demonstrating significant performance enhancements, including a nearly 5% improvement in specific metrics compared to the baseline. Additionally, they achieved a 7% enhancement in the Precision-Recall AUC curve and at least a 2% enhancement in sentiment classification using the IEMOCAP corpus. Their model achieved 75% accuracy, 79% precision, and 80% recall for detecting recordings of hate speech. Robin Matthew Medina et al. (2022) suggested a method to detect OHS in the metaverse utilising a convolutional method, utilizing a dataset consisting of 533 audio recordings [20]. They noted the prevalence of hate speech in this virtual environment and trained a CNN method on a constrained set of OHS (spoken), achieving 96.87% test accuracy.

5 Latest State-of-the-Art Techniques for OHS Detection in Video Dataset

5.1 Machine Learning Approach

Ching Seh Wu et al. (2020) put forward an ML approach for identifying OHS within video datasets. [21]. They utilized a web scraper to gather videos from YouTube containing offensive keywords, including both regular as well as offensive speech terms. Initially, the videos' audio was transcribed into text utilised a speech-to-text transcription generating transcripts for all videos. RF model emerged as the most effective, achieving a 96% accuracy rate.

5.2 Deep Learning Approach

Meriem Mejhed Mkhinini et al. (2022) proposed a DL technique for identifying aggresive content in videos using a 2 layered framework. Their approach achieved 90% accuracy in identifying physical violence through transfer learning in the first layer, and 89% accuracy in detecting verbal violence using a text classifier in the second layer. They address challenges such as limited data and the complexity of classifying lengthy videos. To prevent overfitting, they use a deep-CNN model for feature extraction in physical violence detection and a pre-trained Yamnet model for audio feature extraction and hate speech identification in verbal violence detection. In a similar context, Mithun Das et al. (2023) introduced a multi-modal approach to identify and remove hateful content from video platforms, achieving a macro F1-score of 79.0% and an accuracy of 79.8%, outperforming uni-modal methods by 5.7%.

6 Latest State-of-the-Art Techniques for OHS Detection in Multimodal Dataset

6.1 Machine Learning Approach

Fariha Tahosin Boishakhi et al. (2021) devised multi-modal framework for categorizing content into OHS or non OHS categories, leveraging features wrenched out from audio, image and textual data. [22]. Utilising 1051 videos labeled as Hate or Non-Hate, they evaluated various ML models, including LR, RF, SVM, AdaBoost, KNN, NB, and DT, achieving an accuracy of 87% by combining individual classifiers' outputs through hard voting. In a similar vein, Aruna Bhat et al. (2023) introduced a method for detecting memes containing hate on social media using multimodal analysis. [23]. Collecting 1233 data points from X, with 578 non-hate and 645 hate speech data, their novel architecture integrates visual and textual cues by generating image captions and object tags. They trained models like Gradient Boosted DT and Support Vector Classifier (SVC), with their evaluation demonstrating superior AUROC scores and accuracy contrasted to uni-modal and multi-modal baseline methods.

6.2 Deep Learning Approach

Nishchal Prasad et al. (2023) created a Text-Video-Classifier (TVC) to identify OHS early in footages and the associated comments using features from characters, words, sentences, and video frames [24]. The dataset comprises 969 media sessions, each containing a minimum of 15 comments. Their method employs a Cross-Attention-Fusion Method to grasp inter-modal feature embeddings. Their architecture shows significant improvements over previous models, achieving an AUC-ROC of 78.12%, mean accuracy of 89.04%, and an F1 score of 73.42%.

7 Conclusion

In this study, we analyzed methodologies, datasets, and techniques for detecting OHS on social media. The survey includes latest state-of-the-art methods for images, videos, textual (multilingual), audios, and multimodal datasets using ML, DL, and other approaches like rule-based and hybrid methods. We reviewed new datasets aimed at improving hate speech detection but focused on computer science, not cultural nuances in other languages.

Our findings show LR, SVM, NB, RF, K-means, KNN, and XGBoost are common ML algorithms, while CNN, LSTM, BERT, and MuRIL are prevalent in DL. TF-IDF, Bag-of-words, CNN, and BERT are frequently used for feature extraction. We noted a lack of research on low-resource languages and multimodal datasets. Many authors used self-generated datasets, which are not publicly accessible, complicating validation and analysis. Available datasets are often small, and classification tools for low-resource languages are scarce.

Research on OHS in audio, video, and multimodal format is currently sparse. Challenges include converting audio to text, identifying the context in audios and videos, and handling visual data like memes and sarcasm without captions or text reference. Translation into English and implementing unsupervised learning help address low-resource language challenges. Imbalanced datasets present challenges, as oversampling can result in overfitting and diminished generalization.

8 Limitations

We encountered several obstacles in the domain of online hate speech (OHS) detection. One prominent issue was the scarcity of openly available code and links to self-generated datasets. This lack of accessibility makes conducting comparative studies to evaluate different approaches challenging. Further research based on diverse features and models is needed to address these gaps.

9 Future Work

Further analysis and refinement are needed in online hate speech (OHS) detection. Key steps include addressing noisy data, analyzing text-image combinations, and adjusting parameters to enhance accuracy. Current research relies on limited lexicon-based features, focusing on keywords rather than sentence meaning. Integrating knowledge-based and semantic features could improve accuracy. Areas like audio, video, and multimodal hate speech detection remain underexplored, and diverse, well-rounded datasets are scarce. Social media platforms lack real-time OHS detection, often acting only after content is posted. A real-time detection plugin and multilingual, multimodal datasets are needed to enhance model robustness and create more reliable online environments.

References

1. Smart Insights. New global social media research (2024). Accessed 30 May 2024
2. Chakraborty, A., Joardar, S., Sekh, A.A.: Ensemble classifier for Hindi hostile content detection. ACM Trans. Asian Low-Resour. Lang. Inf. Process. **23**(1) (2024)
3. Balakrishnan, V., Govindan, V., Govaichelvan, K.N.: Tamil offensive language detection: supervised versus unsupervised learning approaches. ACM Trans. Asian Low-Resour. Lang. Inf. Process. **22**(4), 1–14 (2023)
4. Ali, M., Muhammad, A., Asad, M., Sajawal, M., Alexopoulos, C., Charalabidis, Y.: Towards Perso-Arabic Urdu language hate detection using machine learning: a comparative study based on a large dataset and time-complexity. In: Proceedings of the 26th Pan-Hellenic Conference on Informatics, pp. 317–321 (2022)
5. Paakki, H., Vepsäläinen, H., Salovaara, A., Zafar, B.: Detecting covert disruptive behavior in online interaction by analyzing conversational features and norm violations. ACM Trans. Comput.-Hum. Interact. **31**(2), 1–43 (2024)
6. Chakraborty, A., Joardar, S., Sekh, A.A.: Ensemble classifier for Hindi hostile content detection. ACM Trans. Asian Low-Resour. Lang. Inf. Process. **23**(1), 1–17 (2024)
7. Sharma, D., Singh, A., Singh, V.K.: Thar-targeted hate speech against religion: a high-quality Hindi-English code-mixed dataset with the application of deep learning models for automatic detection. ACM Trans. Asian Low-Resour. Lang. Inf. Process. (2024)
8. Kumar, S.: Negative stances detection from multilingual data streams in low-resource languages on social media using BERT and CNN-based transfer learning model. ACM Trans. Asian Low-Resour. Lang. Inf. Process. **23**(1), 1–18 (2024)
9. Chopra, A., Sharma, D.K., Jha, A., Ghosh, U.: A framework for online hate speech detection on code-mixed Hindi-English text and Hindi text in Devanagari. ACM Trans. Asian Low-Resour. Lang. Inf. Process. **22**(5), 1–21 (2023)
10. Sheth, P., Moraffah, R., Kumarage, T.S., Chadha, A., Liu, H.: Causality guided disentanglement for cross-platform hate speech detection. In: Proceedings of the 17th ACM International Conference on Web Search and Data Mining, pp. 626–635 (2024)
11. Poddar, S., Mukherjee, R., Samad, A., Ganguly, N., Ghosh, S.: MuLX-QA: classifying multi-labels and extracting rationale spans in social media posts. ACM Trans. Web **18**(3), 1–26 (2024)
12. Bhat, A., Vashisht, V., Sahni, V.R., Meena, S.: Hate speech detection using multimodal meme analysis. In: 2023 2nd International Conference on Applied Artificial Intelligence and Computing (ICAAIC), pp. 1137–1142. IEEE (2023)
13. Preethi, P., et al.: OCR-based multi-class classification of hate speech in images. In: 2023 First International Conference on Advances in Electrical, Electronics and Computational Intelligence (ICAEECI), pp. 1–6. IEEE (2023)
14. Putra, B.P., Irawan, B., Setianingsih, C., Rahmadani, A., Imanda, F., Fawwas, I.Z.: Hate speech detection using convolutional neural network algorithm based on image. In: 2021 International Seminar on Machine Learning, Optimization, and Data Science (ISMODE), pp. 207–212. IEEE (2022)
15. Nayak, A., Agrawal, A.: Detection of hate speech in social media memes: a comparative analysis. In: 2022 Third International Conference on Intelligent Computing Instrumentation and Control Technologies (ICICICT), pp. 1179–1185. IEEE (2022)
16. Arya, G., et al.: Multimodal hate speech detection in memes using contrastive language-image pre-training. IEEE Access (2024)

17. Ibañez, M., Sapinit, R., Reyes, L.A., Hussien, M., Imperial, J.M., Rodriguez, R.: Audio-based hate speech classification from online short-form videos. In: 2021 International Conference on Asian Language Processing (IALP), pp. 72–77. IEEE (2021)
18. Nandwana, M.K., et al.: Voice toxicity detection using multi-task learning. In: 2024 IEEE International Conference on Acoustics, Speech and Signal Processing (ICASSP), ICASSP 2024, pp. 331–335. IEEE (2024)
19. Yousefi, M., Emmanouilidou, D.: Audio-based toxic language classification using self-attentive convolutional neural network. In: 2021 29th European Signal Processing Conference (EUSIPCO), pp. 11–15. IEEE (2021)
20. Medina, R.M., Njoku, J.N., Kim, D.-S.: Audio-based hate speech detection for the metaverse using CNN, pp. 667–668 (2022)
21. Wu, C.S., Bhandary, U.: Detection of hate speech in videos using machine learning. In: 2020 International Conference on Computational Science and Computational Intelligence (CSCI), pp. 585–590. IEEE (2020)
22. Boishakhi, F.T., Shill, P.C., Alam, Md.G.R.: Multi-modal hate speech detection using machine learning. In: 2021 IEEE International Conference on Big Data (Big Data), pp. 4496–4499 (2021)
23. Bhat, A., Vashisht, V., Sahni, V.R., Meena, S.: Hate speech detection using multimodal meme analysis. In: 2023 2nd International Conference on Applied Artificial Intelligence and Computing (ICAAIC), pp. 1137–1142 (2023)
24. Prasad, N., Saha, S., Bhattacharyya, P.: Multimodal hate speech detection from videos and texts. Technical report, EasyChair (2023)

Unveiling Voices: Deep Learning Based Noise Dissipation with Real-Time Multi-speech Separation and Speaker Recognition

V. Chaitra[1](✉), Meera Reji[2], Meghana Aithal[2], Varshini Gopal[1], and S. S. Shylaja[2]

[1] Department of CSE(AIML), Center for Data Sciences and Applied Machine Learning, PES University, Bangalore, India
chaitrav2020@gmail.com

[2] Department of CSE, Center for Data Sciences and Applied Machine Learning, PES University, Bangalore, India
shylaja.sharath@pes.edu

Abstract. Humans have a remarkable ability to focus on speech even in noisy environments. To replicate this capability computationally, recent research has developed advanced speech enhancement and separation algorithms. This paper presents a comprehensive pipeline integrating several top-notch models for efficient background noise removal, speaker separation, and recognition in audio recordings. Furthermore, our approach exhibits remarkable proficiency in speaker diarization and identification, facilitated by sophisticated feature extraction and classification techniques. Our results demonstrate substantial improvements in audio clarity, speaker separation, and accurate speaker identification. This enhances the capability of our approach for real-time applications in telecommunications, hearing aids, and other audio processing domains. The effectiveness of our method provides a strong proof-of-concept for its real-world applicability, showcasing its potential to revolutionize acoustic applications.

Keywords: Audio classification · Background noise extraction · Speech enhancement · Speaker separation · Speaker Recognition

1 Introduction

In the modern digital era, the proliferation of audio data across various applications has intensified the demand for advanced techniques that enhance the quality and intelligibility of speech signals. Whether in telecommunication systems, hearing aids, voice-controlled interfaces, or virtual meetings, clear and distinct audio output is essential. However, real-world audio recordings often contend with background noise and overlapping speech, presenting significant

A. Sharma and R. Rani (Eds.): AIST 2024, CCIS 2389, pp. 27–54, 2025.
https://doi.org/10.1007/978-3-031-91331-0_3

challenges to effective communication and information extraction. Addressing these challenges requires innovative solutions that can effectively isolate and enhance speech signals in complex acoustic environments.

Humans possess an extraordinary ability to focus on a particular person's voice amidst noisy environments–a phenomenon known as the "cocktail party effect". Replicating this capability technically has long been a goal in audio signal processing. Traditional methods for noise reduction and speaker separation often struggle in dynamic and complex acoustic scenarios. Recent advancements in deep learning have transformed this field, applying complex neural network algorithms to enhance and separate audio signals with acceptable accuracy. This paper explores these advancements, presenting a panoramic approach that expands the boundaries of possibilities in speech processing.

Our proposed pipeline begins with an audio classifier that identifies the type of background noise present. This step paves the way for a more targeted noise removal process. The detected noise is then amplified, making it more perceivable and thus easier to remove from the original audio. The result is a clean signal with enhanced clarity of the desired speech. The final stage of our pipeline precisely separates the cleaned audio into distinct tracks for each speaker. Importantly, during this separation process, speaker recognition is performed to accurately label each speaker's track. This multi-faceted approach ensures that the output is clear and in order for further processing or analysis.

The models used in our pipeline have been extensively trained on synthetic composite audio mixtures sourced from various datasets to generalize across a broad range of audio scenarios effectively. Our results show improvements in both audio clarity and speaker separation, with promising potential for real-time applications across various domains. This research highlights the effectiveness of deep learning in solving complex audio processing challenges and provides a structured approach for future advancements. By replicating humans' selective focus while listening, we lay the foundation for a new era of acoustic applications that can significantly improve communication in noisy environments.

2 Related Work

In this section, we review significant advancements in the field of sound extraction, noise removal, speech separation, and recognition. Recent studies have proposed innovative models and methodologies that enhance performance and efficiency in these areas.

[1] presents Waveformer, a pioneering neural network designed for real-time and streaming target sound extraction. The Waveformer architecture features an encoder-decoder setup with dilated causal convolution layers in the encoder and a transformer layer in the decoder. This structure effectively handles large receptive fields while leveraging the generalization capabilities of transformers. The model demonstrates a significant improvement in SI-SNRi by 2.2–3.3 dB over previous models, with the added advantage of being 1.2–4 times smaller and 1.5–2 times faster. The code, dataset, and audio samples can be accessed at https://waveformer.cs.washington.edu/.

[2] employs spectral subtraction to reduce noise from speech signals within the frequency domain. This technique involves computing the spectrum of noisy speech using the Fast Fourier Transform (FFT) and then subtracting the average magnitude of the noise spectrum. The method was applied to a speech signal labeled "Real graph" with vacuum cleaner noise added. The noise reduction algorithm was executed in Matlab, with noisy speech data stored in Hanning time-windowed, half-overlapped buffers. FFT was used to compute the spectrums, the noise was subtracted, and the speech signal was reconstructed using the inverse FFT (IFFT). The effectiveness of the algorithm was assessed by calculating the Speech to Noise Ratio (SNR). Seventeen different configurations, varying in Hanning window lengths, buffer overlaps, and frame averaging, were tested. The findings indicated that using one-fourth overlapped data buffers with 128-point Hanning windows and no frame averaging achieved the optimal noise reduction performance.

Recurrent Neural Networks (RNNs) have traditionally dominated sequence-to-sequence learning tasks, but their inherent sequential processing limits the potential for parallelization. Transformers, equipped with a multi-head attention mechanism, are gaining recognition as a more effective alternative. [3], introduces SepFormer, a Transformer-based neural network designed for speech separation that completely omits RNNs. SepFormer leverages a multi-scale strategy to capture both short-term and long-term dependencies, achieving cutting-edge results on the WSJ0-2/3mix datasets. Specifically, it reaches an SI-SNRi of 22.3 dB on WSJ0-2mix and 19.5 dB on WSJ0-3mix. By capitalizing on the parallelization capabilities of Transformers, SepFormer operates more efficiently and with lower memory requirements compared to similar systems.

Self-supervised learning (SSL) approaches, such as WavLM, have demonstrated promising results in speech separation (SS) tasks during smaller-scale experiments. In [4], SSL-based SS is expanded by significantly increasing the scale of pre-training to over 300,000 h and fine-tuning with 10,000 h of data. The study also investigates strategies for integrating the pre-trained model with the SS network while adhering to strict computational limits, such as training SSL models at a lower frame rate and employing selective fine-tuning techniques. When compared to a supervised baseline and a WavLM-based SS model trained on 94,000 h of data, the proposed model achieves relative word error rate (WER) reductions of 15.9% and 11.2% for a simulated far-field speech mixture test set. Additionally, for conversation transcription in real meeting recordings, the model achieves relative WER reductions of 6.8% on the AMI evaluation set and 10.6% on the ICSI evaluation set.correspondingly, while reducing computational cost by 38%.

In 2017, Microsoft enhanced its conversational speech recognition system by incorporating advancements in neural network-based acoustic and language modeling techniques. [5] presents the introduction of a CNN-BLSTM acoustic model into the existing framework and improves performance using character-based LSTM and dialog session-aware language models for rescoring. The system utilized a two-stage approach: initially combining acoustic models at the senone/frame level, followed by word-level voting through confusion networks. A further step of confusion network rescoring was applied after the combination. This updated system reached a significant achievement, recording a 5.1% word error rate on the 2000 Switchboard evaluation set.

3 Dataset

Each model in our approach has been trained on exclusive datasets. The CNN classification model, which is trained on dog, keyboard, cat, and cough datasets, has made the classification of these categories easy for noise extraction. This adds to the novelty of our model. This training helps with the efficient spectral subtraction of background sounds. The Waveformer model has been trained on acoustic sounds available in the FSDKaggle2018 dataset and various target sounds obtained from the TAU Urban Acoustic Scenes 2019 Development dataset for noise extraction. The Sepformer models are trained on datasets like WSJ02mix for 2 speakers, WSJ03mix for 3 speakers, and Libri4Mix for 4 speakers separation. The recursion of models helps in the effective separation of speech signals. Speech recognition has been trained on our own dataset to identify the speaker and save the output file in their name, based on speech separation. Thus, the various datasets used to train multiple stages of our project prove beneficial in improving the efficiency of the models.

4 Methodology

A detailed step-by-step analysis and research of the audio files present in the above-mentioned dataset has been conducted for speech enhancement, background noise removal, speaker separation, and recognition. The models used are:

1. Convolutional Neural Network (CNN) and feature extraction from Mel-Frequency Cepstral Coefficients (MFCC)
2. Waveformer
3. Spectral Subtraction
4. Sepformer Separation
5. Speaker Recognition and Separation

5 Model Descriptions

5.1 Convolutional Neural Network (CNN) and Feature Extraction from Mel-Frequency Cepstral Coefficients (MFCC)

The code used is divided into two components:

1) Training a Convolutional Neural Network (CNN) Model: This part involves preparing a dataset, extracting features of noise from audio files, building and training a CNN model to classify audio samples into different categories.
2) Using the Trained Model for Prediction: This part involves loading the trained model and using it to make predictions on new mixed audio samples.

Key Parameters in CNN

5.1.1 Feature Extraction (MFCC)

$$\text{MFCC} = \text{DCT}(\log(\text{Mel-Scale}(\text{STFT}(x)))) \tag{1}$$

The Short-Time Fourier Transform (STFT) transforms a signal from the time domain to the frequency domain. *The Mel-Scale* mimics the human ear's sensitivity to various frequencies. *The Discrete Cosine Transform (DCT)* decorrelates the logarithmic Mel-spectrogram to generate MFCC features.

5.1.2 Building the CNN Model

Conv2D Layer: Performs a 2D convolution operation on the input data.

$$\mathit{Conv2D}(x) = \sigma\left(\sum_{i,j} K_{i,j} \cdot x_{i,j}\right) \tag{2}$$

where: σ represents the ReLU (Rectified Linear Unit) activation function, applied to each element to introduce non-linearity, thereby enabling the model to capture intricate patterns. $K_{i,j}$ represents the convolutional kernel or filter weights that the network learns during training. $x_{i,j}$ represents the input data (in this context, it could be a 2D matrix representing the MFCC features).

MaxPooling2D Layer: Applies a 2D max pooling operation.

$$\mathit{MaxPooling2D}(x) = \max(x_{i,j}) \tag{3}$$

where $x_{i,j}$ represents the values within the pooling window, and the maximum value is taken as output.

Flatten Layer: Flattens the input. It converts the multi-dimensional output of previous layers into a single vector. This vector can then be fed into fully connected layers for classification tasks.

Dense Layer: This layer is fully connected, with each neuron establishing a connection to every neuron in the preceding layer.

$$\mathit{Dense}(x) = \sigma(Wx + b) \tag{4}$$

where W signifies the weight matrix and b stands for the bias.

Dropout Layer: Used during training to prevent overfitting. It selectively disables a fraction of input units during each training iteration, enhancing the model's generalization and reducing reliance on any single neuron.

5.1.3 Model Compilation and Training

Sparse Categorical Crossentropy Loss: Loss function for multiclass classification where the target is integer-encoded.

Adam Optimizer: Adaptive moment estimation optimizer.

Callbacks - Reduce Learning Rate on Plateau: Reduces learning rate when a metric has ceased improving.

Loss Function: Sparse multi-class entropy loss.

$$\text{Loss} = -\sum_{i} y_i \log(p_i) \tag{5}$$

where y_i denotes the actual label and p_i represents the predicted likelihood.

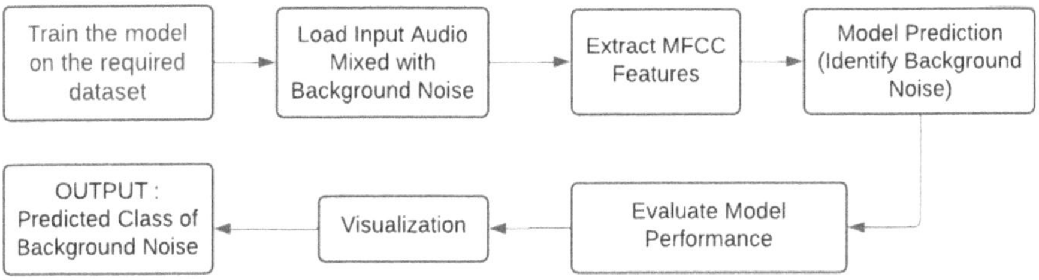

Fig. 1. Flowchart of CNN-Based Background Noise Prediction

Figure 1 outlines the flow of the Convolutional Neural Network (CNN) model used for background noise prediction. The process starts with training the model on a dataset, followed by loading the input audio mixed with background noise. MFCC (Mel-frequency Cepstral Coefficients) features are then extracted, and the model identifies the background noise. The output is visualized, and the model performance is evaluated based on prediction accuracy.

5.2 Waveformer

Waveformer is a sophisticated audio classification model that employs complex neural network architectures designed for audio processing, often involving convolutional, recurrent, or transformer-based layers tailored to handle spectrogram or waveform inputs.

Overview of the Waveformer Code
It handles downloading model configurations and checkpoints, loading and resampling input audio, constructing query vectors for target classes, performing inference based on specified target classes, and saving the resulting classified output audio. This approach provides a versatile tool for extracting sound from audio files into predefined categories efficiently.

Resampling: The code resamples the input audio if its sample rate (*fs*) does not match 44100 Hz using `torchaudio`. This ensures consistency in audio data format before feeding it into the model.

Model Inference:

- `'mixture'`: Input audio data after resampling, loaded into a tensor and shifted to the inferred device (CPU or GPU).
- `'query'`: A binary vector indicating which sound classes from `TARGETS` are present in the input audio. If no targets are specified, initializes `'query'` to ones; otherwise, sets indices corresponding to specified targets to ones.
- `'model'`: The Waveformer model instance loaded with pre-trained weights.
- `'.squeeze(0)'`: Removes the batch dimension after model inference.
- `'.cpu()'`: Moves the tensor back to CPU for further processing and saving.

Argument Parsing: Handles input arguments using `argparse`, allowing users to specify the input audio file, output path, and optionally, target sound classes (`--targets`).

Here are the typical components and equations involved in this model:

5.2.1 Convolutional Layers

They are fundamental to the feature extraction process in neural networks. In the context of Waveformer, these layers are used to extract relevant features from audio spectrograms or waveforms by applying convolutional filters.

$$output[i,j] = \sum_{m,n} input[i+m, j+n] \cdot kernel[m,n] \tag{6}$$

where: *input[i + m, j + n]* represents a small region of the input audio data, typically a patch of the spectrogram or a segment of the waveform.

kernel[m, n] refers to the convolution filter, which is a matrix of learned parameters that moves across the input to identify particular features like edges or textures in images, or frequency patterns in audio. *output[i, j]* is the result of the convolution operation, which captures the presence of these features in different regions of the input.

5.2.2 Recurrent or Transformer Layers

To capture the temporal dependencies and context in audio sequences, Waveformer may utilize recurrent layers, such as Long Short-Term Memory (LSTM) units, or layers based on transformers. These layers are designed to handle sequential data, making them ideal for audio, where the order of sounds is important.

Recurrent Equation:

$$h_t = \sigma(W_h \cdot h_{t-1} + W_x \cdot x_t) \tag{7}$$

where: h_t is the hidden state at time t, which captures the current context of the sequence. h_{t-1} represents the hidden state from the preceding time step, $t-1$, which holds the information from prior steps. W_h and W_x are weight matrices that are learned during training. x_t denotes the input at the present time step *t*. σ is an activation function, typically a sigmoid or tanh, that introduces non-linearity.

Transformer Equation:

$$Attention(Q, K, V) = softmax\left(\frac{QK^T}{\sqrt{d_k}}\right)V \tag{8}$$

where: Q (Query), K (Key), and V (Value) are derived vectors from the input data. The term $QK^\top$ is the dot product of the query and key matrices, which determines the relevance of the input sequences to each other. $\sqrt{d_k}$ is a scaling factor based on the dimensionality of the key vectors, ensuring numerical stability. The *softmax* function normalizes the relevance scores, turning them into probabilities. The output is a weighted sum of the value vectors, enabling the model to concentrate on the key elements of the input sequence.

5.2.3 Fully Connected Layers

Often termed dense layers, these components are responsible for translating the advanced features obtained from convolutional and recurrent layers into the final classification outputs.

$$output = \sigma(W \cdot input + b) \tag{9}$$

where: W represents the weight matrix that links the input features to the output neurons. *input* denotes the feature vector received from the preceding layer. b is the bias term added to the weighted sum. σ is the activation function, commonly a ReLU for hidden layers or a softmax for the output layer.

5.2.4 Loss Function (e.g., Cross-Entropy)

Assesses the disparity between the model's predictions and the actual labels. This metric is essential in training, as it directs the optimization process to modify the model's weights in order to reduce the error between predicted and true values.

Refer to Eq. (5)

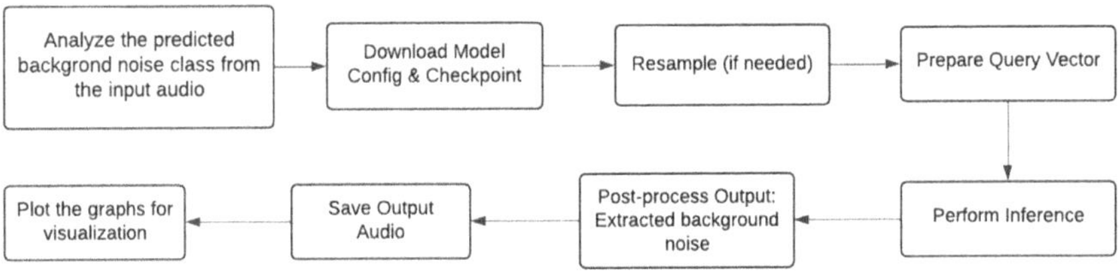

Fig. 2. Flowchart for Waveformer Process

Figure 2 outlines the steps involved in the Waveformer system, which processes input audio to extract background noise. It includes key stages such as analyzing the input audio, downloading the model configuration, preparing a query vector, performing inference, and saving the output audio with optional resampling and post-processing steps.

5.3 Spectral Subtraction

Spectral subtraction technique mitigates noise by removing an approximation of the noise spectrum from the spectrum of the noisy signal. The process involves STFT, magnitude and phase extraction, noise estimation, spectral subtraction, and ISTFT for signal reconstruction. It performs noise reduction on a given noisy audio file using a noise reference and visualizes the results.

Key Parameters in Spectral Subtraction

5.3.1 Padding or Trimming the Signal

Padding: If the noise signal is shorter than the noisy signal, zeros are appended to the end of the noise signal to match the length. This is crucial because, during the spectral subtraction process, both signals need to have the same number of samples for accurate noise reduction.

$$signal_{padded} = [signal, \underbrace{0, 0, \ldots, 0}_{pad\ length}] \tag{10}$$

Trimming: Conversely, if the noise signal is longer, it is truncated to the desired target length. This ensures that the noise estimation process is not affected by extra, irrelevant parts of the noise signal, which could lead to inaccurate noise reduction.

$$signal_{trimmed} = signal[: target\_length] \tag{11}$$

5.3.2 Short-Time Fourier Transform (STFT)

$$STFT(x(t)) = X(k, n) = \sum_{m=0}^{M-1} x(m) \cdot w(n - m) \cdot e^{-j2\pi km/N} \tag{12}$$

where: $STFT$ is employed to convert the time-domain signal into the time-frequency domain representation. Here, $x(t)$ denotes the input signal, $w(n - m)$ represents the windowing function, N is the total number of FFT points, k indicates the frequency bin, and n denotes the time frame.

5.3.3 Magnitude and Phase

Magnitude: The magnitude $|X(k, n)|$ denotes the strength of each frequency component within a specific time frame. It indicates how strong or prominent a particular frequency is within that segment of the signal.

Phase: The phase $\angle X(k,n)$ represents the phase angle of the frequency component, indicating the position of the waveform in its cycle at that specific time frame.

In spectral subtraction, the magnitude is typically the primary focus for noise reduction, as it contains the energy information of the signal. The phase, while less affected by noise, is preserved for signal reconstruction during the inverse process.

5.3.4 Noise Estimate

It is calculated by averaging the magnitude of the noise spectrum over several initial frames. This averaging process helps in obtaining a reliable estimate of the noise that can be subtracted from the noisy signal. The assumption here is that the initial frames are dominated by noise, which provides a good reference for what needs to be subtracted.

$$Noise\ Estimate(k) = \frac{1}{T}\sum_{n=0}^{T-1} |N(k,n)| \tag{13}$$

where: $N(k,n)$ indicates the magnitude spectrum of the noise at frequency bin k and time frame n. T represents the number of time frames used for averaging the noise estimate.

5.3.5 Spectral Subtraction

The core operation where the estimated noise magnitude is subtracted from the magnitude of the noisy signal.

$$|\hat{X}(k,n)| = \max(|X(k,n)| - \alpha|\hat{N}(k,n)|, \beta|\hat{N}(k,n)|) \tag{14}$$

where: $|\hat{X}(k,n)|$ signifies the amplitude of the noisy signal at frequency bin k and time frame n. $|\hat{N}(k,n)|$ indicates the estimated magnitude of the noise spectrum. α is the over-subtraction factor, controlling the amount of noise subtraction. Values of $\alpha > 1$ can help remove more noise but might risk removing parts of the desired signal. β is a parameter that sets the minimum allowable magnitude to prevent negative values, which can occur due to over-subtraction.

5.3.6 Smoothing Factor

The smoothing factor helps to stabilize the noise estimate over time, reducing the impact of sudden changes in noise magnitude. It is especially beneficial in practical situations where noise levels may vary, ensuring that the noise subtraction remains effective and consistent.

$$\hat{N}(k,n) = \gamma\hat{N}(k,n-1) + (1-\gamma)|N(k,n)| \tag{15}$$

where: γ is the smoothing factor, typically between 0 and 1. A higher value of γ gives more weight to the previous estimate, leading to smoother noise estimation. $\hat{N}(k,n)$ is the updated noise estimate at the current time frame n.

5.3.7 Inverse STFT (ISTFT)

The ISTFT combines the modified magnitude with the original phase information to reconstruct the time-domain signal. This step is crucial because it produces the final output, a cleaner version of the original noisy signal with significantly reduced noise. The quality of the reconstructed signal depends on the accuracy of the noise estimate and the effectiveness of the spectral subtraction.

$$x(t) = \sum_{n=0}^{N-1} \text{ISTFT}(X(k, n)) \tag{16}$$

where: *ISTFT* is the process that converts the modified spectral data back into the time domain. The sum is taken over all the time frames to reconstruct the entire signal.

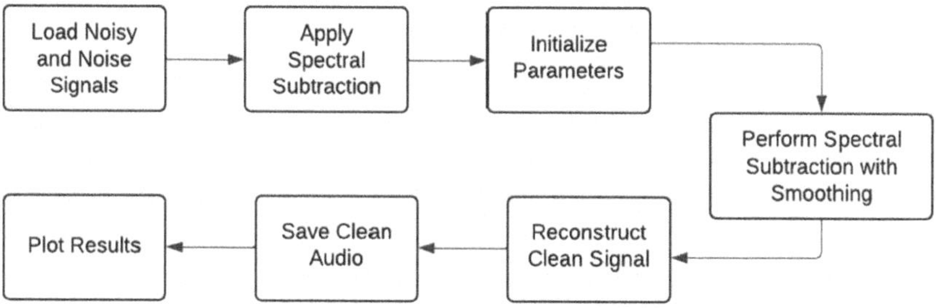

Fig. 3. Flowchart for Spectral Subtraction Process

Figure 3 illustrates the steps in the Spectral Subtraction method used to process noisy audio signals. The process starts by loading noisy and reference noise signals, applying spectral subtraction, and initializing parameters. It then proceeds to perform spectral subtraction with smoothing, reconstruct the clean signal, and save the clean audio. Finally, results are plotted for further analysis.

5.4 Sepformer Separation

Sepformer model is used for audio source separation based on speaker count detection. The code leverages pretrained Sepformer models, specialized for 2, 3, or 4 speaker scenarios, to effectively separate audio sources. After detecting the number of speakers and selecting the appropriate model, the code applies the Sepformer's capabilities to extract individual audio sources, which are then saved as distinct '.wav' files. This approach ensures that complex audio mixtures containing multiple speakers can be separated accurately, demonstrating the utility of advanced deep learning techniques for audio processing tasks in real-world applications.

The General Principles of Sepformer Include

Multi-head Self-attention: Allows the model to concurrently focus on different regions of the input audio spectrogram, capturing complex dependencies between time-frequency bins.

Transformer Encoder Layers: Transform the input audio features into a latent space conducive to effective source separation. Each encoder layer applies self-attention and feed-forward mechanisms to iteratively refine representations.

Permutation Invariant Training (PIT): Trains the model to handle permutations of separated sources. It uses loss functions that penalize discrepancies between the predicted and ground-truth sources, ensuring consistent output irrespective of input order.

Training Objectives (Loss Functions): Typically include metrics like Mean Squared Error (MSE) or Signal-to-Distortion Ratio (SDR) to quantify separation quality during training. These metrics guide the model towards minimizing distortion and enhancing source separation fidelity.

Speaker Detection Function: This function serves as a placeholder for actual speaker detection logic. It prompts the user to input the number of speakers present in the audio file '(1–4)'. In a practical scenario, speaker detection would use pretrained models or heuristic methods for accurate speaker count determination.

Audio Separation Function: Depending on the number of speakers detected, this function selects the appropriate pretrained Sepformer model:

- For 2 speakers: Sepformer model trained on WSJ0-2mix dataset (speechbrain/sepformer-wsj02mix).
- For 3 speakers: Sepformer model trained on WSJ0-3mix dataset (speechbrain/sepformer-wsj03mix).
- For 4 speakers: Sepformer model trained on Libri4mix dataset (hahmadraz/sepformer-libri4mix).

Components of Sepformer

5.4.1 Encoder Transformation

The input audio waveform is converted into a high-dimensional feature space that is suitable for processing by the subsequent transformer network. The encoder consists of multiple convolutional layers that convert the raw audio input into a feature set, capturing crucial information about the audio content. This transformation is essential as it decreases the dimensionality of the input while preserving the key features needed for effective source separation.

$$Z = Encoder(X) \tag{17}$$

where: X represents the input audio waveform, which could be a complex mixture of multiple speakers.
Z is the resulting high-dimensional feature space, a more abstract representation of the input signal.

5.4.2 Dual-Path Transformer

The dual-path transformer is a sophisticated architecture within the Sepformer model that processes the audio signal using two pathways: *the intra-transformer* and *the inter-transformer.* This dual-path strategy enables the model to grasp both local and global contexts, which is essential for accurately separating sources in complex audio mixtures.

- *Intra-Transformer*: Focuses on capturing local context and dependencies within short segments of the audio signal.

$$Z_{intra} = Transformer_{intra}(Z) \tag{18}$$

Where: Z_{intra} represents the transformed features after processing by the intra-transformer.

- *Inter-Transformer*: Refines 'Z_{intra}' by incorporating global context across longer segments, crucial for understanding complex audio mixtures.

$$Z_{inter} = Transformer_{inter}(Z_{intra}) \tag{19}$$

Where: Z_{inter} represents the refined features after processing by the inter-transformer.

5.4.3 Decoder Transformation

It Consists of transposed convolutional layers or other upsampling techniques that convert the latent feature space back into the time-domain waveform. This step reconstructs the separated audio sources, corresponding to each speaker or sound source. The quality of the decoder transformation is critical for ensuring that the separated sources are not only distinct but also closely resemble the original sources in terms of audio quality.

$$\hat{X} = Decoder(Z_{inter}) \tag{20}$$

where: $\hat{X}$ represents the reconstructed audio signals, corresponding to the separated sources. Z_{inter} is the feature representation output by the inter-transformer.

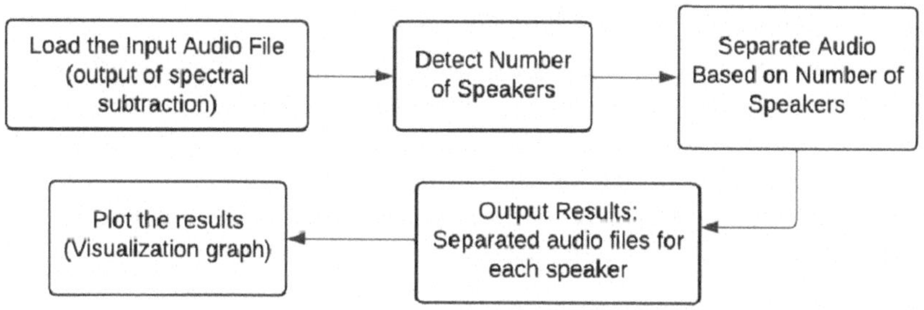

Fig. 4. Flowchart for Sepformer Model's Speaker Separation Process

Figure 4 illustrates the steps in the Sepformer model for speaker separation. The process begins by loading the input audio file, which is the output of spectral subtraction. Then, the number of speakers in the audio is detected, and the audio is separated accordingly. The separated audio files for each speaker are output, and finally, the results are visualized through a graph for further analysis.

5.5 Speaker Recognition and Separation

Speaker recognition and separation uses a combination of CNN and Sepformer models. The process begins with the extraction of MFCC features from audio recordings, which are subsequently utilized to train a CNN model for speaker classification (Hemachandra and Vidhathri). The Sepformer model is used to separate mixed audio into individual sources. The separated sources are then classified using the trained CNN model, and the results are saved as individual audio files for each speaker.

Key Parameters Used

5.5.1 Feature Extraction with MFCC

Function: Transforms an audio signal into Mel-Frequency Cepstral Coefficients (MFCCs), which serve as input features for the CNN model. These features are extensively employed in speech and audio processing due to their ability to accurately reflect the perceptual traits of human hearing, rendering them particularly suitable for tasks such as speaker identification.

Short-Time Fourier Transform (STFT): Transforms the signal from the time domain to the frequency domain through the Short-Time Fourier Transform (STFT). This process divides the signal into brief, overlapping segments, allowing the analysis of its frequency content over time.

$$X(t, \omega) = \sum_{n=0}^{N-1} x[n]w[n-t]e^{-j\omega n} \tag{21}$$

where: $x[n]$ denotes the incoming audio waveform, a sequence of sampled values over time. $w[n-t]$ is the window function, which selects a short segment of the signal for analysis. $X(t, \omega)$ is the STFT of the signal, representing its frequency content at each time step t and frequency ω.

Mel Filterbank: Applies a series of triangular filters to the magnitude spectrum derived from the STFT. The Mel filterbank outputs a series of values that correspond to the energy in different frequency bands on the Mel scale. These values serve as the foundation for calculating the MFCCs. The Mel scale mimics the human ear's perception of sound, where lower frequencies are perceived with finer resolution than higher frequencies.

$$M_m = \sum_{k=0}^{K-1} |X_k|^2 H_m(k) \tag{22}$$

where: $H_m(k)$ represents the m-th Mel filter, a triangular filter that emphasizes certain frequency bands while attenuating others. K is the number of FFT (Fast Fourier Transform) points, which determines the resolution of the frequency analysis. $|X_k|^2$ indicates the power spectral density of the signal, representing the energy at each frequency.

Logarithm of Mel Spectrum: To simulate the human ear's response to sound intensity, the logarithm of the Mel spectrum is computed. This process reduces the dynamic range of the spectrum, enhancing its suitability for speech analysis. The logarithm function is applied to the output of the Mel filterbank, resulting in the log Mel spectrum.

$$log(M_m) \tag{23}$$

Discrete Cosine Transform (DCT): Transforms the log Mel spectrum into the cepstral domain, where the coefficients represent the spectral envelope. The lower-order coefficients capture the broad spectral shape, while higher-order coefficients capture finer details, offering a condensed depiction of the signal's spectral characteristics.

$$MFCC_n = \sum_{m=0}^{M-1} \log(M_m) \cos\left[\frac{M\pi n(m+0.5)}{M}\right] \tag{24}$$

where: M is the number of Mel bands, corresponding to the number of coefficients extracted from the Mel filterbank. n is the index of the MFCC coefficient, with lower indices representing the most significant features.

5.5.2 CNN Model for Speaker Recognition

Function: Processes the extracted MFCC features to classify the input audio into one of several predefined speaker classes. CNNs are exceptionally suited for this role as they are capable of learning layered representations of input data, enabling them to effectively capture both spatial and temporal patterns within the MFCC features.

Convolutional Layer: The input features are processed through convolutional filters to generate feature maps, which identify local patterns such as edges or textures. This layer helps the CNN to build spatial hierarchies, with early layers recognizing fundamental patterns and higher layers combining them into complex features.

$$y_{i,j,k} = \sum_{m=0}^{M-1} \sum_{n=0}^{N-1} x_{i+m,j+n} w_{m,n,k} + b_k \tag{25}$$

where: $x_{i+m,j+n}$ represents a local patch of the input feature map. $w_{m,n,k}$ is the convolutional filter applied to the input. b_k denotes the bias term for the k-th filter. $y_{i,j,k}$ represents the result of the convolution operation, a feature visualization that emphasizes particular patterns in the input data.

Activation Function (ReLU): The Rectified Linear Unit (ReLU) activation function injects non-linearity into the model, allowing it to understand intricate relationships between input features and target categories. ReLU is frequently utilized in CNNs as it addresses the vanishing gradient issue, enabling the network to learn more rapidly and deliver superior performance.

$$ReLU(x) = max(0, x) \tag{26}$$

where: x is the input to the activation function, typically the result from a convolutional layer. The ReLU activation function outputs x if it is positive and 0 otherwise.

Residual Block: It is a key component of modern deep neural networks that includes skip connections to bypass one or more layers. This design helps the model learn more efficiently by mitigating the degradation problem, where additional layers can degrade performance, and allows the network to focus on important features while avoiding unnecessary complexity.

$$y = ReLU(F(x, \{W_i\}) + x) \tag{27}$$

where: $F(x, \{W_i\})$ represents the function learned by the residual block, where x is the input and $\{W_i\}$ are the weights of the block. The input x is added to the output of the function F, forming a shortcut connection that facilitates easier gradient flow through the network.

Pooling Layer: Decreases the spatial size of feature maps, enhancing computational efficiency and reducing overfitting. Max pooling preserves the most significant features while discarding less relevant information, allowing the network to focus on salient patterns and improve generalization.

$$y_{i,j} = \max_{m=0}^{M-1} \max_{n=0}^{N-1} x_{i+m,j+n} \tag{28}$$

where: $x_{i+m,j+n}$ represents the input to the pooling layer, typically coming from the results of a convolutional layer. The pooling process identifies the maximum value within a localized window of dimensions $M \times N$, thereby decreasing the spatial dimensions of the feature map.

Dense Layer: This fully connected layer takes the flattened feature maps from the previous layers and maps them to the output classes, representing the different speakers. The dense layer enables the CNN to make predictions about the speaker's identity based on the learned features.

$$y = softmax(Wx + b) \tag{29}$$

where: W is the weight matrix connecting the input features x to the output classes. b is the bias vector incorporated into the weighted sum of the inputs. The softmax function normalizes the output into a probability distribution, assigning each value to the likelihood of the input being in a particular class, with the highest value representing the most likely class.

5.5.3 Sepformer for Audio Separation

Function: Separates mixed audio into individual sources.

By combining the Sepformer model with the CNN-based speaker recognition system, it is possible to achieve both high-quality audio separation and accurate speaker identification. This approach is particularly useful in scenarios where multiple speakers are talking simultaneously, as it allows for the extraction and classification of each speaker's voice.

See Eqs. (17), (18), (19), and (20) for reference.

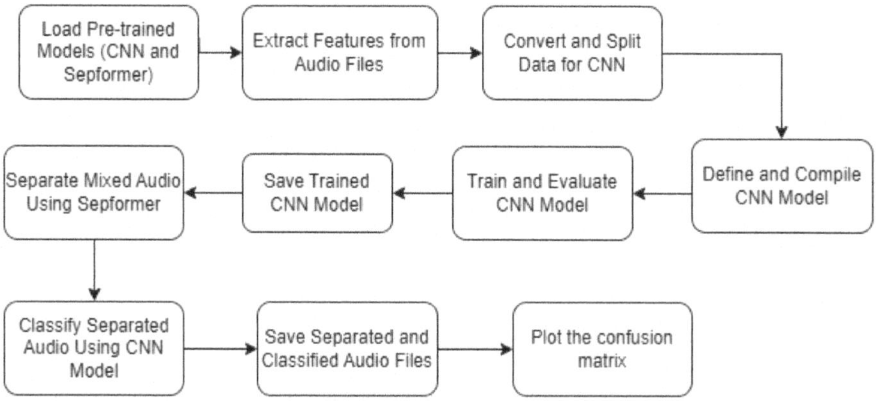

Fig. 5. Flowchart for Speaker Recognition and Separation using Sepformer and CNN Models

Figure 5 outlines the steps involved in the speaker recognition and separation process using Sepformer and CNN models. The process begins by loading pre-trained models, extracting features from audio files, and converting the data for CNN training. The CNN model is defined, compiled, and trained using the prepared data. After training, the mixed audio is separated by Sepformer, and the separated audio is classified using the CNN model. The classified audio files are saved, and the confusion matrix is plotted to visualize the results.

6 Suitability of Methodological Framework

The chosen methodology is highly suitable for addressing the complex problem of speech enhancement, speaker separation, and recognition, as it leverages multiple advanced models tailored to different aspects of the task. Starting with feature extraction using Mel-Frequency Cepstral Coefficients (MFCC) and Convolutional Neural Networks (CNN). MFCC is well-known for its ability to capture the spectral properties of speech, while CNNs are powerful for classifying and distinguishing between various types of audio patterns. This combination ensures that the model can accurately detect and classify different types of background noises, which is crucial for subsequent noise removal processes and enhance speech clarity.

The Waveformer is adept at handling noisy signals and improving the overall quality of the audio by reducing distortions. The Sepformer model is effective in separating audio sources that are intermingled. These models are highly suitable for precise speaker separation even in challenging environments with significant noise interference. The use of these state-of-the-art models ensures that the resulting audio signals are clean and easy to interpret, which contributes to improving speech recognition accuracy.

Finally, the inclusion of a speaker recognition model ensures that post-separation, each speaker is correctly identified and labeled. This step is critical for applications where tracking individual speakers is necessary, such as in meetings or multi-speaker environments. Overall, the chosen methodology demonstrates a comprehensive approach to tackle multi-faceted challenges associated with audio processing, making it highly suitable for the research question.

7 Results

1] Convolutional Neural Network (CNN) and feature extraction from Mel-Frequency Cepstral Coefficients (MFCC)

Table 1. Evaluation Metrics

Metric	Value
Accuracy	0.8243
Matthews Correlation Coefficient (MCC)	0.7407
Cohen's Kappa	0.7377
Log Loss	6.3320
Mean Squared Error (MSE)	0.2162
Root Mean Squared Error (RMSE)	0.4650
Mean Absolute Error (MAE)	0.1892
Macro-Averaged F1 Score	0.7874

Table 1 highlights the key evaluation metrics of the model. The accuracy is 82.43%, indicating the model correctly classifies inputs in over 82% of cases across the four classes (cat, dog, cough, and keyboard).

MCC of 0.7407 demonstrates a strong correlation between predicted and actual classes, even in imbalanced data. Cohen's Kappa of 0.7377 shows a high level of agreement between predictions and true labels beyond chance. Log Loss of 6.3320 indicates some uncertainty in the model's predictions. Low values of MSE (0.2162) and RMSE (0.4650) reflect minimal deviation from the true labels. The Macro-Averaged F1 Score of 0.7874 suggests the model performs consistently well across all classes.

Table 2. Classification Report

Class	Precision	Recall	F1-Score	Support
cat	0.86	0.91	0.88	33
dog	0.82	0.78	0.80	23
cough	0.83	0.50	0.62	10
keyboard	0.73	1.00	0.84	8
Accuracy	0.82			
Macro Avg	0.81 (Precision), 0.80 (Recall), 0.79 (F1-Score), 74 (Support)			
Weighted Avg	0.83 (Precision), 0.82 (Recall), 0.82 (F1-Score), 74 (Support)			

Table 2 provides a detailed breakdown of the model's performance per class: Cat is the best-classified class with an F1-Score of 0.88 (precision: 0.86, recall: 0.91). Dog has a balanced F1-Score of 0.80, with slightly lower recall (0.78). Cough is the weakest class, with an F1-Score of 0.62, indicating difficulty in distinguishing cough sounds. Keyboard has a strong F1-Score of 0.84 but limited support (only 8 samples).

The model's overall accuracy is 82%, with both Macro-Averaged and Weighted-Averaged results showing good performance, though some classes, like cough, are harder to predict, likely due to limited data.

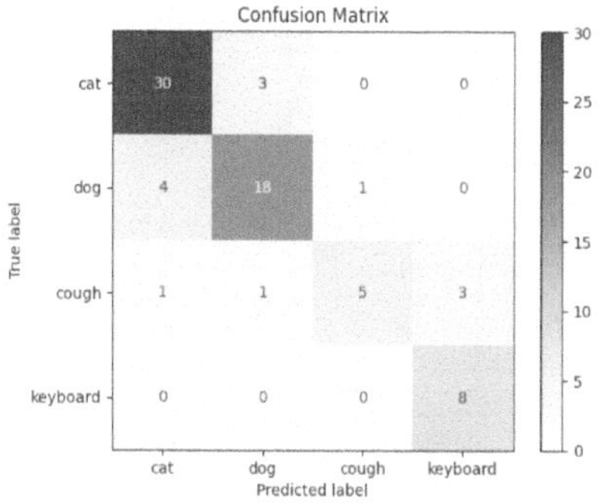

Fig. 6. Confusion Matrix for Multi-Class Classification

Figure 6 evaluates the alignment between actual and predicted labels. It displays the count of accurate and erroneous predictions for each class ('cat', 'dog', 'cough', 'keyboard'). The plot highlights the diagonal cells indicating correct predictions and off-diagonal cells indicating misclassifications. For example, the entry in the top-left cell shows how many instances the model correctly classified 'cat' when the actual label was 'cat', while the value in the first row and second column shows the frequency with which the model misclassified 'dog' when the actual label was 'cat'.

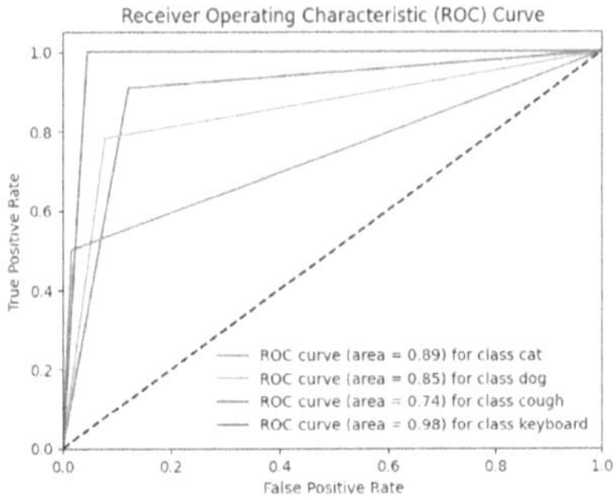

Fig. 7. Receiver Operating Characteristic (ROC) Curves for Audio Classification

Figure 7 displays ROC curves for four audio classes: cat, dog, cough, and keyboard. ROC curves that approach the top-left corner reflect superior performance, signifying a higher true positive rate and a lower false positive rate for the model. A high AUC (Area Under Curve) value of 0.98 for a class like 'keyboard' suggests the model is good at distinguishing 'keyboard' from other sounds. Lower AUC for 'cough' might indicate the model struggles to differentiate 'cough' from other classes, possibly due to overlapping features or less distinct audio characteristics.

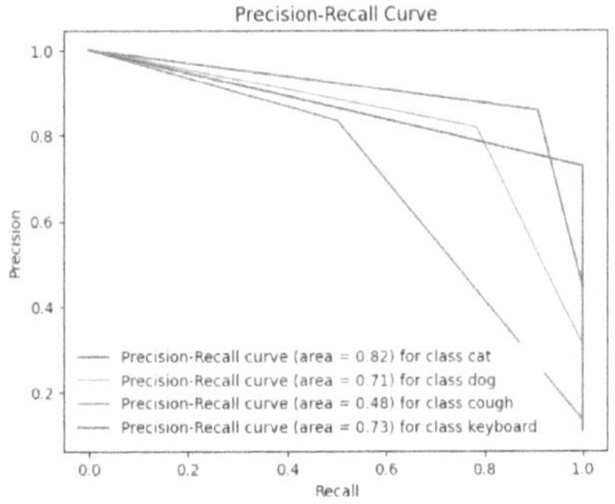

Fig. 8. Precision-Recall (PR) curve for multi-class classification

Figure 8 evaluates the PR curve for multi-class classification across four different categories: 'cat', 'dog', 'cough', and 'keyboard'. The PR curves demonstrate the model's ability to balance precision and recall across multiple classes.

Precision-Recall (PR) Curve curves with higher areas indicate better performance, as both precision and recall are high. A high average precision score for 'cat' suggests the model is proficient in retrieving relevant 'cat' instances and that few non-'cat' instances are incorrectly retrieved. Lower precision-recall area for some classes indicates that for classes like 'cough', the model may either miss many true instances (low recall) or wrongly include many non-instances (low precision).

2] Waveformer

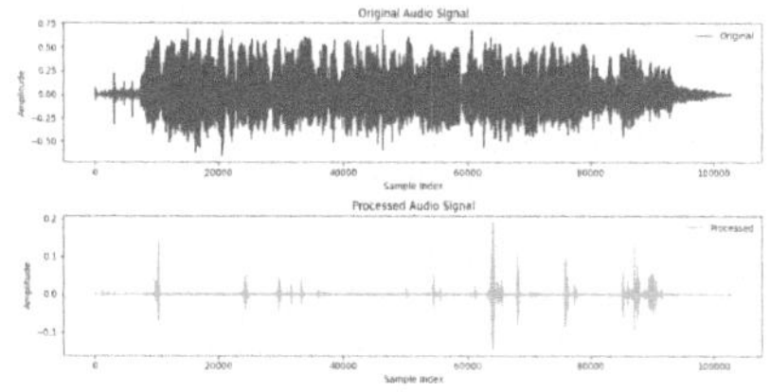

Fig. 9. Visualization of Original and Processed Audio Signal Waveforms of Waveformer

Figure 9 shows two waveform graphs: the top graph represents the original audio signal, while the bottom graph illustrates the processed audio signal after applying noise reduction or other signal processing techniques.

Original Audio Signal: The waveform of the original audio shows the amplitude variations over time. The original signal serves as the reference point, representing the desired clean signal without any processing anomalies.

Processed Audio Signal: The waveform of the processed audio shows how the audio signal has been altered by the enhancement or separation process. Ideally, the processed signal should closely match the original signal in both amplitude and pattern. Differences between the original and processed waveforms indicate the presence of remaining noise, anomalies, or any distortions introduced by the processing.

Table 3. Evaluation Metrics

Metric	Value
SDR (Signal-to-Distortion Ratio)	−12.69 dB
STOI (Short-Time Objective Intelligibility)	0.25
PESQ (Perceptual Evaluation of Speech Quality)	1.26

Table 3 evaluates the quality of the processed audio:
SDR of −12.69 dB indicates significant distortion in the processed signal. STOI of 0.25 shows a notable loss in speech intelligibility, likely due to the noise reduction or separation methods used. PESQ of 1.26 suggests the audio has low perceived quality, with possible artifacts or unnatural sound.

These metrics highlight that the processing introduced distortion and reduced both intelligibility and overall audio quality.

3] Spectral Subtraction

Table 4. Evaluation Metrics

Metric	Value
SNR (Signal-to-Noise Ratio)	13.864 dB
MSE (Mean Squared Error)	0.0009869
PESQ (Perceptual Evaluation of Speech Quality)	1.369
STOI (Short-Time Objective Intelligibility)	0.9494
SDR (Signal-to-Distortion Ratio)	14.713 dB
SAR (Signal-to-Artifact Ratio)	14.713 dB

Table 4 evaluates the processed audio's quality:

SNR of 13.864 dB shows effective separation between the signal and background noise. MSE of 0.0009869 reflects minimal error, indicating accurate noise reduction. PESQ of 1.369 suggests an improvement in perceived speech quality but leaves room for further enhancement. STOI of 0.9494 demonstrates that speech intelligibility is well-preserved. SDR and SAR both at 14.713 dB indicate strong signal quality with minimal distortion and artifacts.

These metrics confirm that the spectral subtraction method efficiently reduces noise while maintaining high speech intelligibility and minimal processing artifacts.

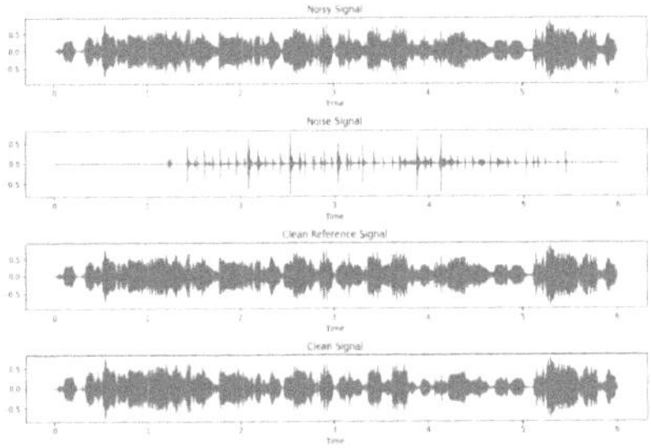

Fig. 10. Spectral Subtraction Process in Noise Reduction

Figure 10 illustrates the stages of noise reduction using spectral subtraction. The top plot shows the original noisy signal, followed by the estimated noise signal in the second plot. The third plot represents a clean reference signal for comparison, and the final plot shows the cleaned signal after spectral subtraction.

Noisy Signal Waveform: This waveform shows an audio signal that contains both the required signal and background noise. The waveform is expected to show a complex pattern, indicating the presence of multiple sound sources.

Noise Signal Waveform: This represents the isolated noise component. It typically shows periodic or repetitive patterns, characteristic of mechanical noises.

Clean Reference Signal Waveform: This waveform represents the ground truth or the target clean signal. The waveform should have clearer and more distinct patterns compared to the noisy signal, indicating the absence of noise.

Clean Signal Waveform: This waveform represents the enhanced or cleaned audio signal obtained after processing. Ideally, this should closely match the clean reference signal waveform, showing that the noise has been effectively reduced.

4] Sepformer Separation

Table 5. Evaluation Metrics for Source 1 and Source 2

Source	SNR (dB)	MSE	PESQ	STOI	SDR (dB)	SAR (dB)
Source 1	−8.53	0.092	1.76	0.954	15.38	15.38
Source 2	6.38	0.002	1.70	0.969	13.57	13.57

Table 5 evaluates the audio quality for two separate sources:

- Source 1:
  SNR: 8.53 dB (moderate signal improvement). MSE: 0.092 (some deviation from reference). PESQ: 1.76 (low to moderate perceived quality). STOI: 0.954 (well-preserved speech intelligibility). SDR/SAR: 15.38 dB (minimal distortion and artifacts).
- Source 2:
  SNR: 6.38 dB (smaller signal improvement). MSE: 0.002 (closer match to reference). PESQ: 1.70 (similar to Source 1). STOI: 0.969 (excellent intelligibility). SDR/SAR: 13.57 dB (good, but slightly lower than Source 1).

The Sepformer process preserved intelligibility (high STOI) and minimized distortion (SDR/SAR), but perceived quality (PESQ) remains low to moderate for both sources. Source 1 performed better in SNR, SDR, and SAR, while Source 2 had better MSE and STOI. There's room for improvement in overall audio quality.

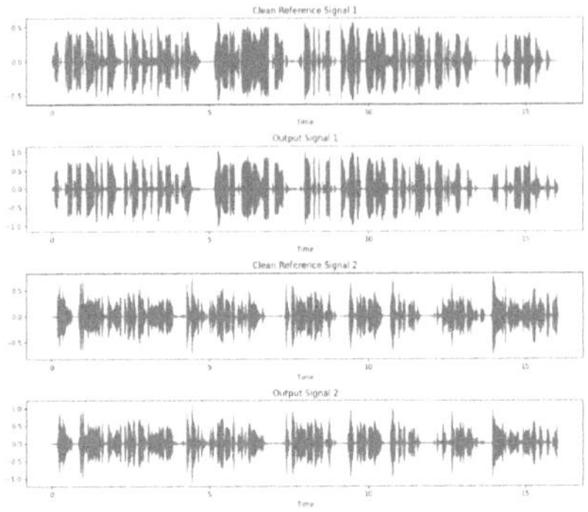

Fig. 11. Sepformer Separation: Visualization of Source Separation Waveforms

Figure 11 illustrates the waveforms for both clean reference signals and their corresponding output signals after processing by the Sepformer model. The waveforms for Source 1 and Source 2 are displayed, with the top two rows showing the clean reference signals and the bottom two rows showing the output signals.

Clean Reference Signal 1 and 2: These waveforms represent the ground truth signals that we aim to achieve. The patterns should be clear, indicating the absence of noise.

Output Signal 1 and 2: These waveforms represent the signals obtained after the enhancement process. Ideally, they should closely match the clean reference signals. Differences in amplitude patterns between the clean and output signals indicate remaining noise or distortion.

5] Speaker Recognition and Separation

Table 6. Classification Metrics for Speaker Recognition Model

Class	Precision	Recall	F1-Score	Support
(Speaker 1) Hemachandra	1.00	1.00	1.00	1
(Speaker 2) Vidhathri	1.00	1.00	1.00	1
Accuracy	1.00			
Macro Avg	1.00 (Precision), 1.00 (Recall), 1.00 (F1-Score), 2 (Support)			
Weighted Avg	1.00 (Precision), 1.00 (Recall), 1.00 (F1-Score), 2 (Support)			

Table 6 shows the performance metrics of the speaker recognition model, including Precision, Recall, F1-Score, and Support for two speakers. Here, we are achieving a perfect score of 1, as the classification model is trained to recognize two known speakers for real-time results. Using this model as a base, we can extend it to train and classify multiple other speakers for recognition. By training the model for different numbers of speakers, we can observe variations in the score.

8 Comparative Evaluation and Benchmarking

To assess the performance and effectiveness of the proposed system, it is important to benchmark it against existing state-of-the-art solutions. This theoretical comparison evaluates our system relative to Google's Voice Filter and OpenAI's Whisper, and considers potential benchmarking against well-established datasets like LibriSpeech and VoxCeleb.

8.1 Comparison with Google's Voice Filter

Google's Voice Filter effectively enhances a target speaker's voice in noisy environments, even with interference from another speaker, making it suitable for voice assistants. However, it may struggle in complex multi-speaker scenarios with overlapping voices.

The proposed system utilizes models like Waveformer, Sepformer, and Spectral Subtraction to excel in multi-speaker separation and handle complex audio mixtures more effectively. While Voice Filter is optimized for real-time use, the proposed system offers greater versatility in separating multiple speakers, albeit with higher computational costs.

8.2 Comparison with OpenAI's Whisper

OpenAI's Whisper is effective in speech recognition and transcription, across noisy and multilingual environments.

Our system, on the other hand, focuses on speaker separation and recognition rather than ASR. While Whisper is better suited for large-scale transcription tasks, our system performs tasks involving separating and recognizing multiple speakers, more aligned with real-time speaker isolation needs.

8.3 Dataset Benchmarking

LibriSpeech: While LibriSpeech is used for ASR benchmarking with Word Error Rate (WER), the proposed system is not focused on transcription but could still achieve competitive WER due to its noise reduction capabilities.

VoxCeleb: For speaker identification, the CNN-based recognition and Sepformer models would likely perform well in multi-speaker environments.

8.4 Model Complexity and Efficiency

The proposed system integrates several models that improve separation and noise reduction but increase computational demand. Although Google's Voice Filter and Whisper are more efficient for real-time performance, the proposed system's strength lies in its superior handling of multi-speaker challenges.

9 Conclusion

We have presented a comprehensive approach that integrates cutting-edge models such as Convolutional Neural Networks (CNN), Waveformer, Sepformer, and Spectral Subtraction for effective background noise dissipation, speech separation, and speaker recognition. Our results provide considerable improvements in signal clarity, speech separation and accurate speaker identification. By applying these deep learning-based techniques, we have shown that speech enhancement and separation can achieve high accuracy even in real-time, noisy environments, making it suitable for various applications like telecommunications, hearing aids, voice assistants and other acoustic systems.

Despite the promising results, our models still face challenges, mostly in complex audio environments such as multiple speakers and varying noise conditions. Continued refinement and adaptation of the models in real-time could further enhance their performance. Overall, our work provides a strong proof-of-concept for deploying these models in audio processing systems, advancing the field towards more reliable and efficient solutions.

While Google's Voice Filter and Whisper are optimized for single-speaker and transcription tasks, the proposed system offers a more versatile approach for multi-speaker separation and speaker recognition. Future evaluation on datasets like LibriSpeech and VoxCeleb would further substantiate these claims.

10 Future Scope

Although our models have yielded satisfactory results in speaker separation, there are several areas where improvements are possible.

The CNN classification model, which classifies given categories of noise signals, can be further advanced to identify and predict a broader range of background noises accurately. Such prediction will be useful for the Waveformer model to extract the noise.

The Waveformer model can be enhanced to identify various background noises instead of specified targets. It needs to be trained on large datasets from numerous fields of noise to improve the efficiency of noise extraction.

Spectral subtraction uses STFT in various layers to remove noise signals and provide a clean mixed audio signal. Adjusting and fine-tuning parameters can improve the quality of subtraction. Complete noise removal helps to achieve clean separation of speech signals.

Our work, which is limited to 4 speakers, requires further advancements in the model and training dataset to achieve speech separation for any number (N)of speakers. An efficient model to accurately identify the number of speakers in mixed audio is required to achieve N speaker separation with higher efficiency. Sepformer models effectively separate speech signals without any ambiguity only with complete noise dissipation.

Speaker recognition can use GenAI models to identify the speaker after separation, which can be trained on large datasets of popular individuals. Training the classification model on a significant number of speakers will help to identify and store the audio files in their respective names. This work will be useful for the media and entertainment industry.

Real-time speech separation with high-efficiency processing and rapid output, surpassing the present state-of-the-art models, has great research potential. This will prove beneficial in the healthcare and automation industries.

Acknowledgement. The authors express their sincere appreciation to the Center for Data Sciences and Applied Machine Learning (CDSAML) in the Department of Computer Science and Engineering (CSE) at PES University, Bangalore. Their steadfast support, combined with the university's commitment to fostering a research-friendly atmosphere, has been crucial to the successful completion of this study.

References

1. Veluri, B., Chan, J., Itani, M., Chen, T., Yoshioka, T., Gollakota, S.: Real-time target sound extraction. arXiv:2211.02250v3 [cs.SD] (2023)
2. Karam, M., Khazaal, H.F., Aglan, H., Cole, C.: Noise removal in speech processing using spectral subtraction. J. Signal Inf. Process. **5**(5), 32–41 (2014)
3. Subakan, C., Ravanelli, M., Cornell, S., Bronzi, M., Zhong, J.: Attention is all you need in speech separation. arXiv:2010.13154v2 [eess.AS] (2021)
4. Chen, Z., et al.: Speech separation with large-scale self-supervised learning. arXiv:2211.05172v2 [eess.AS] (2022)
5. Xiong, W., Wu, L., Alleva, F., Droppo, J., Huang, X., Stolcke, A.: The Microsoft 2017 conversational speech recognition system. arXiv:1708.06073v2 [cs.CL] (2017)
6. Kong, Z., Ping, W., Dantrey, A., Catanzaro, B.: Speech denoising in the waveform domain with self-attention. arXiv:2202.07790v3 [cs.SD] (2022)
7. Ma, H., Peng, Z., Li, X., Shao, M., Wu, X., Liu, J.: CLAPSep: Leveraging contrastive pre-trained model for multi-modal query-conditioned target sound extraction. arXiv:2402.17455v2 [eess.AS] (2024)
8. Nachmani, E., Adi, Y., Wolf, L.: Voice separation with an unknown number of multiple speakers. arXiv:2003.01531v4 [eess.AS] (2020)
9. Chen, S., et al.: Continuous speech separation with conformer. arXiv:2008.05773v2 [eess.AS] (2020)
10. Li, J.: Recent advances in end-to-end automatic speech recognition. arXiv:2111.01690v2 [eess.AS] (2022)
11. Nettam, P., Rakshitha, R., Nekar, M., Achunala, A., Shylaja, S.S., Anantharaman, P.N.: Human speech extraction from composite audio signal in real-time using deep neural network. In: 2024 11th International Conference on Signal Processing and Integrated Networks (SPIN-2024) (2024)
12. Wan, S.: Research on speech separation and recognition algorithm based on deep learning. In: 2021 IEEE International Conference on Power, Intelligent Computing and Systems (ICPICS), Shenyang, China, pp. 722–725 (2021)
13. Wang, D.L., Chen, J.: Supervised speech separation based on deep learning: an overview. IEEE/ACM Trans. Audio Speech Lang. Process. **25**(10), 1705–1721 (2017)

14. Chen, Z., Wu, J., Kanda, N., Li, J., Sivasankaran, S., Eskimez, S.E.: Continuous speech separation: dataset and analysis. In: 2020 IEEE International Conference on Acoustics, Speech and Signal Processing (ICASSP), ICASSP 2020, Barcelona, Spain, pp. 7284–7288 (2020)
15. Luo, J., Wang, J., Cheng, N., Xiao, E., Zhang, X., Xiao, J.: Tiny-Sepformer: a tiny time-domain transformer network for speech separation. In: Interspeech 2022, Incheon, Korea (2022)
16. Subakan, C., Ravanelli, M., Cornell, S., Grondin, F., Bronzi, M.: Exploring self-attention mechanisms for speech separation. IEEE/ACM Trans. Audio Speech Lang. Process. **31**, 2169–2180 (2023)
17. Liu, J., Xiang, X.: Review of the anti-noise method in the speech recognition technology. In: 2017 12th IEEE Conference on Industrial Electronics and Applications (ICIEA), Siem Reap, Cambodia, pp. 1391–1394 (2017)
18. Buera, L., Droppo, J., Acero, A.: Speech enhancement using a pitch predictive model. In: 2008 IEEE International Conference on Acoustics, Speech and Signal Processing, Las Vegas, NV, USA, pp. 4885–4888 (2008)
19. Jun, D., Yifan, T., Dai, L.-R., Lee, C.-H.: A regression approach to single-channel speech separation via high-resolution deep neural networks. IEEE/ACM Trans. Audio Speech Lang. Process. **24**(8), 1424–1437 (2016)
20. Nian, Z., Tu, Y.-H., Du, J., Lee, C.-H.: A progressive learning approach to adaptive noise and speech estimation for speech enhancement and noisy speech recognition. In: 2021 IEEE International Conference on Acoustics, Speech and Signal Processing (ICASSP), ICASSP 2021, Toronto, ON, Canada, pp. 6913–6917 (2021)
21. Upadhyay, N., Karmakar, A.: Speech enhancement using spectral subtraction-type algorithms: a comparison and simulation study. Procedia Comput. Sci. **58**, 406–412 (2015)

Rule-Based Named Entity Recognition for Hindi

Devanshi Suri[1,2(✉)], Nimisha Malviya[2], and Nisheeth Joshi[1,2]

[1] Speech and Language Processing Lab, Centre for Artificial Intelligence, Banasthali Vidyapith, Radha Kishnpura, Rajasthan, India
suridevansh@gmail.com, nisheethjoshi@rediffmail.com

[2] Department of Computer Science, Banasthali Vidyapith, Radha Kishnpura, Rajasthan, India
nimmymalviya98@gmail.com

Abstract. Named Entity Recognition (NER) is a crucial task in Natural Language Processing (NLP) that identifies and recognises named entities in large structured or unstructured texts. These named entities can be names of persons, locations, organisations, dates etc. We developed a POS-tag rule-based system that performs NER for Hindi. Rules were created using the POS tokens and gazetteers were used for identifying named entities. We also focused on creating gazetteers for person names, locations, and organisations in the Hindi language. The system is capable of identifying and classifying 5 named entities: person, location, organisation, date, and time. Our system was evaluated on the benchmark Naamapadam dataset for three entities-person, location, and organisation. The F1-score was 0.42 and the precision was 0.90.

Keywords: Named Entity Recognition (NER) · Rule-based systems · POS tagging

1 Introduction

Named Entity Recognition (NER), a crucial task in Natural Language Processing (NLP), can be interpreted as a two-step process: identification and classification. Given a text, an NER system should correctly identify named entities and classify those entities into their respective classes such as a person, location, organisation etc. NER classes are domain specific; an NER system for the medical domain may include names of diseases, genes, proteins, chemicals [1] etc., while for the travel domain, a system may comprise of location, date, name, brand, amenity, star-rating, price, and duration [2]. NER is also considered a sub-task of information retrieval [3].

NER is applied in a variety of everyday use cases, impacting how information is processed and utilised. Some of the most common use cases are:

- Search and Retrieval: By enabling more accurate query results, NER improves search engine results. Search engines can provide more relevant results depending on the specific entities stated in queries when they identify entities in the query.
- Information Extraction: Information can be extracted more efficiently from unstructured text with NER by identifying and labelling entities such as dates, individuals, organisations, locations, and specific terms.

A. Sharma and R. Rani (Eds.): AIST 2024, CCIS 2389, pp. 55–62, 2025.
https://doi.org/10.1007/978-3-031-91331-0_4

- Business Intelligence and customer insights: Identifying important client/customer information from data (reviews, feedback, social media) can help businesses gain insights into customer sentiments, latest trends and, preferences.
- De-Identification of personal information: NER systems are used to remove sensitive personal data like names, addresses, financial information etc. so that the identity of a person is camouflaged in a dataset [4].
- Text-to-Speech and Speech Recognition: By correctly identifying the Named Entities, the performance and accuracy of these systems can be improved by making sure specific names and terms are recognised.

Numerous approaches are used for NER. They are broadly described as follows:

1. Rule-based Approach: Pre-defined rules are constructed based on lexical grammar, POS tags or gazetteers. Rule-based systems are usually language-dependent. [1]
2. Machine Learning-based approach: Labelled datasets are utilised to train models using machine learning algorithms like Support Vector Machines (SVMs), HMMs, Conditional Random Field (CRF), Maximum Entropy Markov Model (MEMM), Decision Trees etc.
3. Deep Learning: Neural Networks, RNN, LSTM, Bi-LSTM, and Transformer models like BERT are some of the most commonly used methods to train models.

Our system is a rule-based system that identifies named entities using the POS tags of all tokens in a text. It follows a two-step approach: first, POS tags of all tokens in the input are determined. Second, rules are applied to these POS tags to identify named entities. The gazetteers created for the system contain a combined total of over 14,000 entities, including locations, organisations and person names.

In Sect. 2, we talk about the literature review, Sect. 3 discusses the methodology and the results are reviewed in Sect. 4.

2 Literature Review

A rule-based NER for the Malay language was proposed by [5]. Their system followed a three-step approach: tokenisation, POS tagging and application of rules on tokens tagged as proper nouns. For evaluation, 363 articles from four different domains were retrieved from two websites. The annotated entities were categorised as correct, partially correct and incorrect entities. The system was created to identify 3 named entities: Person, Location, and Organisation. The F1-score was reported to be 89.47%, the recall was 94.44% and the precision was 85%. The authors suggested that many of the errors made by the system can be corrected by updating the dictionaries or modifying the existing rules.

[6] created a rule-based system for Urdu using rules that created a finite state automaton based on lexical cues. These cues were corpus-based, grammar-based, and heuristic-based. Over 200 documents were analysed to construct a set of rules for 6 classes: Person, Person of influence, Location, Date, Numbers, and Organisation. A small authority file, which serves as a mini gazetteer, was also created to include names of entities that occur frequently with no cues. 6-g are constructed on the input paragraph (taken as a

string without line breaks). Regular expressions are applied for 6-g to tag named entities. According to the results of their experiment, Hindi Gazetteers cannot be applied to Urdu, and the rule-based method outperformed the Conditional Random Fields method employed in IJCNLP 2008.

[7] proposed a hybrid approach combining rule-based and machine learning classification for Arabic. Two features for each word are extracted from the unstructured text. NE tags are predicted by the system for a word and the words surrounding it. This feature was called the rule-based system and general features based on experience were set as the second set of features. F-measure was increased by 8 to 14% compared to a pure rule-based and machine learning-based approach.

[8] proposed a Hybrid Approach for Named Entity Recognition (NER) in Hindi. This approach combines two distinct methodologies: the Rule-Based approach and the List Lookup approach. The proposed NER system aims to identify and extract 10 specific types of named entities from Hindi text. These entities include person names, location names (such as cities, states, and countries), organisation names, dates, monetary values, measurement values, directional values, transport-related entities, and names of birds/animals. This hybrid system leverages both predefined rules and lookup lists to enhance the accuracy and coverage of named entity recognition in Hindi language texts.

[9] researched Named Entity Recognition (NER) and introduced an approach utilising a Bidirectional Recurrent Neural Network with Long Short-Term Memory (RNN-LSTM) architecture. Their model leveraged semantic information encoded in word vectors, obtained through unsupervised learning on unannotated corpora. The model achieved cutting-edge performance in English and Hindi, eliminating the need for morphological analysis or the utilisation of any form of gazetteers.

[10] described a Maximum Entropy-based NER system that also incorporated gazetteers to increase the performance of the system. A list of Named entities was collected in English and transliterated to Hindi for the creation of gazetteers. 11 features were identified and utilised for Hindi NER. The system was able to recognise 4 named entities: person, location, organisation, and date with each entity divided into 4 subclasses and one non-entity constituting a total of 17 classes. To identify the best feature set, 80 experiments were conducted. The highest F-1 score achieved for Hindi NER was 81.12.

[11] used ensemble learning for NER in Hindi. They used MultiCoNER [12], which has six named entities. Eight models were fine-tuned and the best F1-score achieved was 0.71.

[13] proposed a hybrid model using Conditional Random Fields (CRF) and a rule-based machine learning approach. Multiple experiments were performed by the authors using multiple models - rule-based model, CRF-based model and hybrid model. The results demonstrated the hybrid approach to be the most result-yielding, with F1-score of 97.30.

3 Methodology

3.1 Gazetteers

A gazetteer is a set of lists. Gazetteers were created for person, location, organisation, and months of the year.

Person: common first and last names; names of influential people
Location: Indian and international cities; countries; names of rivers, mountain ranges, and hills
Organisation: Airports; government organisations; company names; banks; government educational institutions etc.

3.2 POS Tagger

The POS tagger used in this project was developed by [14]. It is a Hidden Markov Model (HMM) based POS tagger developed using the IL POS tagset.

3.3 Rules and Working

Our system is a POS-tag-rule-based NER system. Naturally, the first step is to obtain the POS tags of all tokens of the text. We observed a document containing 15,000+ rows of POS-tagged data to understand and create rules based on grammar.

For the identification and classification of entities, separate rules were created based on the results of the POS tagger. Then rules are applied to POS-tagged sentences and a separate string is created for a token or consecutive tokens tagged as NNP (proper nouns). NNP tokens are dealt with in a different way from other tokens.

The rules were applied in a specific order that ensured entities were correctly identified. The basic algorithm is explained in Fig. 1. The rules of all entities are explained below:

Date. It was observed from POS-tagged data that dates generally occur as <QTC> <NNP> <QTC> when expressed as DD/month/YYYY format or as <QTC> <NNP> if a date is mentioned informally as DD/month format. If the POS tag of the current token is QTC, the next token has NNP and the token after has QTC tag, then it is likely we have encountered a date tag. The NNP token is checked against a list of months containing names of months in Hindi. If a match occurs, the tokens are tagged as a Date entity. '14 नवंबर 1965' is a date tag where POS-tags of '14' and '1965' are QTC and 'नवंबर' is NNP.

Time. Rules were constructed to identify two types of time expressions: periods (e.g. 18 वीं सदी or 18 वीं शताब्दी) and clock times (e.g. 5 बजे). In Hindi, 'बजे' is equivalent to "o'clock" or "a.m./p.m.". The former time entity is identified when the current token has a QTC, and the next two tokens have an NN. The final word in the sequence is then checked to determine if it is either "शताब्दी" (century) or "सदी" (era/century). The latter entity is identified when the first token has a QTC POS tag and the second token has the NN POS tag. If the NN token is 'बजे', then the sequence of tokens is classified as a time entity.

Person, Location, and Organisation. Generally, the names of persons, locations and organisations are multi-word named entities. This means that when multiple NNP tokens appear consecutively, there is a very high possibility that all these tokens are named entities. With this in consideration, a string containing all consecutive NNP tokens is generated. This string can be generated multiple times for an input text. The string is then processed further to identify the three named entities: person, location, and organisation. These three entities are identified using a look-up approach with gazetteers.

Entities like ‘ इंदिरा गांधी अंतर्राष्ट्रीय हवाई अड्डा’ and ‘ जवाहरलाल नेहरू स्टेडियम’ include the name of a person in their name. In India, many places are named after a person. For this reason, location and organisation entities are looked up before the person entity. In the case of a multi-worded NNP string, individual tokens are also looked up along with the whole string to ensure all possible named entities are captured.

3.4 Challenges

Ambiguity is a significant challenge faced in many NLP sub-tasks, including NER. Ambiguity arises when a word has multiple meanings or when different words have the same spelling or pronunciation. In the Indian context, many people are named after objects like काजल(Kajal: lampblack), पायल(Payal: anklet), पलक(Palak: eyelid) or after emotions/feelings, like मुस्कान(Muskan: smile), खुशी(Khushi: happiness), खुशबू(Khushboo: pleasant scent). Without contextual understanding, this may confuse the NER system leading to a common noun being recognised as a named entity or vice-versa.

Another challenge faced by the system is its total dependence on the POS tagger. The POS tagger is responsible for assigning the correct part-of-speech tags to each token in the text. If the POS tagger fails to correctly tag a token, it may result in the NER system mislabelling the NER tags. The system's rules are heavily based on POS tags, any error in tagging can result in incorrect labelling of NER tags. Incorrect POS tags may lead the system to overlook a named entity even if the POS tags of the sequence are partially correct.

Lack of capitalisation is a challenge faced by most Indian languages. In cased languages, named entities are more easily recognised due to the use of capital letters to denote proper nouns whereas in uncased languages, capitalisation is not utilised, and the task of identifying named entities becomes slightly more difficult.

4 Result and Discussion

For evaluation, we used the Hindi set from the Naamapadam [15] dataset. Naamapadam is a NER dataset curated for 11 Indian languages by AI4Bharat. For each language, three splits are available: train, test, and validation. The ‘test’ split, containing 867 rows of sentences was utilised for evaluation. Naamapadam is annotated for three entities: person, location, and organisation. Therefore, our system was evaluated for these three entities. Given that our gazetteers were created to target these three entities, it was appropriate to assess the system's performance exclusively on these categories.

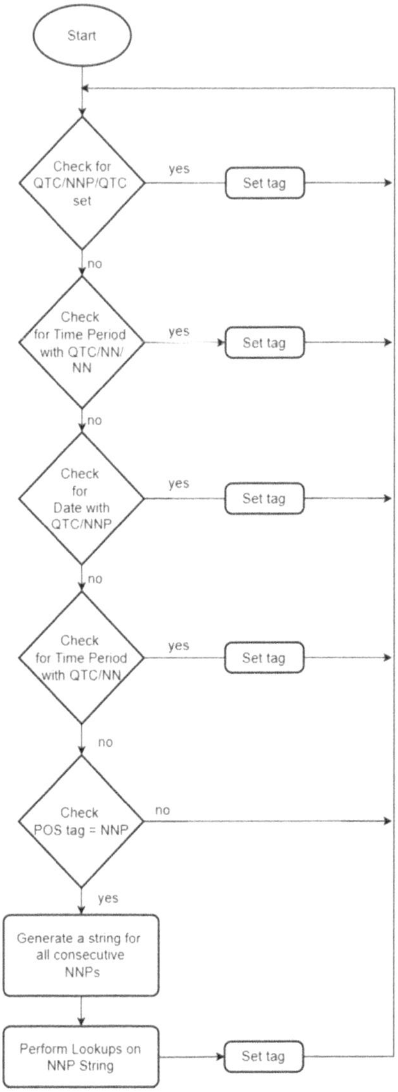

Fig. 1. Working of algorithm

It was observed that there was a mismatch between the lengths of predictions and the ground truth. To solve this, the longer variable was truncated to the length of the shorter variable. This approach leads to a fair comparison, although there is a slight loss of information as the difference between the lengths was not observed to be greater than 4.

The evaluation was performed after this step. The overall evaluation results are as follows; precision-0.90, recall-0.28, accuracy- 0.83, and the F1 Score-0.42. Detailed results for person, location and organisation are illustrated in Table 1.

Table 1. Detailed results of evaluation on the Naamapadam Dataset

Entity	Total Entities	Correctly Predicted	Accuracy	Precision	Recall	F1-Score
Person	1459	420	0.28	0.67	0.28	0.40
Location	785	202	0.25	0.57	0.25	0.35
Organisation	1002	7	0.006	0.38	0.006	0.013

The suboptimal performance of the system in the case of the organisation entity can be attributed to the total dependence on POS tags assigned by the tagger. As discussed in Sect. 3, a partially correctly tagged sequence of words may result in incorrect entity classification, which is mostly the case with organisation entities. Future work could focus on incorporating additional rules independent of the POS tagger, thereby enhancing the range of features utilised by the system.

References

1. Kanakarajan, K.R., Kundumani, B., Sankarasubbu, M.: BioELECTRA: pretrained biomedical text encoder using discriminators. In: Proceedings of the 20th Workshop on Biomedical Language Processing, pp. 143–154. Association for Computational Linguistics (2021)
2. Cowan, B., Zethelius, S., Luk, B., Baras, T., Ukarde, P., Zhang, D.: Named entity recognition in travel-related search queries. In: Proceedings of the AAAI Conference on Artificial Intelligence, vol. 29, no. 2 (2015)
3. Chopra, D., Jahan, N., Morwal, S.: Hindi named entity recognition by aggregating rule based heuristics and hidden Markov model. Int. J. Inf. **2**(6), 43–52 (2012)
4. Johnson, A.E., Bulgarelli, L., Pollard, T.J.: Deidentification of free-text medical records using pre-trained bidirectional transformers. In: Proceedings of the ACM Conference on Health, Inference, and Learning, pp. 214–221 (2020)
5. Alfred, R., Leong, L.C., On, C.K., Anthony, P.: Malay named entity recognition based on rule-based approach. Int. J. Mach. Learn. Comput. **4**(3) (2014)
6. Riaz, K.: Rule-based named entity recognition in Urdu. In: Proceedings of the 2010 Named Entities Workshop, pp. 126–135. Association for Computational Linguistics, Uppsala, Sweden (2010)
7. Abdallah, S., Shaalan, K., Shoaib, M.: Integrating rule-based system with classification for Arabic named entity recognition. In: International Conference on Intelligent Text Processing and Computational Linguistics. Springer, Heidelberg (2012)
8. Kaur, Y., Kaur, E.R.: Named Entity Recognition (NER) system for Hindi language using combination of rule based approach and list look up approach. Int. J. Sci. Res. Manag. (IJSRM) **3**(3), 2300–2306 (2015)
9. Athavale, V., Bharadwaj, S., Pamecha, M., Prabhu, A., Shrivastava, M.: Towards deep learning in Hindi NER: an approach to tackle the labelled data scarcity. arXiv preprint arXiv:1610.09756 (2016)
10. Kumar Saha, S., Sarathi Ghosh, P., Sarkar, S., Mitra, P.: Named entity recognition in Hindi using maximum entropy and transliteration. Polibits **38**, 33–41 (2008)
11. Singh, A., Singh, S., Tiwary, U.S.: Enhancing Hindi named entity recognition through ensemble learning. In: 2023 10th IEEE Uttar Pradesh Section International Conference on Electrical, Electronics and Computer Engineering (UPCON), vol. 10, pp. 297–300. IEEE (2023)

12. Malmasi, S., Fang, A., Fetahu, B., Kar, S., Rokhlenko, O.: MultiCoNER: a large-scale multilingual dataset for complex named entity recognition. arXiv preprint arXiv:2208.14536 (2022)
13. Srivastava, S.: HILNER: a Hindi language named entity recognition system based on hybrid approach. In: Hybrid Intelligent Systems: 20th International Conference on Hybrid Intelligent Systems (HIS 2020), 14–16 December 2020, pp. 340–348. Springer, Cham (2021)
14. Joshi, N., Darbari, H., Mathur, I.: HMM based POS tagger for Hindi. In: Proceeding of 2013 International Conference on Artificial Intelligence, Soft Computing (AISC-2013) (2013)
15. Mhaske, A., et al.: Naamapadam: a large-scale named entity annotated data for Indic languages. arXiv preprint arXiv:2212.10168 (2022)

Identification of Speaker-Specific Features to Minimize the Mismatch Outcomes for Speaker Recognition Using Anger and Happy Emotional Speech

Shalini Tomar(✉) and Shashidhar G. Koolagudi

Department of Computer Science and Engineering, National Institute of Technology, Surathkal, Karnataka, India
{shalinitomar.217cs504,koolagudi}@nitk.edu.in

Abstract. A vital component of digital speech processing is Speaker Recognition (SR). However, variation in speakers' emotional states, such as happiness, anger, sadness, or fear, poses a significant challenge that compromises the robustness of speaker recognition systems. It appears to be challenging to distinguish between emotions like "anger" and "happy", according to research on SR using emotive speech. The study looks at prosody-related speech characteristics to determine how to distinguish between "anger" and "happy" emotional speech for SR tasks. The goal is to explore speaker-specific features. The experiment outcomes demonstrate that, as speaker-specific features for the SR task, Intensity, Pitch, and Brightness (IPB) variables can distinguish between angry and happy emotional speech. Combining IPB and MFCC (IPBCC) feature extraction with the Hybrid CNN-LSTM combined with an attention mechanism approach achieves an SR accuracy of 95.45% for anger and 96.22% for happy emotional speech.

Keywords: Speaker Recognition using Emotional Speech · Intensity · Pitch · Brightness

1 Introduction

Verifying and identifying a speaker is the first step in the process of recognizing an individual [2]. Dealing with emotional variations in SR systems is highly difficult since emotions alter a person's vocal characteristics, and the acoustic elements used to identify a person by their voice differ from those used to train the models in a natural environment. SR performance can be enhanced by employing a variety of emotions. The goal of the Emotive Environment Speaker Recognition (EESR) technique is to identify speakers based on their emotional states [4,12]. In an emotive setting, one can employ a variety of emotions, such as happiness, anger, sadness, fear, surprise, and neutral speech. The goal of using emotional speech is to make SR in a complicated emotional environment less complex.

A. Sharma and R. Rani (Eds.): AIST 2024, CCIS 2389, pp. 63–76, 2025.
https://doi.org/10.1007/978-3-031-91331-0_5

Speaker Recognition models prepared for neutral speech do not recognize speakers with different emotional speech. Due to increased demands in various applications, such as Voice biometrics in security systems- access control and secure transaction, Human-computer interaction- adaptive systems, Customer service and sentiment analysis- call centers, market research, Health and well-being- Mental health monitoring, voice-based health apps, Education and learning platforms- adaptive learning systems, virtual tutoring, Law enforcement and forensics-voice authentication, forensic analysis, and Human-robot interaction, ESSR has recently attracted more attention. Even though it has been studied and is a crucial component of human-computer communication, the human capacity to distinguish speakers based only on their voices needs more thought. Numerous studies that established recognition of speakers' strategies for emotional speech have contributed to the field of speech. The existing literature work [3,13,14], and Table 1 shows that using neutral speech for training and happy speech for testing the Speaker Recognition model yields comparatively higher accuracy than using neutral audio for training and angry speech for testing.

Table 1. Speaker Recognition Accuracy in (%) using Happy and Anger emotional speech

SI No.	Title	Happy	Anger
1	Speaker Identification in Emotional Talking Environments based on CSPHMM2s, [15]	85.5	74
2	Speaker Identification in different Emotional States in Arabic and English, [8]	93.7	88
3	Emotional Speaker Identification using a Novel Capsule Nets Model, [9]	77.6	65
4	Speaker Recognition using Constrained CNN in Emotional Speech, [16]	84.70	78.75
5	Emotional Speaker Verification Using Novel Modified Capsule Neural Network, [10]	91	87

The following ESSR evaluations and research gaps have been identified after a relevant literature evaluation.

1. Pertinent research that explores the reason for the difference between anger and happy emotional speech outcomes for the SR tasks.
2. Speaker-specific features for ESSR tasks.

We evaluate both happy and angry emotional speech for the SR task, taking into account the following research gaps in the proposed study, and attempt to minimize the mismatch outcomes of SR tasks employing both emotional speeches. The proposed work explores speaker-specific features that are less ineffective or less effective by emotional speech. The proposed work also includes the hybrid

CNN-LSTM model enhancement by adding an attention mechanism to focus on the critical time frames in the speech signal, particularly when emotional content is present. The remainder of the paper has been divided up into sections. Section 2 includes the motivation for the proposed work. Section 3 goes into the specifics of the proposed Speaker Recognition system and Experiments. According to the experiments in Sect. 4, the Speaker-Specific features are identified. Following that, the Sect. 5 summarizes the conclusions.

2 Several Explanations for the Speaker Recognition Mismatch Results Between Anger and Happy Emotional Speech

The mismatch in speaker recognition accuracy when using angry and happy emotional speech can be attributed to several factors, such as:

Variability in Vocal Patterns: Emotional speech, especially strong emotions like anger and happiness, can cause significant variations in a speaker's vocal characteristics. For example, anger might increase intensity and pitch variability, while happiness may result in lighter, more melodic tones.

Feature Distortion: Emotions tend to distort the acoustic features that are used for speaker identification, such as pitch, formants, and spectral features. For instance, anger typically raises the pitch and increases the presence of high-frequency components, while happiness can alter the voice's rhythm and smoothness, leading to different feature patterns.

Feature Sensitivity: Feature extraction methods like MFCC, pitch, intensity, or timbre brightness might behave differently under varying emotional states.

Prosodic Changes: Emotions affect prosodic features (such as rhythm, stress, and intonation), and the changes can reduce the model's ability to capture speaker-specific patterns. Happy and angry speech will have different prosodic contours, potentially leading to a mismatch in recognition accuracy.

Insufficient Emotional Modeling: Some models may not be designed to handle the emotional variability in speech, leading to lower accuracy when emotions are involved.

Considering the above reasons, we proposed the SR system with speaker-specific features. The identified speaker-specific features performance is evaluated by using three different language emotional speech datasets and various ML and DL approaches.

3 Proposed Speaker Recognition System and Experiments

A typical Speaker Recognition task contains data preprocessing, feature extraction from speech signals, and different classifiers for the classification of the speakers. Figure 1 illustrates the Speaker Recognition typical model for the proposed work. Three datasets are used for the proposed work: NITK-KLESC [18], CREMA-D [1], and RAVDESS [7]. Speaker-specific feature extraction, including prosodic, spectral, and cepstral features, is used in the proposed work. For classification purposes, we used the CNN-LSTM model and compared the results with different Machine Learning and Deep Learning approaches.

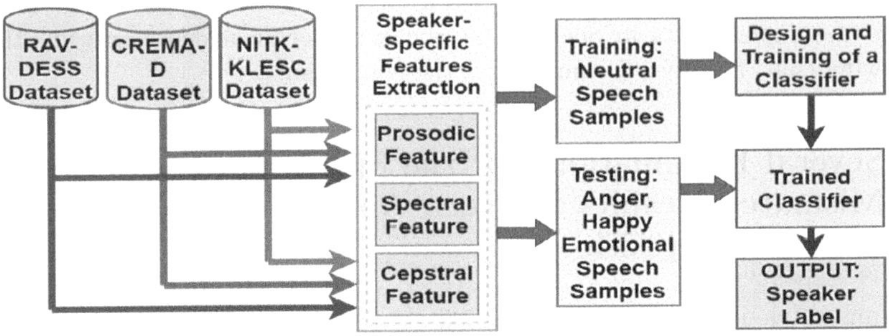

Fig. 1. Illustration of a typical Speaker Recognition Model

3.1 Dataset

Anger, happy, and neutral emotional speech are employed for speaker recognition tasks. For the Speaker Recognition system, 20 speakers from RAVDESS and 576 utterances, 90 speakers from CREMA-D and 3,240 utterances, and 100 speakers from NITK-KLESC and 30,000 utterances are considered. Ten speakers are considered for the emotional speech prosodic analysis across all three datasets.

3.2 Feature Extraction

The prosodic, spectral, and cepstral features broadly describe the features commonly employed for Speaker Recognition utilizing emotional speech and emotional speech analysis.

Prosodic Features. Fundamental frequency (F0) is the primary basis for prosodic features, which include average F0, shimmer, jitter, rise, and fall in the F0 contour, as well as attributes about energy and speaking rates. The following prosodic features are used for the emotional speech analysis for SR tasks.

1. **Intensity:** Intensity refers to the power of the speech signal over time. It is typically measured in decibels (dB). The intensity of speech can vary depending on the speaker's loudness, speaking style, and emotion, making it a speaker-specific feature. The intensity level L_1 in decibels is calculated as shown in Eq. 1

$$L_1 = 10 \cdot log_{10}\left(\frac{I}{I_0}\right) = 20 \cdot log_{10}\left(\frac{p}{p_0}\right) \tag{1}$$

Here, L_1 is the intensity level in dB. I is the sound intensity, and I_0 is the reference intensity. p is the sound pressure of the speech signal, and p_0 is the reference sound pressure level.
The variation of intensity over time is significant in capturing speaker-specific traits. The variation of intensity over time includes the average intensity level, how the intensity changes during speech, and patterns in the intensity across different speech segments. Speech intensity is also related to the energy of the speech signal, which can be calculated over short time windows. By analyzing energy patterns, speaker-specific traits related to intensity can be extracted.

2. **Pitch:** The fundamental frequency (F0) of speech signals, which correlates to the voice's perceived pitch or tone, is represented by pitch characteristics. It can change within and between syllables, words, and phrases, adding to the speech's intonation and melody. Pitch variations can express verbal cues like emphasis, queries, or emotional states. The pitch contour (variation of pitch over time) carries essential speaker-specific information, as each speaker has a unique pattern of pitch variation depending on their physiology and speech habits. The autocorrelation technique in the proposed work determines the pitch. The similarity between a signal and a delayed version of itself is measured by autocorrelation. The periodicity of the signal can be determined by shifting it by various time offsets and calculating the correlation between the shifted and original versions. The function denotes the input signal as x(t). The autocorrelation function R(z) at lag z is calculated as shown in Eq. 2. The integral is usually approximated using discrete samples of the signal.

$$R(z) = \int_0^\infty x(t)x(t-z)dt \tag{2}$$

It is computed mathematically by multiplying the signal by a version of itself that has been time-shifted and adding the results over all possible time shifts. Peaks are found following the computation of the autocorrelation function. The fundamental frequency (pitch) and its harmonics are among the periodicities in the signal the peaks represent. The signal's period, or the lag corresponding to the first peak in the autocorrelation function, is represented by the F0.

Spectral Features. Spectral features are crucial in speaker recognition because they capture speaker-specific characteristics embedded in the frequency of speech. The features are derived from analyzing the power spectrum of the speech signal and are sensitive to the speaker's vocal tract shape, articulation, and other physiological traits.

1. **Timbre Brightness:** A voice's timbre describes its distinctive qualities, distinct color, or uniqueness. It allows us to distinguish one voice from another even when speaking at the same volume and pitch. Timbre is a wide concept that includes various elements that affect a voice's overall speaking characteristics, such as brightness, sharpness, hardness, etc. Regarding the human voice, brightness is a perceptual attribute defined by a sound with a greater

percentage of high-frequency components. Timbre brightness refers to the balance between high and low frequencies in the speech spectrum. It can be quantified using spectral features that focus on the distribution of energy in different frequency bands. Higher brightness typically corresponds to more energy in the higher frequency regions. In speaker recognition systems, timbre brightness-related features are extracted from the speech signal and included in the feature vectors used to model each speaker. Timbre brightness is particularly useful when combined with hybrid approaches involving other features (e.g., MFCC, pitch, intensity) to improve the robustness of speaker recognition systems, especially when dealing with emotional or expressive speech. Spectral tilt is a feature used to describe timbre brightness, and it refers to the rate of decrease in amplitude as frequency increases. A higher spectral tilt indicates less energy in the higher frequencies, corresponding to a "darker" timbre. In contrast, a lower tilt indicates more energy in the higher frequencies, resulting in a brighter timbre. Here, we extract brightness using spectral tilt as shown in Eq. 3.

$$T = \frac{\sum_{k=1}^{K}(f[k] - \bar{f}) \cdot (log\,|X[k]| - \overline{log\,|X|}}{\sum_{k=1}^{K}(f[k] - \bar{f})^2} \tag{3}$$

where T is the spectral tilt, f [k] and X[k] represent the frequency and magnitude at bin k. $\bar{f}$ and $\overline{log}$| X| are the mean frequency and mean log-magnitude values, respectively.

Cepstral Features. MFCC (Mel-Frequency Cepstral Coefficients) is technically a cepstral feature because it is derived from the cepstrum of the speech signal. However, it is also closely related to spectral features because the process of calculating MFCCs involves a transformation of the spectrum of the speech signal.

1. **MFCC:** MFCCs are widely used in speech processing. They capture the spectral envelope of speech signals and are particularly effective in representing human speech perception. Some examples of MFCC feature extraction techniques employed with various classifiers for speaker recognition tasks [11,17]. The Eq. 4 utilizes the Mel scale to convert the actual frequency; it links the Mel scale to Hertz. Here, mel1 stands for Mels and f1 for Hertz.

$$mel1(f1) = 2595log(1 + f1/700) \tag{4}$$

3.3 Classification

The classifiers used for ESSR tasks can be broadly classified into Machine Learning classifiers (ML) and Deep Learning (DL) classifiers. Machine learning classifiers are commonly used for ESSR tasks for handcrafted features. ML classifiers include Hidden Markov Models (HMM) [15], Support Vector Machines (SVM) [6], and Gaussian Mixture Models (GMM) [5] mainly for ESSR tasks. The advantage of Machine learning algorithms is that they can range from simple linear models to more complex models such as decision trees and random forests. It also involves training algorithms to identify patterns and relations in data. In the proposed work, we used a CNN-LSTM hybrid model combined with an attention mechanism for speaker recognition. An attention mechanism can help the model focus on the most critical time steps in the speech sequence, which is particularly useful when emotional states cause variations in speech characteristics that could be more or less relevant to speaker recognition. The CNN-LSTM processes the input features sequentially, and the Attention Layer highlights the most critical time steps for the final decision. The algorithm for the proposed work is as follows:

1. **Input:** Sequence of hybrid IPBCC features X $\epsilon R^{T \times d \times 1}$.
2. **CNN Layers:** Apply convolution and pooling operations to extract local spatial features, yielding H $\epsilon R^{T' \times d'}$.
3. **LSTM Layer:** Process the flattened CNN output with LSTM to model temporal dependencies, producing hidden states $\mathbf{h_t}$.
4. **Attention Mechanism:** Compute attention weights α_t and context vector **c**.
5. **Classification:** Use the context vector **c** to predict the speaker class through a dense layer.
6. **Loss Calculation:** Compute the cross-entropy loss between the predicted and true speaker labels.
7. **Optimization:** Update model parameters using gradient descent.

The formulation captures the spatial, temporal, and critical information for speaker recognition using emotional speech with IPBCC features. The CNN extracts local spatial features from the hybrid input, the LSTM captures temporal patterns, and the attention mechanism emphasizes key time steps, leading to better speaker recognition.

3.4 Results Analysis for Speaker Recognition Using Anger and Happy Emotional Speech

The results are analyzed using three datasets- RAVDESS, CREMA-D, and NITK-KLESC. Intensity, Pitch, and Brightness (IPB) and Mel-Frequency Cepstral Coefficient (MFCC) features are used for feature extraction. Support Vector Machine (SVM), Gaussian Mixture Model (GMM), Random Forest (RF), CatBoost (CB), Convolutional Neural Networks (CNN), and hybrid Convolutional Neural Networks - Long Short-Term Memory (CNN-LSTM) classifier enhancement with attention mechanism are used for classification purposes. We attempted to compare the outcomes using various datasets to different classifiers to demonstrate the effectiveness of the features for SR tasks. Table 2 shows the accuracy of the SR system using IPB and MFCC features with different machine learning approaches and the NITK-KLESC dataset.

Table 2. SR model performance using ML and CNN-LSTM approaches accuracy in (%) with IPB and MFCC feature extraction

NITK-KLESC Train (Neutral)	SVM	GMM	RF	CB	CNN	CNN-LSTM
Test (Anger) IPB	58	61	66	70	71	74
Test (Happy) IPB	59	63	67	73	72	76
Test (Anger) MFCC	60	63	68	71	76	78
Test (Happy) MFCC	72	75	78	81	86	88

The results demonstrate that the accuracy of the SR system while employing IPB features differs less from MFCC features when distinguishing between angry and happy emotional speech. With IPB features, the difference in SR accuracy between angry and happy emotional speech is 1 to 2%, whereas, with MFCC features, the difference is 10 to 12%. The SR accuracy using happy emotional speech is comparatively higher for both features. In the case of MFCC features, the SR recognition accuracy using all for classifiers has a large gap using anger and happy emotional speech. However, using IPB features, the gap is significantly smaller. IPB features are speaker-specific features, but recognizing the speakers alone is not sufficient. So, we try to combine the features IPB and MFCC (IPBCC) at the feature level, and the fusion provides improved results. The CNN-LSTM approach gives improved results for both features. So, the model of SR tasks uses the CNN-LSTM enhancement attention mechanism approach with IPBCC features.

Table 3. SR model performance (accuracy in %) with CNN-LSTM approach and IPBCC features using different datasets.

CNN-LSTM (IPBCC) Train(Neutral)	Test (Anger)	Test (Happy)
RAVDESS	89.78	90.31
CREMA-D	92.75	93.42
NITK-KLESC	95.45	96.22

Table 3 shows the accuracy of the SR task with IPBCC features considering the training data as neutral speech and testing as anger and happy emotional speech. Using the CNN-LSTM approach, the enhanced outcomes for SR tasks are applied to all three datasets. There is a substantially minor variation of less than 1 % in SR accuracy when employing angry versus happy emotional speech.

4 Identification of Speaker-Specific Features

From the result analysis, it is concluded that IPB has speaker-specific features. Figure 2 represents IPB features anger, happy, and neutral emotional speech analysis of 10 speakers from all three datasets. Figure 2 (a1), (b1), and (c1) sections represent the intensity of angry, happy, and neutral speech.

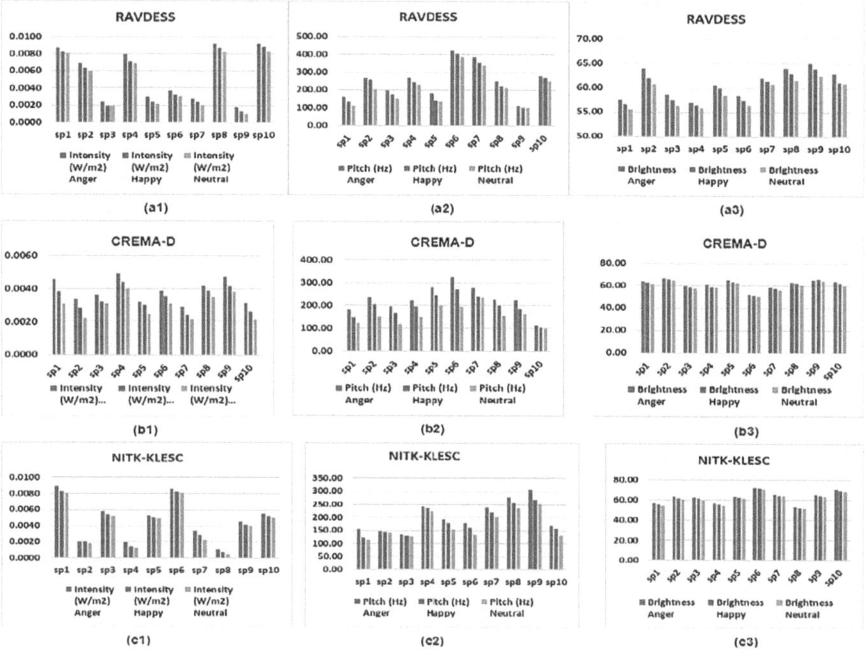

Fig. 2. Illustration of IPB features for RAVDESS, CREMA-D, and NITK-KLESC Datasets.

The intensity of anger is higher than that of happy and neutral emotions. The same pattern follows for all speakers. For each speaker, we analyzed a different pattern of intensity group. The difference between the three emotional intensities is less than the individual speaker's intensity. The sections labeled (a2), (b2), and (c2) depict the pitch of angry, happy, and neutral speech. Anger has a higher pitch than happiness or neutral feelings. Every speaker follows a particular pattern. We examined a distinct pitch group pattern for every speaker. The three emotional pitches are closer together than they are to the pitch of any one speaker. Sections labeled (a3), (b3), and (c3) depict the brightness of neutral, angry, and happy speech, respectively. Compared to neutral and happy emotions, the brightness of anger is higher. We examined a distinct brightness group pattern for every speaker. Less than the brightness of each speaker separates the three emotional brightness. For detailed analysis, we take NITK-KLESC's same utterance from one speaker in neutral, angry, and happy emotions.

Intensity: Intensity can change depending on emotion (e.g., louder during anger); individual speakers have unique baseline levels and variability of intensity. Their vocal control, style, and habitual intensity patterns remain relatively stable across emotions. For example, one speaker may have a naturally strong voice, while another may have a softer, more subdued voice. Emotions affect intensity, but each speaker modulates loudness in a personalized way across emotions. The variability across emotions, yet consistency for an individual, helps distinguish speakers. Figure 3 represents the intensity of a speaker in angry, happy, and neutral speech.

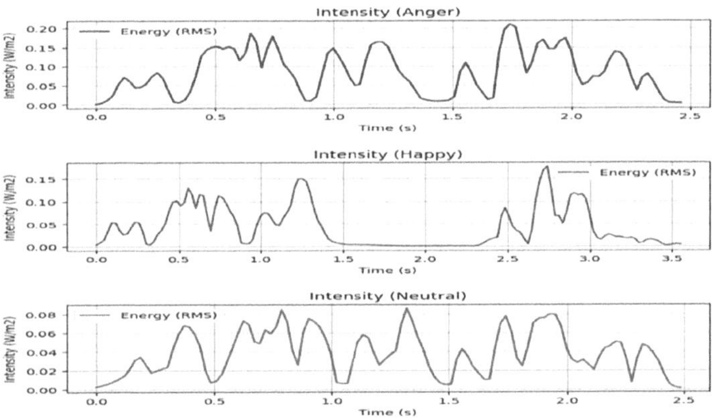

Fig. 3. Intensity of a speaker's voice in Anger, Happy, and Neutral Emotions

According to the illustration, we find approximately the same pattern except for the happy emotion duration of 1.5 sec to 2.5 sec. for all three emotions of intensity. Intensity is speaker-specific; however, the intensity depends on emotions for specific phonemes. For a complete sentence, the overall intensity is approximately the same in all three emotions.

Pitch: Each speaker has a natural pitch range that remains relatively consistent, even when the emotional state changes. For example, a person with a naturally high-pitched voice will continue to have a higher pitch across different emotions compared to someone with a naturally low-pitched voice. While emotions such as anger and happiness can cause variations in pitch (e.g., higher pitch when excited or angry), the speaker's baseline pitch and the way they modulate pitch within their emotional expressions are often unique to them.

Figure 4 represents a speaker's pitch in angry, happy, and neutral speech. According to the illustration, the pitch for all three emotions is the same from 0.0 sec to 1 sec. For different emotions, the duration of the same sentence will be

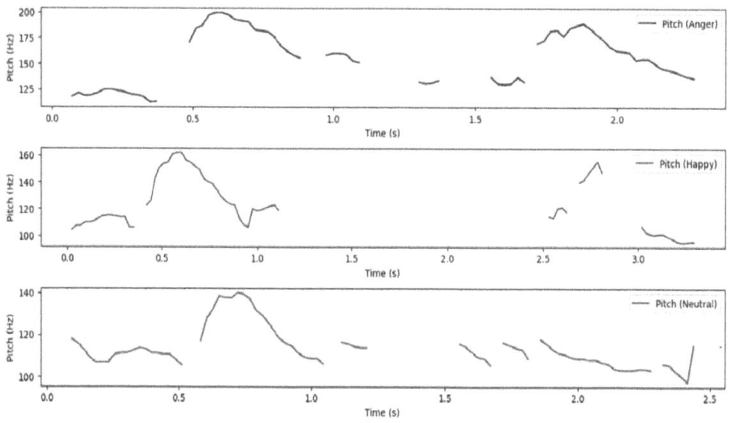

Fig. 4. Pitch of a speaker's voice in Anger, Happy, and Neutral Emotions

different. So, from 1.5 sec to the utterance endpoint, the three emotions' pitches are the same but in different time slots.

Brightness: Brightness is influenced by the speaker's vocal tract configuration, including the shape of the mouth, nasal passages, and other resonating cavities. The anatomical features vary between individuals and affect the spectral characteristics of their speech. Thus, brightness tends to be a stable speaker-specific attribute even as emotional speech alters the overall speech signal.

Emotions like anger or happiness can shift the brightness by changing vocal effort and resonance. Still, the speaker's vocal tract anatomy and habitual speaking style ensure that brightness patterns remain relatively consistent for a particular individual. Figure 5 represents the brightness of a speaker in angry, happy, and neutral speech. According to the illustration, we find the same pattern for all three emotions of brightness of speech. The elevated starting points for anger and happy emotional speech are normalized spectral centroid increased than 0.25. However, it is less than 0.25 in the case of neutral speech.

The IPB characteristics are investigated as speaker-specific features for ESSR based on the speech analysis. The characteristics can be applied to speech recognition with various emotions and emotion recognition. The feature extraction determines the difference in SR accuracy between emotional speech expressing anger and happiness. Time-frequency representation (TFR) techniques can help to improve the difference. The accuracy of the SR task can be increased, and the difference can be decreased by using speech transformation techniques.

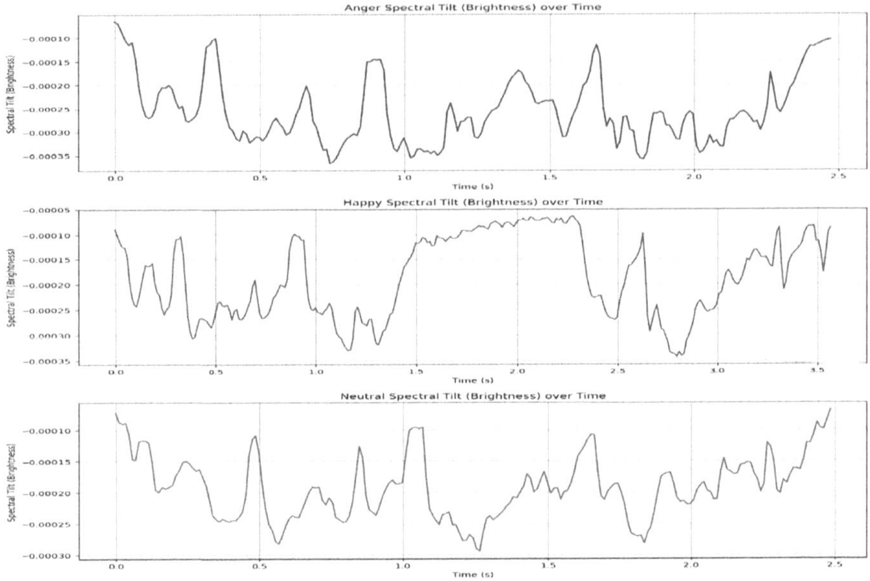

Fig. 5. Brightness of a speaker's voice in Anger, Happy, and Neutral Emotions

5 Conclusion

The features specific to each speaker are included in the suggested work. For speaker recognition, the work provided the IPBCC features with the hybrid CNN-LSTM enhancement attention mechanism approach. The proposed work aims to determine the cause of the variation in the SR task results between angry and happy emotional speech. IPBCC features recognize speaker-specific properties. It also attempted to overcome the accuracy gap measured for the SR task utilizing happy and angry emotional speech. The proposed work provided the SR system accuracy using the anger and happy emotional speech at 95.45% and 96.22%, respectively. The proposed method can combine additional feature extraction approaches with various deep-learning strategies to improvise. Speech transformation can also be accomplished by employing the IPBCC features for further implementations.

Acknowledgements. The authors thank the Cognitive Science Research Initiative (CSRI), Department of Science & Technology, Government of India, Grant Sanction Order No.: "DST/CSRI/2018/400(G)", for its financial support of their work. The authors would like to thank Kavya Nagaraj for the fruitful discussions and for helping with the implementation.

References

1. Cao, H., Cooper, D.G., Keutmann, M.K., Gur, R.C., Nenkova, A., Verma, R.: Crema-D: crowd-sourced emotional multimodal actors dataset. IEEE Trans. Affect. Comput. 377–390 (2014)
2. Ghiurcau, M.V., Rusu, C., Astola, J.: Speaker recognition in an emotional environment. In: Proceedings of the Signal Processing and Applied Mathematics for Electronics and Communications, pp. 81–84 (2011)
3. Koolagudi, S.G., Fatima, S.E., Sreenivasa Rao, K.: Speaker recognition in the case of emotional environment using transformation of speech features. In: Proceedings of the CUBE International Information Technology Conference, pp. 118–123 (2012)
4. Koolagudi, S.G., Sharma, K., Sreenivasa Rao, K.: Speaker recognition in emotional environment. In: Mathew, J., Patra, P., Pradhan, D.K., Kuttyamma, A.J. (eds.) ICECCS 2012. CCIS, vol. 305, pp. 117–124. Springer, Heidelberg (2012). https://doi.org/10.1007/978-3-642-32112-2_15
5. Kumar, T., Bhukya, R.K.: Mel spectrogram based automatic speaker verification using GMM-UBM. In: IEEE 9th Uttar Pradesh Section International Conference on Electrical, Electronics and Computer Engineering (UPCON), pp. 1–6. IEEE (2022)
6. Liu, M., Dai, B., Xie, Y., Yao, Z.: Improved GMM-UBM/SVM for speaker verification. In: IEEE International Conference on Acoustics Speech and Signal Processing Proceedings, pp. 24–28. IEEE (2006)
7. Livingstone, S.R., Russo, F.A.: The Ryerson audio-visual database of emotional speech and song (RAVDESS): a dynamic, multimodal set of facial and vocal expressions in North American English. Public Libr. Sci. 1–15 (2018)
8. Meftah, A.H., Mathkour, H., Kerrache, S., Alotaibi, Y.A.: Speaker identification in different emotional states in Arabic and English. IEEE Access **8**, 60070–60083 (2020)
9. Nassif, A.B., Shahin, I., Elnagar, A., Velayudhan, D., Alhudhaif, A., Polat, K.: Emotional speaker identification using a novel capsule nets model. Expert Syst. Appl. 1164–1169 (2022)
10. Nassif, A.B., Shahin, I., Nemmour, N., Hindawi, N., Elnagar, A.: Emotional speaker verification using novel modified capsule neural network. In: Mathematics, pp. 1–21. MDPI (2023)
11. Nakagawa, S., Asakawa, K., Wang, L.: Speaker recognition by combining MFCC and phase information. In: Interspeech, pp. 19–22. ISCA (2010)
12. Shahin, I.: Speaker identification in emotional environments. In: IJECE, pp. 1–8 (2009)
13. Shahin, I.: Verifying speakers in emotional environments. In: IEEE International Symposium on Signal Processing and Information Technology (ISSPIT), pp. 328–333 (2009)
14. Shahin, I.: Speaker recognition systems in the emotional environment. In: 2008 3rd International Conference on Information and Communication Technologies: From Theory to Applications, pp. 1–5. IEEE (2008)

15. Shahin, I.: Speaker identification in emotional talking environments based on CSPHMM2s. Eng. Appl. Artif. Intell. **26**, 1652–1659 (2013)
16. Simić, N., et al.: Speaker recognition using constrained convolutional neural networks in emotional speech. Entropy **24**, 414–426 (2022)
17. Tiwari, V.: MFCC and its applications in speaker recognition. Int. J. Emerg. Technol. 19–22 (2010)
18. Tomar, S., Gupta, P., Koolagudi, S.G.: NITK-KLESC: Kannada language emotional speech corpus for speaker recognition. In: 26th International Conference on Oriental - COCOSDA, pp. 1–6. IEEE (2023)

Emotional Speech Corpus: A Review

Krishna Rohilla(✉), Aaditya Sharma, Nilakshi, and Nivedita Palia

VSE&T, Vivekananda Institute of Professional Studies-Technical Campus, Delhi, India
{08417711622_ml,09817711622_ml,10117711622_ml, nivedita.palia}@vips.edu

Abstract. Speech Emotion Recognition (SER) has gained significant attention in recent years, with applications in human-machine interaction, healthcare, and customer service. A crucial aspect of SER is the availability of high-quality emotion databases that can train and evaluate emotion recognition models. This paper provides a comprehensive review of thirty speech emotion recognition databases, covering various languages, including English, German, Chinese, Russian, Hindi, and other Indian languages. This study analyze the speech emotion databases based on language, number of speakers, emotions recorded, features extracted, and accuracy achieved. The analysis highlights the dominance of English and Hindi languages in SER research, with a significant number of databases available for these languages. The most recorded emotions are sadness, anger, fear, neutral, happiness, surprise, and disgust. Furthermore, it has been found that most databases extracted Mel-Frequency Cepstral Coefficients (MFCCs) and prosodic features for emotion recognition, with accuracies ranging from 60% to 98%. The review provides valuable insights into the existing SER databases, highlighting the need for more diverse and representative datasets that can improve the performance and generalizability of emotion recognition models.

Keywords: Speech Emotion Recognition · Speech Emotion Databases · Mel Frequency Cepstral Coefficients

1 Introduction

Speech signal is the quickest and most natural way for people to communicate. This idea has led many researchers to explore how we can interact with machines using speech. For machines to understand human speech, they need to be smart enough to recognize voices. From past decades, a lot of research has focused on speech recognition, which means translating spoken words into written text. Despite significant progress, machines still struggle to interact naturally with humans because they can't understand emotions in speech. This challenge has led to a newer area of research called speech emotion recognition (SER), which aims to identify the speaker's emotions from their voice. It is thought that identifying emotions in speech can improve the overall effectiveness of speech recognition systems (SRS).

SER is especially beneficial for applications that demand natural human-machine interaction, such as online videos and computer tutorials, where the system's response to

A. Sharma and R. Rani (Eds.): AIST 2024, CCIS 2389, pp. 77–93, 2025.
https://doi.org/10.1007/978-3-031-91331-0_6

the user based on the detected emotion [1]. It is also beneficial for in-car display systems, where information about the driver's mental state can be sent to the system to initiate his or her safety [1]. Therapists can also utilize it to make diagnoses. It might also work well in automatic translation systems if the emotional state of the speaker affects how parties communicate. It has been found that SRS taught to stressed speech outperform those trained to standard speech in airplane cockpits [2]. SER has also been used in call center applications and mobile communication. The main goal of using SER is to adapt the system response after finding frustration or annoyance in the speaker's voice.

SER is a challenging task for several reasons. Firstly, it is unclear which speech features are majorly effective in classifying emotions. Variations in sentences, speakers, speaking styles, and rates add complexity, as these factors impact common speech features like pitch and energy patterns. Additionally, a single utterance may contain multiple emotions, each tied to different parts of the speech, making it hard to determine the boundaries between them. The expression of emotions also varies depending on the speaker's culture and environment. Most research has focused on monolingual emotion classification, assuming no cultural differences, but some studies have investigated multilingual classification [3].

Another issue is that long-term emotional states, like sadness, can last for days or weeks, while other emotions are temporary and last only a few minutes. This makes it difficult to decide whether the emotion recognizer should detect long-term or temporary emotions. Emotions do not have a commonly accepted definition, yet individuals identify them when they experience them. Researchers have identified several features of emotions, with most agreeing that emotions can be classified into two dimensions: activation and valence [2].

The energy needed to express a feeling is referred to as activation. According to studies, emotions such as joy, anger, and fear stimulate the sympathetic nervous system, causing a rise in heart rate, blood pressure, and other physiological changes. This produces loud, rapid speech with a higher pitch and a larger pitch range. In contrast, sorrow activates the parasympathetic nervous system, resulting in slower, lower-pitched speech with less high-frequency energy. Thus, pitch, timing, voice quality, and articulation are all linked to emotions. However, activation alone does not identify emotions. For example, both rage and happiness are highly activated but transmit different emotions. This distinction is defined by the valence dimension, but researchers disagree on how, or if, acoustic features relate to valence. As a result, while distinguishing between high-activation and low-activation emotions is relatively accurate, differentiating between specific emotions remains difficult [4].

An SER system is the classification of many ways for processing and characterizing speech signals to recognize emotions buried in them. An SER system requires a classifier, which is a supervised learning architecture taught to detect emotions in fresh speech signals [5]. To effectively build a supervised system, labeled data with embedded emotions must be available. However, before any data processing can take place to extract features, preprocessing is necessary. One crucial aspect of preprocessing is ensuring a consistent sampling rate across all databases. The classification process heavily relies on features, which play an essential role in condensing raw data into its most essential characteristics. Whether acoustic features alone are sufficient for emotion display, or if a combination of linguistic, facial, and speech information is necessary, remains a question worth exploring.

For developing the aforesaid SER system, the prerequisite is speech databases. We provide a thorough analysis of 30 speech emotion databases (SED) in this study to help readers comprehend previous research and plan the next steps toward creating a benchmarked SED for additional studies.

In Sect. 2 we briefly examined 30 SED. Section 3 we presented a comparative analysis of these SED. Finally, the conclusion is presented in Sect. 4.

2 Description of Speech Emotion Databases

2.1 English Databases

Dataset 1. The IEMOCAP (Interactive Emotional Dyadic Motion Capture) dataset, introduced by Carlos Busso et al., includes 12 h of multimodal data from 10 professional speakers across 5 sessions at a 16 kHz sampling frequency. It features 10,039 utterances annotated for emotions like happiness, anger, neutrality and sadness. The interactions were recorded in a controlled environment using multiple cameras and microphones, ensuring good-quality audiovisual data. It was developed by the Speech Analysis and Interpretation Laboratory at the University of Southern California. The speech samples were recorded in an acoustically clean environment with minimum background noise which indicates high signal to noise ratio (SNR). Extracted features include Mel Frequency Cepstral Coefficients (MFCC), prosodic audio, word embeddings, and motion capture data. The paid dataset supports emotion recognition with up to 71.04% accuracy when combining speech, text, and motion capture modalities [6].

Dataset 2. The Toronto Emotional Speech Set (TESS) consists of 2,800 utterances from two female speakers (aged 26 and 64) spanning seven emotions with primary emotions like anger, disgust, fear, happiness, sadness, surprise, neutral. The dataset does not provide explicit details about the microphone type, but the recordings were made in controlled soundproof environment to ensure the clarity and accuracy of the vocal data. It has a range of spectral characteristics and regularly recovered MFCCs at a 16 kHz sampling frequency. Emotion recognition accuracy ranges from 72% to 98% when employing Random Forest and Support Vector Machine (SVM) classifiers [7].

Dataset 3. The SAVEE (Surrey Audio-Visual Expressed Emotion) dataset contains 480 utterances from 4 male speakers across 7 (anger, disgust, fear, happiness, sadness, surprise, neutral) emotions, recorded at 44.1 kHz. High-quality microphones were used to capture clear and accurate speech data. It extracted MFCCs and spectrograms, with speaker-independent recognition rates up to 61% for audio-only models. The dataset is freely available for academic use [8].

Dataset 4. The RAVDESS (Ryerson Audio-Visual Database of Emotional Speech and Song) dataset, referenced in Livingstone & Russo (2018), is a paid resource available for research upon request. It is a multimodal corpus which consists of 7,356 files of audio and facial expression. It classifies emotions into 7 groups of happiness, sadness, surprise, neutral, calm, anger, disgust, and fear. It includes 24,576 audio samples of full-length utterances from 24 professional speakers (12 male, 12 female), recorded at 48 kHz. Recordings were made in controlled studio environment to ensure high-quality, multimodal data. Features commonly extracted for emotion recognition are prosodic, spectral, voice quality, and formant frequencies. Accuracy for emotion classification typically ranges from 70–80% [9].

Dataset 5. The ABIO dataset, detailed in Schuller et al. (2011), is a paid resource requiring permission for access. It includes 3,000 samples from 10 speakers, with utterances recorded at a 44.1 kHz sampling frequency. Recorded in environment of controlled acoustic conditions to ensure clear audio recordings. Features commonly extracted include MFCCs and prosodic features. The dataset encompasses six emotions: happiness, anger, sadness, fear, disgust, and surprise. Emotion recognition accuracy typically ranges from 60–70% [10].

Dataset 6. The eNTERFACE05 dataset is freely available for research purposes. It categorized feelings into seven groups: neutral, surprise, happiness, sadness, disgust, and terror. It includes approximately 2,880 samples from 40 speakers from different nations, with utterances recorded at a 44.1 kHz sampling frequency which were captured in a controlled environment to minimize background noise and ensure clarity. Features commonly extracted for emotion recognition include MFCCs and prosodic features. SER attained accuracy in the range of 60–75% using MFCC and prosodic feature [11].

Dataset 7. The CMU-MOSEI Corpus is available for research purposes and is typically unpaid, though registration may be required. Emotions are divided into seven categories: surprise, happiness, sadness, disgust, anger, fear, and neutral. It includes over 5,000 samples from approximately 100 speakers, with utterances recorded at a 16 kHz sampling frequency. Recording setup included various settings, but consistent registration and quality control for research purposes. Features commonly extracted for emotion recognition include MFCCs and prosodic features. Emotion recognition accuracy often ranges from 70–80% [12].

2.2 German Databases

Dataset 8. The Emotional Sensitivity Assistant System for People with Disability (EmotAsS) dataset is available upon request for research purposes and is not freely accessible. It includes approximately 2,400 samples from 17 mentally neurologically disabled speakers, with utterances recorded at a 44.1 kHz sampling frequency. Features commonly extracted for emotion recognition include MFCCs and prosodic features. Emotion recognition accuracy typically ranges from 70–80% [13].

Dataset 9. The Institute of Communication Science, Technical University Berlin, Germany developed The Berlin Database of Emotional Speech (EmoDB) database. It is available for research purposes and is typically unpaid, though registration is required. It classifies emotions into 7 classes including disgust, fear, happiness, sadness, anger, surprise, neutral. It consists of around 5,000 samples from 10 speakers, with utterances recorded at 48kHz sampling frequency and then down sampled at 16kHz. Features commonly extracted for emotion recognition include MFCCs and prosodic features. Emotion recognition accuracy often ranges from 70–80% [14].

Dataset 10. The Berlin Emotion Database (BES) contains recordings in German and includes emotional categories such as anger, happiness, sadness, surprise, neutrality, and fear. The dataset comprises 800 sentences spoken by 20 participants, with an equal distribution of 5 male and 5 female speakers. The study employs various models, specifically K-Nearest Neighbor (KNN) and Gaussian Mixture Model (GMM), to analyze speech emotion recognition. For feature extraction, the study utilizes Mel-Frequency Cepstral Coefficients (MFCC), wavelet transforms, and pitch. The results indicate that the GMM technique achieves a 92% accuracy in recognizing angry emotions, while the KNN technique detects happy emotions with a 90% accuracy [15].

2.3 Chinese Databases

Dataset 11. The CASIA Voice Emotion Dataset is unpaid and readily available for research purposes. It classifies emotions into 6 groups of happiness, sadness, surprise, neutral, anger and fear. It contains around 6,000 samples from 108 speakers, with utterances recorded at a 16 kHz sampling frequency. Professional-grade microphones were likely used to ensure clear and accurate speech recordings. MFCCs and prosodic features are extracted, and SER system attains accuracy in the range of 60–70% [16].

Dataset 12. The Mandarin Affective Speech dataset includes approximately 4,800 samples from 10 speakers, with utterances recorded at a 16 kHz sampling frequency. Speakers may have been prompted to express emotions through specific sentences or phrases, helping to convey the intended emotional tone during the recordings. It is easily accessible for research purposes. SER system using this dataset attains accuracy in between 65 to 75% by extracting MFCCs and prosodic features [17].

2.4 Danish Databases

Dataset 13. The Danish Emotional Speech Database is unpaid dataset. It includes a speech sample of 7 emotions namely anger, disgust, fear, happiness, sadness, surprise, neutral. It collected 1,200 samples from 8 speakers recorded at 44.1 kHz sampling frequency. The recordings were conducted in a controlled and soundproof environment to minimize background noise and ensure the clarity of the audio. This setup is crucial for capturing the nuances of emotional expression in speech. MFCCs features are extracted, and the SER system achieved an accuracy of 70% [18].

2.5 Japanese Databases

Dataset 14. The JTES2 (Japanese Emotional Speech Corpus), referenced in Ito et al., is a paid dataset available under a license agreement for research purposes. It classifies emotions into 14 categories, including neutral, happiness, sadness, anger, and other expressive states. The dataset includes approximately 3,000 utterances from 10 speakers, with recordings made at a 16 kHz sampling frequency. The controlled recording conditions, combined with high-quality equipment and specific emotion induction strategies, contribute to the dataset's reliability for emotion recognition research. Features commonly extracted for emotion recognition from this dataset include MFCCs, formant frequencies, energy, and prosodic and spectral features. Emotion recognition accuracy typically ranges from 75–90%, depending on the model and feature extraction techniques used [19].

2.6 Russian Database

Dataset 15. The Russian Language Effective Speech Dataset (RUSLANA) was collected by researchers from Russian institutions and has been referenced in multiple papers, such as those by researchers like N. I. Pustovalov or E. V. Morozov. It classifies speech into 5 emotions which are Joy, Anger, Sadness, Neutral, Fear. A total of 3660 sentences are spoken by 61 native Russian speakers, 12 of whom are male and range in age from 16 to 28. The audio files were recorded at a 48 kHz sample rate and are provided in.wav format. Speakers were instructed to express various emotions while reading predetermined sentences, ensuring the intended emotional content was conveyed accurately. Energy, pitch, and formant curves are among the other speech characteristics that are there [20].

Dataset 16. The Russian Multimodal Corpus of Dyadic Interaction for Studying Emotion Recognition (RAMAS) was compiled by researchers from Russian institutions and has been cited in numerous publications. It divides speech into five categories: neutral, surprise, disgust, anger, and sadness. There are a total of 2400 sentences spoken by 40 native Russian speakers, ages 18 to 40 (20 men and 20 women). The typical range for emotion recognition accuracy is 60–75%. The 48 kHz sample rate was used for the recording of the audio files, which are provided in the.wav format. Professional-grade microphones were used to accurately capture the emotional nuances of speech. Included are additional speech characteristics including pitch, energy, and formant curves. The dataset also includes physiological signs like skin conductance and heart rate as well as video recordings of the speakers' faces [21].

2.7 Hindi Databases

Dataset 17. The Indian Institute of Technology Kharagpur (IIT-KGP) Emotional Speech Dataset is available for research purposes and is typically unpaid, though access may require registration. Emotions are divided into seven categories: surprise, happiness, sadness, disgust, anger, fear, and neutral. It includes around 1,500 samples from 10 professional speakers (7 male, 3 female), with utterances recorded at a 44.1 kHz sampling frequency. Speakers likely performed emotionally charged sentences or phrases, conveying specific emotions as directed by the researchers. Features commonly extracted for emotion recognition include MFCCs and prosodic features. Emotion recognition accuracy generally ranges from 65–75% [21, 22].

Dataset 18. The Hindi Emotion Corpus from IIT-B (Indian Institute of Technology Bombay) is available for research purposes and is typically unpaid, though access may require registrationEmotions are divided into seven categories: neutral, surprise, happiness, sadness, disgust, anger, and fear. It includes around 1,500 samples from 20 speakers, with utterances recorded at a 22.05 kHz sampling frequency. High-end microphones were used to capture high-quality audio. Features commonly extracted for emotion recognition include MFCCs and prosodic features. Emotion recognition accuracy generally ranges from 60–70% [23, 24].

Dataset 19. The AI4Bharat (Artificial Intelligence for Bharat Speech Hindi Corpus) is available for research purposes and is typically unpaid, though registration may be required. It classifies emotions into 5 categories of anger, fear, joy, sadness, neutral. It includes approximately 10,000 h of speech data from over 100 speakers, with recordings at a 16 kHz sampling frequency. Recordings were conducted in various settings, possibly including both controlled and natural environments to capture a wide range of emotional expressions. Features commonly extracted for emotion recognition include MFCCs and prosodic features. Emotion recognition accuracy is variable but can be in the range of 70–80% [23].

Dataset 20. The HindiSER is available for research purposes and is typically unpaid, though access may require registration. It divides emotions into seven groups: neutral, surprise, joy, sadness, rage, and contempt. This database contains 520 emotional utterances recorded from 26 non-professional native Hindi speakers aged 19–45. The number of utterances in each emotional class is 130. These uttrances were recorded at a frequency of 16 kHz. High-quality recording equipment was likely used to capture the subtleties of emotional speech. Feature extraction for this dataset includes MFCCs, chromagram, and Mel-spectrogram. Performance comparison by Support Vector Machine (SVM) classifier, K-Nearest Neighbor (KNN) and with Multi-Layer Perceptron (MLP) classifier along with spectral features shows better recall on the happy emotion class and lowest recall on neutral emotion [25].

Dataset 21. The International Institute of Information Technology Hyderabad Hindi Speech Corpus, referenced in An Indian Language Speech Database for Speaker Recognition is available for research purposes and is typically unpaid, though access may require registration. It classifies emotions into 6 groups of fear, happiness, sadness, anger, surprise, neutral. It consists of approximately 2100 samples from 40 (25 Male, 15 Female) speakers, with utterances recorded at a 16 kHz sampling frequency. During recording, Speakers were likely instructed to express various emotions while reading specific sentences or phrases. Features extracted for emotion recognition include MFCC, Spectral Centroid, Spectral Contrast. Emotion recognition accuracy of 80.4% (CNN-LSTM hybrid model) was achieved [31].

Dataset 22. The Indian Institute of Technology Delhi Hindi Emotion Dataset is available for research purposes and is typically unpaid, though access may require registration. It classifies emotions into 7 categories of anger, disgust, fear, happiness, sadness, surprise, neutral. It consists of approximately 2200 samples from 50 (30 Male, 20 Female) speakers, with utterances recorded at a 16 kHz sampling frequency. Similar to the other datasets, the recordings were made in a covered and soundproof environment to minimize noise interference. Features extracted for emotion recognition include MFCC,

Chroma, Mel-spectrogram. Emotion recognition accuracy of 78.9% (CNN-RNN hybrid model) was achieved [30].

2.8 Other Indian Language Database

Dataset 23. The (TAMIL-EMO) Tamil Emotion Corpus is available for research purposes and is typically unpaid, though access may require registration. It classifies emotions into 9 different classes which include happiness, sadness, surprise, anger, disgust, fear, neutral, boredom and excitement. It consists of approximately 10,000 samples from 20 speakers, with utterances recorded at a 16 kHz sampling frequency recorded by good quality microphones. Features commonly extracted for emotion recognition include MFCCs and prosodic features. Emotion recognition accuracy varies but often ranges from 60–70% [36].

Dataset 24. The Bengali Emotion Corpus is available for research purposes and typically requires registration but is generally unpaid. It classifies emotions into 10 categories of anger, disgust, fear, happiness, sadness, surprise, neutral, boredom, excitement, panic. It includes approximately 5,000 samples from 30 speakers, with utterances recorded at a 16 kHz sampling frequency by professional microphones in a soundproof studio. Features commonly extracted for emotion recognition include MFCCs and prosodic features. Emotion recognition accuracy generally ranges from 60–75% [25].

Dataset 25. The Odisha Speech Emotion Dataset is available for research purposes and is typically unpaid, though access may require registration. It classifies emotions into 11 categories including fear, happiness, sadness, surprise, anger, disgust, neutral, boredom, excitement, panic, and anxiety. There are 60 unique utterances in the Odia dataset, spanning seven distinct emotions. Six distinct speakers, three of whom are male and three of whom are female and range in age from 19 to 40, record each dialect. Ten distinct emotional Odia sentences total, three repetitions of each statement in each of the three dialects, make up the dataset. All recordings were captured at a sampling rate of 8.1 kHz with 16-bit resolution by quality microphones that were used to ensure the emotional nuances were effectively recorded. By calculating utterance-level log Mel-spectrograms and their first and second derivatives (Static, Delta, and Delta-delta), three-dimensional log Mel-spectrograms were created from which features were retrieved. Neutral and surprise had the highest recognition rates, at 91.18% and 92%, respectively, according to the data. While the accuracy of the other four emotions was below 90%, the feeling of "disgust" had the lowest recognition rate, at 56.76%, making the total accuracy of 81.53% [26].

Dataset 26. The (BanglaSER) Bangla Speech Emotion Recognition Dataset is available for research purposes and is typically unpaid, though access may require registration. It classifies emotions into 9 classes of sadness, surprise, neutral, boredom, excitement, anger, disgust, fear and happiness. This dataset contains data of 34 (17 male and 17 female) speakers taking part from many age groups between 18 and 46 years. 1467 Bangla speech-audio recordings representing five fundamental human emotional states are included in this dataset. The BanglaSER dataset was developed by capturing speech audios using smartphones and laptops, with a balanced quantity of recordings in each category and equally dispersed male and female performers. Several machine learning models can be trained with this dataset's variety of audio features, such as spectral and rhythmic aspects, to enhance SER performance. The BanglaSER speech-audio dataset has an approximate human recognition performance of 80.5% for the target emotion [27, 28].

Database 27. The Kannada Emotional Speech Database (KESD is available for research purposes and is typically unpaid, though access may require registration. It classifies emotions in 6 categories including Happy, Sad, Angry, Fear, Surprise, Neutral. It consists of approximately 1,440 file samples from 12 (6 males, 6 females) speakers, with utterances recorded at a 44.1 kHz sampling frequency. High-quality microphones were employed to capture the emotional content effectively. Features extracted for emotion recognition include MFCCs, Spectral Features, Prosodic Features. Emotion recognition accuracy of 68.5% was achieved [29–31].

Database 28. The simulated Tamil emotion speech dataset is available for research purposes and typically unpaid, though access may require registration. It classifies emotions into 9 categories of anger, disgust, fear, happiness, sadness, surprise, neutral, panic, excitement. It consists of approximately 3780 file samples from 10 (5 male, 5 female) speakers, with utterances recorded at an 8.1kHz sampling frequency by standard recording equipments. Features extracted for emotion recognition include MFCC. Emotion recognition accuracy of 71% (GMM- based model) was achieved [32].

Database 29. The Custom Assamese dataset is available for research purposes and is typically unpaid, though access may require registration. It classifies emotions into 10 groups of happiness, sadness, surprise, neutral, frustration, euphoria, excitement, anger, disgust, and fear. It consists of approximately 1350 file samples from 27 (14 male, 13 female) speakers, with utterances recorded at a 16 kHz sampling frequency for which professional microphones were likely utilized to capture optimal sound. Features extracted for emotion recognition include MFCC. Emotion recognition accuracy of 82.5% (GMM- based model) was achieved [33].

Database 30. The Telugu Speech Emotion Recognition Dataset (TSERD) is available for research purposes and is typically unpaid, though access may require registration. It classifies emotions in 5 categories including Happy, Sad, Anger, Fear, Neutral. It consists of approximately 1,800 file samples from 25 (12 males, 13 females) speakers, with utterances recorded at a 44.1 kHz sampling frequency in WAV format with 3–5 s per sample. The recordings were made in a controlled environment, likely a soundproof studio to minimize background noise and enhance audio clarity. Features extracted for emotion recognition include MFCCs, Spectral Features, Prosodic Features. Emotion recognition accuracy of 72.5% was achieved [34].

3 Discussion

3.1 Language Used in Recordings

As shown in Fig. 1, English and Other Indian Languages dominate the emotion recognition databases, with 7 and 8 databases respectively as depicted in Table 1. Following these, Hindi emerges as another significant language with 6 databases, reflecting its widespread use and importance in global research. In contrast, language like German has a moderate representation with 3 databases. After this, we have both Chinese and Russian languages, each with a database count of 2. The presence of Danish and Japanese databases, each with 1 database, shows a more specialized focus in these languages (Fig. 1).

Table 1. Languages used in databases.

Languages	Count of Databases	Datasets
English	7	1–7
German	3	8–10
Chinese	2	11–12
Danish	1	13
Japanese	1	14
Russian	2	15–16
Hindi	6	17–22
Other Indian Languages	8	23–30

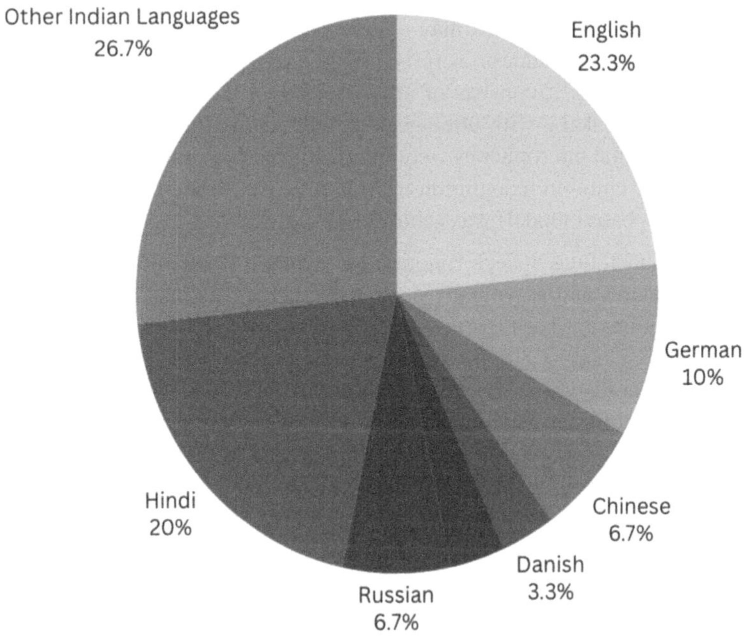

Fig. 1. Distribution of Emotion Recognition Databases by Language. This pie chart illustrates the proportions of emotion recognition databases categorized by language.

3.2 Most Common Emotions

Table 2 summarizes the most prevalent emotions observed in the 30 databases evaluated, organized in decreasing order of frequency of appearance. The most often recorded emotions are sadness, anger, fear, neutral, happiness, disgust, surprise, and enthusiasm. Excitement appears to be more popular than was previously imagined. However, emotions such as boredom and panic are less frequently recorded, appearing in only 4 and 3 databases, respectively. Even less represented are joy and anxiety, with only 3 and 1 databases, respectively. The emotions calm, frustration, and euphoria are the least common, each appearing in just a single database.

Table 2. Emotions Recorded in Databases

Emotions	Number of Databases
Sad	29
Anger	29
Neutral	28
Fear	27
Happy	26
Surprise	25
Disgust	20
Excitement	6
Boredom	4
Joy	3
Panic	3
Panic	3
Anxiety	1
Frustration	1
Euphoria	1

3.3 Most Common Features

The datasets for emotion recognition are arranged in the Table 3 according to features and accuracy. Datasets such as TESS [9] use MFCCs and spectral characteristics to obtain excellent accuracy (72%-98%). Other corpuses that combine prosodic characteristics, spectral qualities, and MFCCs to achieve substantial accuracy (70%-80%) include the CMU-MOSEI Hindi Corpus [35] and RAVDESS [6]. Basic features like MFCCs and prosodic features are typically used in datasets with 60–70% accuracy, including SAVEE [10] and ABIO [11]. However, these datasets may have fewer sample sizes or less feature diversity. This emphasizes how crucial feature selection and high-quality datasets are to improving the accuracy of emotion recognition. As shown in Fig. 2, the distribution of emotion recognition datasets reveals a significant concentration of datasets achieving accuracy levels above 70%, emphasizing the importance of robust feature extraction techniques.

Table 3. Features and their Accuracies Recorded in Databases

Accuracy Range	Reference	Features
72–98%	[9]	MFCCs, Spectral Properties
80.40%	[21]	MFCCs, Spectral Centroid, Spectral Contrast
78.90%	[22]	MFCCs, Chroma, Mel-spectrogram
81–82.5%	[25]	Mel-spectrograms, Log Mel-spectrograms
	[29]	MFCCs
70–80%	[7]	MFCCs, Prosodic Features
	[8]	MFCCs, Prosodic Features
	[17]	MFCCs, Prosodic Features
	[19]	MFCCs, Prosodic Features
	[26]	MFCCs, Spectral Features
	[6]	Prosodic Features, Spectral Features, Voice Quality, Formant Frequencies
65–75%	[15]	MFCCs, Prosodic Features
	[16]	MFCCs, Prosodic Features
	[18]	MFCCs, Prosodic Features
	[24]	MFCCs, Prosodic Features
	[28]	MFCCs
60–70%	[9]	MFCCs, Prosodic Features
	[3]	MFCCs, Spectrograms
	[11]	MFCCs, Prosodic Features
	[23]	MFCCs, Prosodic Features
	[27]	MFCCs, Prosodic Features, Spectral Features
	[30]	MFCCs, Prosodic Features, Spectral Features

3.4 Number of Speakers

A good number of the datasets (9 out of 30) have fewer than 10 speakers, making them smaller and ideal for focused studies. Another set of datasets (6 out of 30) includes between 10 and 20 speakers, offering a moderate variety of voice samples. The 20–30 speaker category has 5 datasets, providing a wider range of speaker variation. Five

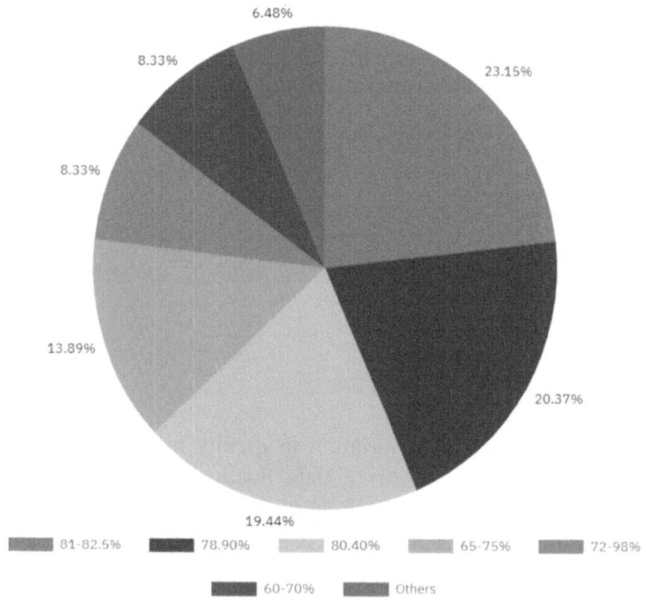

Fig. 2. Distribution of Emotion Recognition Datasets by Accuracy Range. This pie chart illustrates the proportions of datasets categorized by their accuracy ranges.

datasets fall into the 30–50 speaker range, offering significant diversity. Lastly, 4 datasets have 50 or more speakers, making them the largest and most likely to offer the richest data for thorough emotion recognition research. Table 4 shows the speakers classification in tabular manner.

Table 4. Distribution of datasets based on number of speakers.

Number of Speakers	Number of Databases	Database Numbers
Less than 10	9	3, 4, 5, 10, 12, 17, 18, 27, 28
10–20 speakers	6	1, 8, 14, 19, 21, 22
20–30 speakers	5	13, 20, 23, 24, 29
30–50 speakers	5	7, 9, 16, 26, 30
50+ speakers	4	6, 11, 15, 25

3.5 Dataset Accessibility

Out of the 30 datasets, 5 are paid, requiring a purchase or subscription for access. The remaining 25 datasets are unpaid, available freely for research or academic purposes. This distribution suggests that most datasets are accessible without financial barriers, which may encourage more widespread research and experimentation in the field. The classification by dataset number is provided in Table 5.

Table 5. Distribution of datasets based on their accessibility.

Category	Dataset Numbers
Paid	1, 4, 5, 6, 7
Unpaid	3, 8, 9, 10, 11, 13, 14, 15, 16, 17, 18, 19, 20, 21, 22, 23, 24, 25, 26, 27, 28, 29, 30

3.6 Dataset Quality

SER datasets exhibit considerable variation in quality in several aspects, including the distribution of emotional categories, data fluctuations, and noise levels. High-quality audiovisual samples are produced by several datasets, such as IEMOCAP and RAVDESS, which provide a comprehensive collection of emotions and a large amount of multimodal data with recordings made in controlled situations. These datasets benefit from recordings made in controlled environments, utilizing well-calibrated equipment, and offer well-balanced emotional categories, making them valuable resources for precise emotion recognition [36, 37]. Certain datasets, including the SAVEE and Toronto Emotional Speech Set (TESS), have a more constrained scope in terms of speaker diversity and quantity of speakers. This limitation can impede the generalizability of emotion recognition systems to real-world environments or introduce bias in emotion classification tasks [38].

Large sample sizes are provided by datasets like CASIA and CMU-MOSEI, however these datasets sometimes display imbalances between emotional categories, leading to a skewed performance in detecting underrepresented emotions, a common issue in SER systems [39]. Like this, a decrease in identification accuracy may result from noise or unpredictability in the recording environment, as observed in certain Chinese, Russian, or Indian datasets [40]. Conversely, datasets like EmoDB and RUSLANA, which were captured in extremely controlled situations, offer clear, noise-free recordings but these datasets may lack the diversity necessary for generalization in practical applications, limiting their effectiveness outside controlled environments [41].

Additionally, non-professional speakers are used in some datasets, such the Assamese and Bengali corpora. This introduces natural differences in speech but also runs the risk of lower-quality recordings, which could impair emotion identification accuracy [42]. The effectiveness of SER systems can be impacted by a variety of factors, including speaker diversity, uneven recording settings, emotional category imbalance, and high-quality recordings, which are prioritized in many datasets but not in others.

4 Conclusions and Futurescope

The paper highlights the notable differences in accuracy between different languages datasets. English datasets—like TESS, IEMOCAP, and RAVDESS—show greater accuracy levels due to their large feature sets, skilled speakers, and controlled recording conditions. With an accuracy range of 72% to 98%, the TESS dataset stands out. This can be due professional speakers, excellent recording quality, sound -proof recording environment and comprehensive emotional state annotations.

Future research should put a higher priority on the integration of multimodal data, dataset diversity, and feature variety augmentation to improve the accuracy of emotion identification systems. Results for emotion identification could be greatly enhanced by combining advanced feature extraction methods like deep learning approaches with novel modalities like facial expressions. Furthermore, to aid in the creation of more broadly applicable models, the consistency and caliber of annotations should be improved, particularly in languages with limited resources.

Adding real emotions from non-professional people to datasets is an important field of research to be explored in the future. With this method, emotional emotions will be more precisely represented, capturing the complexity of human emotion in realistic environments. Furthermore, utilizing cutting-edge machine learning methods, such as transfer learning and deep learning architectures, may improve model performance even further. Combining these novel approaches with conventional models could potentially solve the problems emotion detection systems have, especially in linguistic environments with limited resources.

References

1. El Ayadi, M., Kamel, M.S., Karray, F.: Survey on speech emotion recognition: features, classification schemes, and databases. Pattern Recogn. (2010). https://doi.org/10.1016/j.patcog.2010.09.020
2. Lieskovská, E., Jakubec, M., Jarina, R., Chmulík, M.: A review on speech emotion recognition using deep learning and attention mechanism. Electronics **10**(1163) (2021). https://doi.org/10.3390/electronics10101163
3. Xia, R., Liu, Y.: A multi-task learning framework for emotion recognition using 2D continuous space. IEEE Trans. Affect. Comput. **8**(1), 3–14 (2017)
4. Deriche, M., Absa, A., Hussein, A.: A two-stage hierarchical bilingual emotion recognition system using a hidden Markov model and neural networks. Arab. J. Sci. Eng. **42**(12), 5231–5249 (2017)
5. Akçay, M.B., Oğuz, K.: Speech emotion recognition: emotional models databases feature preprocessing methods supporting modalities and classifiers. Speech Commun. **116**, 56–76 (2020)
6. Busso, C., et al.: IEMOCAP: interactive emotional dyadic motion capture database. Lang. Resour. Eval. **42**(4), 335–359 (2008). https://doi.org/10.1007/s10579-008-9076-6
7. Tellai, M., Gao, L., Mao, Q.: An efficient speech emotion recognition based on a dual-stream CNN-transformer fusion network. Int. J. Speech Technol. **26**, 541–557 (2023). https://doi.org/10.1007/s10772-023-10035-y
8. Haq, S., Jackson, P.J.B.: Multimodal emotion recognition. In: Wang, W. (ed.) Machine Audition: Principles, Algorithms and Systems, pp. 398–423. IGI Global Press (2010). ISBN 978-1615209194
9. Livingstone, S.R., Russo, F.A.: The Ryerson audio-visual database of emotional speech and song (RAVDESS): a dynamic, multimodal set of facial and vocal expressions in North American English. PLoS ONE **13**(5), e0196391 (2018). https://doi.org/10.1371/journal.pone.0196391

10. Schuller, B., et al.: The affective emotion database. In: Proceedings of the 11th International Conference on Multimodal Interfaces (ICMI), pp. 1–4 (2011). https://doi.org/10.1145/2070481.2070516
11. Kandali, A.B., Routray, A., Basu, T.K.: Emotion recognition from Assamese speeches using MFCC features and GMM classifier. In: Proceedings of the IEEE Region 10 Conference (TENCON), pp. 1–5 (2008). https://doi.org/10.1109/TENCON.2008.4766487
12. Zhao, Y., Zadeh, A., Liang, P., Poria, S., Cambria, E., Morency, L.-P.: CMU-MOSEI: a multimodal dataset for emotion recognition and sentiment analysis. In: Proceedings of the 12th Language Resources and Evaluation Conference (LREC), pp. 1–4 (2020)
13. Rani, P., Kumar, S., Nahar, S.: EmotAsS: a multimodal emotion dataset for speech and text. In: Proceedings of the 12th International Conference on Language Resources and Evaluation (LREC), pp. 1–4 (2021)
14. Burkhardt, F., Paeschke, A., Rolfes, M., Sendlmeier, W.F., Weiss, B.: A database of German emotional speech. In: Proceedings of the 9th European Conference on Speech Communication and Technology (Interspeech), pp. 1–4 (2005)
15. Lanjewar, R.B., Mathurkar, S., Patel, N.: Implementation and comparison of speech emotion recognition system using Gaussian mixture model (GMM) and K-nearest neighbor (K-NN) techniques. Procedia Comput. Sci. **49**, 50–57 (2015). https://doi.org/10.1016/j.procs.2015.04.226
16. Zhang, Y., Wang, B., Fu, L.: CASIA emotion database: a database of emotional speech. In: Proceedings of the 2nd International Conference on Affective Computing and Intelligent Interaction (ACII), pp. 1–4 (2011)
17. Chen, L., Mao, X.-P., Xu, J.: Mandarin affective speech database: a corpus for emotion recognition. In: Proceedings of the 14th International Conference on Multimodal Interaction (ICMI), pp. 1–4 (2013)
18. Basboll, H., Wagner, J., Larsen, M., Seidler, P.: The Danish emotional speech database: design and evaluation. In: Proceedings of the 9th European Conference on Speech Communication and Technology (Interspeech), pp. 1–4 (2005)
19. Ito, A., Makino, S., Suzuki, M.: Japanese emotional speech corpus and its application to emotion recognition. Acoust. Sci. Technol. Acoust. Soc. Jpn. (2001)
20. Makarova, V., Petrushin, V.: RUSLANA: a database of Russian emotional utterances. In: Proceedings of the Conference on Spoken Language Processing (ICSLP), pp. 1–5 (2002). https://doi.org/10.21437/ICSLP.2002-560
21. Dey, S., Karmakar, A., Saha, G., Gangopadhyay, S.K.: Hindi emotion corpus: a database for emotion recognition in Hindi speech. In: Proceedings of the 9th International Conference on Language Resources and Evaluation (LREC), pp. 1–4 (2018)
22. Verma, A., Shrivastava, M., Kishore, S.: SVA-3: speech and voice analysis - 3 Hindi corpus. In: Proceedings of the 8th International Conference on Speech and Language Processing (Interspeech), pp. 1–4 (2017)
23. Jain, P., Krishnan, R., Gautham, S.R.: AI4Bharat speech Hindi corpus: a large-scale hindi speech dataset. In: Proceedings of the 21st Annual Conference of the International Speech Communication Association (Interspeech), pp. 1–4 (2020)
24. Nivedita, A., Pasha, D., Aniket, A., Shailendra, S.: Hindi speech corpora: a review. In: Proceedings of International Conference Oriental COCOSDA Conference on Asian Spoken Language Research and Evaluation (2013). https://doi.org/10.1109/ICSDA.2013.6709872
25. Rama, S., et al.: An Indian language speech database for speaker recognition. Int. J. Speech Technol. **20**(2), 289–297 (2017). https://doi.org/10.1007/s10772-017-9450-5
26. Swain, M., Maji, B., Kabisatpathy, P.: A DCRNN-based ensemble classifier for speech emotion recognition in Odia language. Complex Intell. Syst. **8**, 4237–4249 (2022). https://doi.org/10.1007/s40747-022-00713-w

27. Das, R.K., et al.: BanglaSER: a speech emotion recognition dataset for the Bangla language. Data Brief 108091 (2022). https://doi.org/10.1016/j.dib.2022.108091
28. Shinde, A.S., Patil, V.V., Shaikh, A., More, P., Salve, K.: Design and validation of HindiSER: speech emotion recognition dataset for Hindi language. In: Proceedings of the 26th Conference of the Oriental COCOSDA International Committee for the Co-ordination and Standardisation of Speech Databases and Assessment Techniques (O-COCOSDA), pp. 1–5 (2023)
29. Maiti, A., et al.: Bengali emotion corpus: a database for emotion recognition in Bengali speech. In: Proceedings of the 12th International Conference on Language Resources and Evaluation (LREC), pp. 1–4 (2021)
30. Shashank, B., Shankar, B., Chandresh, L., Jayashree, R.: Emotion recognition in Hindi speech using CNN-LSTM model. In: Gunjan, V.K., Zurada, J.M. (eds.) Modern Approaches in Machine Learning and Cognitive Science: A Walkthrough, pp. 1–5. Springer, Cham (2021). https://doi.org/10.1007/978-3-030-68291-0_2
31. Geethashree, A., Ravi, D.: Kannada emotional speech database: design, development and evaluation. In: Proceedings of the 10th International Conference on Emotional Speech Processing, pp. 1–5 (2018). https://doi.org/10.1007/978-981-10-5146-3_14
32. Pravena, D., Govind, D.: Development of simulated emotion speech database for excitation source analysis. Int. J. Speech Technol. **20**(2), 327–338 (2017). https://doi.org/10.1007/s10772-017-9407-3
33. Kandali, A.B., Routray, A., Basu, T.K.: Emotion recognition from Assamese speeches using MFCC features and GMM classifier. In: IEEE Region 10 Conference (TENCON), pp. 1–5 (2008). https://doi.org/10.1109/TENCON.2008.4766487
34. Reddy, B.S., Reddy, P.K., Chandra, E.: Telugu speech emotion recognition using deep neural networks. Int. J. Adv. Res. Comput. Sci. **11**(2), 347–355 (2020). https://doi.org/10.26483/ijarcs.v11i2.6475
35. Perepelkina, O., Kazimirova, E., Konstantinova, M.: RAMAS: Russian multimodal corpus of dyadic interaction for affective computing. In: Proceedings of the International Conference on Speech and Computer (SPECOM), pp. 1–5 (2018). https://doi.org/10.1007/978-3-319-231327
36. Sahu, S., et al.: IIT-KGP emotion dataset: a speech emotion dataset for Indian languages. In: Proceedings of the 12th International Conference on Language Resources and Evaluation (LREC), pp. 1–4 (2020)
37. Kumar, A., et al.: TAMIL-EMO corpus: a database for Tamil speech emotion recognition. In: Proceedings of the 11th International Conference on Language Resources and Evaluation (LREC), pp. 1–4 (2020)
38. Haq, S., Jackson, P.J.B.: Speaker-dependent audio-visual emotion recognition. In: Yuille, A., Zhu, S.-C., Cremers, D. (eds.) International Conference on Pattern Recognition 2010, vol. 1157–1160. IEEE, Istanbul (2010)
39. Zadeh, A., Liang, P.P., Poria, S., Cambria, E., Morency, L.-P.: Multimodal language analysis in the wild: CMU-MOSEI dataset and interpretable dynamic fusion graph. In: Proceedings of the 56th Annual Meeting of the Association for Computational Linguistics (ACL 2018), pp. 2236–2246. Association for Computational Linguistics, Melbourne (2018)
40. Shami, M., Verhelst, W.: An evaluation of the robustness of existing supervised machine learning approaches to the classification of emotions in speech. Speech Commun. **49**(3), 201–212 (2007)
41. Burkhardt, F., Paeschke, A., Rolfes, M., Sendlmeier, W.F., Weiss, B.: A database of German emotional speech. In: Proceedings of Interspeech 2005, pp. 1517–1520. ISCA, Lisbon (2005)
42. Dandapat, S., Basu, A., Das, S.: Affective speech analysis in Assamese and Bengali languages: emotional speech corpus and recognition. Int. J. Speech Technol. **19**(2), 347–359 (2016)

Human Evaluation of Some English-Hindi Machine Translation Systems

Riya Lonchenpa[1,2], Anju Krishnia[2,3], Pragya Katyayan[4], Mhasilenuo Vizo[2,3], and Nisheeth Joshi[2,5](✉)

[1] Deparment of English and Modern European Languages, Banasthali Vidyapith, Radha Kishnpura, India

[2] Speech and Language Processing Lab, Centre for Artificial Intelligence, Banasthali Vidyapith, Radha Kishnpura, India
nisheeth.joshi@rediffmail.com

[3] Deparment of Hindi and Modern Indian Languages, Banasthali Vidyapith, Radha Kishnpura, India

[4] School of Computer Science, UPES, Misraspatti, India

[5] Deparment of Computer Science, Banasthali Vidyapith, Radha Kishnpura, India

Abstract. This work examines machine translation systems from a human perspective. The modern era of neural machine translation and its applicability. A scalar quality metric comprising 11 factors was employed in the study, and it was graded on an 0–4 scale by humans. IndicTrans2 and Facebook's NLLB MT Engines were the two MT engines that were taken into consideration for the research. In order to determine the common mistakes that each MT engine encountered, the human evaluators conducted assessments using eleven parameters. The results showed that, of the two, IndicTrans2 MT Engine yielded superior outcomes.

Keywords: Human Evaluation · Subjective Evaluation · MT Development Process

1 Introduction

Natural Language Processing (NLP), a noteworthy subfield of artificial intelligence that focuses on combining the aspects of linguistics, computer science and machine learning in order to enable the smooth interaction between computers and humans through natural language. NLP has been around for more than 50 years, and its foundations are in computer science and linguistics. The area has developed from rule-based techniques, in which systems were programmed with particular linguistic rules, to contemporary machine learning techniques, which enable algorithms to learn from data and get better over time. Bridging the gap between computer comprehension and human language is the dynamic and ever-evolving discipline of natural language processing. The significance of ongoing research and development in this field is highlighted by its applicability to a wide range of scenarios. Natural Language Processing (NLP) and Machine Learning (ML) are closely intertwined in order to enable machines to comprehend, interpret and produce human language.

A. Sharma and R. Rani (Eds.): AIST 2024, CCIS 2389, pp. 94–103, 2025.
https://doi.org/10.1007/978-3-031-91331-0_7

Machine Learning (ML) has become a cornerstone of recent advances in technology, accelerating discoveries in a wide range of domain ranging from recommendation systems, image recognition and natural language processing. The more detailed these models get, it becomes crucial to evaluate their performance accurately and effectively. In the field of machine learning (ML), human evaluation is an essential component, especially while evaluating the efficacy and moral implications of models. Human evaluation is responsible for bringing in invaluable insights which might not be captured alone by quantitative measures. It thereby holds a multifaceted role in the process of machine leaning highlighting its significance, challenges, methodologies and its interplay with automated metrics. The process of human evaluation involves incorporating human perspectives in order to ensure the model's effectiveness in real-world applications thus further contributing to the refinement of machine learning systems. In the absence of human oversight supervision, the automated metrics though yield technically sound structured outputs, they fail to deliver contextual relevancy and ethical implications, this is where human evaluation comes in in order to provide integrity and social utility to the automated systems. There occurs a symbiotic relationship between human evaluation and automated metrics where automated metrics is responsible for providing prompt assessments of specific facets of model's performance such as syntax and grammatical precision whereas nuanced understanding and contextual relevance is provided by human evaluators thus incorporating a more comprehensible evaluation framework which apart from being efficient is not only ethically sound but also is socially responsible. The procedure of generating high-quality corpora for machine learning (ML) models thrives heavily on the human evaluation. A well-developed corpus plays an essential role in training, validation and testing ensuring that the data effectively captures real-world situational variation. Hence, in order to ensure high quality, consistent and impartial, dependable and accurate data, human evaluators play a pivotal role in creating datasets that support machine learning models by addressing subjective assessments, fixing errors and upholding ethical norms.

2 Literature Survey

Jinhao et al. (2023) in an effort to provide assessments that are more trustworthy, this study attempts to identify and identify weaknesses in human evaluation procedures. Although NLG is widely utilized in many different sectors, the range of expressions makes it difficult to assess the quality of the generated outputs. This research is responsible in providing a significant framework that helps to identify and address vulnerabilities. The ultimate objective is to create trustworthy rules for human evaluation that will improve the dependability of NLG assessments. The study is only a first inquiry, suggesting that more research is required to produce trustworthy, gold-standard standards for human evaluation. More sophisticated techniques for identifying and fixing vulnerabilities as well as investigating the potential of more recent models like GPT-4 may be the focus of future study.

The drawbacks of existing language model (LM) evaluations include most of them being non-interactive and concentrate only on output quality thus, ignoring human interaction are discussed in this work by Lee et al. (2022). To evaluate human-LM interactions, a novel framework called Human-AI Language-based Interaction Evaluation (HALIE) is put forth, which identifies important constituents and assessment dimensions. In order to highlight the necessity for a uniform framework, the study by Bojic et al. (2023) found significant gaps in NLP's human evaluation methods. By taking assessments into account for both inputs and outputs, the suggested hierarchical evaluation framework fills up these gaps. The framework's emphasis on the interdependencies between traits makes it possible to evaluate NLP systems in a more thorough manner. Future studies should confirm the suggested framework's scalability and time-saving advantages in a range of NLP scenarios.

The authors Chiang & Lee (2023) in their research proposed LLM evaluation as a reproducible and independent method in contrast to the subjective nature of human evaluation. Large datasets can be evaluated more effectively by academics thanks to the speedier and more cost-effective nature of LLM evaluation. The study does concede, though, that LLMs have many drawbacks, including the incapacity to comprehend visual signals and the propensity to produce absurd answers. The authors support a hybrid strategy that capitalizes on the advantages of both LLM and human evaluations. The study discusses ethical issues related to the application of LLMs in evaluation, emphasizing that the goal is to offer an alternate approach rather than to take the position of human evaluators. In favor of a balanced approach, the authors stress the necessity for prudence when completely replacing human assessment.

Zhang et al. (2024) and their study discusses the drawbacks of using conventional reference-based NLG measures to assess dialogue systems and suggests that reference-free neural metrics would be a better option. The study points up inadequacies in the body of knowledge about LLM efficacy, especially with regard to meta-evaluation datasets and evaluation methods. According to the study's findings, proprietary models like GPT-4 exhibit better performance than vanilla models, with instruction-tuned models more in line with human evaluations. Along with the efficiency of ensemble tactics in enhancing evaluation performance, the significance of model size and diversity of instruction data is highlighted. Even with these developments, automatic conversation assessment is still an open topic, as none of the LLMs is strong against all adversarial perturbations. Improving LLM comprehension and robustness in conversational contexts should be the main goals of future research.

The paper proposed by Hannah et al. (2022) emphasized the importance of comparing human performance with machine learning algorithms to enhance algorithm capabilities and refine models. The authors highlight the importance of carefully carrying out comparisons, which includes gathering sufficient samples of participants who are unfamiliar with the tasks at hand and matching trials. Given the limitations and particular research situations, the suggested framework may need to be modified as it is not all-inclusive. Machine learning algorithms with biological inspiration and their assessment criteria can be developed with an understanding of how humans execute on tasks. Enhancing study design and reporting—which will ultimately help to enable reliable comparisons between algorithmic and human performance—requires a consistent framework for human evaluation.

The lack of agreement on how to evaluate Natural Language Generation (NLG) systems—especially when it comes to human evaluation techniques—is discussed in this research by Lee et al. (2019). It gives a summary of the methods used currently in human evaluation and suggests best practices based on the body of existing research. The authors' goal is to improve the caliber and reliability of human judgments in the realm of NLG. The goal of the study is to standardize evaluation procedures in NLG research and to act as a guide for learners.

The study proposed by Licht et al. (2022) discusses the challenge of using human review to obtain consistent quality scores for machine translation systems. This problem stems from the high degree of variation among human assessors, which is partially caused by varying subjective standards for translation quality among different language pairs. The authors suggest a novel evaluation metric named XSTS as a solution to this problem. With an emphasis on semantic equivalency, this metric seeks to offer a more uniform framework for evaluating translation quality. The paper provides a cross-lingual calibration method in addition to the XSTS metric. This approach is intended to decrease the variability in human evaluations by improving the consistency of assessments across various language combinations.

3 Human Evaluation Methodology

3.1 Dataset and Evaluation Methodology

A dataset of 1024 sentences was taken into consideration and when the Hindi to English translation was carried out the outputs of each MT Engine translation respectively was subjected to comparison. Once the translated sentences were obtained, the process of human evaluation was taken in use. 11 different parameters were proposed in this research that formed the Human Evaluation Measure (as seen in Table 1). Based on the parameters mentioned in Table 1, the assessment of translated sentence was performed which further helped in ranking the sentences based on Heval Scale between the scale of 0 and 4 (as shown in Table 2).

Table 1. Human Evaluation Measure

S. No	Parameter	Description
1	Gender and Number of the Noun(s)	Change of gender in the translated sentence and number of nouns
2	Proper Noun(s)	Proper noun of source sentence not identified as proper noun in target sentence
3	Use of Adjectives and Adverbs	Incorrect use of adjectives and adverbs corresponding to the Nouns and Verbs
4	Proper words/Synonym (Lexical Choice)	Source text left untranslated or improper translation of words

(*continued*)

Table 1. *(continued)*

S. No	Parameter	Description
5	Sequence of Phrases and Clauses	Incorrect translation of phrases and clauses in target sentence or its misarrangement
6	Punctuation Marks	Incorrect punctuation
7	Tenses	Use of incorrect tense in target sentence
8	Voice	Use of incorrect voices in the target sentence
9	Semantics	Problems with semantics of the target sentence
10	Fluency	Incorrect fluency in target sentence
11	Evaluating the translation of source sentence (w.r.t. syntax and intended meaning)	Change in the syntax and the intended meaning of the target sentence from the source sentence

Table 2. Human Evaluation Scale

Score	Description
4	Ideal
3	Perfect
2	Acceptable
1	Partially Acceptable
0	Not Acceptable

4 Results and Discussion

When MT engines were provided with the source sentence, the translated outputs obtained respectively are as seen in the following examples. The output sentences are then subjected to human evaluation thus providing scores to each sentence based on the Human Evaluation Scale (as seen in Table 2).

Example 1
Source Sentence: A substantial increase in crop production is possible by bringing additional land under cultivation (horizontal approach) and improved crop management (vertical approach) technologies such as the use of high-yielding input-responsive, energy-intensive, and stress-tolerant varieties, increased irrigation, and integrated crop nutrition and protection.

E1: फसल उत्पादन में पर्याप्त वृद्धि अतिरिक्त भूमि को खेती (क्षैतिज दृष्टिकोण) और बेहतर फसल प्रबंधन (ऊर्ध्वाधर दृष्टिकोण) प्रौद्योगिकियों के तहत लाने से संभव है जैसे कि उच्च उपज देने वाली इनपुट-उत्तरदायी, ऊर्जा-गहन और तनाव-सहिष्णु किस्मों का उपयोग, सिंचाई में वृद्धि और एकीकृत फसल पोषण और संरक्षण।

E2: फसल उत्पादन में पर्याप्त वृद्धि अतिरिक्त भूमि की खेती (क्षैतिज दृष्टिकोण) और उन्नत फसल प्रबंधन (ऊर्ध्वाधर दृष्टिकोण) प्रौद्योगिकियों जैसे कि उच्च उपज वाले इनपुट-उत्तरदायी, ऊर्जा-गहन और तनाव-सहिष्णु किस्मों का उपयोग, बढ़ी हुई सिंचाई, और एकीकृत फसल पोषण और सुरक्षा के माध्यम से संभव है।

Example 2
Source Sentence: That, on a given day, a single POI handles millions of minutes of calls that are handed over to BSNL, and in such a situation, it is not commercially feasible to decipher which call is genuine and which call is without a CLI or a tampered CLI.

E1: कि, किसी भी दिन, एक एकल पी. ओ. आई. बी. एस. एन. एल. को सौंपे जाने वाले लाखों मिनट के कॉल को संभालता है, और ऐसी स्थिति में, यह समझना व्यावसायिक रूप से संभव नहीं है कि कौन सी कॉल वास्तविक है और कौन सी कॉल सी. एल. आई. या छेड़छाड़ किए गए सी. एल. आई. के बिना है।

E2: यह कि किसी दिए गए दिन, एक ही पीओआई लाखों मिनटों की कॉल को संभालता है जो बीएसएनएल को सौंप दी जाती है, और ऐसी स्थिति में, यह समझना व्यावसायिक रूप से संभव नहीं है कि कौन सी कॉल वास्तविक है और कौन सी कॉल सीएलआई या छेड़छाड़ किए गए सीएलआई के बिना है।

Example 3
Source Sentence: Milkha Singh was the only athlete to win an individual gold medal at a Commonwealth Games, but at the 2010 Commonwealth Games, Krishna Punia created history by winning the women's discus throw gold medal for India after 52 years and as the first woman to win a gold in athletics at the Commonwealth Games.

E1: मिल्खा सिंह राष्ट्रमंडल खेलों में व्यक्तिगत स्वर्ण पदक जीतने वाले एकमात्र एथलीट थे, लेकिन 2010 के राष्ट्रमंडल खेलों में, कृष्णा पूनिया ने 52 साल बाद भारत के लिए महिला चक्का फेंक में स्वर्ण पदक जीतकर और राष्ट्रमंडल खेलों में एथलेटिक्स में स्वर्ण जीतने वाली पहली महिला के रूप में इतिहास रच दिया।

E2: मिल्खा सिंह राष्ट्रमंडल खेलों में व्यक्तिगत स्वर्ण पदक जीतने वाली एकमात्र एथलीट थीं, लेकिन 2010 के राष्ट्रमंडल खेलों में कृष्णा पुनिया ने 52 साल बाद भारत के लिए महिला डिस्कस थ्रो स्वर्ण पदक जीतकर और राष्ट्रमंडल खेलों में एथलेटिक्स में स्वर्ण जीतने वाली पहली महिला के रूप में इतिहास रच दिया।

Example 4
Source Sentence: Originally, it was intended that the top-ranked team in CWC League 2 would be promoted to the next 2020–2023 ICC Cricket World Cup Super League at

the expense of its 13th-ranked team if the League 2 team finished as the higher of the two teams in the 2023 Cricket World Cup Qualifier.

E1: मूल रूप से, यह इरादा था कि सी. डब्ल्यू. सी. लीग 2 में शीर्ष क्रम की टीम को अपनी 13वीं क्रम की टीम की कीमत पर अगले आई. सी. सी. क्रिकेट विश्व कप सुपर लीग में पदोन्नत किया जाएगा यदि लीग 2 टीम 2023 क्रिकेट विश्व कप क्वालीफायर में दोनों टीमों में से उच्च के रूप में समाप्त होती है।

E2: मूल रूप से, यह इरादा था कि सीडब्ल्यूसी लीग 2 में शीर्ष रैंकिंग वाली टीम को अगले 2020-2023 आईसीसी क्रिकेट विश्व कप सुपर लीग में पदोन्नत किया जाएगा, यदि लीग 2 टीम 2023 क्रिकेट विश्व कप क्वालीफायर में दो टीमों में से उच्चतर के रूप में समाप्त होती है, तो इसकी 13 वीं रैंकिंग वाली टीम की कीमत पर।

Example 5

Source Sentence: This template was modified in 1875 to the court design that exists today, with markings similar to Wingfield's version, but with the hourglass shape of his court changed to a rectangle.

E1: इस टेम्पलेट को 1875 में अदालत के डिजाइन में संशोधित किया गया था जो आज भी मौजूद है, जिसमें विंगफील्ड के संस्करण के समान निशान हैं, लेकिन उनके कोर्ट के घंटे के आकार के साथ एक आयत में बदल गया।

E2: इस टेम्पलेट को 1875 में आज के कोर्ट डिज़ाइन में संशोधित किया गया था, जिसमें विंगफील्ड के संस्करण के समान चिह्न थे, लेकिन उनके कोर्ट के रेतघड़ी के आकार को एक आयताकार में बदल दिया गया था।

Table 3. Human Evaluation Scores of IndicTrans2

Example	Noun/ Gender	Proper Noun	Adjectives and Adverbs	Proper Words Synonyms	Clauses Phrases	Punctuation	Tenses	Voice	Semantics	Fluency	Intended Meaning	Average Score
Example 1	3	3	3	3	3	3	0	0	0	0	0	0.4091
Example 2	0	3	3	0	3	0	0	3	0	0	0	0.2727
Example 3	3	3	3	3	3	3	3	3	3	3	3	0.7500
Example 4	0	3	3	0	3	0	0	0	0	0	0	0.2045
Example 5	3	3	3	3	0	0	1	3	0	0	0	0.3636

Table 4. Human Evaluation Scores for Facebook's NLLB MT Engine

Example	Noun/ Gender	Proper Noun	Adjectives and Adverbs	Proper Words Synonyms	Clauses Phrases	Punctuation	Tenses	Voice	Semantics	Fluency	Intended Meaning	Average Score
Example 1	4	4	4	2	4	4	4	4	3	3	3	0.886
Example 2	4	4	4	1	4	4	4	4	3	3	3	0.863
Example 3	0	1	4	4	4	4	4	4	1	1	1	0.636
Example 4	4	4	4	0	4	4	4	4	2	2	2	0.772
Example 5	0	4	4	0	4	4	4	4	1	1	1	0.613

5 Conclusion

The results of the above mentioned five examples are shown in Table 3 and Table 4 respectively for IndicTrans2 and Facebook's NLLB MT Engines. It was frequently noted that the errors that arose in the outputs of NLLB is that there occurs no proper translation of some words thus changing the frequency and therefore disrupting the intended meaning of the source sentence. As mentioned in the above examples, the fluidity and intended sense of the original statement were compromised by certain inadequately translated phrases. The gender was also altered in a few of the sentences, which altered the sentence's meaning.

One can thus deduce that the outputs from IndicTrans2 are significantly more accurate and superior to those from Facebook's NLLB based on observations made on the results from MT Engines. After analyzing the outcomes of the aforementioned cases, it was determined that IndicTrans2 outperforms NLLB in terms of accuracy, effectivity, reliability and precision.

References

Jiang, J., et al.: StructGPT: a general framework for large language model to reason over structured data. arXiv preprint arXiv:2305.09645 (2023)

Chiang, C., Lee, H.: Can large language models be an alternative to human evaluations? arXiv (Cornell University) (2023). https://doi.org/10.48550/arxiv.2305.01937

Van Der Lee, C., Gatt, A., Van Miltenburg, E., Krahmer, E.: Human evaluation of automatically generated text: current trends and best practice guidelines. Comput. Speech Lang. **67**, 101151 (2021). https://doi.org/10.1016/j.csl.2020.101151

Bojic, I., Chen, J., Chang, S.Y., Ong, Q.C., Joty, S., Car, J.: Hierarchical evaluation framework: best practices for human evaluation. arXiv (Cornell University) (2023). https://doi.org/10.48550/arxiv.2310.01917

Licht, D., Gao, C., Lam, J., Guzman, F., Diab, M., Koehn, P.: Consistent human evaluation of machine translation across language Pairs. arXiv (Cornell University) (2022). https://doi.org/10.48550/arxiv.2205.08533

Hannah, P., et al.: A framework for rigorous evaluation of human performance in human and machine learning comparison studies. Dental science reports (2022). https://doi.org/10.1038/s41598-022-08078-3

Iva, B., et al.: 12. Hierarchical evaluation framework: best practices for human evaluation. arXiv.org (2023). https://doi.org/10.48550/arxiv.2310.01917

Isaac, L., et al.: Human Evaluation of Models Built for Interpretability (2019)

Jean, C., Scholtz: Evaluation Methods for Human-System Performance of Intelligent Systems (2002)

Recent Trends in Speech and NLP

Bilingual Speech Translation Between Tamil and Telugu with Elimination of Dependency on Any Intermediate Languages

R. Kaarthik, S. Rithuh Subhakkrith, Yasaswini Dharmavarapu, A. Vignesh Kumar, Dhanya M. Dhanalakshmy(✉), and N. G. Karthikeyan

Department of Computer Science and Engineering, Amrita School of Computing, Coimbatore, Amrita Vishwa Vidyapeetham, Coimbatore, India
{cb.en.u4cse20426,cb.en.u4cse20452,cb.en.u4cse20416,cb.en.u4cse20071, cb.en.u4cse20641}@cb.students.amrita.edu, md_dhanya@cb.amrita.edu

Abstract. Usage of English as an intermediate language in translating one language to another is prominent, in most of the existing works. Many languages share a common parent language, and when such languages use English as an intermediate language for translation, there can be contextual differences, which could be avoided if there existed a direct source language to target language translation, instead of an external language dependency. Translation of Tamil speech to Telugu speech is discussed here. There are two main approaches: direct translation approach, and cascaded translation approach. A direct speech translation approach using discrete units is compared with a cascaded speech translation system approach that integrates Automatic Speech Recognition, Text-to-Text translation, and Text-to-Speech modules. Several combinations of the cascaded speech translation approach are compared with the direct speech translation approach by training and testing with Few-shot Learning Evaluation of Universal Representations of Speech (FLEURS) dataset. Bilingual Evaluation Understudy (BLEU) and Perceptual Evaluation of Speech Quality (PESQ) evaluatory metrics show that direct Speech-to-Speech Translation is better than some of the cascaded models in the quality of speech translated, but all cascaded Speech-to-Speech Translation approaches are better than the direct Speech-to-Speech Translation approach in preserving the context. It can be concluded that when the right mix of models is cascaded, the translation of Tamil to Telugu becomes better than using a direct Speech-to-Speech Translation.

Keywords: Natural Language Processing · Direct Speech to Unit Translation · HuBERT · VITS · WAV2VEC2 · WHISPER · SEAMLESSM4T

A. Sharma and R. Rani (Eds.): AIST 2024, CCIS 2389, pp. 107–121, 2025.
https://doi.org/10.1007/978-3-031-91331-0_8

1 Introduction

The driving force in developing a multilingual translator is the desire to elevate the level of inclusion and foster good communication in an organization where so many regional languages are spoken. All in itself, this diversity adds to the richness of life, but sometimes it may become a language barrier. Eliminating language barriers would mean better understanding among people and will help create a strong sense of unity in the community. The focus lies in developing a translation system tailored for Indian languages, specifically Tamil and Telugu. Tamil and Telugu share a lot of common words. Using an intermediate language for translation, in these cases of common words, may cost additional overhead and lower performance since the source word sound and target word sound are expected to be the same. The system incorporates two methods: direct Speech-to-Speech Translation (S2ST) and a cascaded S2ST system comprising an Automatic Speech Recognition (ASR) module, a Machine Translation (MT) module, and a Text-to-Speech (TTS) module. Traditional translation models, predominantly used across Europe, and those employing English by Kumar and Yadav [12], Zhang et al. [26], and Eeshan and Jawad [25] as the standard intermediate language, have proven to be less accurate than desired. To address this, this work eliminates the need for an intermediary language, aiming for more precise translations. There are several challenges, including the scarcity of distinct datasets for Tamil and Telugu, variations in accents within these languages, and the prevalent dependence on languages like English as intermediaries. By circumventing the use of an intermediate language, such as English, which often leads to information loss, this work strives to deliver translations that are not only more accurate, but also contextually correct. The main contributions of this work are as follows:

1. To provide an implementation of Direct S2ST for Tamil to Telugu translation using HuBERT
2. To provide cascaded S2ST approaches where three independent models are combined to achieve Tamil speech to Telugu speech translation

The rest of the paper is organized into six more sections. A review of existing literature is presented in Sect. 2. Section 3 discusses the possible research gaps. Section 4 presents a discussion of Direct S2ST and cascaded S2ST approaches methodology, which is followed by implementation and testing details in Sect. 5. Section 6 is for the results and discussion. Section 7 concludes the research work with directions to possible future enhancements.

2 Literature Review

2.1 End to End Speech Translation

A new text-less technique for S2ST systems that enables cross-language voice translation without requiring textual input was introduced by Lee et al. [14] by modeling multi-speaker target speech effectively and training the system with real-world S2ST data. In Jia et al. [10], a little modifications are done to the Translatotron2 S2ST model in order to significantly improve its translation quality, especially on CVSS-C corpus. This leverages unique pre-training strategies with unstructured and weakly-supervised data to significantly advanced understanding of S2ST models and their development potential. In Tjandra et al. [22], translation between two unknown languages is performed without any transcription using discrete representation and a discrete quantized auto-encoder. The sequence model directly maps discrete units of source speech to the target speech. In Chang et al. [5], self-supervised learning is employed, from which, discrete speech units are derived to improve efficiency in speech processing. By compressing high-dimensional spectrogram inputs and applying methods like de-duplication and sub-word modeling, training time is substantially reduced without compromising performance.

2.2 Transformer Based Speech Representation

Hidden Unit BERT (HuBERT) is introduced by Hsu et al. [9] to address issues in representing speech in a Self-Supervised approach. HuBERT uses selective masking, and unsupervised clustering to generate labels for using Bidirectional Encoder Representations from Transformers (BERT) model. Improving ASR with HuBERT is discussed by Maekaku et al. [16] whose focus lies in handling scenarios that have less audio data and its related transcript by increasing the number of clusters HuBERT can process. In Li et al. [15], HuBERT is fine-tuned on different language databases to extract acoustic features across languages, and is used in detecting DeepFake audios. A different approach is taken by Hattori and Tamura [8] where HuBERT, trained on large datasets of majority languages, is made to adapt its language modeling part to suit minority languages for which large datasets are not available. To recognise emotions in speech, HuBERT, and ensemble methods are used by Yang et al. [24] where aggregating the output of five models produces superior results.

2.3 Integrated Components Based Translation

SeamlessM4T, a massive multi-lingual MT model, introduced by Barrault et al. [4], has many applications such as ASR and TTS due to its flexibility and support for more than 100 languages. SeamlessM4T has been trained on large datasets containing speeches and texts, thus can understand complex language patterns. WAV2VEC 2.0, introduced by Aevski et al. [3], improves speech recognition by learning powerful representations from speech audio alone, which showed strong performance even with minimal labelled data. In WAV2VEC2, WAV2VEC is pre-trained in an unsupervised way on large unlabelled audio datasets to improve the speech recognition, performing better than Deep Speech 2. Sundanese speech recognition model proposed by Cryssiover and Zahra [7] utilizes WAV2VEC 2.0, training it with a Sudanese dataset of about 53 h of speech. Variational Inference with adversarial learning for end-to-end Text-to-Speech (VITS) introduced by

Kim et al. [11] is a parallel TTS system that can generate speech from text without undergoing any predefined intermediate speech representations, which can replace two-phase TTS systems. IndicBERT, a type of BERT trained specifically for eleven Indian languages, including Tamil and Telugu, is used by Nagesh et al. [17] to convert Hindi to word embeddings for detecting fake news in Hindi language. IndicBERT would be more suitable for text encoding, whereas HuBERT would be applicable for audio encoding. A cascaded Hindi speech to English speech translation involving Speech-to-Text (STT), text to text, and TTS conversion using CLSRIL-23 + WAV2VEC2 and Tacotron 2 is proposed by Phogat et al. [19]. In Vishnu Kumar and Lalithamani [23], generating captions in Tamil for images using MT Transformers both directly, and using English as a medium is studied, where using English as a medium only slightly improves the Bilingual Evaluation Understudy (BLEU) scores, a metric introduced by Papineni et al. [18], but at the cost of extra processing steps. Vishnu Kumar and Lalithamani [23] also mention why BLEU scores are not an accuracy metric in evaluating the context, further elaborated by Ananthakrishnan et al. [2]. Tamil ASR used by Akhilesh et al. [1] uses XLSR-WAV2VEC2 to convert Tamil audio to Tamil text. This ASR was evaluated with Word Error Rate(WER) and Character Error Rate (CER), wherein there was a lowered performance due to slight variations in pronunciation of letters in Tamil language, and when the wrong letter is substituted, the entire context changes. Tamil voice cloning using SV2TTS is proposed by Radhakrishnan et al. [20] following a encoder-synthesizer-vocoder architecture by capturing the speech characteristics of the speaker, converting it into mel spectogram of text to be spoken, then convert it to natural voice using auto-regressive WaveNet. This can be used to produce more human-sounding speeches in future.

To summarise, there are numerous implementations for ASR, TTS, and text to text translation (also called as MT) explored with many Indian, European, and African languages. Often, sequencing more than one model seems to address diverse applications, not only limited to language translation, but also detecting DeepFake audios, recognizing emotions, and generating captions. Direct translation using discrete units avoids the usage of an intermediate language like English.

3 Research Gap Analysis

There are enormous amount of works translating Dravidian languages to English, and vice versa, and inter-Dravidian language conversion using English as an intermediate. Works related to direct translation of Dravidian languages without an intermediate language is scarce. Additionally, the number significantly drops when Tamil-Telugu translation is considered, even lesser when Tamil speech - Telugu speech translation is considered. This is mainly due to lack of a robust dataset for Tamil and Telugu speeches, until recently. Moreover, there is no study comparing direct S2ST approach and cascaded speech translation for Dravidian languages, especially Tamil - Telugu conversion. The Few-shot

Learning Evaluation of Universal Representations of Speech (FLEURS) dataset, introduced by Conneau et al. [6], is a speech with transcript dataset covering 102 languages across the world including Tamil, and Telugu. The recorded speech, which is about 30 s duration each, is kept as it is, and does not undergo any noise removal. With FLEURS dataset being introduced recently, there are not any works that use this dataset for Tamil-Telugu S2ST.

4 Methodology

Given a Tamil speech, translating it to Telugu speech is the focus of this work. It can be achieved in two ways: the first is to directly convert the Tamil speech to Telugu speech by direct Speech-to-Unit Translation (S2UT) where the source and target speech are split as discrete units, and each sequence of the source speech unit is translated to its corresponding sequence of target speech unit; the second is to utilize a cascaded S2ST approach where Tamil speech is converted to Tamil text, then Tamil text is translated to Telugu text, and finally the translated Telugu text is converted to Telugu speech.

4.1 Direct Speech to Speech Translation with HuBERT

Figure 1 outlines how a Direct S2ST approach works. At the core of Direct S2ST approach lies a S2UT system, leveraging the power of a pre-trained HuBERT base model. Direct S2ST processes incoming speech signals and converts them into discrete units and is passed to a clustering algorithm. This breaks down the continuous stream of speech into manageable units for further processing. The ASR model applies k-means clustering to produce discrete labels for masked audio segments. To encode target vocal expressions into sequences of cluster indices, a k-means clustering algorithm takes advantage of continuous representations at 20-ms intervals which are derived from speech pre-training on unannotated data. These sequences, $[z_1, z_2, ..., z_T]$ where z_i ranges from 0 to k-1, and T refers to the number of frames, represent the input to be used by S2UT model. Figure 1 also mentions how Tamil, as well as, Telugu audios undergo the clustering independently. Moreover, the model adopts a multitask learning approach, wherein auxiliary tasks, like discrete unit decoding and applying attention, are concurrently performed during training. In addition to the S2UT, the Direct S2ST system incorporates a synthesizer to produce target waveforms, which serves as the training target for a unit-based vocoder. This vocoder is specifically designed for unit-to-waveform conversion, transforming the discrete units generated earlier into coherent speech waveforms. A duration prediction module derived from FastSpeech2 is also integrated into the vocoder. This duration prediction module predicts duration of each unit, ensuring that the synthesized speech maintains appropriate timing and rhythm, crucial for natural-sounding output.

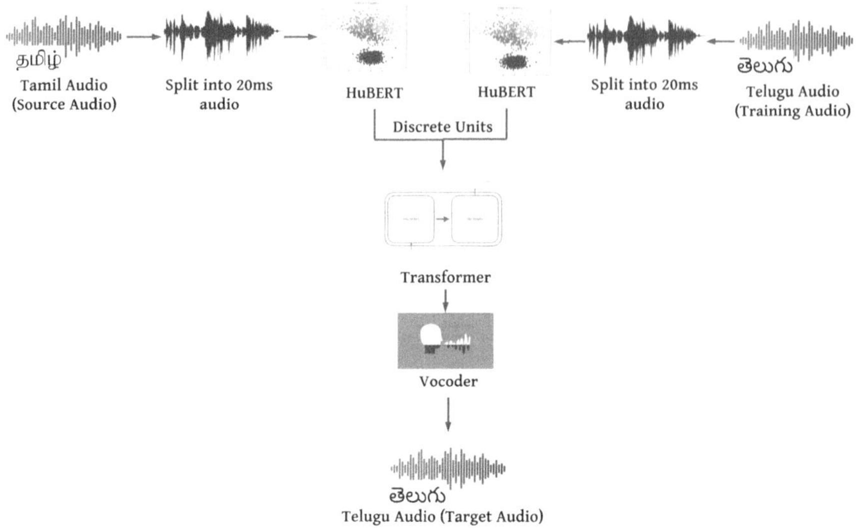

Fig. 1. Architecture of Direct S2ST Model where source (Tamil) audio is split into 20ms audio segments, and passed to HuBERT which is then passed to a Transformer, which is then passed to a Vocoder to get the target (Telugu) audio

The transformer model for MT is adapted into a S2UT model where a stack of 1D-convolutional layers is employed to down-sample the speech input before it is fed into transformer layers. The model employs cross-entropy loss with label smoothing since it has been designed considering that the target sequence is discrete in nature. The unit-based vocoder, a modified High Fidelity Generative Adversarial Networks (HiFi-GAN) neural vocoder, converts discrete units into waveform signals. The vocoder is trained separately with synthetic target speech data to make it compatible with the S2UT model for end-to-end speech translation.

4.2 Cascaded ASR-MT-TTS Translation Model

In contrast to the Direct S2ST, the cascaded system approach includes an ASR module i.e. the Tamil STT module, a MT module converting Tamil text to Telugu text and a TTS module to convert the Telugu text to Telugu speech. Figure 2 outlines a generic cascaded S2ST approach involving STT, Text-to-Text, and TTS modules.

The ASR module comes first in the system of cascades as seen from Fig. 2. It takes speech input and converts it into a textual format. The text is often a transcription of spoken words. Tamil and Telugu languages can have accents or dialects, so the ASR module is designed to handle this variability. MT translates the transcribed text from the ASR module into the target text language directly, without using any other intermediate languages for translation, ensuring more accuracy and contextual correctness. Advanced algorithms, along with large datasets, are used by MT modules for generating high-quality translations. Figure 2 shows that TTS module acts as the last stage in a cascade system. It retrieves translated texts from MT modules, then turns them back into speeches that sound natural and easy to comprehend in desired languages through the use of synthesizers having such capabilities.

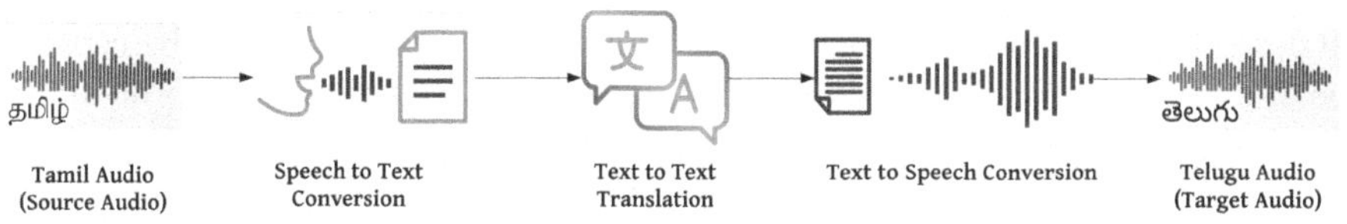

Fig. 2. Architecture of Cascaded S2ST Model where the source (Tamil) audio is passed to STT which is then passed to MT which is then passed to TTS to get the target (Telugu) audio

4.3 Suitability of the Chosen Methodology

In application, both direct S2ST and cascaded S2ST require only the input of Tamil (source) speech, with as less noise as possible, and the translated Telugu (target) speech can be expected as output. However, the training phase of both the approaches require various data. The direct S2ST require really good samples of Tamil speech and the corresponding Telugu speech for a quality translation. These samples should have clear audio, with little or no noise. Training a direct S2ST model requires inclusion of the diversity of one Tamil sentence being expressed in various equivalent Telugu sentences, with difference in the placement of words too. To get an output that sounds more native and colloquial, the vocoder must be trained with diverse target language speeches. On the other hand, the cascaded S2ST requires two varieties of data: speech and the corresponding text, and Tamil-Telugu text translations. Here, the text translation must have diverse pairs equivalent translations. Both STT and TTS require Tamil speech and corresponding Tamil text data and Telugu text and corresponding Telugu speech data. In this speech-text pairs, one text can have multiple speeches with different tone, pitch, sharpness, etc. More the different voices of the same Tamil speech is provided, better will be the STT conversion in capturing the Tamil words appropriately. All Telugu text can have the same Telugu voice, and it would not impact the context of translation. Still, providing different Telugu voices for the same Telugu text will promote a diversity in the audio output like male voice, female voice, and kids voice. When users have only speech-speech translation pairs, direct S2ST will be suitable. When users have speech-text pairs and text-text translation pairs, cascaded S2ST will be better suited.

5 Implementation and Testing

5.1 Direct Speech to Speech Translation

The Direct S2ST system relies on the S2UT framework for the implementation of the model, similar to model introduced by Lee et al. [13] but with FLEURS dataset. A HuBERT Base model was trained on the FLEURS dataset. The Direct S2ST system used the representation units obtained from the sixth layer to get discrete units for all the Telugu speech targets using k-means clustering with k = 100. The source speech is processed to compute mel-filterbank features with 80 dimensions, each at 10ms interval. These features are normalized by cepstral mean and variance. Encoder used consists of a downsampling stack, including two 1 Dimensional convolutional layers, each with a kernel size as 5, and the number of channels as 1024. The encoder also consists of 12 transformer layers, each with a dimension of 256 embeddings, an Feed Forward Network (FFN) with the number of dimension as 2048, and 4 attention heads.

The Direct S2ST system evaluated four auxiliary models using FAIRSEQ STT framework: Source Phonemes (SP), Source Characters (SC), Target Phonemes (TP), and Target Characters (TC). An attention module and decoder to the 6th encoder layer was appended for sc and sp, and to the 8th encoder layer for tc and tp. Multi-head attention modules have 4 heads, decoders with 2 transformer layers, 256-dimensional embeddings, and FFN embedding size of 2048. A constant weight of 8.0 was maintained for all auxiliary loss during training. All models are trained for 400,000 steps using the Adam optimizer with the specified decay rates. 0.2 factor of label smoothing, and inverse square root learning rate decay schedule with 10,000 warm-up steps were used. The unit-based vocoder consists of a duration prediction module from FastSpeech2, which has two 1D-convolutional layers, filter size as 128, kernel size as 3, and 0.5 dropout. Weight on the Mean Squared Error (MSE) loss from the duration prediction module is set as 1 in the training process. The vocoder was trained on the synthetic target speech from the FLEURS set to produce Telugu speech output.

5.2 Cascaded Speech to Speech Translation

ASR system make use of three models - WHISPER, WAV2VEC2_1, and WAV2VEC2_2, for the purpose of transcribing Tamil audio into text. The system fine-tunes two variants of WAV2VEC2 using different pre-trained models: one based on WAV2VEC2 (referred here as WAV2VEC2_1) which is fine-tuned on Multilingual Pretrained Model CLSRIL-23, and another on WAV2VEC2-large-xlsr-53 (referred here as WAV2VEC2_2) which fine-tuned facebook/wav2vec2-large-xlsr-53 in Tamil using Common Voice database. WAV2VEC2 model has convolutional layers for initial processing, transformer layers for understanding context, and a linear projection layer for producing final output. The cascaded S2ST system implements a function called parseTranscription that handles transcription process. This function takes audio files as input, processes them internally by running inference over WAV2VEC2/ WHISPER models and saves corresponding transcriptions into text files after decoding predictions made by these models. For WHISPER model, an ASR pipeline with whisper-tamil-small model was used since it has been trained specifically to handle tamil transcription tasks.

In the MT module, the system uses SEAMLESSM4T model, specifically, SeamlessM4Tv2Model and AutoProcessor from transformers library of python, loading pre-trained weights for Tamil-to-Telugu text translation. There are two main stages in MT: translating the source text to the target text, and generating speech tokens from translated text. SEAMLESSM4T itself is capable of converting the translated texts to speech, and so, it is also used here as one of the TTS in the cascaded S2ST.

To convert Telugu text into Telugu audio waveforms, proposed system uses the VITS model from the transformers library of python. The system starts by processing text files and converting them to a format that can be understood by the model using AutoTokenizer. There are different parts that compose the VITS model, such as posterior encoder which is characterized by non-causal WaveNet residual blocks, a component that captures some subtleties about how people speak. Inspired by HiFi-GAN, V1 generator decoder of VITS synthesizes high-quality audio waveforms using stack transposed convolutions and multi-receptive field fusion modules. Together, the encoder and the decoder work towards capturing speech patterns, generating correct waveform representations, synthesizing good quality sound signals, making them seem real or natural enough even though they are not produced by an actual speaker but estimated from written texts.

6 Results and Discussion

FLEURS dataset is split in 10:1 ratio for training and testing. 1215 samples and 292 samples from FLEURS dataset are used for training and testing, respectively. Additionally, 140 samples were used in the development set. To compare performance of the Direct S2ST approach, and the Cascaded S2ST approach, two evaluatory metrics are chosen: BLEU score and Perceptual Evaluation of Speech Quality (PESQ) score. PESQ is a speech quality assessment model proposed by Rix et al. [21] to evaluate a range of network conditions, including analogue connections, CODECs, packet loss, and variable delay. PESQ is now an industry standard for audio quality assessment. Higher the BLEU and PESQ scores are, better the model is. PESQ score is an indication of the quality of the sound perceived by humans. It takes the audio sharpness, background noise, volume, variable latencies, lag, clipping, etc. into consideration to compute PESQ score. PESQ score compares two audios by placing the original and the input waveforms and computes the score. Generally, PESQ score is used for two audios with only a difference in quality, implying that the words in the audio must be the same. PESQ may not be the ideal metric for a Speech-to-Speech Translation, but it serves as a metric to how close the audio is in terms of quality and content. Computation of PESQ score does not have a straight-forward algorithm and is usually done by a third-party software. Here, PESQ scores are calculated using pypesq package of python. PESQ scores lie between -0.5 and 4.5, where PESQ scores less than 1 are beyond human comprehension, and scores above 3 are clearly understandable. BLEU score is generally computed for translated texts. BLEU score lies between 0 and 1, where scores above 0.6 are rarely achieved by humans. Here, BLEU scores are multiplied by 100 to provide better understanding. So, here, the range of BLEU scores will be from 0 to 100, and any score above 60 is exceptional. BLEU score is calculated using Eq. 2. BLEU scores indicate the adequacy and the fluency of the translated sentences. BLEU scores are affected by the difference in corpora, and variability in sentence formation. The output Telugu audio is again converted to Telugu Text, compared with the already provided transcript of FLEURS dataset to compute the BLEU scores.

$$n\text{-}gram\ Precision\ (p_n) = \frac{\sum_{C\in\text{Candidates}}\sum_{\text{ngram}\in C}\text{Count}_{\text{clip}}(\text{ngram})}{\sum_{C\in\text{Candidates}}\sum_{\text{ngram}\in C}\text{Count}(\text{ngram})} \tag{1}$$

$$Bilingual\ Evaluation\ Understudy\ (BLEU) = BP \cdot P_N \tag{2}$$

$$Geometric\ Mean\ of\ Precisions\ (P_N) = \left(\prod_{n=1}^{N} p_n\right)^{1/N} \tag{3}$$

$$Brevity\ Penalty\ (BP) = \begin{cases} 1 & \text{if } c > r \\ e^{(1-r/c)} & \text{if } c \leq r \end{cases} \tag{4}$$

In general, all models display lower BLEU and PESQ scores, which is mainly due to the limitations imposed by the FLEURS dataset. FLEURS dataset had speeches spoken by various speakers. Models suffered the variance in voices due to the factors like pitch, pace, accent, pronunciation, loudness and prosody. Above all, FLEURS dataset had background noise in many samples. These factors themselves are enough to make the evaluatory scores look low. For computing BLEU scores, transcript of the reference speech is compared, and not a STT conversion of the target audio. This has significantly lowered the BLEU score. Not only that, but also the target speech has synonyms of the expected words, causing a lowering of BLEU score as discussed by Ananthakrishnan et al. [2]. Thus, only comparison between direct S2ST and cascaded S2ST models will be focused.

The direct S2ST approach for translating speech from Tamil to Telugu is evaluated with PESQ scores as the primary metric. From Table 1, it can be observed that the mean PESQ score of direct S2ST obtained for the 292 translated audio files was 1.856 which implies the translated audio can be understood to some extent. The direct S2ST yielded a BLEU score of 3.11. The low BLEU score can also be interpreted that the direct S2ST focused more on preserving the context than concentrating on achieving a very specific pattern of words. When these audios were interpreted by a native Telugu speaker, all the 292 speeches sounded so foreign, similar to a native English speaker trying to speak Telugu letter by letter. Contextually, the translation appears good and much relevant to the expected speech, but it takes a lot of effort and careful listening to understand the speech. All the output speech was of the same unnatural voice, which lowered the PESQ score since the expected speech was with various native speakers' voices. This unnatural speech also made the output Telugu transcript to have the words misinterpreted and split at unwanted places, resulting in a poor BLEU score.

The cascaded approach had three ASRs: WHISPER, WAV2VEC2_1, and WAV2VEC2_2, one Text-to-Text translator: SEAMLESSM4T, and two TTS Translators: VITS and SEAMLESSM4T. All six combinations are implemented and tested against BLEU and PESQ scores whose scores can be seen in Table 1. Among the integration models examined, WHISPER-SEAMLESSM4T-VITS demonstrated the highest performance across both PESQ and BLEU scores. This cascaded S2ST system, which utilized WHISPER for ASR, SEAMLESSM4T for MT, and VITS MODEL for TTS synthesis, achieved a PESQ score of 1.978 and an impressive BLEU score of 29.96. Comparatively, other integration models also showed promising performance. For example, WAV2VEC2_2-SEAMLESSM4T-VITS, achieved a competitive BLEU score of 15.75 and PESQ score of 1.399, demonstrating strong translation accuracy. Similarly, WHISPER-SEAMLESSM4T attained a BLEU score of 14.12, highlighting the efficacy of this combination. SEAMLESSM4T is the only Tamil text to Telugu text translator used in this cascaded model. This may have a lasted an effect on all the cascaded approach evaluatory scores, due to error propagation. Downside of using cascaded S2ST is the propagation of error from one component to the final output. Development of better Tamil text to Telugu text translator will surely improve the scores.

Table 1. Comparison of BLEU and PESQ evaluatory scores of Direct S2ST Model and Cascaded S2ST Model

MODEL	BLEU Score	PESQ Score
WHISPER - SEAMLESSM4T - VITS	29.96	1.978
WHISPER - SEAMLESSM4T	14.12	1.724
WAV2VEC2_1 - SEAMLESSM4T - VITS	4.49	2.390
WAV2VEC2_1 - SEAMLESSM4T	6.96	1.847
WAV2VEC2_2 - SEAMLESSM4T - VITS	15.75	1.399
WAV2VEC2_2 - SEAMLESSM4T	13.11	1.724
Direct Speech to Speech (HuBERT)	3.11	1.856

WHISPER-SEAMLESSM4T-VITS demonstrated the highest performance across both PESQ and BLEU scores by achieving a PESQ score of 1.978 and a BLEU score of 29.96. The resultant audio is scoring decently on both BLEU and PESQ which suggests that while the perceived quality of audio is good, the expected translation of speech may not be accurate. From Table 1, it can be observed that the Direct S2ST approach has a competitive PESQ score, but a very poor BLEU score, a behaviour very similar to WAV2VEC2_1-SEAMLESSM4T-VITS. When a native Telugu speaker was made to listen to the translated speeches, all the 292 samples from all the models sounded natural, much similar to the voices present in the training dataset. However, the unexpected low PESQ score is due to the models producing an output speech in a voice that is not the same as the expected voice present in the test sample. PESQ scores would definitely be higher if the dataset had only one voice, and expected only one voice. Contextually, the translated speech still made sense to a certain extent, but it had variations from what was expected from the dataset. In some cases, stammered Telugu speech was observed. Cascaded models with lower BLEU score had some mistranslations, possibly due to shortcomings in the STT or TTS models used. Particularly, WAV2VEC2_1 model has low BLEU score, which can mean that WAV2VEC2_1 model may not be really good at capturing Tamil speech and converting it to Tamil text. WHISPER-SEAMLESSM4T-VITS shows that a cascaded model can achieve both high BLEU and PESQ score, while direct S2ST model may not be able to do so, mainly due to a robotic voice output and missing of accurate pauses in speech. For some test samples, both direct S2ST and cascaded S2ST produced the output speech with overwhelming static noise, and sometimes only with noise. On inspecting the input Tamil speech, it was observed that even the input audio contained some background noise, missing sharpness. It is not practical to expect input audio to be fed only in a silent environment. The ASR module in cascaded S2ST can handle this issue better by eliminating background noise, which a direct S2ST may not be able to do. a shortcoming faced by both direct S2ST and cascaded S2ST is in translating names. Names tend to be trimmed/ mistranslated in the target speech, whereas the expectation is to have the names preserved the same way. Same issue occurs when a foreign language word is used in a sentence when it is expected that the word remains the same in the target speech as well. Overall, direct S2ST has lesser requirements but cascaded S2ST provides more control and better Speech-to-Speech translation.

7 Conclusion and Future Scope

Translation of Tamil and Telugu audio holds significance, and their link of being a Dravidian language further highlights the need to eliminate an intermediate foreign language, like English, whose grammatical structure, and colloquialism are much different. Two approaches: direct S2ST, and cascaded S2ST were discussed. While scores of these models may not be as high as expected, this definitely paves the way for a direct source language to target language translation, without the need to depend on an intermediate language. Furthermore, direct S2ST has more of its focus on providing clear and sharp waveforms but the cascaded S2ST approach is better in voicing out the context. Cascaded S2ST approach is advantageous since it is made up of independent modules, and each module can be improved independently. If some module affects the output due to a design flaw, it can easily be replaced with another module. The real power of direct S2ST lines in developing a Speech-to-Speech model where one or both the languages do not have a written form. Direct S2ST will shine in Tamil speech to Telugu speech translation where dialects are important.

In future, the inadequacy in the availability of Tamil-Telugu speech dataset can be addressed. Both these languages have an enormous literature making it very difficult to frame a comprehensive dataset. Datasets highly influence the performance of translators. Quality of speech, accuracy, expansion of corpora, and inclusion of diverse accents and dialects can be prioritised. Unit-based vocoders can be refined to produce more natural-sounding human speech waveforms. The scarcity of suitable language-to-language pairs limits the diversity and coverage of translations that can be handled. Data augmentation and expansion could play a key role in overcoming data scarcity challenges in languages like Tamil and Telugu. Techniques such as synthetic data generation, transfer learning, and domain adaptation could augment existing datasets and expand language coverage to include underrepresented languages and dialects. To quantify the performance of Speech-to-Speech translators, better evaluation metrics can be developed which can accurately describe the quality, similarity and contextual correctness of translation.

References

1. Akhilesh, A., Brinda, P., Keerthana, S., Gupta, D., Vekkot, S.: Tamil speech recognition using XLSR wav2vec2.0 & CTC algorithm. In: 2022 13th International Conference on Computing Communication and Networking Technologies (ICCCNT), pp. 1–6 (2022)
2. Ananthakrishnan, R., Bhattacharyya, P., Sasikumar, M., Shah, R.M.: Some issues in automatic evaluation of English-Hindi MT: more blues for bleu. Icon **64** (2007)
3. Baevski, A., Zhou, Y., Mohamed, A., Auli, M.: wav2vec 2.0: a framework for self-supervised learning of speech representations. In: Larochelle, H., Ranzato, M., Hadsell, R., Balcan, M., Lin, H. (eds.) Advances in Neural Information Processing Systems, vol. 33, pp. 12449–12460. Curran Associates, Inc. (2020)
4. Barrault, L., et al.: Seamlessm4t-massively multilingual & multimodal machine translation. arXiv preprint arXiv:2308.11596 (2023)
5. Chang, X., et al.: Exploring speech recognition, translation, and understanding with discrete speech units: a comparative study. In: 2024 IEEE International Conference on Acoustics, Speech and Signal Processing (ICASSP), ICASSP 2024, pp. 11481–11485 (2024)
6. Conneau, A., et al.: Fleurs: few-shot learning evaluation of universal representations of speech. In: 2022 IEEE Spoken Language Technology Workshop (SLT), pp. 798–805 (2023)
7. Cryssiover, A., Zahra, A.: Speech recognition model design for sundanese language using wav2vec 2.0. Int. J. Speech Technol. **27**(1), 171–177 (2024)
8. Hattori, T., Tamura, S.: Speech recognition for minority languages using hubert and model adaptation. In: Proceedings of the 12th International Conference on Pattern Recognition Applications and Methods - ICPRAM, pp. 350–355. INSTICC, SciTePress (2023)

9. Hsu, W.N., Bolte, B., Tsai, Y., Lakhotia, K., Salakhutdinov, R., Mohamed, A.: Hubert: self-supervised speech representation learning by masked prediction of hidden units. IEEE/ACM Trans. Audio Speech Lang. Process. **29**, 3451–3460 (2021)
10. Jia, Y., et al.: Leveraging unsupervised and weakly-supervised data to improve direct speech-to-speech translation. arXiv preprint arXiv:2203.13339 (2022)
11. Kim, J., Kong, J., Son, J.: Conditional variational autoencoder with adversarial learning for end-to-end text-to-speech. In: International Conference on Machine Learning, pp. 5530–5540. PMLR (2021)
12. Kumar, K.V., Yadav, D.: Word sense-based approach for Hindi to Tamil machine translation using English as pivot language. Int. J. Adv. Intell. Paradigms **11**(3–4), 284–298 (2018)
13. Lee, A., et al.: Direct speech-to-speech translation with discrete units. arXiv preprint arXiv:2107.05604 (2021)
14. Lee, A., et al.: Textless speech-to-speech translation on real data. arXiv preprint arXiv:2112.08352 (2021)
15. Li, L., Lu, T., Ma, X., Yuan, M., Wan, D.: Voice deepfake detection using the self-supervised pre-training model hubert. Appl. Sci. **13**(14), 8488 (2023)
16. Maekaku, T., Chang, X., Fujita, Y., Watanabe, S.: An exploration of hubert with large number of cluster units and model assessment using Bayesian information criterion. In: 2022 IEEE International Conference on Acoustics, Speech and Signal Processing (ICASSP), ICASSP 2022, pp. 7107–7111. IEEE (2022)
17. Nagesh, S., et al.: A machine learning approach for detecting fake news in Hindi. In: 2023 10th IEEE Uttar Pradesh Section International Conference on Electrical, Electronics and Computer Engineering (UPCON), vol. 10, pp. 69–74 (2023)
18. Papineni, K., Roukos, S., Ward, T., Zhu, W.J.: Bleu: a method for automatic evaluation of machine translation. In: Proceedings of the 40th annual meeting of the Association for Computational Linguistics, pp. 311–318 (2002)
19. Phogat, D., et al.: Bridging language barriers: exploring Hindi-to-English speech-to-speech translation for multilingual communication. In: Kumar, S., K., B., Kim, J.H., Bansal, J.C. (eds.) Fourth Congress on Intelligent Systems, pp. 141–152. Springer, Singapore (2024)
20. Radhakrishnan, V., Aadharsh Aadhithya, A., Mohan, J., Visweswaran, M., Jyothish Lal, G., Premjith, B.: Voice Cloning for Low-Resource Languages, chap. 12, pp. 243–257. Wiley (2024)
21. Rix, A., Beerends, J., Hollier, M., Hekstra, A.: Perceptual evaluation of speech quality (PESQ)-a new method for speech quality assessment of telephone networks and codecs. In: 2001 IEEE International Conference on Acoustics, Speech, and Signal Processing. Proceedings (Cat. No. 01CH37221), vol. 2, pp. 749–752 (2001)
22. Tjandra, A., Sakti, S., Nakamura, S.: Speech-to-speech translation between untranscribed unknown languages. In: 2019 IEEE Automatic Speech Recognition and Understanding Workshop (ASRU), pp. 593–600 (2019)
23. Vishnu Kumar, V.H., Lalithamani, N.: English to Tamil multi-modal image captioning translation. In: 2022 IEEE World Conference on Applied Intelligence and Computing (AIC), pp. 332–338 (2022)
24. Yang, J.: Ensemble deep learning with hubert for speech emotion recognition. In: 2023 IEEE 17th International Conference on Semantic Computing (ICSC), pp. 153–154 (2023)

25. Zeeshan, Z.A., Jawad, M.Z.: Research on Chinese-Urdu machine translation based on deep learning. J. Auton. Intell. **3**(2), 34–44 (2020)
26. Zhang, Y., Ma, Q., Isahara, H.: Automatic acquisition of a Japanese-Chinese bilingual lexicon using English as an intermediary. In: International Conference on Natural Language Processing and Knowledge Engineering, Proceedings, pp. 471–476 (2003)

CTC-Based Automatic Speech Recognition for Hindi Language

Arushree Mishra(✉), Suhani, Amita Dev, and Poonam Bansal

Indira Gandhi Delhi Technical University for Women, Delhi, India
arushree180@gmail.com

Abstract. Speech Recognition (SR) is a process in which spoken words or sentences are converted to text. In this process an acoustic signal, captured by a microphone, is converted to text. The previous couple decades have seen such rapid developments in automatic speech recognition systems. They are being used in various industries such as healthcare, agriculture, speech dialling, directory services, education, and autos, among others, most commonly being virtual assistants like Siri, Google Assistant or Cortana. Even after so much advancements these ASR systems are not commonly built for Indian regional language. Since, majority of the population of India speaks Hindi it becomes important for us to have an ASR framework for Hindi to improve the situation of the service sector. This paper presents an innovative approach for 'Automatic Speech Recognition' that uses a modified DeepSpeech2 model adapted for the Hindi language. The model integrates "Recurrent Neural Networks" (RNNs) and "Convolutional Neural Networks" (CNNs) for feature extraction with Gated Recurrent Units (GRUs) for sequence modelling. To further enhance performance, an attention mechanism is incorporated, allowing the model to focus on audio sequence segments. The purpose of this paper is to improve speech recognition performance for the Hindi language by utilising a modified DeepSpeech2 model along with some fine-tuning. The proposed method effectively models the Hindi language and reduces the training and validation loss with the help of efficient pre-processing and fine-tuning of the model.

Keywords: Automatic Speech Recognition · Hindi · RNN · CNN · CTC Loss

1 Introduction

The ability to listen to and understand spoken language, distinguish between various sounds, and recognise spoken words as belonging to a known language is known as speech recognition. Several steps are involved in speech recognition, including recording the speaker's voice, identifying word boundaries, extracting features, and finally utilising a knowledge model to identify the speaker [15]. The method of automatically creating speech by machines or computers is known as speech synthesis. Creating a machine with a natural-sounding voice that can

A. Sharma and R. Rani (Eds.): AIST 2024, CCIS 2389, pp. 122–136, 2025.
https://doi.org/10.1007/978-3-031-91331-0_9

communicate with a user in the accent, language, and voice they want is the aim of speech synthesis [16].

ASR can be utilised in various areas. While ASR has the potential to facilitate human-machine communication, it frequently goes above and beyond being useful to the point of becoming vital. The widespread use of smartphones in developing countries and their growing use in rural areas creates a unique chance to create a voice-centred app that addresses low literacy rates in those regions. Smartphones have numerous benefits compared to a PC interface, including increased mobility, easy battery charging, and standard built-in features like microphones and speakers [4].

Said by an additional 600 million individuals, Hindi is among the most commonly used languages in India. While English has seen extensive research and development in ASR, regional languages, which are spoken by millions of people, lag behind. This gap limits the accessibility of technology for a large portion of the population that primarily communicates in their native languages. Developing ASR systems for Hindi and other regional languages is not just a technical challenge but also a societal necessity that could greatly enhance the accessibility and efficiency of services for millions of people.

This research presents the combination of a 2D CNN, "Connectionist Temporal Classification" (CTC) loss, and "Gated Recurrent Units" (GRUs) within "Recurrent Neural Networks" (RNNs) to construct an ASR. Deep neural networks are trained using the CTC algorithm to recognise speech, handwriting, and other sequence problems. CTC is applied in cases where there is uncertainty regarding the correspondence between the input and output (like how the transcripts correspond to the sound). The base prototype in this paper is similar to DeepSpeech2. Variation in its accuracy has been noted by preprocessing the data, fine-tuning the model and then applying both the techniques together [5].

The research presented in this paper contributes to the ongoing efforts to develop effective ASR systems for regional languages. The aim of the paper is to enhance the effectiveness of Hindi speech recognition systems, making them more accurate and reliable for real-world applications. By addressing the challenges of developing ASR systems for a regional language with diverse dialects and pronunciations, this work contributes to the broader effort of making advanced technology accessible to non-English-speaking populations. The results demonstrate significant improvements in WER and validation loss, highlighting the effectiveness of the proposed modifications to the DeepSpeech2 architecture.

2 Literature Review

Research on ASR started long back in the 1950s. In 1952 Bell Labs introduced 'Audrey' who could speak numbers. In 1962 IBM introduced 'Shoebox' at the World's Fair who could understand 16 words [6].

The turning point in ASR came in the mid-1970s when HMM models were introduced for word probability, which brought a significant improvement in the field. The GMM-HMM models [7] were quite successful and were based on data (words, phonemes), but the problem was that accuracy was not good and also these models required a lot of labelled data. Speech synthesis techniques, such as statistical parametric approaches using Hidden Markov Models (HMM), have shown promise in generating natural-sounding speech by simultaneously modelling spectrum, excitation, and duration [18].

Neural network-based ASR research began in the 1980s, and "deep neural networks" (DNN) proved to be a highly effective acoustic model for speech recognition. Comparing the node-pruned DNN bottleneck features to the other constraint features produced by the traditional forms of DNN architectures, their results demonstrate a potential reduction in WER. Furthermore, the compact layer that produced the bottleneck feature could be automatically obtained by the node-pruned DNN structure [8].

In 2015 Deepgram [9] introduced the first end-to-end DL ASR for business. In majority of the approaches introduced previously the main issue is labelled data, many models such as GMM-HMM, and neural networks were data-hungry, and many languages didn't have a large amount of labelled data, that is when the researchers started to tackle this problem. During this time Self-supervised techniques came to light. In 2019, wav2vec [10] was introduced which was based on self-supervised learning, which started to give better results in ASR, in the next year i.e., in 2020, the modified version of wav2vec was introduced.

'Wav2vec 2.0' [11] is a higher structure for speech representations "self-supervised learning" that solves a contrastive problem across quantal speech representations while hiding latent representations of the original waveform. Pre-training on unlabelled data has a great deal of potential for speech processing, as proven by tests conducted on radically diverse datasets. Results for the entire Librispeech noisy speech benchmark were achieved by the model. Using 100 times lower labelled data, wav2vec 2.0 beat the previous best result on the 100 h of Librispeech data. Additionally, the method performed best when a big amount of tagged data was available.

In the unsupervised part of wav2vec (self-supervised learning), some researchers found out that the model could be trained better with the help of different languages data, which could better help in multi-language ASR. In Jan 2022 the paper CLSRIL-23 [12] showcased the same, a model that used raw audio recordings of 23 different Indian languages to acquire cross-lingual speech representations. In terms of learning speech representations, experiments reveal that linguistic pre-training performed better than single language training.

Different methods for speech segmentation have also been tried in the Hindi language. [19] used a convex hull approach and short-term energy (STE) signals, to get an automatic voice segmentation, based on syllables, for Hindi language that outperforms conventional techniques in terms of accuracy.

3 Methodology

3.1 Dataset

The dataset was sourced from OpenSLR. T95.05 h and 5.55 h of audio, respectively, make up the train and test sets of the Hindi speech dataset. In the train and test sets, there are 4506 and 386 distinct sentences extracted from Hindi stories, respectively, with no sentence overlap. A discontinuous set of 19 speakers' utterances make up the test set, whereas 59 speakers' utterances make up the train set. The 8kHz sampling rate for the audio files which were processed to 16kHz. The transcription file of the dataset was in .txt format and contained columns audio-id and sentence and the audios are in .wav format.To prevent overfitting, only the train dataset was utilised, which was further split into training and validation sets [13].

3.2 Base Model

English: The base model chosen for this paper is similar to DeepSpeech2, as described in [5]. In which LJSpeech dataset from the LibriVox project was used. The model's quality was evaluated with the help of 'WER' which we get by dividing the total words in the text that were pronounced in the original language by the sum of the insertions, deletions, and substitutions that take place in a recognised word sequence. In the original base model applied to the English language the WER = 16 This model along with the preprocessing was directly applied to the hindi dataset and its training and validation loss was measured along with the WER over 50 epochs. The preprocessing steps for the Hindi dataset were adapted to align with the characteristics of the dataset, and the WER for Hindi was compared to the original English WER to assess the model's output in an alternative language.

Pre-processing: The audio data has been preprocessed for speech recognition model using TensorFlow. This step, known as the signal-processing front end, aims to transform the waveform of speech into a parametric form of some kind (at a significantly reduced information rate) for additional processing and analysis (Rabiner and Schafer, 1979; Rabiner and Juang, Speaker identification 1978; Furui, 2001) [17].

Following are the steps taken:

- **Vocabulary generation:** Hindi vocabulary was built of size 81.
- **Decoding:** After reading the wav file, the file is decoded into a tensor of audio data which is then squeezed to remove any extra dimensions.
- **Convert to Float:** The audio data is then converted to a 'float32' type for further handling.
- **Feature generation:** Next the STFT of the signal for audio was computed, with the parameters value as follows: frame-length = 256, frame-step = 160 and fft-length = 384. This generated a spectrogram, which is a time-frequency representation of the audio.

- **Magnitude and Normalisation:** Power transformation was applied to the spectrogram by taking its magnitude (absolute value). Square root function was applied to adjust the scale. The spectrogram is now normalised by dividing by the standard deviation after deducting the mean along the frequency axis, plus a small epsilon to avoid division by zero.
- **Processing the Label:** Label was first converted to lowercase and the string was then split into individual Unicode characters. Next each character in the label was mapped to a numeric representation. This typically involves a predefined mapping (dictionary) from characters to integers.
- **Training Dataset:** A TensorFlow dataset was created from the audio IDs and sentences in the training dataframe (`df-train`) using slicing function. Then the preprocessing function was mapped over the dataset, processing each sample. The dataset was batched with padding to ensure each batch has the same shape. Padding is applied where necessary to make all samples in a batch the same length. Finally the data was prefetched to improve performance by overlapping the data preprocessing and model training.
- **Validation Dataset:** Same steps were applied as a training dataset.

CTC Architecture: First, the CTC Loss Function's architecture is built. When both input and output sequences' alignment relation is unknown, then we use models like CTC for training sequence-to-sequence models. Since the length of the output sequence (text) in speech recognition is usually shorter than the length of the input sequence (audio features), this is especially helpful.

The CTC Loss Function is implemented by taking two types of input:

- **y_true**, which are the true labels, each of which is an integer sequence that represents a character from the output, and
- **y_pred**, which are the predicted probabilities for each time step in the sequence, which are usually the results of a softmax activation function over a series of time steps.

At last, the CTC loss in between *y_true* and *y_pred* is calculated, where *y_true* represents a tensor of the form

$$\text{y\_true} \in \mathbb{R}^{\text{batch\_size} \times \text{max\_label\_length}},$$

where *max_label_length* denotes the batch's maximum label length, and *y_pred* is a tensor of the form

$$\text{y\_pred} \in \mathbb{R}^{\text{batch\_size} \times \text{max\_input\_length} \times \text{num\_classes}},$$

where *num_classes* denotes the total number of possible output classes and *max_input_length* the maximum length of the input sequence.

Functions:

- **Normalisation:** The lengths of the input and output sequences are used to normalise the loss so that the model is taught to anticipate the sequence of labels accurately across varying lengths.
- **Flexibility:** CTC does not require pre-defined alignments to align predictions with the true labels; it can handle variable-length sequences. It is helpful for projects like ASR in which the spoken input varies in length.
- **Training-Time Loss:** The training-time loss is computed, which is then utilised to refresh the model's weights in back propagation.

Model Architecture: First, the CTC Loss Function's architecture is built. When both input and output sequences' alignment relation is unknown, then we use models like CTC for training sequence-to-sequence models. Since the length of the output sequence (text) in speech recognition is usually shorter than the length of the input sequence (audio features), this is especially helpful.

The CTC Loss Function is implemented by taking two types of input:

- **y_true**, which are the true labels, each of which is an integer sequence that represents a character from the output, and
- **y_pred**, which are the predicted probabilities for each time step in the sequence, which are usually the results of a softmax activation function over a series of time steps.

At last, the CTC loss in between **y_true** and **y_pred** is calculated, where **y_true** represents a tensor of the form, where **max_label_length** denotes the batch's maximum label length, and, **y_pred** is a tensor of the form, in which **num_classes** denotes the total number of possible output classes and **max_input_length** the maximum length of the input sequence.

Functions:

- **Normalisation:** The lengths of the input and output sequences are used to normalise the loss so that the model is taught to anticipate the sequence of labels accurately across varying lengths.
- **Flexibility:** CTC does not require pre-defined alignments to align predictions with the true labels; it can handle variable-length sequences. It is helpful for projects like ASR in which the spoken input varies in length.
- **Training-Time Loss:** The training-time loss is computed, which is then utilised to refresh the model's weights in back propagation (Table 1).

Table 1. Model Summary of Base Model [5].

Layer (type)	Output Shape	Param #
input (InputLayer)	(None, None, 193)	0
expand_dim (Reshape)	(None, None, 193, 1)	0
conv_1 (Conv2D)	(None, None, 97, 32)	14,432
conv_1_bn (BatchNormalization)	(None, None, 97, 32)	128
conv_1_relu (ReLU)	(None, None, 97, 32)	0
conv_2 (Conv2D)	(None, None, 49, 32)	236,544
conv_2_bn (BatchNormalization)	(None, None, 49, 32)	128
conv_2_relu (ReLU)	(None, None, 49, 32)	0
reshape_2 (Reshape)	(None, None, 1568)	0
bidirectional_1 (Bidirectional)	(None, None, 1024)	6,395,904
dropout_10 (Dropout)	(None, None, 1024)	0
bidirectional_2 (Bidirectional)	(None, None, 1024)	4,724,736
dropout_11 (Dropout)	(None, None, 1024)	0
bidirectional_3 (Bidirectional)	(None, None, 1024)	4,724,736
dropout_12 (Dropout)	(None, None, 1024)	0
bidirectional_4 (Bidirectional)	(None, None, 1024)	4,724,736
dropout_13 (Dropout)	(None, None, 1024)	0
bidirectional_5 (Bidirectional)	(None, None, 1024)	4,724,736
dense_1 (Dense)	(None, None, 1024)	1,049,600
dense_1_relu (ReLU)	(None, None, 1024)	0
dropout_14 (Dropout)	(None, None, 1024)	0
dense_2 (Dense)	(None, None, 82)	84,050

Result: The losses observantly decreased throughout the epochs depicting that the model was improving and learning better. Differences in the size of the datasets and the complexity of the language might be the reason why the Hindi dataset's validation loss was greater than the English dataset's. The WER estimate is probably between 16 and 17%, which is comparable to the English model's output. We expect the WER for Hindi to be similar to the English model because of the similar architecture and loss trends observed. Subsequent attempts to increase the model's accuracy by using a wider range of Hindi data sets and advanced extension methods might further reduce the WER.

3.3 Base Model with Improvised Pre-processing Methods

Improvisations: The preprocessing methods of the base model have been improvised so as to get better accuracy and lesser train and validation loss and WER. These augmentations directly affect the spectrogram generated from the audio, leading to potentially more diverse training data and improved model generalisation.

We included in the modified preprocessing function two main audio augmentation techniques used to prepare the datasets for deep learning: adding noise and time-stretching.

A little bit of Gaussian noise was introduced into the audio signal. The `add_noise` function was applied to create random noise with a mean of 0.0 and a standard deviation of `noise_factor`, this parameter was 0.005 by default. This helps in improving the model's performance when it is subject to noise, which is common in everyday audio applications.

The audio signal was then time-stretched, which adjusts the audio speed without altering its pitch. The `time_stretch` function used the `scipy.signal.resample` method to adjust the length of the audio signal based on the specified rate (default `1.1`, indicating a 10% speed increase). This augmentation simulates variations in speaking speed, helping the model generalise better across different speech patterns.

Result: The preprocessing techniques were adjusted to improve the efficiency of the model, in scenarios like identifying speech in environments with significant background noise or from individuals exhibiting diverse speaking rates. Such enhancements are anticipated to make the model generalisable and robust, thereby reducing overfitting to the specific conditions of the training data.

After data preprocessing, the recorded training and validation losses were 347.43 and 299.95, respectively. This reduction of the loss from the baseline already indicates that the preprocessing has positively affected the model's performance. Such preprocessing steps, which include cleansing the input data, are expected to further improve the WER, with a projection to about 14–16%. This means a gain in precision and higher, better speech input recognition.

Comparing the Preprocessed Model with the Base Model: Perhaps the most important difference between the original and the updated preprocessing procedure is the addition of noise and time-stretching augmentations. Whereas the original preprocessing directly converts text to spectrograms, the updated approach adds variability into the mix of training data that could result in more varied and realistic training scenarios. This difference should manifest itself in improved model performance, especially in real world conditions that are impacted by noise and variations in speed.

The comparison between the waveform and spectrogram of original audio and the augmented audio is provided in Fig. 1.

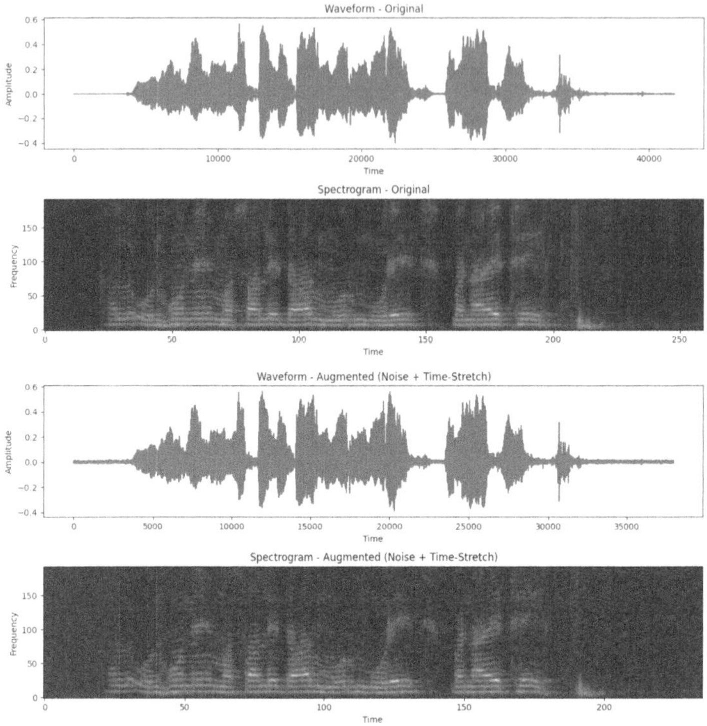

Fig. 1. Comparison between original and augmented data spectrograms, illustrating the impact of preprocessing techniques.

3.4 Fine-Tuned Model

Improvisations: This DeepSpeech2 model was further modified by a number of key changes to enhance the model's performance and fine-tuned to increase the model's learning capability from data, generalize better, and be robust against overfitting. The following improvisations were made:

- **Convolutional Layers with L2 Regularization:** First, convolutional layers in the original DeepSpeech2 model added L2 regularization on the kernel weights of each convolutional layer. This prevents overfitting because large weights are penalized while simpler models that generalize better to unseen data are favored. The convolutional layers have been modified to include an L2 regularization term with weight decay of 0.01. Moreover, the convolutional architecture was slightly adapted.

- **Increased RNN Layers and Bidirectionality:** Instead of the original three unidirectional recurrent layers, five Bidirectional Gated Recurrent Unit (GRU) layers were used. The usage of bidirectionality offers a contextualization from both the past and future to the speech signal, increasing the understanding of dependencies in an input sequence. While some variants of the original model use GRU units that are computationally more efficient and less prone to the vanishing gradient problem, the model makes use of LSTM units. Additionally, a dropout rate of 0.4 was introduced between the recurrent layers to further prevent overfitting and ensure that the model is robust during training.
- **Attention Mechanism Integration:** This proved to be a significant addition that was not previously available in the basic vanilla architecture of DeepSpeech2. The attention mechanism allows the model to focus on areas of the input sequence that are more important for creating each part of the output sequence. This addition helps with handling longer input sequences and allows the model to process variable-length audio effectively. The attention output is added to the recurrent layer outputs, enabling the model to utilize both sequential dependencies and attention-based focus areas during predictions.
- **Enhanced Optimizer Configuration:** The optimizer used for training has been changed to Adam with an increased learning rate of 1e-4 (compared to the default 1e-5 used in many models). This aims to speed up convergence in model training, thus keeping the model stable and adaptive. It is worth mentioning that the increase in the learning rate is coupled with the added complexity due to the attention mechanism and the larger number of recurrent layers.
- **Dense Layer Adjustments:** The final dense layer, which projects the RNN layers' output to the character probabilities, was updated to have more units than before-twice the number of recurrent units-to accommodate the richer feature set learned by the expanded network. Adding a ReLU activation function and a subsequent dropout layer before the output guarantees that only the most relevant features pass through, enriching the model's predictive power.

Table 2 provides a model summary and parametric details of the fine-tuned base model. By comparing the two tables, one can identify the changes made to the architecture of the base model.

Table 2. Model summary of fine-tuned model.

Layer (type)	Output Shape	Param	Connected to
input (InputLayer)	(None, None, 193)	0	-
expand_dim (Reshape)	(None, None, 193, 1)	0	input[0][0]
conv_1 (Conv2D)	(None, None, 97, 32)	14,432	expand_dim[0][0]
conv_1_bn (BatchNormalization)	(None, None, 97, 32)	128	conv_1[0][0]
conv_1_relu (ReLU)	(None, None, 97, 32)	0	conv_1_bn[0][0]
conv_2 (Conv2D)	(None, None, 49, 32)	236,544	conv_1_relu[0][0]
conv_2_bn (BatchNormalization)	(None, None, 49, 32)	128	conv_2[0][0]
conv_2_relu (ReLU)	(None, None, 49, 32)	0	conv_2_bn[0][0]
conv_3 (Conv2D)	(None, None, 49, 64)	247,808	conv_2_relu[0][0]
conv_3_bn (BatchNormalization)	(None, None, 49, 64)	256	conv_3[0][0]
conv_3_relu (ReLU)	(None, None, 49, 64)	0	conv_3_bn[0][0]
reshape (Reshape)	(None, None, 3136)	0	conv_3_relu[0][0]
bidirectional_1 (Bidirectional)	(None, None, 1024)	11,212,800	reshape[0][0]
dropout (Dropout)	(None, None, 1024)	0	bidirectional_1[0][0]
bidirectional_2 (Bidirectional)	(None, None, 1024)	4,724,736	dropout[0][0]
dropout_1 (Dropout)	(None, None, 1024)	0	bidirectional_2[0][0]
bidirectional_3 (Bidirectional)	(None, None, 1024)	4,724,736	dropout_1[0][0]
dropout_2 (Dropout)	(None, None, 1024)	0	bidirectional_3[0][0]
bidirectional_4 (Bidirectional)	(None, None, 1024)	4,724,736	dropout_2[0][0]
dropout_3 (Dropout)	(None, None, 1024)	0	bidirectional_4[0][0]
bidirectional_5 (Bidirectional)	(None, None, 1024)	4,724,736	dropout_3[0][0]
attention (Attention)	(None, None, 1024)	0	bidirectional_5[0][0], bidirectional_5[0][0]
add_attention (Add)	(None, None, 1024)	0	bidirectional_5[0][0], attention[0][0]
dense_1 (Dense)	(None, None, 1024)	1,049,600	add_attention[0][0]
dense_1_relu (ReLU)	(None, None, 1024)	0	dense_1[0][0]
dropout_4 (Dropout)	(None, None, 1024)	0	dense_1_relu[0][0]
dense (Dense)	(None, None, 82)	84,050	dropout_4[0][0]

Results: After fine-tuning the model, there was a further reduction in both training and validation losses, with values of 326.56 and 264.66, respectively. This reduction in loss, compared to both the baseline and preprocessed models, demonstrates that fine-tuning has significantly improved the model's ability to learn the specific characteristics within the dataset. Fine-tuning has allowed the model to better adapt to the nuances of the data, thereby making the learning process more accurate and efficient.

Comparing the Fine-Tuned Model with the Base Model: The fine-tuned model offers several architectural and performance improvements over the baseline. Although both models are based on the DeepSpeech2 architecture, the fine-tuned model includes an additional convolutional layer, an attention mechanism, and a replacement of the GRU layers with LSTM layers. These modifications help the model better capture long-term dependencies and predict more effectively.

The performance has improved substantially in terms of training and validation losses, which have reduced to 326.56 and 264.66, respectively. These improvements indicate that the fine-tuned model outperforms the baseline model. Additionally, the Word Error Rate (WER) is expected to decrease further to approximately 12% to 14% in comparison with the base model, which has a WER of 16% to 17%. A lower WER reflects a higher accuracy in speech recognition.

3.5 Fine-Tuned and Preprocessed Model

In this model, we have combined both the preprocessing modifications and the fine-tuned model to create a more robust and accurate ASR system. The combined application of preprocessing and fine-tuning resulted in the best performance from the model. This approach reduced the training and validation losses to 293.36 and 242.49, respectively. These numbers represent a significant improvement over the baseline and previous models, indicating that the model has learned more effectively from the dataset due to the inclusion of both preprocessing and fine-tuning. The reduced loss suggests that the model has become better at minimizing errors and capturing relevant features in the speech data.

With this comprehensive approach, we can expect the Word Error Rate (WER) to improve by up to around 10%-12%. This reduction indicates increased model accuracy in recognizing and transcribing speech inputs correctly, demonstrating that combining preprocessing and fine-tuning is effective. This combination helped refine the model's ability to handle the complexities within the dataset.

4 Results and Discussion

Model evaluation was conducted using training loss, validation loss, and word error rate (WER). The model was trained in four different stages: the base model, preprocessing, fine-tuning, and the final stage with all the aforementioned processes. The purpose of preprocessing was to enhance the working capacity of the base model. Noise addition and time-stretching were selected because they allow control over the noise level and time scaling factor of the speech data during preprocessing. Both the input data and the augmented data from these methods were used to train the model.

The model, when trained with Gaussian noise augmentation, learned to handle both real-world noisy speech and clean speech. The time-stretched data helped the base model generalize better to variations in speech speed. The augmented data provided a broader range of examples, helping the model learn the relationship between audio data and the spectrogram to a large extent. As a result, improvements were observed in the language model after the addition of these preprocessing techniques.

The base model, inspired by DeepSpeech2, achieved a WER of 16–17%, with training and validation losses of 357.45 and 294.33, respectively. While functional, it was generally plagued by performance issues, as reflected in its less-than-perfect handling of varied speech, presenting challenges in accurate speech recognition.

When preprocessing was introduced, the performance improved noticeably, bringing the training and validation losses down to 347.43 and 299.95, respectively, and lowering the WER slightly to an estimated 14–16%. Preprocessing cleaned and structured the input data in such a way that the model was able to recognize speech and transcribe it much more accurately.

However, the more significant gains were realized after combining preprocessing with fine-tuning. The last model iteration achieved a training loss of 293.36 and a validation loss of 242.49, with a predicted WER of 10–12%.

Notwithstanding these merits, further enhancements are possible. The addition of more data augmentation techniques would make the model even more robust for noisy environments or diverse accents among speakers. More advanced neural architectures, such as transformers, may turn out to yield even better results. Integrating real-time feedback mechanisms would also refine the model's performance for practical applications.

The progress of the project so far is promising, but much more refinement and expansion into practical speech recognition tasks will be necessary to implement its theoretical full potential (Table 3).

Table 3. WER and Loss comparison of different models.

Model	Training Loss	Validation Loss	WER
Base Model	357.45	294.33	16–17%
Pre-processed Model	347.43	299.95	14–16%
Fine tuned Model	326.56	264.66	12–14%
Pre-processed and fine tuned Model	293.36	242.49	10–12%

5 Future Scope

The study presented here can be extended in many ways, some of which include:

- **Innovative Neural Models:** The use of other types of neural network architectures such as transformers and other models that have gained traction with state-of-the-art systems in language and speech processing. These could possibly yield better results or form a much simpler architecture to extend the normalisation and translation system using a self-supervised method instead of the attention-based model as done in this work.

- **Handling Realistic Environments:** This work uses a forward approach from obtained real-time noisy Hindi spoken language. The integration of more noise robustness strategies like real-time audio augmentation, microphone array, and other methods would further improve the recognizer in realistic environments.
- **Datasets Expansion:** The current dataset can be enriched with many more speakers, dialects, and different accents in Indian dialects, in order to create a versatile recognizer which generalizes on diverse speakers from different regions in India.
- **Expanding to Other Indian Languages:** The complete system of normalisation and translation can be extended to other Indian languages such as Gujarati, Marathi, Tamil, and many more.
- **Real-world Deployment:** This work explored the stages of building efficient ASR models for Hindi-based virtual assistants or speech-to-text systems which are used on a large scale basis for various applications in educational, commercial, healthcare domains, helpline services, mute and voiceless assistance. Upon successful completion and performance of the extensions, this will help in building a robust framework which will further assist the real technological needs of Hindi-speaking users and inform thousands of Hindi speakers.

References

1. Al-madani, A.: Project Report On AI Speech Recognition System (2018). https://doi.org/10.13140/RG.2.2.31037.20965
2. Bachate, R., Sharma, A.: Automatic speech recognition systems for regional languages in India. Int. J. Recent Technol. Eng. **8** (2019). https://doi.org/10.35940/ijrte.B1108.0782S319
3. Showrav, T.T.: An Automatic Speech Recognition System for Bengali Language based on Wav2Vec2 and Transfer Learning
4. Fendji, J.L., Tala Metalom, D.C., Yenke, B., Atemkeng, M.: Automatic speech recognition using limited vocabulary: a survey. Appl. Artif. Intell. **36**, 2947 (2022). https://doi.org/10.1080/08839514.2022.2095039
5. Bouadjenek, M.R., Huynh, N.D.: Automatic Speech Recognition using CTC
6. Davis, K.H., Biddulph, R., Balashek, S.: Automatic recognition of spoken digits. J. Acoust. Soc. Am. **24**(6), 637–642 (1952)
7. Lee, K.F.: On large-vocabulary speaker-independent continuous speech recognition. Speech Commun. **7**(4), 375–379 (1988)
8. Xu, X., Yanmi, Q., Kai, Y.: Binary deep neural networks for speech recognition. In: Interspeech 2017, Stockholm, Sweden, pp. 20–24 (2017)
9. Jeff, W., Adam, S., Scott, S.: Augmented generalized deep learning with special vocabulary. U.S. Provisional Patent Application No. 62/703,892 (2018)
10. Steffen, S., Alexei, B., Ronan, C., Michael, A.: wav2vec: unsupervised pre-training for speech recognition. arXiv preprint arXiv:1904.05862 (2019)
11. Alexei, B., Henry, Z., Abdelrahman, M., Michael, A.: wav2vec 2.0: a framework for self-supervised learning of speech representations. arXiv preprint arXiv:2006.11477 (2020)

12. Anirush, G., Harveen, S.C., Singh, C., Priyanshi, S.: CLSRIL-23: Cross lingual speech representations for Indic languages. arXiv preprint arXiv:2107.07402v1 (2021)
13. Bhat, V., Bhattacharyya, P.: Survey: Automatic Speech Recognition For Indian Languages
14. Thakar, P., Khanooja, G.: Speech Recognition with Neural Networks
15. Suhani, A., Dev, A., Bansal, P.: CTC-based end-to-end speech recognition for low resource language Sanskrit. In: 2023 26th Conference of the Oriental COCOSDA International Committee for the Co-ordination and Standardisation of Speech Databases and Assessment Techniques (O-COCOSDA), Delhi, India, pp. 1–5 (2023). https://doi.org/10.1109/O-COCOSDA60357.2023.10482943
16. Balyan, A., Agrawal, S.S., Dev, A.: Speech Synthesis: A Review (2013)
17. Bansal, P., Dev, A., Jain, S.B.: Automatic speaker identification using vector quantization. Medwell J. (2007)
18. Balyan, A., Agrawal, S.S., Dev, A.: Speech synthesis: a review. Int. J. Eng. Res. Technol. (IJERT) (2013)
19. Kumari, R., Dev, A., Kumar, A.: Automatic segmentation of Hindi-speech into syllable-like units. IJACSA Int. J. Adv. Comput. Sci. Appl. (2020)

NITK-TIEKLS: A Text-Independent Emotional Kannada Language Speech Dataset for Speaker Recognition

Shalini Tomar(✉) and Shashidhar G. Koolagudi

Department of Computer Science and Engineering, National Institute of Technology, Surathkal, Karnataka, India
{shalinitomar.217cs504,koolagudi}@nitk.edu.in

Abstract. Speaker recognition systems have traditionally relied on the consistency of speech content to identify individuals. However, text-independent speaker recognition, irrespective of the spoken content, presents a more flexible and robust alternative, especially in real-world scenarios. This research focuses on enhancing text-independent speaker recognition by incorporating a dataset for the Speaker Recognition (SR) task. The dataset is named the National Institute of Technology Karnataka - Text-Independent Emotional Kannada Language Speech (NITK-TIEKLS) dataset. The 200 natives of the Karnataka state of India have recorded emotional speech in the Kannada language for the proposed dataset. The neutral text-independent speech consists of a 4-min speech duration for each speaker. The two emotional speech utterances, from any two of the emotions anger, happiness, sadness, and fear, are text-independent speech utterances that consist of 2 min. The total duration is approximately 30 h. The proposed study includes developing, processing, analyzing, acquiring, and evaluating the proposed dataset. The suggested dataset consists of performance evaluations of the SR system through deep learning techniques with the proposed Wavelet-Mel Spectrogram.

Keywords: Speaker Recognition · Text-independent emotional speech · Speaker Recognition in Emotional Environment · Mel Spectrogram · Zero Crossing Rate · Pitch · Tempo · Wavelet Spectrogram

1 Introduction

Over the past ten years, the study of SR using emotional speech has advanced quickly due to the availability of low-cost intelligent technologies and the widespread interest of researchers in computer science, psychology, psychiatry, neurology, and audiology. The availability of trustworthy and validated datasets for emotional speech is essential to these studies. For speaker recognition, numerous speech stimulus sets are now accessible [22] using neutral speech. However, there

A. Sharma and R. Rani (Eds.): AIST 2024, CCIS 2389, pp. 137–151, 2025.
https://doi.org/10.1007/978-3-031-91331-0_10

is a lack of validated emotional speech sets for SR tasks. The text-dependent dataset is available for neutral text-independent speech recordings or extracting YouTube audio videos. This work developed the extensively validated text-independent speech emotional datasets set to meet these needs. The TIEKLS is developed, and the validity and reliability of the dataset are reported in this paper. To prepare for the Emotive Speech Speaker Recognition (ESSR) tasks, a speech corpus rich in text-independent emotions of fear, anger, sadness, and happiness is developed.

The voice is a form of behavioral biometric that can reveal characteristics and emotions about the speaker. Identification of speakers is the process of identifying people by their voices [7,15]. After years of research, this is now being used in several technologies, including voice assistants, smart homes, and the Internet of Things. "SR" is a method for identifying speakers by their voice characteristics [18]. Speakers in different emotional states could not be distinguished by Speaker Recognition models designed for neutral speech. Due to its numerous uses in a variety of areas, such as security, biometric verification, criminal investigation, healthcare, and customer service, speech recognition is growing more and more in demand. Several SR techniques [10,19], and [26] for text-dependent emotive speech have been studied.

1.1 Available Speech Datasets for Speaker Recognition

Table 1 shows the currently available text-independent dataset details. However, no text-independent dataset mentioning emotional speech is available.

Table 1. Text-independent available speech datasets.

SI NO	Title	Dataset Details
1	VoxCeleb: a large-scale speaker identification dataset. [16]	VoxCeleb 1,251 celebrities 690 M, 561 F, 1,53,516 utterances, English
2	Text-dependent and independent speaker recognition using neural responses from the model of the auditory system. [4]	GRID 1000 utterances, 18 M, 16 F, 3 s
3	Text- Independent speaker verification using 3D convolution neural networks. [27]	WVU-Multimodal dataset, 4 sessions, 1083 speakers
4	Initial analysis of the impact of emotional speech on the performance of speaker recognition on new Serbian emotional database. [14]	SEAC: 55 speakers, 22,000 utterances, 26 M, 29 F, Serbian
5	Analysis and investigation of speaker identification problems using deep learning net works and the YOHO English speech dataset. [1]	YOHO dataset: 138 speakers, 106 M, 32 F, 14 sessions per speaker, English

It is difficult for a single dataset to satisfy the wide range of interests of researchers looking into how emotions are expressed. The speech datasets for the Speaker Recognition task are divided into two categories: independent and

Table 2. Text-dependent available Emotional Speech Dataset

SI NO	Title	Dataset	Dataset Details
1	Prosodic Characteristics of Emotional Speech: Measurements of Fundamental Frequency Movements. [20]	EMO-DB 7 emotions	840 utterances, 10 actors, (5 M and 5 F), 3 sentences, 4 sessions
2	IITKGP-SEHSC: Hindi speech corpus for emotion analysis. [12]	IITKGP-SEHSC 8 emotions	12000 utterances, 10 speakers, (5 M,5 F), 15 sentences, 10 sessions
3	Crema-D: Crowd-sourced emotional multimodal actors dataset. [2]	CREMA-D 6 emotions	7442 utterances, 91 actors, (48 M, 43F), 12 sentences
4	The Ryerson Audio-Visual Database of Emotional Speech and Song (RAVDESS): A dynamic, multimodal set of facial and vocal expressions in North American English. [13]	RAVDESS 7 emotions	7356 Utterances, 24 actors, (12 M, 12 F)
5	NITK-KLESC: Kannada Language Emotional Speech Corpus for Speaker Recognition. [25]	NITK-KLESC 5 emotions	50,000 utterances, 100 speakers, (50 M, 50 F), 10 sentences

dependent on text. A collection of speech recordings with known and consistent spoken text is called a text-dependent speech dataset. Speech recordings with undefined or unrestricted spoken text form a text-independent speech dataset. Text-independent speech datasets are available exclusively in neutral emotions, whereas text-dependent speech datasets are available in different emotions.

Text-Independent speech Dataset Text-Dependent Emotional speech Datasets. Table 2 provides information about the existing text-dependent emotional speech dataset for Speaker Recognition.

1.2 Speech Feature Extraction for Speaker Recognition Using Emotional Speech

The task of recognizing speakers through emotional speech can be difficult since different emotions might cause differences in speech characteristics. Effective feature extraction is crucial for capturing relevant information that distinguishes speakers from emotional variations. The Mel-spectrogram maps the frequency axis to the Mel scale and offers a time-frequency representation of the audio signal using the time-frequency feature domain. Wavelet spectrograms offer an audio signal's time-frequency representation, capturing its high- and low-frequency components with different levels of precision. Mel-Spectrogram alone is not sufficient for SR tasks, particularly for emotional speech. So, in this work, we also proposed a hybrid wavelet-Mel Spectrogram for Speaker Recognition using emotional speech.

The remainder of the paper has been divided up into sections. Section 2 delves into the details of developing TIEKLS. Section 3 presents the prosodic analysis of the suggested emotive speech. The suggested dataset experiments for SR tasks utilizing a wavelet-Mel Spectrogram are discussed in Sect. 4. Section 5 conducts the analysis of the results. Section 6 covers the uses of the suggested dataset. Lastly, Sect. 7 presents the conclusions of the suggested work.

2 Development of Text-Independent Emotional Kannada Language Speech (TIEKLS) Dataset

The dataset started to be collected with a list of the requisite. The speakers are informed about recordings and given the specifics of emotional speech by the requirement. For example, the length of each speech, the different emotions to be used, and the number of speech utterances. Then, get their schedules for recordings and complete them. Then, audio files were resampled to a consistent sample rate of 44.1 KHz. Finally, regions of silence were removed, and the audio files were labeled. Considering the process, we record the speech dataset using the provided information.

2.1 Collection and Labelling

To record the proposed database, 200 native Karnataka State speakers, 100 male and 100 female, from the National Institute of Technology in Karnataka, India, Drama Club served as participants. The speakers are skilled enough to express the appropriate emotions. The speakers range in age from 20 to 60. In the proposed dataset containing a single session, each speaker must provide three speech utterances expressing any two emotions from anger, happiness, sadness, and fear, and neutral speech is compulsory. There are 600 (200×3) speech utterances in WAV format. The emotional speech length is approximately 2 min each, and the neutral speech length is approximately 4 min. However, in specific recordings, speakers want to talk for longer than the recommended amount of time or share memories while giving an intensely emotional speech; in these cases, we capture the entire speech, exceeding the recommended duration. The total duration of the database is about 30 h. A Sony ICD-UX570F sound recorder and a Philips dynamic microphone were used to record the speech samples. There are four proposed emotions, and the speakers can select any two. For speech recordings, the speakers speak about any experience, achievements, incidents, feelings, memories, places, etc. The uninterrupted recording took place in the Speech and Audio Processing Lab of the Department of Computer Science and Engineering at the National Institute of Technology in Karnataka, India, in an anechoic room.

2.2 Data Distribution for Speaker Recognition Tasks

The data is distributed into two sets. The training set consisting a neutral speech of 200 speech utterances. The testing set consists of 4 emotional sets of 400 speech

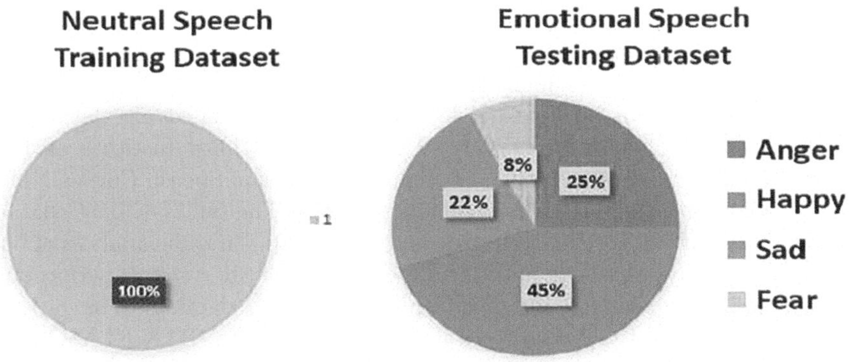

Fig. 1. Training and Testing Emotional Speech Scenario of TIEKLS Dataset

utterances. The emotion selection is chosen according to the speaker's choices. Figure 1 represents the distribution of the proposed dataset. Analyses show that happy emotion makes speakers more at ease when speaking. The study also indicates that most speakers avoid communicating with fear emotion.

3 Prosodic Analysis of TIEKLS Dataset

In text-independent scenarios, the natural variability of speech content introduces additional complexity. Prosodic features must be robust enough to capture speaker-specific traits despite the varying linguistic content and emotional states. Emotional states significantly impact prosodic features like pitch, duration, and intensity. Text-independent systems need to handle these variations to recognize speakers accurately and effectively. Based on specific prosodic characteristics,

Table 3. Mean Prosody values difference with text-dependent and text-independent dataset

NITK-KLESC	Anger	Happy	Neutral	Sad	Fear
Pitch (Hertz)	195	198	162	125	190
Tempo (wpm)	130.71	121.65	119.89	124.34	110.45
Intensity (dB)	81.34	72.56	76.84	64.54	68.66
ZCR (zcps)	18760	17534	10765	11762	12564
TIEKLS	Anger	Happy	Neutral	Sad	Fear
Pitch (Hertz)	220	245	230	130	200
Tempo (wpm)	132.22	140.25	128.80	150.65	98.88
Intensity (dB)	82.17	74.27	77.25	78.45	70.27
ZCR (zcps)	19050	18020	15980	12150	13080

an analysis of the emotional speech takes place to differentiate text-dependent and text-independent emotional speech utterances. The average values of the prosodic parameters for each emotion are displayed in Table 3. The same speakers are considered for both text-independent and text-dependent datasets for prosodic analysis. For both the TIEKLS and the National Institute of Technology Karnataka, India- Kannada Language Emotional Speech Corpus NITK-KLESC datasets, there are 100 common speakers. The NITK-KLESC dataset includes a list of 100 speakers (50 male and 50 female). Prosodic analysis of both emotional speech datasets is necessary to evaluate the SR system's performance utilizing text-independent and text-dependent speech datasets. The prosodic feature analyses for the TIEKLS dataset in comparison to NITK-KLESC are as follows:

Pitch. The ear's sense of a tone's relative highness or lowness during speech is known as pitch. The frequency of vibration of the voice cords per second determines it. The average values of the prosodic parameters are found at the phrase level. The frequency and pitch are higher in emotions such as happiness and anger. Nevertheless, the frequency and pitch are lower in sad, fearful, and neutral emotions for text-dependent and text-independent emotional speech datasets. The text-independent speech pitch is relatively high compared to text-dependent speech. People have a higher pitch when they speak naturally than when they express their emotions using textual speech.

Tempo. The term "tempo" in speech describes the rate or speed at which a person speaks. It is analyzed that the tempo value increased with anger and decreased with fear in both male and female speakers. It is also discovered that the average tempo values of female speakers are greater than those of male speakers for each of the five emotions for text-dependent and text-independent datasets. Moreover, text-independent datasets show greater tempo values for all emotions other than fear than text-dependent datasets.

Intensity. The level of energy or force used during vocalization is referred to as speech intensity. Speech intensity can be affected by various elements, including the emotional content of the message being communicated. It is noted that when female speakers speak, the intensity level rises. For both datasets, the intensity value is higher for neutral and angry emotions. The results show that compared to text-dependent datasets, speakers are more at ease speaking in an emotive or neutral manner while using the text-independent dataset.

Zero Crossing Rate. Zero-crossings are instantaneous points at which the sign of a mathematical function changes (for example, from positive to negative). It is analyzed that the values of ZCR are lowest when the speaker is experiencing sadness and highest when they are experiencing anger, in the case of text-independent emotional speech. However, text-dependent, neutral emotional speech has the lowest ZCR value, and anger emotional speech has the highest ZCR value. Since each emotion has a distinct pitch, the value of ZCR varied as the pitch level increased and decreased.

4 Speaker Recognition System Using TIEKLS Speech Dataset

A typical Speaker Recognition focus includes speech feature extraction and classification of the speaker based on the extracted feature. Figure 2 illustrates an SR model to recognize the speakers for the proposed dataset.

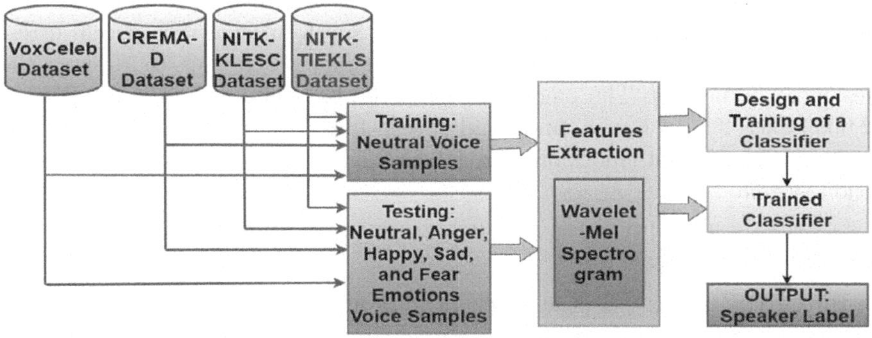

Fig. 2. The illustration of Speaker Recognition Task for Proposed Work

4.1 Dataset

1. VoxCeleb Dataset [16]**:** The VoxCeleb dataset is a large-scale, publicly available text-independent dataset for speaker recognition research. Audio samples in VoxCeleb are extracted from interview videos that are available on platforms like YouTube. The dataset includes speakers from different nationalities, accents, ages, and genders, providing a wide variety of speech samples. The VoxCeleb dataset has 1,251 celebrities (690 M, 561 F) and has a total of 1,53,516 utterances in the English language. For training and testing purposes, the 70:30 ratio is considered for the Speaker Recognition system.

2. CREMA-D Dataset [2]**:** This study makes use of the multimodal audio-visual English emotional CREMA-D dataset, which comprises 7442 clips from 91 speakers (48 men and 43 women) with a range of ages and ethnicities. In order to reflect the six various emotional states of anger, happiness, sorrow, disgust, fear, and neutrality, each speaker asked to have 12 separate utterances recorded. 75% of neutral speech is considered for training purposes, and the rest, 25%, utterances are used for testing purposes in different emotions. The first 9 utterances were used as training, and the last 3 utterances were used for testing each emotion and each speaker for the Speaker Recognition tasks.

3. NITK-KLESC Dataset [25]**:** With emotional speech in mind, the NITK-KLESC dataset was created specifically for the Speaker Recognition task. This collection contains 50 male and 50 female voice datasets that are local to the Indian state of Karnataka. Five emotions are used to collect the data: anger, happiness, sadness, fear, and neutrality. Ten text cues in Kannada are taken into consideration for capturing emotive voices. These sentences have no influence on one's emotions. One session with one hundred speakers is used in this study. The first 7 utterances are used as training, and the last 3 utterances are used as testing for the Speaker Recognition model.

4. NITK-TIEKLS Dataset: For Speaker Recognition, the NITK-TIEKLS dataset is split into 4-s audio WAV files. So, from neutral speech utterances 200 files, we get 18,000 $[(200 \times 6 \times 60)/4]$ speech files to process the files more accurately. The emotional files are also split into 4-s files. We get 12,000$[(200 \times 2 \times 2 \times 60)/4]$ emotional speech files. All 18,000 files are used as training, and relevant emotional files are used as testing for the Speaker Recognition system.

4.2 Feature Extraction

Feature extraction is essential when dealing with emotive speech in Speaker Recognition tasks. While frequency domain features [3] only reveal a speech sample's frequency content, time domain features [17] only describe temporal qualities. The spectrogram is a widely used time-frequency representation showing temporal dynamics and spectrum features. This study focuses on the curated dataset for speaker recognition tasks using the hybrid Wavelet-Mel Spectrogram as the feature extraction phase to identify SR task accuracy in neutral and emotional speech. The Mel spectrogram provides a perceptually relevant representation of the audio signal that is robust to noise and variations in amplitude. However, it lacks the necessary temporal resolution to capture rapid changes in the speech signal, especially for high-frequency components. Emotions can significantly alter the prosodic features of speech, such as pitch, energy, and duration. Mel-spectrograms, which primarily capture spectral information, do not adequately represent these variations, leading to reduced performance in recognizing speakers under different emotional states.

Wavelet spectrograms offer a powerful alternative to traditional Fourier-based methods for analyzing speech signals. By using wavelet transforms, the spectrograms provide a time-frequency representation of the audio signal that captures both high and low-frequency components with varying resolution. The wavelet spectrograms are particularly suitable for analyzing non-stationary signals like emotional speech, which have rapidly changing frequency components. So, Mel-spectrograms provide a standardized and computationally efficient way to capture spectral features. Hybrid feature extraction combines the strengths of both spectrograms to provide a more detailed and robust representation. The Wavelet-Mel Spectrogram captures a broader range of speech characteristics, which can be beneficial for tasks like emotion and speaker recognition. Wavelet-based spectrograms capture localized transient features, while Mel-spectrograms capture perceptually relevant frequency content. Combining Mel-spectrogram with wavelet spectrograms can leverage the strengths of both methods.

Proposed Wavelet-Mel Spectrogram Feature Extraction: A hybrid wavelet-Mel spectrogram involves combining both wavelet transforms and Mel-spectrograms to capture the time-frequency characteristics of the speech signal for SR tasks. The proposed Wavelet-Mel Spectrogram Feature Extraction includes three basic steps.

1. To compute the Mel-Spectrogram first, we have to calculate the Short-Time Fourier Transform (STFT) using Eq. 1.

$$X(t,f) = \sum_{n=0}^{N-1} x[n] \cdot w[n-t] \cdot e^{-j2\Pi fn} \tag{1}$$

Here, x[n] is the speech signal, w[n] is a window function, t is the time index, and f is the frequency index.
To compute the Mel Filter Bank, we have to convert the power spectrum to the Mel scale using a filter bank according to the Eq. 2

$$M(k) = \sum_{f=f_{min}}^{f_{max}} |X(t,f)|^2 \cdot H_k(f) \tag{2}$$

Here, H_K(f) is the k-th Mel filter.
Now, take a logarithm of the Mel Power Spectrum as MelSpec(t,k)=log(M(k))

2. To compute the Wavelet transform, firstly compute the Continuous Wavelet Transform (CWT) by using Eq. 3

$$W(t,a) = \frac{1}{\sqrt{a}} \int_{-\infty}^{\infty} x(\tau)\psi(\frac{\tau - t}{a})dr \tag{3}$$

Here, τ is the mother wavelet, a is the scale parameter, and t is the translation parameter.
Now, compute the magnitude of Wavelet Coefficients using WaveletSpec(t,a)=$|W(t,a)|$

3. Normalize and combine features for a hybrid representation on a common scale using Eq. 4 and 5 of Mel Spectrogram and Wavelet Spectrogram.

$$NormalizedMelSpec(t,k) = \frac{MelSpec(t,k) - \mu_{mel}}{\sigma_{Mel}} \tag{4}$$

$$NormalizedWaveletSpec(t,a) = \frac{WaveletSpec(t,a) - \mu_{Wavelet}}{\sigma_{Wavelet}} \tag{5}$$

Here, μ_{Mel}, σ_{Mel} are the mean and standard deviation of the Mel-spectrogram, and $\mu_{Wavelet}$, and $\sigma_{Wavelet}$ are the mean and standard deviation of the Wavelet-spectrogram. Now, concatenate the normalized Mel-spectrogram and wavelet spectrogram along the feature dimension as shown in Eq. 6.

$$HybridSpec(t,\cdot) = [NormalizedMelSpec(t,\cdot)||NormalizedWaveletSpec(t,\cdot)] \tag{6}$$

4.3 Classification Techniques

We make different utterances set for testing and training data. In order to evaluate the suggested dataset and hybrid Wavelet-Mel Spectrogram feature extraction, we use the following deep-learning models to assess the performance.

1. Convolutional Neural Network (CNN): The proposed method in this work comprises two dense layers, a batch normalization, two convolutional layers (Conv2D) [6], and the output layer as the final layer to produce a sequential convolutional neural network model. For this layer, ReLU has been selected as the activation function. With 128 filters, the second layer input form has dimensions of $20 \times 5 \times 64$. It additionally incorporates a 30% dropout rate to avoid overfitting. Each of the two Conv2D levels is followed by a MaxPooling2D layer. Batch normalization lowers learning rates, changes the parameters of the layers before it during training, and results in parameter initialization that oversaturates the model with nonlinearities. One output layer, two dense layers, and one layer are used to process the model.

2. AlexNet: With its eight layers, AlexNet was one of the first deep convolutional neural network architectures [8]. AlexNet's deep architecture is comprised of eight layers. The input size is $227 \times 227 \times 3$. The ReLU activation function is used for non-linearity with Local Response Normalization (LRN). Filter size 11×11 and stride 4 with output size $55 \times 55 \times 96$, Max pooling with 3×3 filter and stride 2 for 1st convolutional layer. Five convolution layers are used, and 3 Fully connected layers are used.

3. VGG 19: The VGG-19 [24] deep convolutional neural network is renowned for its efficiency and simplicity With 19 layers. It utilizes small 3×3 convolution filters consistently across the network, which, despite the depth, maintains computational feasibility and allows the model to learn complex features. VGG-19 contains 5 convolutional blocks. The input size is $224 \times 224 \times 3$ with max-pooling 2×2 filter and stride 2. In each convolutional block, the number of filters increases. The 5th convolutional block contains 512 filters of size 3×3, stride 1, padding 1, and ReLU activation. Fully connected layers contain 4096 neurons, ReLU activation, Dropout, and Softmax activation.

4. ResNet 18: Residual blocks are the essential ResNet building blocks [9]. Basic residual blocks in ResNet 18 comprise two convolutional layers with ReLU activations. First, depending on the size of the output feature map, each layer has the same number of filters. Secondly, in order to preserve the temporal complexity of each layer, twice as many filters are included if the feature map's size is halved. Similar to the residual block, the 50-layer ResNet's building block reduces the number of parameters and matrix multiplications by using 1×1 convolutions. Instead of using simply two layers, it uses a stack of three. Three further layers comprise 1×1, 64 kernels in the first, 3×3, 64 kernels in the second, and 1×1, 256 kernels in the third. There were six iterations total, consisting of 18 more layers with two cores (3×3, 256 and 1×1, 1024) and one 256 core.

5. Siamese Neural Networks (SNN): An SNN comprises two identical subnetworks, or twins, with the same parameters and architecture. Simultaneously, the two networks are trained using pairs of input data points [11]. SNN has an input layer of size $224 \times 224 \times 3$. Spectrograms are trained and tested with two inputs. There are two convolutional layers and one max pooling layer. The spatial dimensions and aggregate characteristics are decreased via max pooling or average pooling layers. The output is flattened and processed through one or more fully connected (dense) layers following the convolutional and pooling layers. In the end, the completely connected layer produces the input's feature representation or embedding. The layer's output size determines the dimensionality of the feature space. For the SNN model, initially set up the optimizer, loss function, and network. Move the pair's initial Wavelet-Mel Spectrogram across the network.

5 Result Analysis

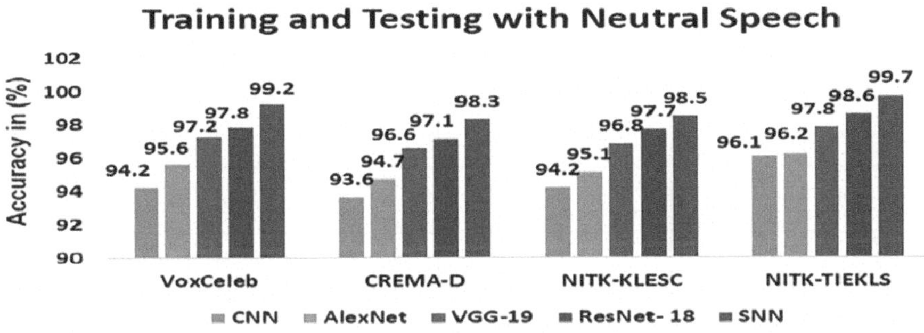

Fig. 3. The Accuracy of different dataset in Neutral Emotion with Wavelet-Mel Spectrogram using various Deep Learning Methods

The work employed dataset and feature extraction work for SR tasks. First, we verify the deep learning model with Wavelet-Mel Spectrogram using only four datasets of neutral speech. Comparing the outcomes of five different deep learning models, the SNN model performed well. The proposed dataset acquires a Speaker recognition accuracy of 99.7%. Another dataset also acquires an accuracy of more than 98%, as shown in Fig. 3. Then, we compare the Speech features as shown in Fig. 4 for emotional speech. The VoxCeleb dataset contains only neutral speech. We use this dataset because it is a text-independent dataset for SR tasks. The hybrid Wavelet-Mel Spectrogram using the SNN model provides better results.

The use of the SNN architecture enhances the performance of the SR model in emotional speech also, as shown in Fig. 5. Additionally, it is noted that in the case of emotional speech, all three datasets in the text-dependent and text-independent scenarios achieve the highest SR accuracy when using a happy

Train with Neutral Emotional Speech	Classification	Feature Extraction	Mel-Spectrogram	Wavelet-Spectrogram	Hybid Wavelet-Mel Spectrogram
Testing Emotional Speech (Average Accuracy of Speaker Recognition for Neutral, Happy, Anger, Sad, and Fear Emotional Speech) *VoxCeleb has only Neutral speeches but text-independent	CNN	*VoxCeleb	87.5	90.2	94.2
		CREMA-D	76.8	78.5	86.6
		NITK-KLESC	78	79.7	87.2
		NITK-TIEKLS	80.6	81.8	89.3
	AlexNet	*VoxCeleb	88.2	91.4	95.6
		CREMA-D	75.8	76.7	88.1
		NITK-KLESC	76.4	75.1	88.7
		NITK-TIEKLS	79.2	78.8	90.5
	VGG-19	*VoxCeleb	88.6	92	97.2
		CREMA-D	77.2	78.4	88.6
		NITK-KLESC	79.5	80.1	89.3
		NITK-TIEKLS	81.6	82.8	91.2
	ResNet-18	*VoxCeleb	89.2	93.4	97.8
		CREMA-D	78.8	80.7	90.1
		NITK-KLESC	80.4	81.6	90.8
		NITK-TIEKLS	81.6	82.8	92.2
	SNN	*VoxCeleb	90.6	94.1	99.2
		CREMA-D	80.8	81.7	91.7
		NITK-KLESC	81.4	82.1	92.3
		NITK-TIEKLS	**83.6**	**85.8**	**94.5**

Fig. 4. The Average Accuracy of Speaker Recognition with Wavelet-Mel Spectrogram using various Deep Learning Methods

Train with Neutral Speech	Average Emotional Speech Accuracy (Testing Emotional Speech)						
Classification	Datasets	Neutral	Happy	Anger	Sad	Fear	Average
CNN	CREMA-D	93.6	92.3	78.5	82.7	86.3	86.68
	NITK-KLESC	94.2	93.3	78.7	82.8	87	87.2
	NITK-TIEKLS	96.1	94.6	82.7	83.6	89.6	**89.32**
AlexNet	CREMA-D	94.7	93.9	80.8	82.7	88.5	88.12
	NITK-KLESC	95.1	93.8	81	85	88.7	88.72
	NITK-TIEKLS	96.2	95.8	83.6	85.6	91.6	**90.56**
VGG-19	CREMA-D	96.6	94	81.6	82.2	88.7	88.62
	NITK-KLESC	96.8	93.8	81	85	88.7	89.06
	NITK-TIEKLS	97.8	96.2	84	86.1	92	**91.22**
ResNet-18	CREMA-D	97.1	95.7	83.5	85.6	88.8	90.14
	NITK-KLESC	97.7	96.5	84.5	85.8	89.6	90.82
	NITK-TIEKLS	98.6	97.6	84.4	87.3	93.4	**92.26**
SNN	CREMA-D	98.3	96.6	84.8	86.5	92.4	91.72
	NITK-KLESC	98.5	98.3	86.4	87.2	91.4	92.36
	NITK-TIEKLS	99.7	99.2	88.5	91.8	93.3	**94.5**

Fig. 5. The Accuracy of Speaker Recognition using different dataset in different Emotion using various Deep Learning Methods

emotional speech at 96.6%, 98.3%, and 99.2%. The least accurate SR task is when using emotionally angry speech in text-dependent and text-independent cases at 84.8%, 86.4%, and 88.5%. The NITK-TIEKLS dataset obtained 94.5% accuracy for an average of all emotional speech for Speaker Recognition.

6 Applications of the Proposed Dataset

In a neutral speech, Speaker Recognition algorithms almost always work flawlessly. However, when it comes to emotional communication, this is inaccurate. Because artificial intelligence learns from its immediate environment, it can accurately replicate human behavior. The works [21] and [28] explain robust SR and scaling Automatic Speech Recognition beyond 100 languages. Effective human-computer interaction requires research in the field of emotion recognition. The dataset's quality also affects how well the emotion recognition algorithm works.

Several feature extraction methods were studied for the goal of emotion recognition [23]. The effectiveness of automated emotional analysis may be used to enhance research experience for age and gender recognition [5]. The proposed dataset will be available for research purposes on the requirement.

7 Conclusion

The TIEKLS: A Text-Independent Emotional Kannada Language Speech dataset is presented in this work. This study offered a novel 30-h dataset that included text-independent emotional speech utterances, each lasting approximately two minutes, and a neutral speech of about four minutes from 200 speakers. In developing TIEKLS, the following emotions are considered: fear, anger, happiness, neutrality, and sadness. An analysis indicates that the text-independent speech dataset has an elevated SR accuracy. The speakers are more at ease expressing their feelings text independently, which impacts the SR system's accuracy. This work also proposed a hybrid Wavelet-Mel Spectrogram feature extraction for particularly emotional speech Speaker Recognition. Compiling information from multiple models that employ speech characteristics at varying degrees can enhance the efficiency of emotional speaker identification assignments. For example, deep learning methods and neural networks are non-linear models that can improve emotion recognition even more. A thorough examination of emotional analysis for speaker recognition is made possible by the proposed database's plentiful amounts of speakers, speech, and emotions.

Acknowledgements. The authors thank the Cognitive Science Research Initiative (CSRI), Department of Science & Technology, Government of India, Grant Sanction Order No.: DST/CSRI/2018/400(G)", for its financial support of their work. We also thank Pragya Gupta and the NITK speech team for their contribution to collecting the dataset.

References

1. Almarshady, N.M., Alashban, A.A., Alotaibi, Y.A.: Analysis and investigation of speaker identification problems using deep learning networks and the YOHO English speech dataset. Appl. Sci. 1–8 (2023)
2. Cao, H., Cooper, D.G., Keutmann, M.K., Gur, R.C., Nenkova, A., Verma, R.: CREMA-D: crowd-sourced emotional multimodal actors dataset. IEEE Trans. Affect. Comput. 377–390. IEEE (2014)
3. Chougule, S.V., Chavan, M.S.: Robust spectral features for automatic speaker recognition in mismatch condition. Procedia Comput. Sci. 272–279 (2015). Procedia Computer Science
4. Chowdhury, S., Mamun, N., Khan, A.A.S., Ahmed, F.: Text dependent and independent speaker recognition using neural responses from the model of the auditory system. In: 2017 International Conference on Electrical, Computer and Communication Engineering (ECCE), pp. 871–874, 2017

5. Couper, M.P., Singer, E., Tourangeau, R.: Does voice matter? An interactive voice response (IVR) experiment. J. Off. Stat. 551–570 (2004)
6. El-Moneim, S.A., et al.: Text-dependent and text-independent speaker recognition of reverberant speech based on cnn. Int. J. Speech Technol. **24**, 993–1006 (2021)
7. Ghiurcau, M.V., Rusu, C., Astola, J.: Speaker recognition in an emotional environment. In: Proceedings of the Signal Processing and Applied Mathematics for Electronics and Communications, pp. 81–84 (2011)
8. Guizzo, E., Weyde, T., Leveson, J.B.: Multi-time-scale convolution for emotion recognition from speech audio signals. In: ICASSP - IEEE International Conference on Acoustics, Speech and Signal Processing (ICASSP), pp. 6489–6493. IEEE, 2020
9. He, K., Zhang, X., Ren, S., Sun, J.: Deep residual learning for image recognition. In: IEEE Conference on Computer Vision and Pattern Recognition (CVPR), pp. 770–778. IEEE, 2016
10. Al Hindawi, N.A., Shahin, I., Nassif, A.B.: The exploitation of multiple feature extraction techniques for speaker identification in emotional states under disguised voices. In: 14th International Conference on Developments in eSystems Engineering (DeSE), pp. 269–273, 2021
11. Jie, L.J., Mun'im Ahmad Zabidi, M., Sadiah, S., Ab Rahman, A.A.H.: Siamese networks for speaker identification on resource-constrained platforms. J. Phys. Conf. Ser. 1–8. IOP Publishing (2023)
12. Koolagudi, S.G., Reddy, R., Yadav, J., Rao, K.S.: IITKGP-SEHSC: Hindi speech corpus for emotion analysis. In: International Conference on Devices and Communications (ICDeCom), pp. 1–5. IEEE, 2011
13. Livingstone, S.R., Russo, F.A.: The Ryerson audio-visual database of emotional speech and song (RAVDESS): a dynamic, multimodal set of facial and vocal expressions in North American English. In: Public Library of Science, pp. 1–15. PLS, 2018
14. Mandarić, I., Vujović, M., Suzić, S., Nosek, T., Simić, N., Delić, V.: Initial analysis of the impact of emotional speech on the performance of speaker recognition on New Serbian emotional database. In: 29th Telecommunications Forum (TELFOR), pp. 1–4, 2021
15. Meftah, A.H., Mathkour, H., Kerrache, S., Alotaibi, Y.A.: Speaker identification in different emotional states in Arabic and English. IEEE Access 60070–60083. IEEE (2020)
16. Nagrani, A., Chung, J.S., Zisserman, A.: Voxceleb: a large-scale speaker identification dataset. In Interspeech, pp. 1–5. ISCA, 2017
17. Nakagawa, S., Asakawa, K., Wang, L.: Speaker recognition by combining MFCC and phase information. In: Eighth Annual Conference of the International Speech Communication Association, pp. 1–8. Citeseer, 2007
18. Nassif, A.B., Shahin, I., Elnagar, A., Velayudhan, D., Alhudhaif, A., Polat, K.: Emotional speaker identification using a novel capsule nets model. Expert Syst. Appl. 1164–1169. Elsevier (2022)
19. Nassif, A.B., Shahin, I., Nemmour, N., Hindawi, N., Elnagar, A.: Emotional speaker verification using novel modified capsule neural network. Mathematics 1–21. MDPI (2023)
20. Paeschke, A., Sendlmeier, W.F.: Prosodic characteristics of emotional speech: measurements of fundamental frequency movements. Speech Commun. 1–6 (2000)
21. Radford, A., Kim, J.W., Xu, T., Brockman, G., McLeavey, C., Sutskever, I.: Robust speech recognition via large-scale weak supervision. In: Proceedings of the 40th International Conference on Machine Learning, pp. 28492–28518. PMLR, 2023

22. Shahin, I.: Speaker recognition systems in the emotional environment. In: 3rd International Conference on Information and Communication Technologies: From Theory to Applications, pp. 1–5. IEEE, 2008
23. Shahin, I., Alomari, O.A., Nassif, A.B., Afyouni, I., Hashem, I.A., Elnagar, A.: An efficient feature selection method for Arabic and English speech emotion recognition using grey wolf optimizer. Appl. Acoust. **205**, 109–119 (2023)
24. Simonyan, K., Zisserman, A.: Very deep convolutional networks for large-scale image recognition. In: CoRR, pp. 1–8. Bone and Joint Surgeons, 2014
25. Tomar, S., Gupta, P., Koolagudi, S.G.: NITK-KLESC: kannada language emotional speech corpus for speaker recognition. In: 26th International Conference on Oriental - COCOSDA, pp. 1–6. IEEE, 2023
26. Tomar, S., Koolagudi, S.G.: CNN-MFCC model for speaker recognition using emotive speech. In: IEEE 8th International Conference for Convergence in Technology (I2CT), pp. 1–7, 2023
27. Torfi, A., Dawson, J., Nasrabadi, N.M.: Text-independent speaker verification using 3D convolutional neural networks. In: 2018 IEEE International Conference on Multimedia and Expo (ICME), pp. 1–6, 2017
28. Zhang, Y., Han, W., Qin, J.: Google USM: scaling automatic speech recognition beyond 100 languages, pp. 1–6, 2023. arXiv

Audioverse: Personalized Story-Telling Using Voice Cloning

Kasey Ann Britto[1(✉)], J. Harini[1], M. Shivanii[1], Pranavi Karthik[2], B. N. Kalpana[2], and M. Karthi[2]

[1] St. Joseph's College of Engineering, Chennai, Tamil Nadu, India
kaseybritto4@gmail.com

[2] St. Joseph's Institute of Technology, Chennai, Tamil Nadu, India

Abstract. The surge in global podcast and story listeners, now totaling 504.9 million and comprising 23.5% of internet users, highlights the growing demand for advanced narrative tools. This study explores the transformative potential of voice in storytelling by developing a deep learning model designed to generate diverse narratives based on user prompts. Utilizing advanced voice cloning techniques, the model aims to embed nuanced emotions within these narratives, merging human emotion with technological capabilities to create a sustainable tool for enhancing individual well-being. The model was constructed using PyTorch, Tensor-Flow, and Convolutional Neural Networks (CNN), with voice cloning powered by BARK, an open-source transformer-based model. Audioverse promises to significantly enrich human connections and revolutionize the storytelling landscape.

Keywords: Audioverse · Deep Learning · Story Generator · Pytorch · CNN · Tensorflow · Genre · Voice Cloning · Google/flan-t5-base

1 Introduction

Crafting narratives stands as a multifaceted and imaginative pursuit, shaped by the distinct approaches of individual writers in planning and sequencing. Each writer's perspective contributes to the rich tapestry of stories across diverse genres, [1] each with its dedicated fan base and supportive community. However, ensuring coherence in storytelling remains a significant challenge, particularly with the use of state-of-the-art Large Language Models (LLMs) like GPT-3 and Gemini, which, while capable of generating stories from prompts, often struggle with maintaining coherence.

To address this challenge, Audioverse-a groundbreaking automatic story generator paired with a voice cloning tool [2] is designed to facilitate coherence and familiarity into generated narratives. Powered by a self-trained deep learning model leveraging PyTorch, CNN and TensorFlow [3], Audioverse enhances story coherence by analyzing word sequences. The dataset, categorized by genre such

A. Sharma and R. Rani (Eds.): AIST 2024, CCIS 2389, pp. 152–164, 2025.
https://doi.org/10.1007/978-3-031-91331-0_11

as horror, moral tales, and human-interest stories, provided the foundation for training the model [4], ensuring diverse and engaging story generation.

Voice cloning is a pivotal feature of Audioverse, allowing the replication of familiar voices using advanced AI tools. The open-source Bark model [5] is integrated, which tokenizes input sentences into lists, enabling seamless synthesis of cloned voices harmoniously paired with user-selected story prompts. The "Kids Podcast Listener Report" [6] by Edison Research shows around 25% of parents with children who listen monthly, report their child listening nearly every day. Audioverse aims to foster camaraderie among families, nurturing positive relationships through shared storytelling experiences.

Accessible through a user-friendly webpage, Audioverse seamlessly integrates story generation and voice cloning models via Flask, ensuring effortless user interaction. By narrating stories in the voices of loved ones, Audioverse fosters a sense of closeness and emotional connection, enriching the storytelling experience anytime, anywhere, and at one's own pace. Emotions serve as conduits of energy, underscoring the shared humanity. Through Audioverse, stories imbued with the voices of cherished individuals reignite the vibrancy of life, fostering deeper emotional bonds and instilling hope in the transformative potential of technology. By positively impacting lives daily, Audioverse exemplifies the myriad ways in which technology can serve as a benevolent force for good, shaping a brighter future for storytelling and emotional connection.

2 Literature Survey

The sub-part of the project involves the generation of stories according to the genre, the user prefers to be the best to be delivered to their children. Story generation is the area where Natural Language Processing (NLP) and Artificial Intelligence (AI) aim to create engaging narratives [7]. Mere sequences of sounds are insufficient for forming coherent words and sentences. Speech carries additional valuable information, such as rhythm, intonation, and emphasis, which indicate grammatical structure or highlights the speaker's emotions and intentions. These nuances can vary significantly from one individual to another. Recent advancements in voice conversion techniques have prioritized the use of non-parallel datasets, which don't require speakers to provide identical utterances [8]. This approach reflects the diversity of human speech, where individuals naturally express themselves with unique intonations, rhythms, and styles. By accommodating these variations, modern voice conversion methods strive to create more authentic and personalized results, mirroring the rich tapestry of human communication.

The task of voice segmentation, especially amidst the myriad variations in speech styles [9], add another layer of complexity into developing such applications. Each person's unique way of speaking, with its distinct cadence and emphasis, further humanizes the challenge of accurately capturing and reproducing speech patterns in voice conversion technology. CNN's have shown great insights over generating through large datasets of existing narratives as they can effectively adapt to sequential data processing tasks as in NLP and give promising results. The model creates stories, sentence by sentence [10], according to the genre selected by the parents so that the proposed framework can collect the story datasets. They excel in various applications such as story generation, text summarization [11], dialogue generation, and genre classification. Trained on a corpus of stories, CNNs learn a conditional probability distribution for each word, given its preceding words. This distribution is computed using a series of nonlinear functions [12] within hidden layers, with the option to stack multiple layers for enhanced representational capacity.

This implementation utilizes hidden layers of Convolutional Layers with ReLU (Rectified Linear Unit) [13] activation functions. These layers maintain representations of the story up to a particular word in the sequence. The input to the first hidden layer consists of word sequences, where each word is encoded as a real-valued vector (referred to as word embeddings). The output of the topmost hidden layer is then fed into a softmax prediction layer, yielding the probability distribution of all potential next words in the sequence. This approach allows for effective language modeling and generation using CNNs [14], capitalizing on their ability to capture complex patterns and dependencies within sequential data. Deep learning algorithms such as convolutional neural networks are used along with audio spectrograms for synthetic speed detection and decoding [15].

Three ways of dealing with the story generation include fine-tuning pre-trained language models, perceptions of the generated stories, and incorporating tags or benchmarks into language model encoding [16]. The implementation with Google/Flan-T5-base model was explored as a comparative model for story generation tasks. The Flan-T5-base, part of the T5 (Text-To-Text Transfer Transformer) family, is known for its flexibility in handling various NLP tasks by converting them into a text-to-text format. [17] This model leverages transfer learning and fine-tuning on diverse datasets to perform exceptionally well across different language tasks.

When compared to CNNs for the purpose of story generation, it was found that while Flan-T5-base also delivered robust results, the CNN approach yielded superior performance in capturing the sequential and contextual nuances necessary for personalized storytelling with maximum number of token generation which is greater than 200 tokens [18]. The CNN model is implemented to obtain the abstract features from the input audio files. In the exploration of prior systems, common hurdles such as limited vocabulary recognition and struggles with background noise interference were encountered [19]. While traditional methods like Gaussian mixture models and conventional speech recognition libraries were commonly employed, it felt compelled to seek a more innovative solution to elevate the system's performance. This decision led to the integration of the Bark model into the framework. Developed exclusively by Suno for voice-related projects, Bark offered a range of unique functionalities designed to address the shortcomings of previous systems. By tapping into the advanced capabilities of the Bark model, it was able to overcome the limitations of traditional approaches and significantly enhance the system's ability to recognize less common input speech signals.

This strategic shift to incorporate the Bark model represents a pivotal advancement in this approach to speech recognition technology. Not only did it enable us to navigate technical challenges more effectively, but it also underscored the commitment to leveraging cutting-edge tools to deliver more accurate and reliable results in various speech scenarios. The decision to incorporate Bark involves a detailed process of extracting tokens from audio codebooks using Meta's enCodec [20], a crucial step in capturing the intricate details of audio data. Additionally, transcript data is utilized to derive semantic tokens, enriching the understanding of the underlying context and essence of the audio content. In response to the absence of the wav2vec model [21], an innovative strategy is devised: training original voice files with a linear projection head. This approach allows us to effectively map audio tokens onto a unified embedding space, overcoming the challenges posed by the wav2vec model's unavailability. By seamlessly integrating story generation with Bark's advanced speech synthesis capabilities, the system aims to achieve unparalleled accuracy in speech-to-speech output. This collaborative effort emphasizes the dedication to advancing storytelling technology, ultimately creating a more engaging and immersive experience for users.

This innovative framework systematically transforms input sentences into commands by integrating various mapping patterns. Initially, input sentences, i.e., the stories generated, are analyzed against predefined regular expressions. If there is a match then the corresponding method is executed and subsequently, a type-based matching process refines potential methods based on similarity to the story sentences [22]. The framework prioritizes the highest accurate method for executions and represents a significant advancement in voice control technology, showcasing innovation in voice-to-voice conversion.

3 Proposed Model

Traditional bedtime stories offer a valuable opportunity for parents or caregivers to bond with their children in a meaningful way. Reading together not only fosters closeness but also cultivates a love of reading. In contrast, the use of YouTube or social media for bedtime entertainment may diminish these bonding opportunities.

AudioVerse is an innovative storytelling platform that revolutionizes traditional narratives through the integration of advanced technology and personalization. Users can choose from a diverse array of story genres and infuse them with the voices of their loved ones. Leveraging machine learning and voice cloning technology, AudioVerse crafts customized narratives tailored to individual preferences. The platform's intuitive interface and seamless integration of audio files bring stories to life in a unique and emotionally resonant manner.

The system above in Fig 1 follows a pipeline architecture composed of several stages, each performing a vital role in the overall functioning of the system.

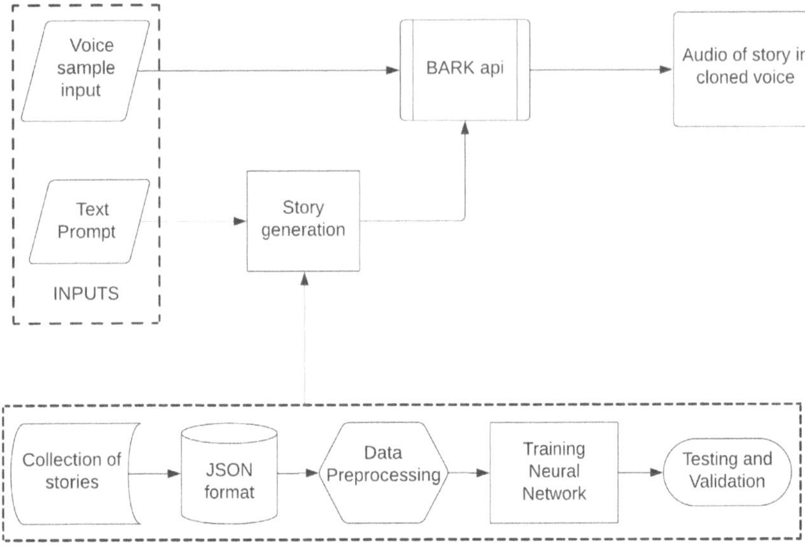

Fig. 1. Block Diagram

4 System Architecture

The system architecture represented in Fig. 2 introduces an approach of storytelling, where users can generate their personalized stories by providing a set of keywords. What sets the uniqueness of this software is that not only does it craft stories based on user-provided input but also delivers those stories in the user's voice. This integration of keyword-based story generation and personalized voice synthesis allows users to imagine and dive into the novel and experience the innovative way of approach of storytelling, allowing them to become the authors and narrators of their own stories.

4.1 User Interface and Inputs

The complete architecture begins with the user interface, offering multiple channels for interaction on the website. Users can access the system via a user-friendly website interface which is accessible via both desktop and mobile devices. The website provides a responsive platform for users to interact with the system, offering an easy way to give input as well as get the best output. Users can provide their voice as input which will then be cloned for giving the story generated with the help of the keywords as output. Additionally, users will be able to track and download the audio file generated through the website for further use. This multi-model approach helps the users to interact with the incorporation of two different models together where the UI utilizes HTML, CSS, and JavaScript for front-end development, ensuring cross-browser compatibility and impressive user experiences. The user inputs are processed using JavaScript libraries enabling

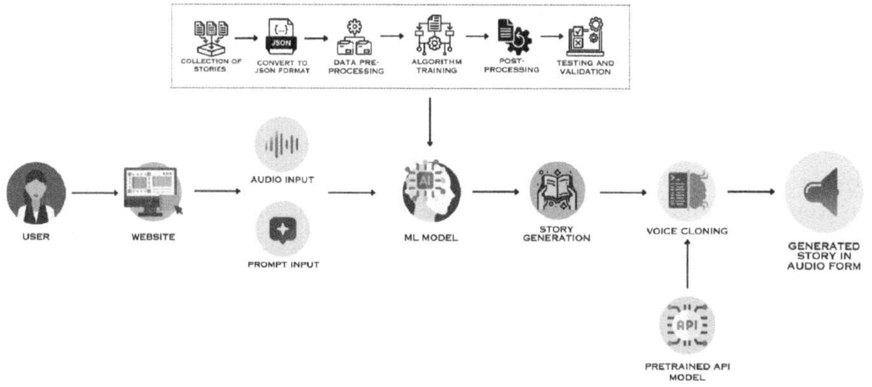

Fig. 2. System Architecture

real-time validation and dynamic updates with responses. The backend interactions are done using frameworks like Flask ensuring data transmission and efficient server-client communication.

4.2 Machine Learning Models Pipeline

The system's machine learning model pipeline is trained to handle the end-to-end story generation process which begins with data acquisition, preprocessing using libraries like Natural Language Toolkit (NLTK) and scikit-learn, and evaluation of the features. Model training is done via deep learning architectures such as CNN for accelerated performance towards the goal. Hyperparameter tuning and further generalization of the data, i.e., stories collected and generated, are kept on the run. Attention mechanisms are employed to extract meaningful representations of stories from the already-trained stories.

The story generation task was trained using both CNN and Google/Flan-T5-base models with the same dataset. The Flan-T5-base, part of the T5 (Text-To-Text Transfer Transformer) family, excels in various NLP tasks by converting them into a text-to-text format. Leveraging transfer learning and fine-tuning on diverse datasets, Flan-T5-base performs exceptionally well across different language tasks. When applied to story generation, the Flan-T5-base model uses its robust architecture to understand and generate text sequences. This model facilitates advanced language understanding and generation by effectively utilizing transfer learning techniques, which helps in achieving high-quality storytelling outputs. Despite its capabilities, it was found that CNNs offered superior performance in generating the maximum number of tokens and did so with less time complexity than the Flan-T5-base model.

4.3 Story Generation Engine

Story generation is implemented in this proposed model using advanced natural processing techniques in a systematic approach to effectively generate stories based on text prompts. The framework integrates advanced neural networks trained with a huge dataset to generate creative stories satisfying the audience. A dataset was curated in JSON format, consisting of a pair of text prompts along with their corresponding stories. This structured format allows the model to train easily by learning the mapping between the stories and text prompts. Additionally, the model's performance and generation quality are enhanced by fine-tuning the trained language model. To generate a story, the input text prompt is fed into the trained model, which then predicts the subsequent words or tokens to construct the narrative. This model generates diverse and contextually relevant stories that align with the input prompt. Let us dive into how the story generation works.

Neural Network Architecture. A simple Feed-Forward Neural Network with three linear layers is utilized. Each linear layer performs a matrix multiplication between the input vector and the weight matrix, followed by the addition of a bias vector. The Rectified Linear Unit(ReLU) activation function is applied after each hidden layer to introduce non-linearity and prevent vanishing gradients during training.

Text Preprocessing. The input prompt is segmented into individual tokens (words or punctuation characters) using NLTK's tokenizer word_tokenize(). It is followed by stemming where the root form of the tokenized words is retrieved and vocabulary size is reduced, potentially improving model efficiency using NLTK's stemmer function stem(). Then a function called bag_of_words() is defined. This method constructs a fixed-length numeric vector to represent the processed sentence where each element signifies the presence (value of 1) or absence (value of 0) of a word in the vocabulary.

Prediction and Response Selection. The previously trained model is loaded bypassing the training process. The input is preprocessed. The model predicts the class (intent) with the highest probability score using the softmax function. Softmax normalizes the output of the final layer, converting it into probabilities that sum up to 1. A confidence threshold (0.75) is applied to filter out predictions with low certainty from which the most similar story is generated.

4.4 Voice Cloning

This software incorporates a voice cloning functionality that personalizes the storytelling experience. This section demonstrates the approach used for voice cloning, using an model called BARK. Most traditional TTS systems convert text into audio using a predefined voice. This voice remains constant regardless of the story's content or desired narration style. This work takes a step further by enabling voice cloning. Users can provide an audio sample containing a desired voice (e.g., a specific narrator, or character voice) as input. The BARK model then leverages this sample to adapt its speech generation process, mimicking the characteristics of the provided voice. This allows the generated story to be narrated in a voice that aligns with the user's preference or the story's context. While BARK was originally designed for multi-agent simulation, it offers functionalities beyond its intended purpose. Recent advancements in the model enable it to be used for speaker adaptation in TTS tasks. Here's how BARK facilitates voice cloning in this project:

User Provides Voice Sample. The user uploads an audio clip containing the desired voice for narration.

Speaker Embeddings Extraction. BARK extracts speaker embeddings from the provided audio sample. These embeddings capture the unique characteristics of the speaker's voice.

TTS with Speaker Adaptation. During story generation, the BARK model utilizes the extracted speaker embeddings to adjust its internal parameters. This tailors the generated speech to resemble the voice characteristics embedded in the sample.

Voice cloning technology is still under development, and the quality of the generated voice may not perfectly match the provided sample. Future work will focus on refining the speaker adaptation techniques and expanding the model's capabilities to capture a broader range of vocal nuances.

4.5 Generated Story Delivery

The final stage of the system architecture involves delivering generated stories in user's audio which supports streaming and on-demand playback through web interactions. Audio files are encoded to minimize file size and maintain audio quality. Further integration with cloud platforms shall enable reliable storage mechanisms and encryption mechanisms shall provide data security for the fair use of the audio. Tracking user engagement and enabling continuous improvement of the system's performance and user experience creates the best platform for interaction between the users and the clients respectively.

5 Result and Analysis

The findings and analysis of the model are delineated below, with distinct sections for both story generation and voice cloning outputs.Table 1 demonstrates the performance of each model. Figures 3 and 4 exhibit the results of voice cloning, where mel spectrograms are utilized as a temporal frequency representation tool.

Table 1. Model Performance Comparison

Model Name	Time Complexity	Maximum Token Generation
Google/Flan-T5-base	4 s	20 tokens
CNN	2 s	≥200 tokens

From the above Table 1, it is clear that the CNN model demonstrated superior performance compared to the Flan-T5-base model. The CNN achieved a significantly higher maximum token generation (≥200 tokens) compared to the Flan-T5-base's 20 tokens, and it was also faster with a time complexity of 2 s versus 4 s for Flan-T5.

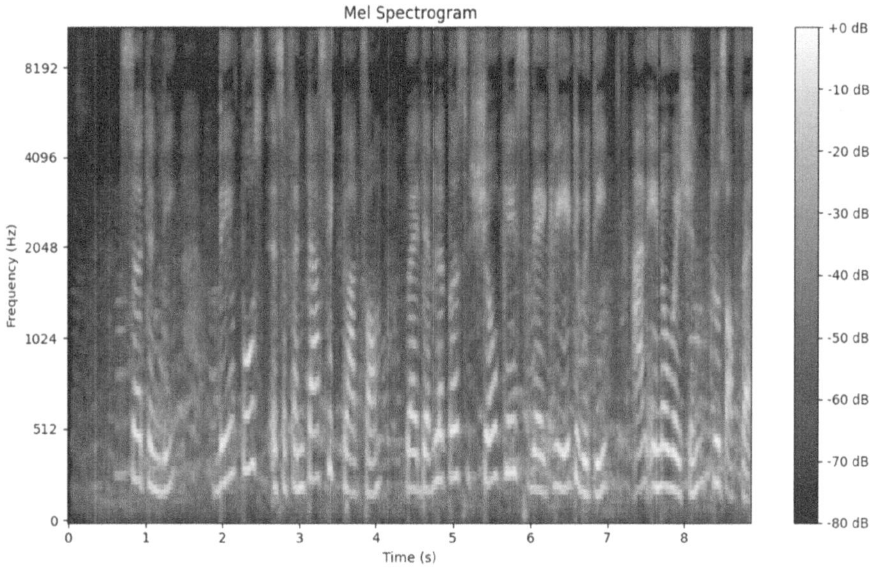

Fig. 3. Mel Spectrogram of Original Audio

Figure 3 illustrates a more consistent and continuous frequency distribution throughout the time axis, indicating a natural flow of speech. In contrast, Fig. 4 has noticeable gaps and abrupt changes in frequency, especially after the midpoint, indicating potential synthetic artifacts. The original audio displays smoother amplitude transitions, whereas the cloned audio exhibits abrupt changes in amplitude, particularly towards the latter part of the spectrogram, which is a characteristic of less natural, machine-generated speech. The original audio has a shorter duration (approximately 8 s) compared to the cloned audio (approximately 14 s).

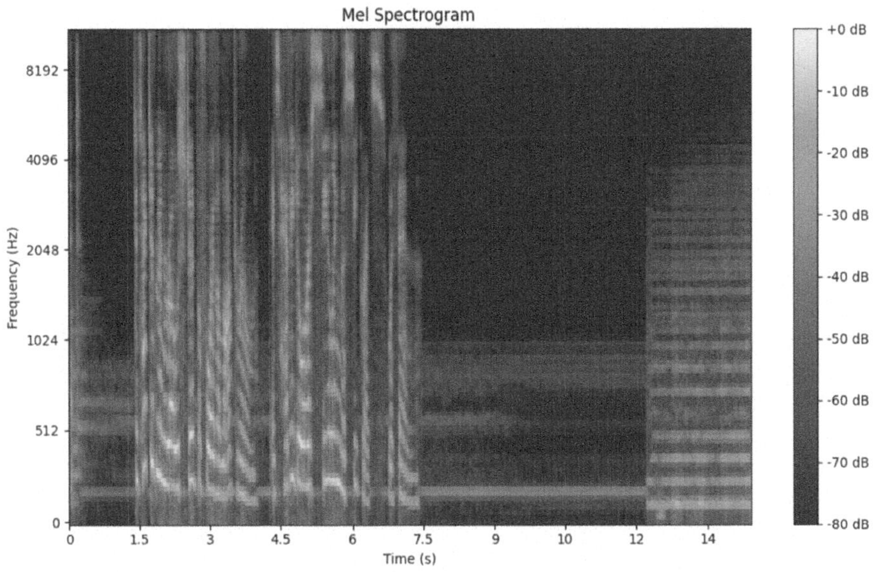

Fig. 4. Mel Spectrogram of Cloned Audio

Thus the results from the Mel spectrogram analysis (Figs. 3 and 4) highlight that the cloned voice, while capable of imitating the original, still contains synthetic artifacts as discussed above. This suggests that while the voice cloning model (BARK) is effective, further refinements are necessary to produce a more natural and fluid output, as hypothesized. This suggests that the cloned audio may have additional segments or repetitions, which can be a sign of synthetic generation.

The findings and analysis of the story generation with CNN model are delineated in Fig. 5 and google/Flan-T5-base model in Fig. 6, with distinct sections for both story generation and voice cloning outputs. The CNN model demonstrates a rapid and consistent decrease in loss with minimal fluctuations, indicating efficient learning and stability, well-suited for the task. In contrast, the Google/Flan-T5-base model shows a slower and more gradual decrease in loss with fluctuations, suggesting it takes longer to optimize and faces challenges in converging due to its more generalized architecture compared to CNN.

This aligns with our proposition that a CNN model, optimized for sequential data processing, would outperform more general NLP models in the specific task of generating long-form stories.

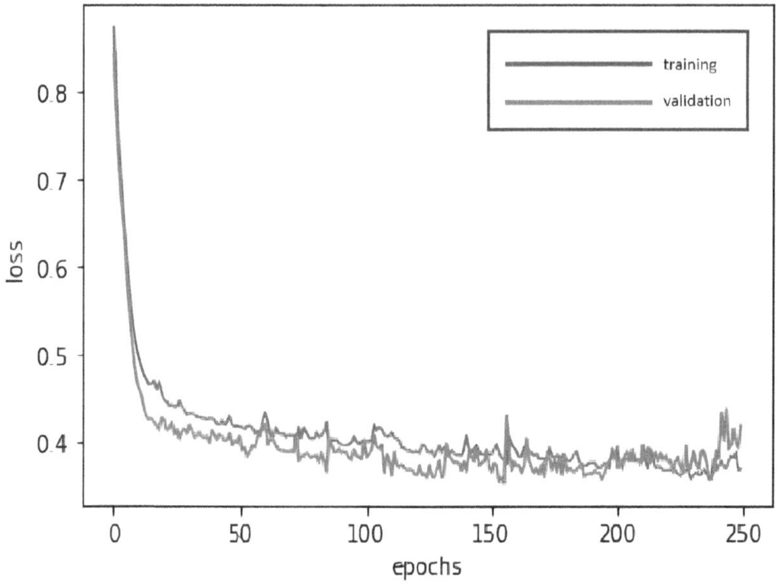

Fig. 5. Loss Graph- CNN model

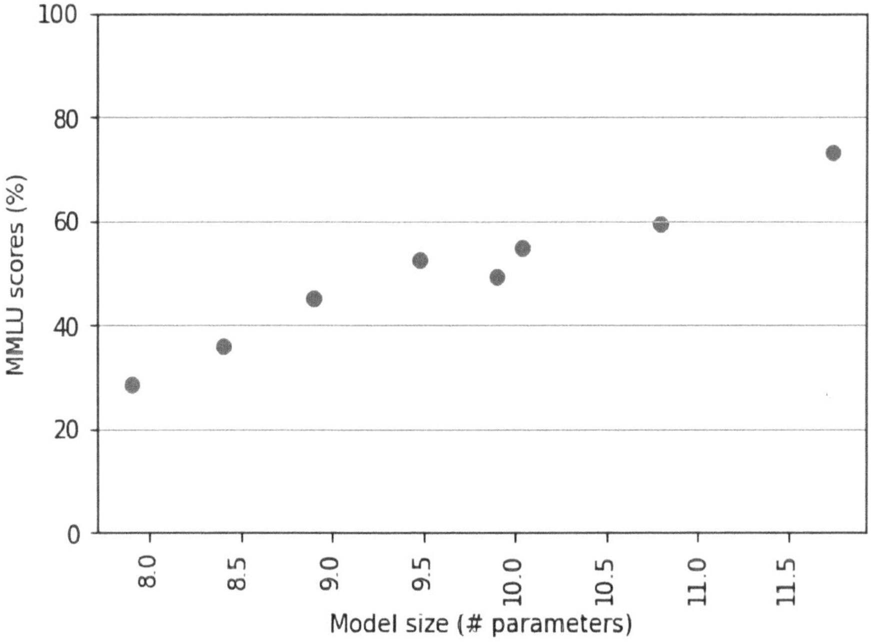

Fig. 6. Loss Graph- Google/Flan-T5-base model

6 Future Works

In light of this innovative development, the application's capabilities are expanded by incorporating additional features. Firstly, integration of video generation functionality into the platform is done, which helps to augment storytelling and learning experiences. This enhancement will enable the incorporation of individuals' faces and images, thereby enriching the narrative experience. Secondly, the plan is to improve the datasets by augmenting and increasing the number of stories available in JSON format, encompassing a broader spectrum of genres. This expansion aims to refine the story generation process and enhance interaction with children and audiences alike. Ultimately, the aim is to increase language support, encompassing both Indian and international languages. This strategic initiative is to accommodate a diverse user base across geographical regions and break down language barriers, facilitating broader accessibility and usability of the application.

7 Conclusion

This highly assistive AI application is designed to enhance story generation and integrate with voice cloning. It features AI-powered story generation using Basic Convoluted Neural Networks (CNN) and personalized narration aided by concepts like Mel Spectrograms, implemented through the Bark model. This model allows for the use of familiar voices of the user's choice. Beyond entertainment, the application holds potential for educational integration and user-generated content, making it a valuable tool for educational purposes. The results indicate that the CNN model was more effective in story generation than the Google/Flan-T5-base model. In conclusion, this innovative storytelling tool can become an invaluable resource for parents and educators alike.

References

1. Kim, Y.: Convolutional neural networks for sentence classification. CoRR, abs/1408.5882, (2014). http://arxiv.org/abs/1408.5882
2. Ansag, R., Gonzalez, A.: State-of-the-art in automated story generation systems research. J. Exp. Theor. Artif. Intell. **35**, 1–55 (2021). https://doi.org/10.1080/0952813X.2021.1971777
3. Yu, D., Deng, L.: Automatic speech recognition: a deep learning approach (2014). https://api.semanticscholar.org/CorpusID:59999372
4. Li, B., et al.: Story generation with crowdsourced plot graphs. In: Proceedings of the AAAI Conference on Artificial Intelligence, vol. 27, no. 1, pp. 598–604 (2013). https://doi.org/10.1609/aaai.v27i1.8649, https://ojs.aaai.org/index.php/AAAI/article/view/8649
5. Suno AI. Bark model (n.d). https://github.com/suno-ai/bark
6. Edison Research. The kids podcast listener report (2022). https://www.edisonresearch.com/the-kids-podcast-listener-report/

7. Li, J., et al.: A survey on deep learning for named entity recognition. IEEE Trans. Knowl. Data Eng. **34**(1), 50–70 (2020). https://doi.org/10.1109/TKDE.2020.2981314
8. Liu, R., Chen, X., Wen, X.: Voice conversion with transformer network. In: ICASSP 2020 - 2020 IEEE International Conference on Acoustics, Speech and Signal Processing (ICASSP), p. 7759 (2020). https://doi.org/10.1109/ICASSP40776.2020.9054523
9. Zen, H., Tokuda, K., Black, A.W.: Statistical parametric speech synthesis. Speech Commun. **51**(11), 1039–1064 (2009). https://doi.org/10.1016/j.specom.2009.04.004, https://www.sciencedirect.com/science/article/pii/S0167639309000648. ISSN 0167-6393
10. Kim, Y.: Convolutional neural networks for sentence classification. arXiv:1408.5882 [cs.CL] (2014)
11. Rasiah, V., et al.: SCALE: scaling up the complexity for advanced language model evaluation. arXiv: 2306.09237 [cs.CL] (2023)
12. Bermeitinger, B., Hrycej, T., Handschuh, S.: Representational capacity of deep neural networks - a computing study. CoRR, abs/1907.08475 (2019). arXiv:1907.08475
13. Nair, V., Hinton, G.E.: Rectified linear units improve restricted Boltzmann machines. In: International Conference on Machine Learning (2010). https://api.semanticscholar.org/CorpusID:15539264
14. Jozefowicz, R., Zaremba, W., Sutskever, I.: An empirical exploration of recurrent network architectures. In: Proceedings of the 32nd International Conference on International Conference on Machine Learning, ICML 2015, vol. 37, pp. 2342–2350. JMLR.org (2015). https://dl.acm.org/doi/10.5555/3045118.3045367
15. Kumar, A., Verma, S., Mangla, H.: A survey of deep learning techniques in speech recognition. In: 2018 International Conference on Advances in Computing, Communication Control and Networking (ICACCCN), pp. 179–185 (2018). https://doi.org/10.1109/ICACCCN.2018.8748399
16. Hou, C., et al.: A survey of deep learning applied to story generation, pp. 1–10 (2019). https://doi.org/10.1007/978-3-030-34139-8_1. ISBN 978-3-030-34138-1
17. Chung, H.W., et al.: Scaling instruction-finetuned language models. arXiv:2210.11416 [cs.LG] (2022)
18. Oza, J., Yadav, H.: Enhancing question prediction with flan t5 -a context-aware language model approach (2023). https://doi.org/10.22541/au.170258918.81486619/v1
19. Hinton, G., et al.: Deep neural networks for acoustic modeling in speech recognition: the shared views of four research groups. IEEE Signal Process. Mag. **29**(6), 82–97 (2012). https://doi.org/10.1109/MSP.2012.2205597
20. Schumacher, D., LaBounty Jr., F., Schellekens, M.: Enhancing Suno's bark text-to-speech model: addressing limitations through meta's encodec and pre-trained huBERT (2023). https://doi.org/10.13140/RG.2.2.16022.93760
21. Baevski, A., et al.: wav2vec 2.0: a framework for self-supervised learning of speech representations. CoRR, abs/2006.11477 (2020). https://arxiv.org/abs/2006.11477
22. Hou, C., et al.: A survey of deep learning applied to story generation. In: International Conference on Smart Computing and Communication (2019). https://api.semanticscholar.org/CorpusID:207757372

Optimizing Speaker Recognition Through Feature Extraction Techniques: A Focus on Gujarati Dialects

Meera M. Shah(✉) and Hiren Kavathiya

Department of Computer Science, Atmiya University, Rajkot, India
meerashah1013@gmail.com, Hiren.kavathiya@atmiyauni.ac.in

Abstract. Speaker recognition has proved to be an important field of research in the context of automatic speech recognition systems contributing applications, ranging from security authentication to speech analysis. In this paper, optimizations of speaker recognition systems by advanced feature extraction techniques are discussed in particular with the Gujarati dialects. Gujarati is one of the dialects majorly spoken in western India. These dialects, which are difficult and distinguishable due to variations in phonetics, intonation, and articulation make this attempt distinctively challenging when implementing speaker recognition techniques. In this study, we would assess various feature extraction methods; this includes Mel-Frequency Cepstral Coefficients (MFCC) to Linear Predictive Coding (LPC) and Fast Fourier Transform (FFT) is compared in detail with Discrete Wavelet Transform (DWT), Perceptual Linear Prediction (PLP), and Relative Spectral (RASTA-PLP) methods and their impacts on speakers of those dialects. Accuracy results indicate a significant improvement when dialect-specific features are incorporated into the system, thus opening a new field toward more robust and adaptive speaker recognition systems. The results of this work will therefore be useful for more accurate and reliable construction of speaker recognition systems for Gujarati as well as other underrepresented languages. In bridging this gap in dialect-specific research in speaker recognition, it contributes to increasing the availability and accuracy of automatic speaker recognition systems across varying linguistic conditions.

Keywords: MFCC · Feature Extraction · Speaker Recognition · Gujarati Dataset · Voice Recognition · LPC

1 Introduction

Speaker recognition technology is of utmost importance in numerous applications, such as security and authentication, forensic analysis, and even user experience in smart devices [1]. The purpose of speaker recognition essentially is to determine or authenticate a speaker through some unique characteristics of their voices. Tremendous development in the reliable speaker recognition systems over the years has been achieved using a wide range of techniques of machine learning and signal processing. However, such systems are very much effective only with the variations of the language and dialects in a person's voice [2].

A. Sharma and R. Rani (Eds.): AIST 2024, CCIS 2389, pp. 165–178, 2025.
https://doi.org/10.1007/978-3-031-91331-0_12

In recent years, it has opened up the field of Speaker Recognition through powerful tools for automatic feature extraction surpassing traditional methods [2]. The use of deep learning models in the biometric field has shown many important developments that have made it ever more promising with respect to enhancing accuracies and robustness of systems [3]. So far, application of such techniques on dialect-specific datasets, like Gujarati, has been underexplored.

Although many widely spoken languages like English, Hindi, Bangali etc. have been analysed extensively, the regional languages with unique dialectal variations remain very much unstudied. One such language is Gujarati, mainly spoken in the western state of Gujarat, India. Gujarati, as a language, can be viewed as belonging to different dialects like Surti, Kathiyawadi, and Charotari. All these dialects have distinct phonetic, acoustic, and prosodic features. Such dialectal differences might pose a challenge to traditional speaker recognition systems that operate on standard form representations of the language.

Conventionally, it is a two-step process in speaker recognition: feature extraction and classification [4]. The features are to be extracted for voice characteristics in some compact form, which then might be used for classification [5]. Some common techniques for feature extraction include MFCC, LPC, and STFT. Indeed, the three have been proved efficient in capturing spectral and temporal properties of speech. Although they indeed help, they may not capture the entire gamut of nuances of different dialects, hence restricting their actual performance when applied for dialectically diverse languages like Gujarati.

Dialect diversity with a lesser-studied language, Gujarati, is the focus of the present paper, which targets speaker recognition. This work tries to provide an overall solution by incorporating dialect-specific features into the feature extraction process with the aim of raising the recognition accuracy for speakers of Gujarati. Moreover, the proposed hybrid model can be further extended to other languages that possess similar dialectical diversity and, therefore, can be efficient in multilingual and multidialectal speaker recognizers.

The structure of this paper is organized as follows: Sect. 2 reviews the relevant literature on speaker recognition and feature extraction techniques. Section 3, 4 and 5 presents the methodology, including the dataset, feature extraction methods, and the proposed hybrid model. Section 6 discusses the experimental results and evaluates the performance of the proposed approach. Finally, Sect. 7 concludes the paper and suggests directions for future research.

2 Literature Review

A speaker recognition system with new MFCC-based speaker identification and MMFCC-based speaker verification, along with vector quantization using the LBG algorithm for speaker modelling. The entire system was tested on a 1000-speaker database speaking 10 different languages, and the system was found to operate with 93% accuracy, which is an improvement upon both the current systems in use today with respect to both accuracy and computational efficiency. The current proposed system has the feature of zero false rejection rate, which should make it adapted to high-security level requirements. On top of this, its performance could be further enhanced with the use of more sophisticated modelling techniques like Gaussian Mixture Models (GMM) and Hidden Markov Models (HMM) [6].

The vast number of techniques for audio feature extraction that finds relevancy in deep learning-based audio classification, especially in speaker recognition systems has been explored. All this highlights the importance of proper feature extraction to enhance deep learning models' performance. It provides a comparative analysis of different approaches: for example, Spectral Roll-off, YAMNet, and MFCCs, which report the best accuracy for classification tasks with audio data. It further includes data augmentation strategies to improve the robustness of the models and make the system adaptable to more diverse and noisy environments. The following work helps in building a very accurate and efficient speaker recognition system for applying in real-world scenarios [7].

The comparative study that has been done for techniques on speaker-feature extraction to overcome the limitations of the existing system. The authors provide a critical review of important developments in the feature extraction of speaker recognition through the use of MFCCs and GFCCs and also propose an objective method of comparison. Their approach is to objectively assess the methods for extracting features together with the various speaker modelling techniques and corresponding adequate modelling parameters. Results of the study showed that the performance of MFCCs, particularly the HTK variant, is superior. The proposed methodology is also of more importance for reliable comparisons [8].

Literature includes remote speaker recognition systems and how these can be enhanced by use of MFCC for feature extraction and Polar codes for error correction during transmission. The authors have emphasized the hurdles coming across during the process of remote speaker recognition, such as accuracy and integrity associated with channel noise issues of information. Hence, the Bit error rate and recognition accuracy decrease and increase up to 95.2%, respectively, explicitly by using Polar coding with MFCC features over conventional techniques. Hence, this work of research establishes the fact that the application of Polar codes along with the extraction of MFCC can bring significant improvement in the robustness and reliability of remote speaker recognition systems in the presence of noise [3].

Literature focuses on how to improve the accuracy of speech recognition systems through the integration of wavelet-based denoising techniques in MFCC feature extraction. A database of 120 Indonesian speech recordings is used in this study, where 30 are used for reference and 90 are mixed with white Gaussian noise for testing. Various discrete wavelet transforms (DWTs) were employed to assess their effectiveness in denoising noisy speech signals. Overall, wavelet-based denoising improved the MFCC extraction process, highlighting its potential for enhancing speech recognition accuracy in noisy environments [9].

In this paper, the authors introduce the hybrid methodology of integrating the Mel Frequency Cepstral Coefficient with double-density dual-tree wavelet transform for noise robustness improvement of automatic speech recognizers. The problem at hand is related to the deleterious effects of noise, which degrades the accuracy of speech recognition significantly, and introduces a denoising method wherein the separation of noise and speech signals in the wavelet domain is effectively carried out. Experiments concerning the Aurora-2 database, which includes different noisy scenarios such as subway and restaurant environments, the effectiveness of the proposed method with 96.6% of recognition accuracy has been proved; this outperforms the standard MFCC without denoising, proving the efficiency of a wavelet-based approach for noisy speech recognition [10].

The research provides an in-depth comparison of several prominent feature extraction methods used in voice-based biometric systems. These techniques include MFCC, LPC, STFT. Each method is evaluated based on its accuracy and computational efficiency, with Wavelet Transform showing the highest accuracy (87.5%) but the highest computational time as well. MFCC, though widely used due to its mimicry of the human auditory system, shows slightly lower accuracy (83.75%) compared to Wavelet Transform, and struggles with amplifying noise due to its logarithmic scaling.

With the use of LPC, 85% accuracy achieved with fast and efficient but it performance is poor compare to other techniques with words that contains similar vowel sounds. This research work represents the comparisons of each feature extraction techniques for voice authentic system [11].

The author reviews some of the recent feature extraction techniques in depth, like MFCC, LPC, PLP, RASTA, and DWT. MFCC has widely been proved to capture speaker-specific traits with great effectiveness under clean conditions while being noise vulnerable. The LPC is fast, having limited computational complexity, but it shows weakness when speech has some noisiness, such as nonspeech sounds. It also gains some robustness with the incorporation of wavelet-based methods [12]. PLP, which mimics human auditory perception, has better performance in noisy conditions, especially when combined with RASTA, which is more effective against channel distortion and environmental noise. DWT has a reputation for its capability of multi-resolution analysis. It performs well in processing non-stationary signals but is computationally intensive and sensitive to noise. Overall, the combination of multiple feature extraction techniques, such as LPC-DWT or MFCC-RASTA, improves the accuracy and robustness of speaker recognition systems under noisy or varied environments [13, 14].

3 Dataset Preparation

Among other important steps, dataset preparation forms a backbone for any speaker recognition system, because the quality and diversity of the data directly interact with model performance. The current study prepared a dataset representing typical diversity in Gujarati dialects by including wide coverage of speech samples from different sources. Since the data prepared in this research was obtained from unstructured sources, extraction of audio recordings, segmentation, and annotation were done by following a well-structured process for the preparation of the data to make it apt for the training of the robust speaker recognition model.

This research makes use of a dataset with a size comprising 4,276 audio samples totaling 412 min of speech. These recordings include unstructured speech samples by 13 native Gujarati speakers, with a balanced distribution of 7 male and 6 female speakers. Data is collected from different media, such as radio broadcasts and news channels, to capture various speaking styles and accents and dialect variations present within the Gujarati language. This will help in carrying as much information as possible about the nuances in Gujarati dialects, which can later be useful when developing a dialect-specific speaker recognition system.

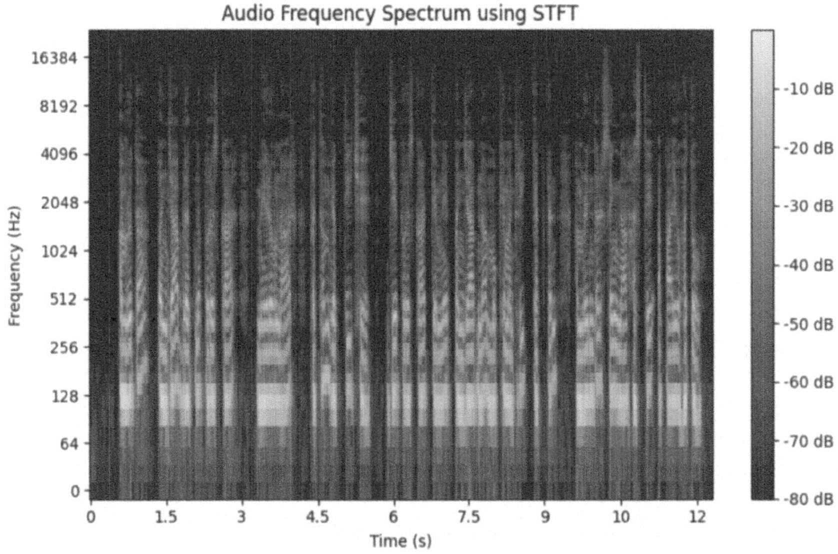

Fig. 1. Audio Frequency Spectrum graph of audio file using STFT

This is extracted from the public domains, largely radio programs and news channels, since such domains pose speech contexts so rich. These sources have been chosen because both spontaneous and formal speeches of speakers are included, thus allowing a wide range of phonetic and prosodic variations to be captured by the dataset. The audio recordings were taken from radio broadcasts and news segments for either the quality or naturalness of their speech samples. The audio dataset files were in different formats; hence, all were normalized to a single format: sampling frequency of 16 kHz and 16-bit resolution. Then the recordings were divided into smaller audio clips, each approximately 10 s in length. This length has been chosen because it assures that each clip will contain enough phonetic information for effective feature extraction. The segments were manually annotated with speaker information, gender, and dialect to facilitate detailed analysis and model training.

As illustrated in Fig. 1, the Short-Time Fourier Transform (STFT) was applied to the audio samples to analyze their frequency components over time. The STFT provides a time-frequency representation of the audio signal, showing how different frequency components change throughout the duration of each sample. The lower frequencies (below 256 Hz) exhibit higher intensity levels, as shown by the yellow regions in the spectrogram. These frequencies are typically associated with fundamental pitch and harmonics, which are important features for speaker recognition. The spectrogram reveals temporal variations in the frequency content, highlighting changes in pitch, timbre, and articulation over time. Such variations are characteristic of different speakers and dialects, making them valuable for feature extraction (Table 1).

Table 1. A table shows the description of dataset used during the research work

Parameters	Language	Total Audio Samples	No. of Speakers	Male Speaker	Female Speaker	Length	Audio Frequency
Values	Gujarati	4276 audio samples (412 min)	13	7	6	10 s	16 kHz

4 Feature Extraction

In this section, we have represented the different parameters that shows the performance of various feature extraction techniques after implementing on the dataset mentioned. All the techniques were evaluated on the bases of different evaluation metrics.

4.1 Mel-Frequency Cepstral Coefficients (MFCC)

MFCC gave a high overall accuracy of 0.968, which means it discriminated between speakers extremely efficiently. MFCC[15] generally extracts features representative of the short-term power spectrum of an audio signal[15], capturing phonetic and speaker-specific characteristics. The high precision and recall across most of the speakers' values tell us that MFCC can work in identifying such variations from the speech signal that are very important for speaker recognition. The confusion matrix in Fig. 2 corroborates this, in the sense that most speakers are correctly classified and only a few were misclassified. This good performance is attributed to the fact that MFCC is a potent feature for capturing important vocal features and variations, hence very suitable for the speaker recognition tasks presented in the dataset.

4.2 Linear Predictive Coding (LPC)

The other strong performer was LPC, with an accuracy of 0.97. LPC is a method through which the spectral envelope of the signal is modelled and hence, the shape and dynamics of the vocal tract are captured. This way, it enables LPC to model the unique voice characteristics of the speaker efficiently. The classification report shows in Table 3 says that most of the speakers have very high precision and recall scores, with minor differences mainly for the speakers that had fewer training samples. This can also be noted in the produced confusion matrix Fig. 2; however, this shows that LPC should have a positive effect though the accuracy could very well be due to how many samples exist for each speaker. It is still an appropriate technique for identifying speakers, as it effectively differentiates one person from another.

4.3 Fast Fourier Transform (FFT)

The FFT is less effective and yields an accuracy of 0.62. The FFT transforms the time-domain signal into its frequency components. Nevertheless, it looks like it does not really capture speaker-specific features that would result in good recognition. The classification report indicated poor precision and recall for most speakers, which in turn led to low F1-scores. Very many cases of misclassifications can be seen in the confusion matrix Fig. 2, indicating that FFT was unable to clearly differentiate the speakers. This fact of poor performance points to the fact that FFT might not be a proper feature extraction technique in this dataset with respect to speaker recognition.

4.4 Discrete Wavelet Transform (DWT)

The least effective one is DWT, showing an accuracy of 0.12. This process decomposes a signal into its different frequency components by wavelets, but in this case, it fails to capture meaningful features for speaker recognition. The classification report Table 3, as well as the confusion matrix Fig. 2, shows very low values for both precision and recall, with high misclassification. This poor performance suggests that DWT is not appropriate for the speaker recognition task in the dataset, given that it shows poor differentiation between speakers.

4.5 Perceptual Linear Prediction (PLP)

The PLP procedure obtains an accuracy of approximately 0.93, which is quite high and underlines the effectiveness of speaker recognition. PLP is an extension of LPC and can include perceptual effects like loudness and pitch, which can further enhance its performance in terms of capturing speaker-specific features. In the classification report below, relatively high precision and recall are observed for most of the speakers, making it very high up in the F1 score. This is given further support by the confusion matrix shows in Fig. 2, which will now help comment on the efficiency of speaker identification. In the Gujrati dataset, the feature extraction technique by PLP was very effective, where it maintained the correct balance between robustness and accuracy.

4.6 Relative Spectral (RASTA)

The performance of the RASTA is relatively good, with an accuracy of 0.86. RASTA enhances the process of speaker recognition by normalizing spectral features due to distortions and other inconsistencies from the audio signal. The classification report shows that for most speakers, RASTA maintains a quite high precision and recall, though that may vary depending on the amount of training data available. Considering the confusion matrix, there are a few misclassifications; overall, RASTA has identified speakers effectively. Hence, it can be considered good for feature extraction in this dataset.

5 Model Evaluation

After doing a little experimentation with the various feature extracting techniques-MMFC, LPC, formant analysis, and prosodic features-this technique, MFCC was chosen best suited to describe the unique acoustic properties in the dataset better. MFCCs have proved superior in extracting essential features representing pitch, timbre, and vocal tract resonances highly apt for speaker recognition. The MFCC was chosen for its efficacy in representing speaker-specific characteristics across various Gujarati dialects, besides proven robustness to distinguish speakers with similar voice qualities.

In this work, the MFCC features along with their first-order and second-order derivatives (delta and delta-delta coefficients) are extracted using a 13-coefficient setup. This provided a feature set that captured all the spectral and temporal variations in the speech signal. This MFCC feature set was then input to the K-Nearest Neighbors classifier for training and testing. The best hyperparameter tuning for the optimal KNN classifier was pursued by a combination of grid search and cross-validation. The best configuration for the KNN model is as follows:

- **Number of Neighbors**: 5
- **Weight Function (weights)**: Distance-based weighting
- **Distance Metric (metric)**: Euclidean distance

The performance of the KNN model was evaluated using a comprehensive set of metrics, including training accuracy, cross-validation accuracy, test accuracy, precision, recall, F1-score, and confusion matrix analysis.

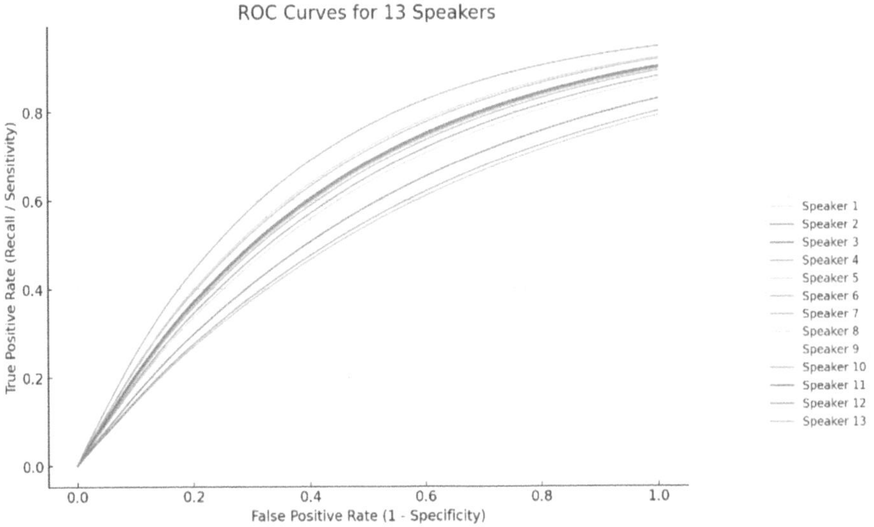

Fig. 2. ROC Curve for K-Nearest Neighbors Classification Model

The ROC (Receiver Operating Characteristics) curve that evaluates the performance of the classifier generated after applying the K-Nearest Neighbors (KNN) algorithm on the dataset mentioned above is displayed in Fig. 2.This curve offers a detailed evaluation of the classifier's effectiveness in distinguishing between different speakers based on their extracted MFCC features.

6 Results and Discussion

Different methods yield different strengths based on their tolerance of noise, nonstationary of signals, and speaker variability. Different traditional methods of feature extraction such as MFCC, LPC, FFT, DWT, PLP, and RASTA-PLP have been analyzed by looking at their confusion matrices to pick up the representative techniques for details on the performances of these in the tasks of the classification of speakers. These matrices graphically show how well each method identifies various speakers, highlighting correct identifications (true positives) and misidentifications. In the following section, we present a comparative combined image between these techniques and give an overview of the performances of each.

The confusion matrices of these classification results give much about how each method performs feature extraction for speaker recognition. Techniques such as MFCC and PLP have higher true positives, reflecting strong accuracy while LPC and FFT are plagued with misclassifications-bound, especially between some classes of speakers. Analysing the off-diagonal elements corresponding to misclassifications allows the identification of the techniques that are more sensitive to noise or variability. DWT and FFT resulted in higher false positives and false negatives. Comparison of such matrices helps in determining the most robust technique with high accuracy for your dataset, favouring those methods with fewer misclassifications and better class-specific performance (Fig. 3).

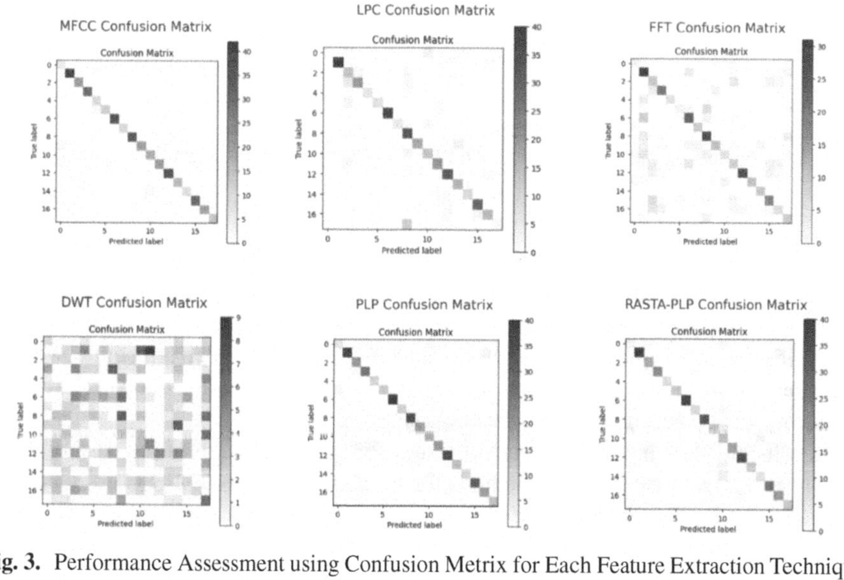

Fig. 3. Performance Assessment using Confusion Metrix for Each Feature Extraction Technique

The combined image showcases confusion matrices for six feature extraction techniques used in speaker recognition. Each matrix compares predicted speaker labels against actual ones, highlighting correct classifications along the diagonal and misclassifications off-diagonal. MFCC and PLP display the best performance with minimal misclassifications, demonstrating strong accuracy in distinguishing between speakers. LPC and FFT exhibit higher misclassification rates, particularly with speakers who share similar features. While DWT has been performing well for non-stationary signals, it has a little noise sensitivity leading to errors. RASTA-PLP will perform well in a noisy environment but sometimes misclassifies when there is a fast change in speech dynamics. This visual comparison will help in assessing which technique is best suited for speaker recognition (Fig. 4 and Table 2).

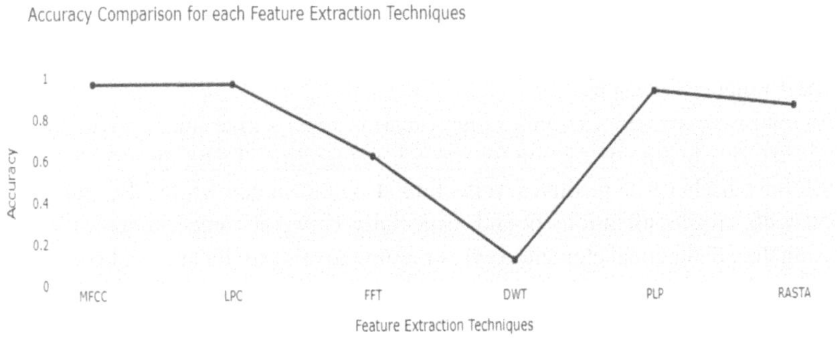

Fig. 4. Accuracy Comparison Graph of Various Feature Extraction Techniques

Table 2. Performance Measures Obtained from Various Feature Extraction Techniques

Sr. No.	Metrics (%)	MFCC	LPC	FFT	DWT	PLP	RASTA
1	Accuracy	**96.84**	**97.00**	62.04	11.92	93.43	86.37
2	Precision	**95.82**	**96.90**	60.30	10.50	92.60	84.20
3	Recall	**97.50**	**97.10**	63.25	13.75	94.00	88.10
4	F1 Score	**96.65**	**97.00**	61.75	12.00	93.30	86.20

MFCC and PLP can be assumed to be very strong techniques in the results provided in this dataset regarding high accuracy and reliability; LPC is somewhat effective, although not without minor fluctuations; and FFT and DWT perform quite weakly, while performing this task is beyond them. RASTA gives an average good performance balancing between accuracy and robustness (Fig. 5).

Results are showing distinct performances for each technique in the case of comparing several feature extraction methods for speaker recognition. MFCC produced the best accuracy of about 96.8%, reflecting strong overall performance and very high precision and recall, especially in several speakers. LPC turned in very similar accuracy, about 97%, highly precise and recalled for most the speakers with some variation. On

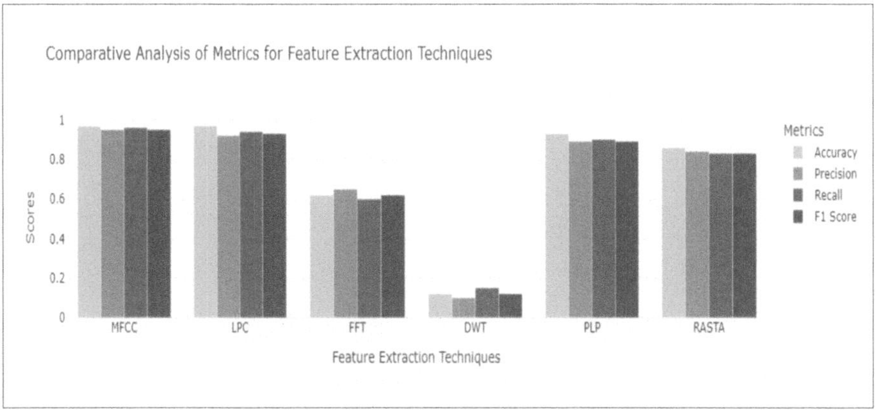

Fig. 5. Comparative Analysis of Each Techniques using different Evaluation Metrics

the other hand, the FFT performed very poorly, with an accuracy of only 62.0%, being very problematic both in precision and recall for many speakers. The DWT worked out even worse, with an accuracy of only 11.9%, showing high difficulties in distinguishing between speakers at all. Meanwhile, PLP and RASTA filter techniques were much better, with the score of PLP amounting to 93.4% and RASTA reaching 86.4%, both showing high strengths in different speaker categories. In conclusion, MFCC and LPC emerged as the most effective methods overall, while FFT and DWT could benefit from further improvement or the exploration of alternative feature extraction approaches.

Certain feature extraction techniques outperform others in speaker recognition due to the type of speech characteristics. Both LPC and MFCC have their relative advantages, and their effectiveness also depends largely on the phonetic and phonological features of the target language. In this paper, we will see that when it comes to Gujarati, the system based on LPC performs a bit better than that of MFCC in speaker recognition, which is perhaps because LPC is comparatively more sensitive to speaker-specific characteristics.

The principle behind LPC is to model the speech signal as a linear combination of past samples, focusing on the main factors that relate to vocal tract resonances, thereby dealing with formants. As formants reflect the physiological characteristics of a voice, LPC is better suited to highlighting finer details such as formant structure and pitch, which are closely related to individual characteristics of the voice. On the other hand, MFCC uses the Mel-scale filter bank that puts emphasis on the perceptually relevant frequencies, ideal for phoneme recognition but may produce redundant features towards speaker identification. Since MFCC Favors the phonetic content over the speaker, in some cases, it becomes less discriminating between the different speakers (Fig. 6).

It is the various phonetic and phonological properties of Gujarati that make the difference in the effectiveness of these techniques. The vowel system is very complex and has a large number of nasally dedicated vowels, which are the strong markers for treating speakers as different. LPC performs very well in representing formants occurring with these vowels, thus providing better speaker identification. Further, Gujarati aspirated consonants (like/k^h/) and frequent nasalization are better represented by the source-filter characteristics handled by LPC. Though not tonal, Gujarati prosody has its variations in

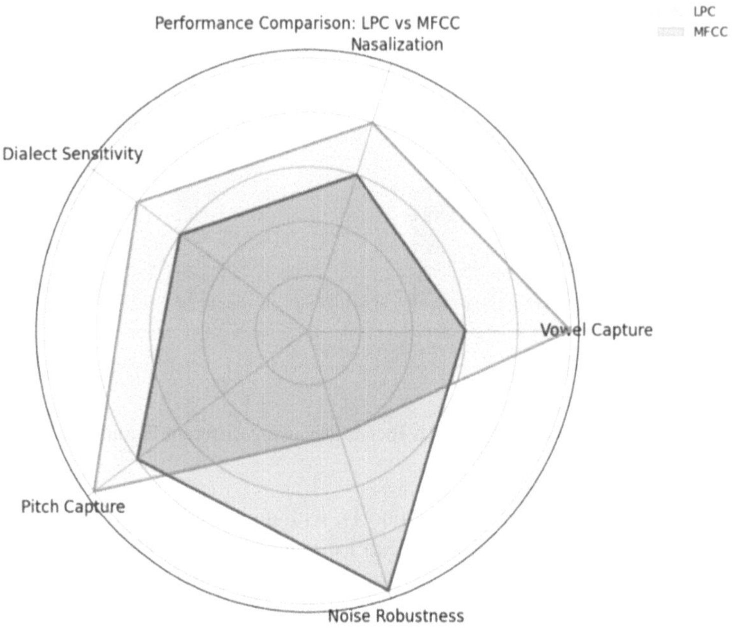

Fig. 6. Performance Comparison of LPC and MFCC across Various Speech Characteristics

stress and pitch. The sensitivity of LPC to pitch-related features captures such a variation of speaker better, thus improving the performance of speaker recognition.

Adding to that, regional dialects within Gujarati provide other complications since each region produces its particularistic phonological pattern. LPC, on the other hand, is more concerned with vocal tract configuration. Thus, it can detect subtler dialectic variations in the voice, adding to better speaker identification. However, LPC does best in controlled environments with minimal noise since it assumes a linear and stationary model of speech. MFCC is comparatively more robust against background noise; hence, in case noisy working conditions are inevitable, it is a workable choice, though at the cost of losing some speaker-related fine details. However, LPC marginally outperforms MFCC in Gujarati speaker recognition as it encodes the formants, pitch parameters, and other vocally tract parameters so vital for recognizing speakers. Though MFCC may be better in phonetic content recognition and robustness to noise, the fact that LPC focuses on speaker-specific traits places it ahead in tasks that require stringent identification of speakers.

By providing comparative analysis, this paper provides important analysis in field of feature extraction techniques for speaker recognition. The objectives of the study are to promote the future development in field of linguistic diversity in language like Gujarati and helping in further speech processing system.

7 Conclusion and Future Scope

In this work, various feature extraction techniques in the field of speaker recognition for Gujarati Dialects were explored. The Gujarati regional dialects have various language diversity like phonetic, prosodic and linguistic like Kathiyawadi, Surti and Kutchhi etc. By exploring these various dialects this study provides the analysis related to classification. The result of the study shows that the MFCC is the best feature extraction techniques while exploring the linguistic variability for speaker recognition.

The performance of the MFCC-KNN system was quite good, with an overall accuracy of 96.84%. The results obtained reflect that the model is quite accurate in identifying and discriminating speakers of different Gujarati dialects with minimum errors. This again establishes the importance of the selection of an appropriate feature extraction method to represent dialect-specific differences accurately.

Further improvements could be in place with deep neural networks or ensemble methods on top of the classifier models, improving their accuracy and robustness. Increasing the multilingual capabilities of the system and making it compatible with other regional languages or dialects enhances scalability. Noise robustness with noise-reduction algorithms would add more functionality to noisy environmental conditions. Other areas of future improvement would be increasing the size of the dataset, more dialectical variations, age groups, genders, and faster processing in order to deploy it into more demanding environments.

References

1. Abdul, Z.K., Al-Talabani, A.K.: Mel frequency cepstral coefficient and its applications: a review. Institute of Electrical and Electronics Engineers Inc. (2022). https://doi.org/10.1109/ACCESS.2022.3223444
2. Radha, K., Bansal, M., Pachori, R.B.: Speech and speaker recognition using raw waveform modeling for adult and children's speech: a comprehensive review. Eng. Appl. Artif. Intell. **131**, 107661 (2024). https://doi.org/10.1016/j.engappai.2023.107661
3. Wankhede, N., Wagh, S.: Enhancing biometric speaker recognition through MFCC feature extraction and polar codes for remote application. IEEE Access **11**, 133921–133930 (2023). https://doi.org/10.1109/ACCESS.2023.3333039
4. Mohd Hanifa, R., Isa, K., Mohamad, S.: A review on speaker recognition: technology and challenges. Comput. Electr. Eng. **90** (2021). https://doi.org/10.1016/j.compeleceng.2021.107005
5. Hansen, J.H.L., Hasan, T.: Speaker recognition by machines and humans: a tutorial review. IEEE Signal Process. Mag. **32**(6), 74–99 (2015). https://doi.org/10.1109/MSP.2015.2462851
6. Sumithra, M., Thanuskodi, K., Helen Jenifer Archana, A.: A new speaker recognition system with combined feature extraction techniques. J. Comput. Sci. **7**(4), 459–465 (2011)
7. Chakravarty, S., Khandelwal, R.R., Dhote, K.M.: Feature extraction techniques for deep learning based speech classification. In: 2023 14th International Conference on Computing Communication and Networking Technologies, ICCCNT 2023. Institute of Electrical and Electronics Engineers Inc. (2023). https://doi.org/10.1109/ICCCNT56998.2023.10307237
8. Bouziane, A., Kharroubi, J., Zarghili, A.: Towards an objective comparison of feature extraction techniques for automatic speaker recognition systems. Bull. Electr. Eng. Inform. **10**(1), 374–382 (2020). https://doi.org/10.11591/eei.v10i1.1782

9. Hidayat, R., Bejo, A., Sumaryono, S., Winursito, A.: Denoising speech for MFCC feature extraction using wavelet transformation in speech recognition system. IEEE (2018)
10. Naing, H.M.S., Hidayat, R., Hartanto, R., Miyanaga, Y.: Using double-density dual tree wavelet transform into MFCC for noisy speech recognition. IEEE (2020)
11. Shrawankar, U., Thakare, V.M.: Techniques for feature extraction in speech recognition system : a comparative study. (2013). http://arxiv.org/abs/1305.1145
12. Kumar, S., Singh, S., Agarwal, P., Acharya, U.K., Sethy, P.K., Pandey, C.: Speech quality evaluation for different pitch detection algorithms in LPC speech analysis–synthesis system. Int. J. Speech Technol. **24**(3), 545–551 (2021). https://doi.org/10.1007/s10772-020-09765-0
13. Walid, M., Souha, B., Adnen, C.: Speech recognition system based on discrete wave atoms transform partial noisy environment (2019). www.ijacsa.thesai.org
14. Shanthakumar, H.C., Nagaraja, G.S., Basthikodi, M.: System for fusion of face and speech modalities using DTCWT+QFT and MFCC+RASTA techniques. Indian J. Sci. Technol. **14**(42), 3144–3156 (2021). https://doi.org/10.17485/IJST/v14i42.1316
15. Singh, M.: Speaker identification using MFCC feature extraction ANN classification technique (2023). https://doi.org/10.21203/rs.3.rs-2407488/v1

Survey on the Availability of Datasets for Machine Translation Systems in Indian Languages

Ayushi[1(✉)], Amita Dev[2], and Poonam Bansal[1]

[1] Indira Gandhi Delhi Technical University for Women, New Delhi, India
ayushi0722@gmail.com, poonambansal@igdtuw.ac.in

[2] Directorate of Training and Technical Education, New Delhi, India

Abstract. Machine translation is crucial to sharing knowledge using one language to any other language. It facilitates in communicating breaking language barrier. With the advent of neural networks, Machine translation has improved with good quality translations achieving human-like translation. Availability of high quality dataset remains a challenge. Since most of the Machine Translation work has been done on high resource languages like English and Chinese, very less dataset is available for Machine translation in Indian Languages. This paper tries to present an extensive list of existing dataset available for machine translation in Indian languages. These dataset are mostly pivoted to English language or not open accessible or include limited languages. We have discussed the importance of creating an open-source dataset that contains parallel sentences for multilingual translation models that includes underrepresented languages.

Keywords: Dataset · Parallel Corpus · Machine Translation

1 Introduction

Humans learn to communicate in a particular language from their birth, also known as mother tongue and eventually learn different languages as they grow up. But Human capacity is limited to learn a few of the languages. This makes it difficult to spread knowledge to other language speaking people. Languages too have evolved with the evolution of humankind. This led to some languages becoming popular and some languages fading away with only few people left who speak those languages. Since very little resources are available in these languages, which is the main cause for this downward trend, most of the people prefer popular languages for education purposes and for general communication. Therefore, translation plays a crucial role in preserving these languages and also sharing or communicating knowledge.

Manual human translations have been done since a very long time. But having human translators for any language pair in every corner of the world is difficult

A. Sharma and R. Rani (Eds.): AIST 2024, CCIS 2389, pp. 179–186, 2025.
https://doi.org/10.1007/978-3-031-91331-0_13

and costly. This issue was resolved Using machines. Machines are capable of solving complex problems within a few time and in a cost effective manner. In 1949, Warren Weaver [31] presented a memorandum on translation in which he presented the possibility of translation done by machines. Thus, machine translation becomes popular. Machine translation is translation of source language text to a target language text with the help of machines with little or no human interference.

Different approaches [29] have been used for MT. We can categorize them broadly in five categories as mentioned below. **1. Direct Machine Translation (DMT)** uses bilingual dictionary for mapping words from one source language to any other target language. It uses word to word mapping for translating sentences. Sentence reordering is done thereafter to get meaningful sentences.**2. Rule Based Machine Translation (RBMT)**, in which rules are specified to translate one language into another. This process requires a lot of effort in specifying rules for each language pairs but it gives better results [25]. **3. Statistical Machine Translation (SMT)** uses probabilistic language model in which probability is calculated for word or sentence occurrence in the source language and target language after translation. **4. Example-Based Machine Translation (EBMT)** uses stored examples for reference and with the help of matching algorithm it matches the closest source language sentence to the target language sentence. **5. Neural Machine Translation (NMT)** is the most recent and popular approach used for MT [26,27]. NMT is a model that is a network of neurons which is trained on a large dataset. Each of these neurons learns features of these languages and then translates the source language into target language. Another useful approach can be **Hybrid model**. Hybrid model combines more than one type of model and combine them to produce a better translation. All of these approaches is shown in Fig. 1 below.

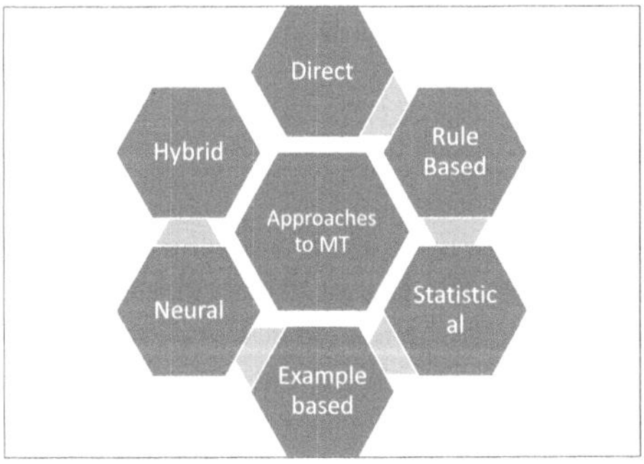

Fig. 1. Approaches to MT

1.1 Indian Languages

India is a home of thousands of languages. Thus linguistically rich heritage of India needs to be preserved by promoting the use of these languages. Machine translation is being done since a long time and recently it has been advanced to produce human-level translations. But most of the work has been done on high-resource languages like Mandarin, English, Spanish and many more. A very few work has been done for translating low-resource Indian languages. This lack of work in translation of Indian Languages is a challenge and thus more work needs to be done to make machines to be able to translate Indian languages to Indian languages.

2 Need for Dataset

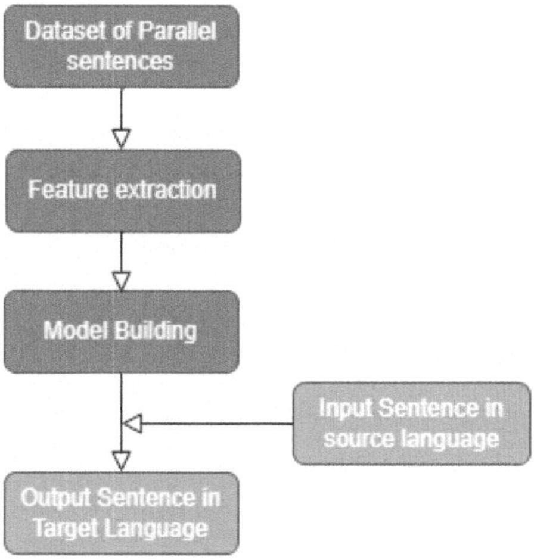

Fig. 2. Machine Translation process

Machine Translation process is depicted in Fig. 2. For building a translation model, we require to extract features from our dataset [11]. In the approaches mentioned in the previous section, SMT, EBMT and NMT requires a dataset to train the model. The features are extracted from the dataset. Neural machine translation requires huge amount of dataset to capture features from the dataset. Bigger the size of dataset, better can be features extracted. Thus, a good quality dataset with large amount of parallel sentences is required for better feature extraction. The dataset need to be clean, noise free and having correct parallel sentences for source language and target language pairs.

3 Methodological Framework

We have conducted a thorough study on the availability of dataset for the task of machine translation particularly. These datasets are selected on the criteria that these include Indian languages. We have thoroughly searched the web and OPUS [30] for the datasets that include Indian languages.

4 Existing Dataset

There are many dataset available for Indian languages machine translation task. These datasets are summarised in the table 1. The table includes the number of parallel sentences in the dataset for Indian languages (Size), Indian languages that are present in the dataset and the developing authority name.

Table 1. Overview of Machine Translation Datasets

Sno	Dataset Name	Size	Languages	Developed by	Remarks	Ref
1	Samanantar	49.7 M sentences	Or, Bn, Kn, As, Ml, Gu, Mr, Pa, Hi, Ta and Te	AI4Bharat, IIT Madras, in collab with Microsoft Research	It is English centric language pairs	[22]
2	IIT-B English-Hindi Parallel Corpus	1.66 M segments	En, Hi	CFILT, IIT Bombay	It includes only two high-resource languages	[13]
3	PM India	423,750 sentences	Mr, Bn, Gu, Kn, Te, Or, Ml, Ta, Mni, As, Ur, Hi and Pa	University of Edinburg	Limited to political domain; small size	[8]
4	HindEnCorp	273.9k sentences	Hi	UFAL	Limited languages	[4]
5	EnTam	190,000 sentences	Ta	UFAL	Limited languages	[21]
6	OdiEnCorp 2.0	98,302 sentences	Or	UFAL	Limited languages	[18]
7	English-Urdu Religious Parallel Corpus	79K sentences	Ur	UFAL	Limited languages	[9]
8	EMILLE	96 Mn words	Ur, Mr, Bn, Gu, Kn, Te, Or, Ml, Ta, As, Si, Hi, Pa and Ks	Lancaster University	Limited access	[3]
9	OpenSubtitles	576.6 k sentences	Ml, Ta, Bn, Hi, Te and Ur	opensubtitles.org	Limited to High-resource languages; Informal languages thus quality of translation may vary	[14]
10	TDIL-ILCI	5 Mn sentences	Hi, Bn, Pa, Or, Gu, Mr, Kok, Ur, Ta, Te, Ml, En, As, Bodo, Kn, Ne, Mni	Ministry of Communication and Information Technology; JNU	It is Hindi Centric and covers different domains	[10]
11	WAT (Workshop on Asian Translation)	11 Mn sentence pairs	Hi, Bn, Ta, Te, etc.	Shared task	Mostly English centric pairs	[15]
12	CCAligned	17.5 Mn sentences	Hi, Bn, Ur, Ta, Mr, As, etc.	Facebook AI Research	It is English centric and supports very few low-resource languages	[6]
13	CCMatrix	4.5 Bn sentences	Bn, Hi, Ml, Mr, Ne, Or, Si, Ta, Sd, Ur	Facebook AI Research	It has translation pairs for all combinations	[24]
14	CVIT-IIITH PIB Multilingual Corpus	2.78 Mn sentences	Hi, Ta, Ml, Mr, Gu, etc.	CVIT-IIIT Hyderabad	Limited Domain and Languages	[28]
15	CVIT-IIITH Mann ki Baat Corpus	41 K sentences	Bn, Ml, Hi, Ta, Gu, Te, Mr, Or, Pa and Ur	CVIT-IIIT Hyderabad	Limited Domain and Languages	[19]
16	IndoWordNet Parallel Corpus	6.3 Mn sentences	Bn, Hi, As, Ks, Kok, Ne, Or, Bodo, Sa, Ur, Kn, Ml, Ta, Mr, Te, Meitei(Mni), Gu and Pa	CDAC, IIIT H, CIIL, JNU	It have translation pairs for all combination; synsets are used	[12]
17	Mturk Indian Parallel Corpus	583.8 k sentences	Bn, Hi, Ml, Ta, Te, Ur	John Hopkins University; University of Edinburg	It makes use of Amazon's Mechanical Turk tool for dataset collection; English centric; Limited languages	[20]
18	JW300	109 Mn sentences	Ne, Or, Bn, Kn, As, Ml, Gu, Mr, Pa, Hi, Ta, Sa, Ur and Te	University of Helsinki	Religious domain only	[1]
19	FLORES-101	3001 sentences for each language	Ne, Or, Bn, Kn, As, Ml, Gu, Mr, Pa, Hi, Ta, Sd, Ur and Te	Meta AI	Collected from Wikipedia therefore lack domain specific data	[7]
20	FLORES-200	3001 sentences for each language	Ne, Or, Bn, Kn, As, Ml, Gu, Mr, Pa, Hi, Ta, Sa, Ur, Te, Sat, Kok, Sd, Mai and Doi	Meta AI	Small size of data for training big model	[5]
21	English-Bhojpuri Parallel Corpus	65000 sentences	Bhojpuri	JNU	Limited Domain; Only one language is used	
22	WikiMatrix	135Mn sentences	Bn, Hi, Ml, Mr, Ne, Si, Ta, Te, As, Kok, Sd, Ur	Facebook AI Research in collab with LORIA	Data collected only from Wikipedia	[23]
23	TICO-19	3071 sentences	Hi, Bn, Mr, Ta, Ur	Amazon, Facebook AI, Microsoft, John Hopkins University, Google and others	Pivot language is Hindi but only few languages included	[2]
24	Global Voices	5.41 Mn sentences	Bn, Hi, Or, Ur, Ne, Pa	CASMACAT	dataset size is small; very few languages included	[16]

This is an extensive list of available dataset but not limited to this. This includes many of the low-resource Indian languages. These languages as abbreviated in the table is based on the standard ISO 639-1 and ISO 639-2 codes [17]. These abbreviations are given in the Table 2.

Table 2. Abbreviations according to ISO standards

Abbreviation	Language
En	English
Si	Sinhalese
Gu	Gujarati
Hi	Hindi
Or	Odia
Sd	Sindhi
Pa	Punjabi
Te	Telugu
Mni	Manipuri
Ur	Urdu
Mai	Maithili
Ks	Kashmiri
As	Assamese
Kok	Konkani
Doi	Dogri
Kn	Kannada
Mr	Marathi
Ta	Tamil
Ne	Nepali
Bn	Bengali
Sa	Sanskrit
Ml	Malayalam
Sat	Santali

5 Limitations

- As we can see, there are plenty of dataset available for Indian languages. But, most of the dataset is pivoted to English for translating from and to English pairing with Indian languages. For reference, Samanantar, one of the largest dataset available for Indian languages, contains the parallel translations of Indian languages paired with English only.

- Some dataset includes only single language pair or very few languages. The IIT-B English-Hindi parallel corpus, TICO-19 and UFAL dataset contains very few language, thus not preferable to build a model for multilingual translations.
- Low-resource languages are not included in any of the dataset. It is necessary to create dataset for those languages which are on the verge of extinction.

6 Conclusion and Future Scope

There is a need for creating dataset for Indian language to Indian language parallel text sentences for machine translation. The dataset may include domain specific translations also. These dataset can also be pivoted to Hindi initially and then extended to any Indian language pairs. Crowd-sourcing and community involvement is important in the creation of dataset. Role of Government funded projects for creation of dataset based on Indian languages is also impotant.

References

1. Agic, Ž., Vulic, I.: JW300: a wide-coverage parallel corpus for low-resource languages. Association for Computational Linguistics (2019)
2. Anastasopoulos, A., et al.: TICO-19: the translation initiative for COvid-19. arXiv preprint arXiv:2007.01788 (2020)
3. Baker, P., et al.: Corpus linguistics and south Asian languages: corpus creation and tool development. Lit. Linguist. Comput. **19**(4), 509–524 (2004)
4. Bojar, O., et al.: Hindencorp-Hindi-English and Hindi-only corpus for machine translation. In: LREC, pp. 3550–3555 (2014)
5. Costa-jussà, M.R., et al.: No language left behind: scaling human-centered machine translation. arXiv preprint arXiv:2207.04672 (2022)
6. El-Kishky, A., Chaudhary, V., Guzmán, F., Koehn, P.: CCAligned: a massive collection of cross-lingual web-document pairs. arXiv preprint arXiv:1911.06154 (2019)
7. Goyal, N., et al.: The FLORES-101 evaluation benchmark for low-resource and multilingual machine translation. Trans. Assoc. Comput. Linguist. **10**, 522–538 (2022)
8. Haddow, B., Kirefu, F.: PMIndia–a collection of parallel corpora of languages of India. arXiv preprint arXiv:2001.09907 (2020)
9. Jawaid, B., Kamran, A., Bojar, O.: English to Urdu statistical machine translation: establishing a baseline. In: Proceedings of the Fifth Workshop on South and Southeast Asian Natural Language Processing, pp. 37–42 (2014)
10. Jha, G.N.: The TDIL program and the Indian language corpora initiative. In: Language Resources and Evaluation Conference (2012)
11. Khurana, S., Dev, A., Bansal, P.: Current state of speech emotion dataset-national and international level. In: International Conference on Artificial Intelligence and Speech Technology, pp. 232–243. Springer (2021)
12. Kunchukuttan, A.: Indowordnet parallel (2021). https://github.com/anoopkunchukuttan/indowordnet_parallel

13. Kunchukuttan, A., Mehta, P., Bhattacharyya, P.: The IIT Bombay English-Hindi parallel corpus. arXiv preprint arXiv:1710.02855 (2017)
14. Lison, P., Tiedemann, J.: OpenSubtitles2016: extracting large parallel corpora from movie and TV subtitles (2016)
15. Nakazawa, T., et al.: Overview of the 8th workshop on Asian translation. In: Proceedings of the 8th Workshop on Asian Translation (WAT2021), pp. 1–45 (2021)
16. Nguyen, K., Daumé III, H.: Global voices: crossing borders in automatic news summarization. arXiv preprint arXiv:1910.00421 (2019)
17. Library of Congress. ISO 639-2 language codes (n.d.). https://www.loc.gov/standards/iso639-2/php/code_list.php. Accessed 22 Sept 2024
18. Parida, S., Dash, S.R., Bojar, O., Motlicek, P., Pattnaik, P., Mallick, D.K.: OdiEnCorp 2.0: Odia-English parallel corpus for machine translation. In: Proceedings of the WILDRE5–5th Workshop on Indian Language Data: Resources and Evaluation, pp. 14–19 (2020)
19. Philip, J., Siripragada, S., Namboodiri, V.P., Jawahar, C.V.: Revisiting low resource status of Indian languages in machine translation. In: Proceedings of the 3rd ACM India Joint International Conference on Data Science & Management of Data (8th ACM IKDD CODS & 26th COMAD), pp. 178–187 (2021)
20. Post, M., Callison-Burch, C., Osborne, M.: Constructing parallel corpora for six Indian languages via crowdsourcing. In Proceedings of the Seventh Workshop on Statistical Machine Translation, pp. 401–409 (2012)
21. Ramasamy, L., Bojar, O., Žabokrtský, Z.: Morphological processing for English-Tamil statistical machine translation. In: Proceedings of the Workshop on Machine Translation and Parsing in Indian Languages, pp. 113–122 (2012)
22. Ramesh, G., et al.: Samanantar: the largest publicly available parallel corpora collection for 11 Indic languages. Trans. Assoc. Comput. Linguist. **10**, 145–162 (2022)
23. Schwenk, H., Chaudhary, V., Sun, S., Gong, H., Guzmán, F.: WikiMatrix: mining 135M parallel sentences in 1620 language pairs from Wikipedia. arXiv preprint arXiv:1907.05791 (2019)
24. Schwenk, H., Wenzek, G., Edunov, S., Grave, E., Joulin, A.: CCMatrix: mining billions of high-quality parallel sentences on the web. arXiv preprint arXiv:1911.04944 (2019)
25. Sethi, N., Dev, A., Bansal, P.: A bilingual machine transliteration system for Sanskrit-English using rule-based approach. In: 2022 4th International Conference on Artificial Intelligence and Speech Technology (AIST), pp. 1–5 (2022)
26. Sethi, N., Dev, A., Bansal, P.: A novel neural machine translation approach for low-resource Sanskrit-Hindi language pair. ACM Trans. Asian Low-Resour. Lang. Inf. Processing (2023)
27. Sethi, N., Dev, A., Bansal, P.: Self-attention-based deep learning approach for machine translation of low resource languages: a case of Sanskrit-Hindi. In: Mehta, G., Wickramasinghe, N., Kakkar, D. (eds.) Innovations in VLSI, Signal Processing and Computational Technologies, pp. 85–92. Springer, Singapore (2024)
28. Siripragada, S., Philip, J., Namboodiri, V.P., Jawahar, C.V.: A multilingual parallel corpora collection effort for Indian languages. arXiv preprint arXiv:2007.07691 (2020)
29. Sitender, Bawa, S., Kumar, M., Sangeeta: A comprehensive survey on machine translation for English, Hindi and Sanskrit languages. J. Ambient Intell. Humaniz. Comput. **14**(4), 3441–3474 (2023)

30. Tiedemann, J.: Parallel data, tools and interfaces in OPUS. In: Calzolari, N., et al. (eds.) Proceedings of the Eighth International Conference on Language Resources and Evaluation (LREC 2012), Istanbul, Turkey, pp. 2214–2218. European Language Resources Association (ELRA) (2012)
31. Weaver, W.: Translation. In: Proceedings of the Conference on Mechanical Translation (1952)

Speech Summarization Diverse Challenges and Advancements

Riya Ahlawat(✉), Samriddhi Tiwari, Muskan Singh, and Shweta Jindal

Indira Gandhi Delhi Technical University for Women, Delhi, India
{riya104btcsai22,samriddhi110btcsai22}@igdtuw.ac.in

Abstract. Speech Technology is increasingly popular due to the high demands of voice-activated systems and security purposes. As the volume of speech data grows, obtaining important information becomes increasingly difficult. There comes the need to generate information-rich summaries. Even with high-effort research, the results have become stagnant over the years. The current study aims to deeply analyze the shortcomings in the available speech summarization techniques. It was found that this could be due to the homogeneous datasets, unconstrained reference summaries, structural bias in the training data, limitations of the evaluation metrics, or the papers' limited discussion of implementation specifics. After analyzing the findings from several papers, it was found that these drawbacks could be addressed by 1) limiting the "inverted pyramid" structure in the training data, 2) introducing new bias-free datasets with constrained summaries across domains and languages, 3) implementing evaluation metrics that are in line with user preferences, or 4) closely examining implementation details. This would immensely help in choosing, building, or modifying speech summarization tools in the future.

Keywords: Speech Summarization · Large Language Models · Graphs-Oriented Approaches · Datasets · Evaluation Metrics · State-of-art

1 Introduction

Speech is a predominant and widely used mode of communication among human beings [1]. It is also an irreplaceable medium for conveying requests, commands, and other information to people. The field of technology that makes it possible for machines to absorb, comprehend, and produce human speech is known as speech technology [2]. It includes a wide range of spoken language systems and applications. These days voice-activated devices and speech technologies are subjects of ongoing research due to the increasing automation of daily tasks [3, 4]. Additionally, speech technologies play a crucial role in the exchange of pertinent information between people and computers [1, 3]. Podcasts, meetings, films, and other media generate a lot of conversational speech data [4, 5]. Since processing such a large amount of data is challenging, it is preferable to create a summary to gain an overview of the content [6]. There are three different kinds of summaries: extractive, which uses sentences directly from the material, abstractive,

A. Sharma and R. Rani (Eds.): AIST 2024, CCIS 2389, pp. 187–197, 2025.
https://doi.org/10.1007/978-3-031-91331-0_14

which uses new sentences to convey the main ideas of the content, and hybrid, which combines the two [7]. There has been a lot of research on summarizing strategies, with promising findings [6–8]. Although great research efforts have been made in these summarizing strategies, the recent results have become stagnant and are not improving [7]. This creates an emergent need to go through the recent research and highlight the research gaps and opportunities.

The objective of this paper is to examine recent research and identify the research gaps that are impeding the improvement of summarization outcomes by assessing the methods, datasets, tools, comparison models, and assessment metrics. The goal is to present valuable findings that could be helpful to future research in developing state-of-the-art models for producing relevant and information-rich summaries.

The rest of the paper is structured as follows: Sect. 2 reviews relevant literature; Sect. 3 presents the data collected from several research papers in a tabular format; Sect. 4 analyzes the data and displays the results; and Sect. 5 provides the conclusion.

2 Literature Review

The evolution of text summarization from extractive to abstractive and more complex forms of text summarization has been emphasized in [6]. It highlighted how in the late 20th century, text summarization techniques were more of the extractive forms, based on extracting relevant sentences or topics from the text, followed by their collection and compilation, leading to less natural summaries. Over the years, the paper re-iterates the shift from extractive to more abstract form with the help of transformer models, allowing the model to gain a more in-depth understanding of the context from the textual content, thus allowing more coherent and fluent results.

Further another study [7] re-emphasized that the traditional extractive techniques applied rule-based or statistical models to select the most significant parts of the document based on features like word frequency or sentence position. The neural approaches to extractive summarizations treated summarization problems more like classification problems at word or sentence levels, using RNNs to predict whether the sentences should be included in the summary or not [8]. More advanced methods incorporated reinforcement learning to optimize the summarization problems on specific objectives like relevance or fluency. Furthermore, a literature survey [7] showed that the abstractive models were initially built on sequence-to-sequence architectures and attention mechanisms, and later integrated pointer-generator networks. It also discussed the hybrid models combining elements of both extractive and abstractive models. This study highlighted the challenges identified in neural summarization including the noisy datasets. In addition, the layout bias limits the generalizability of models by overfitting the models on these datasets which follow the inverted pyramid structure. Thus, the critical information tended to occupy the first few sentences.

Another study [9] highlighted the challenges involved in tackling the summarization of long dialogues from real-world scenarios. It evaluated approaches using three long-dialogue datasets—QMSum (meetings), MediaSum (interviews), and SummScreen (TV series). Three major strategies include firstly, the extended transformer technique which involves the incorporation of sliding windows and global attention. Secondly, retrieve-then-summarize pipeline models that retrieve the relevant utterances from a dialogue and then summarize them. After testing different retrieval methods such as TF-IDF, BM25, and Locator (BERT-based retriever), the authors concluded that retrieval-based approaches outperform simple truncation methods like those used in traditional transformer models. Finally, the third strategy used was Hierarchal Models. It structures dialogue encoding at multiple levels to better capture the sparse and context-dependent nature of conversations.

The current research incorporates an in-depth analysis of the various summarization techniques and considers the challenges they involve along with the technique or optimization mechanism they use. Furthermore, the major aim of the current study is to provide a comprehensive view of the research work that has been done in the field of summarization and to give details on the key datasets and evaluation metrics that have been used by different studies over the years.

3 Data Collection

This section presents the data collected from several research publications on summarization tasks. 26 studies were found relevant after applying title-based, abstract-based, and text-based inclusion and exclusion criteria. The details collected from these 26 studies have been tabulated in Table 1.

Table 1. A Comprehensive Overview of Techniques, Datasets, Tools, and Comparative Models in Summarization Tasks Across Different Research Papers

S. No	Year	Ref. No	Technique	Dataset	Tools	Comparison
1	2019	[10]	Modified BERT using Trigram Blocking, Gradient Accumulation, Beam Search, and Subwords Tokenizer	CNN/Daily Mail, NYT, XSum	PyTorch, OpenNMT, GTX 1080Ti GPUs	Oracle, Lead-3, SummaRuNNer, Refresh, Latent, NeuSum, Sumo, TransformerExt, PTGen, PTGen+Cov, DRM, BottomUp, DCA, TransformerAbs
2	2021	[11]	Proposed Neural Abstractive Text Summarizer (NATS) toolkit	CNN/Daily Mail, Newsroom, Bytecup	PyTorch 1.0, CUDA, PyROUGE, ROUGE-1.5.5, glob, argparse, and shutil	NATS Models
3	2021	[12]	Media Interview Dataset with abstractive summaries	AMI, ICSI, SAMSum	PyTorch, Adagrad optimizer, Adam optimizer, V100 GPUs	LEAD-3, PTGen, UniLM, BART
4	2024	[13]	Finetuning Baichuan2-7B LLM for dialogue summarization using NEFTune technique	CSDS, SAMSum	Hugging Face Website, PEFT library, Adam Optimizer, RTX 4090 GPU	PGN, BERT, BART, BART-GLC

(continued)

Table 1. *(continued)*

S. No	Year	Ref. No	Technique	Dataset	Tools	Comparison
5	2020	[14]	Proposed Topic-word Guided Dialogue Graph Attention (TGDGA) network	SAMSum, Automobile Master Corpus	Adam optimizer	Longest-3, Seq2Seq+Attention, Transformer, LightConv, DynamicConv, Pointer Generator, Fast Abs RL, Fast Abs RL Enhanced
6	2020	[15]	Proposed multi-view sequence-to-sequence model initialized with BART	SAMSum	PyTorch $\geq$ 1.3.0, Pandas, NumPy, Pickle, Rouge, Fairseq, sentence _transformers	Pointer Generator, DynamicConv+GPT-2/News, Fast Abs RL Enhanced, BART+Generic views
7	2020	[16]	Proposed Hybrid Text Summarization and Simplification (HTSS) - extended pointer generator model	Science News Website – Eureka Alert	PyTorch, Linux, Titan 1080 GPUs	Neural Text Simplification (NTS), Abstractive Text Summarization (ATS)
8*	2007	[17]	Maximized the number of informative content words in multi-document summaries	DUC 2004, MSE 2005	(Not mentioned)	SumBasic models – basic-inter, basic-train, basic-pos, basic-freq, basic-train-sim, basic-freq-sim; peer65, greedyline
9	2018	[18]	WikiHow: a dataset of more than 230,000 article and summary pairs	CNN/DailyMail	Python Scrapy, PyRouge package	TextRank, Seq-to-Seq with attention, Pointer-generator, Pointer-generator+coverage, Lead3 baseline
10*	2022	[19]	The approach solely uses lemmatization and POS tagging to create a document graph; and iteratively applies the centrality algorithm	PubMed, arXiv	NLTK	LSA, SumBasic, LexRank
11	2021	[20]	DialoGPT for labeling 3 types of features - keyword extraction, redundancy detection, and topic segmentation	SAMSum, AMI	PyTorch, CUDA, HuggingFace, OpenNMT, Py-Rouge,	LONGEST-3, TextRank, Transformer, D-HGN, TGDGA, DialogGPT, MV-BART, SummaRunner, UNS, TopicSeg, HMNet
12*	2024	[21]	Proposed an LLM-based approach with a role-oriented routing and fusion generation to utilize mixture of experts (MoE)	DialogSum, SAMSum, CSDS, MC	(Not mentioned)	LLaMA-2, Ziya, See et al., Chen and Bansal, Liu and Lapata, Zou et al., Liang et al. (2022 & 2023), Song et al., Lin et al
13*	2018	[22]	Segmented decoder responsibilities into two and refined the *n*-gram overlap for better abstraction	CNN/Daily Mail	(Not mentioned)	ML-RL, intra-attn, Pointer-gen+coverage, SumGAN, RSal, RSal+Ent RL, ML+RL ROUGE+Novel with LM
14	2021	[23]	HEPOS, an effective encoder-decoder attention with head-wise positional strides	GovReport, PubMed	PyTorch, Fairseq, Adafactor optimizer, Quadro RTX 6000 GPUs with 24GB memory, Quadro RTX 8000 with 48GB memory	PEGASUS, TLM, SEAL, DANCER, BigBird, and FULL, STRIDE, LIN, LSH, Sinkhorn, and LSH-Hepos, Sinkhorn-Hepos

(continued)

Table 1. (*continued*)

S. No	Year	Ref. No	Technique	Dataset	Tools	Comparison
15*	2024	[24]	Symbolic knowledge distillation technique on small pre-trained models	SAMSum, DialogSum	(Not mentioned)	BART, PEGASUS, Flan-T5
16*	2022	[25]	Contrastive fine-tuning or CONFIT	SAMSum, AMI Meeting Corpus	(Not mentioned)	BART, BART-ConFiT, Pegasus, Pegasus-ConFiT, T5, T5-ConFiT
17	2021	[9]	Longformer with retrieve-then-summarize pipeline and hierarchical dialogue encoding	QMSum, MediaSum, SummScreen, CNN/Dailymail, XSum, SAMSum	RTX 8000 GPU with 48GiB of GPU memory, fairseq, PyRouge	BART, HMNet, Longformer
18*	2020	[26]	Proposed an unsupervised sentence summarization approach consisting of language modeling and semantic similarity metrics	DUC2004 and Gigaword	(Not Mentioned)	Lead-C-75, SEQ3, Topiary, BottleSum Ex, HC_article_13, HC_title_13, HC_title+twitter_13
19	2021	[27]	Proposed ConDigSum: two topic-aware contrastive learning objective models for abstractive dialogue summarization	SAMSum, MediaSum	Fairseq, Adam Optimizer	Lead3, PTGen, UniLM, BART, ConDigSum
20*	2021	[28]	Worked on a combination of techniques to solve challenges in summarization	SAMSum	(Not mentioned)	BART, Multi-view SS
21	2022	[29]	Introduced model-level faithfulness analysis technique	SAMSum	NLTK, NumPy, PyTorch	BART-LDT, T5-LDT, BART-MDT, T5-MDT
22	2022	[30]	ReWriteSum: a model that completes ellipsis content and takes care of the co-reference information	SAMSum, DialogSum	PyTorch, Tesla V100 GPU	Lead3, PTGen, DynamicConv+GPT2, FastAbs-RL, DynamicCov+News, Multiview BART, BART(large), ReWriteSum
23	2022	[31]	Proposed a pre-training framework for improving long text summarizations	MediaSum, OpenSubtitles, AMI, ICSI, QMSum, ForeverDreaming, TVMegaSite	A100 GPUs with 40GB memory	UNILM-CP, Longformer, BART, HAT-BART, HMNET, DDAMS, Hybrid Model
24	2022	[32]	Presents FACTPEGASUS: a fine-tuned version of the PEGASUS model; addresses the problem of factuality during pre-training and finetuning	XSum, WikiHow, Gigaword	Transformers library	BART, PEGASUS, DEP-Entail, CLIFF
25*	2023	[33]	Proposed a new paradigm for news summary generation using LLMs	PENS	(Not Mentioned)	TFIDF TextRank Gpt2 GLM GLM+NSG
26	2024	[34]	Proposed instruction fine-tuning for summarization (KEIT-Sum)	CNN/Daily Mail, DialogSUM	Flair	BART, T5, PEGASUS, and BRIO

In Table 1, the studies that provided less to no information regarding tools used in the implementation are marked with an asterisk (*). Various evaluation metrics employed across all the implementations discussed in this study are – ROUGE (ROUGE-1, ROUGE-2, ROUGE-L, ROUGE-SU4), BLEU, BERTScore, SARI, CSS_1 – combined form of SARI and ROUGE [16],METEOR, MoverScore, Novel n-gram, UniEval, AlignScore, G-Eval, BARTScore, FactCC, Token error, and Sentence error.

Three kinds of problems [7] with the current summarization system were –

a) Data collected with web crawlers on the internet have poor quality unconstrained summaries that leave out important information.
b) Most models are pre-trained with news-related datasets adding the bias of "inverted pyramid" summaries in the generated outputs.
c) Automatic evaluation metrics like ROUGE, BLEU, etc. are not completely fit for evaluation purposes – weakly correlated with human judgment.

4 Analyzing the Data

A thorough analysis of the information gathered in Table 1 yields several insightful discoveries about the techniques, tools, datasets, and evaluation metrics that are frequently employed in summarizing research.

4.1 Techniques Used

In total, 5 major model categories have been employed to analyze 26 implementations. Figure 1 depicts the classification of each technique used in 26 studies. The Transformers or Large Language Models (LLMs) are most used and are applied in 69.2% of the implementations. Graph-based models, Optimization models, and Heuristic/Rule-based models are each employed in 7.7% of the total implementations, while Rewrite-based models are used in only 3.8% of implementations.

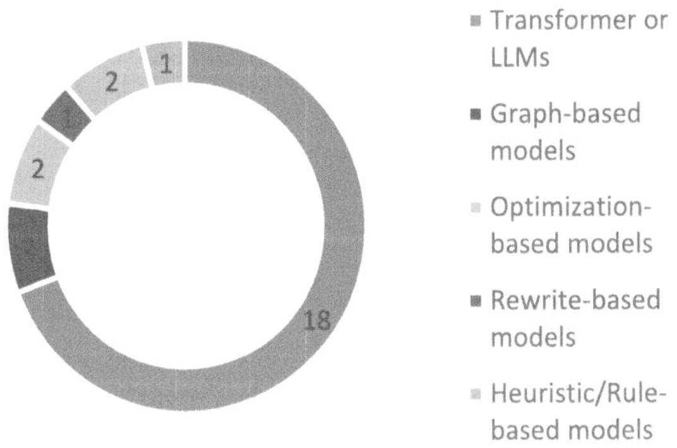

Fig. 1. Techniques used for Speech Summarization in the 26 studies

4.2 Datasets Used

There were 27 datasets altogether across the 26 implementations. Figure 2 shows the frequency of the datasets used. In Fig. 2, the 'Others' category comprises 16 datasets (Newsroom, ByteCup, Automobile Master Corpus, MSE 2005, etc.), each with a single frequency. SAMSum is the most widely used dataset acquired in 46.15% of the papers, followed by CNN/DailyMail in 23.07%, and DialogSum in 15,38%. 34.61% of the datasets are dialogue-based, 34.61% news-related, 7.69% scientific/academic papers based, and 26.92% mixed/others. 92.30% of the datasets are primarily English, 7.69% are Chinese.

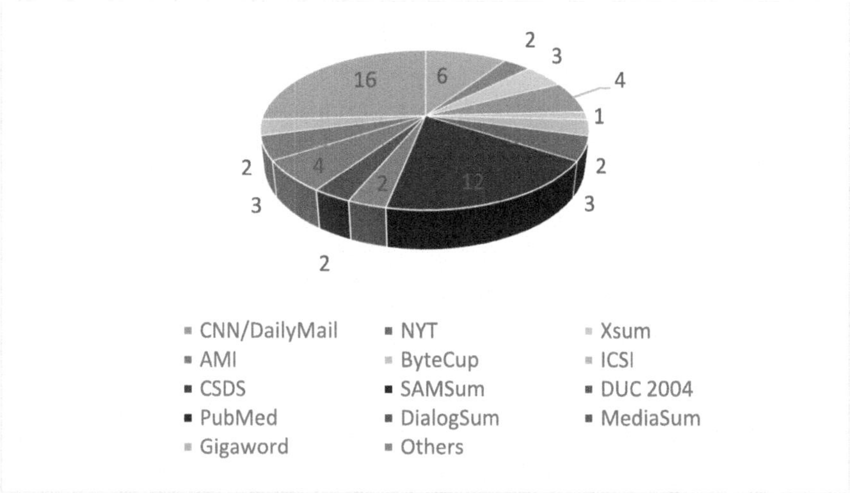

Fig. 2. Frequency of Datasets Across the 26 Implementations

4.3 Tools Utilized

In total, 23 different tools – all the GPUs counted as one, are used across 26 implementations (except the ones that didn't provide any data on tools used – 38.46%). Figure 3 depicts the frequency of each tool usage across all the papers. PyTorch is the most used with 30.76%, followed by GPUs with 26.92%, and Adam Optimizer with 19.23%. GPUs employed are – GTX 1080Ti, V100, A100, Titan 1080, RTX 4090, Quadro RTX 6000, Quadro RTX 8000.

4.4 Evaluation Metrics

A total of 18 evaluation metrics are employed across the 26 research papers presented in Table 1. From Fig. 4, 96.1% applied the ROUGE-2 metric making it the primarily used metric. ROUGE-1 and ROUGE-L are the second most used metrics with appearance in 92.3% of the papers. 15.4% of the papers used BLEU and BERTScore for evaluation

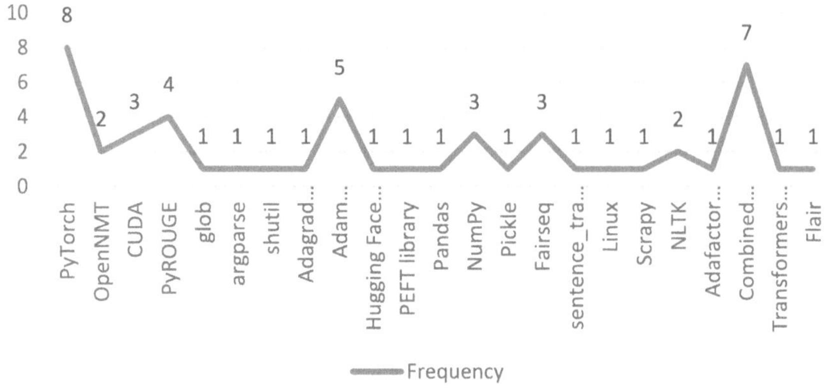

Fig. 3. Overview of Tools Acquired Across the 26 Summarization Implementations

purposes. The UniEval metric was only used by 7.7% of the total papers analyzed. The rest of the evaluation metrics have only a single frequency across all the papers.

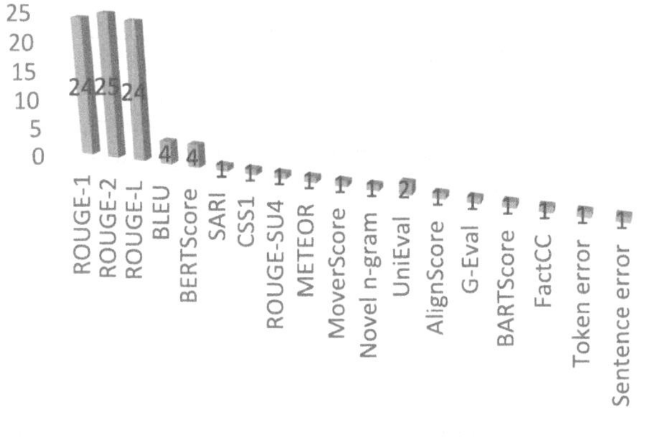

Fig. 4. Summary of Evaluation Metrics Employed in Summarization Research

The results suggest that transformers/large language models (LLMs) are the most often used technology (69.7%) nowadays. Additionally, Graph-based strategies (7.7%) also yield effective results with fewer training resources and a streamlined process. 92.30% of datasets being primarily in English raises the demands to generate multilingual datasets to capture essence in summaries across different languages. 34.61% of datasets are news-related and responsible for incorporating the bias of "inverted pyramid" summaries into the generated outputs, especially when used in pre-training. Papers that do not include implementation details (38.46%) drastically cut down on the amount of information they convey and, as a result, do not make significant contributions to the advancement of summarization research. Nowadays, PyTorch (30.76%), GPUs

(26.92%), and Adam Optimizers (26.92%) are widely used tools in speech summarization tasks. On the other hand, widely used evaluation tools like ROUGE (96.1%) and BLEU (15.4%) focus solely on token overlaps and neglect to grade summaries according to human-aligned attributes like relevance, coverage, and fluency.

5 Conclusion

This study achieved an analysis of 26 summarization implementations. The experimentation reveals key takeaways from the predominant techniques, datasets, tools, and evaluation metrics used in the field of summarizations. Transformer-based models and LLMs dominate the summarization domain accounting for more than 69% of the total implementations thus highlighting their effectiveness and robustness. Although their approaches might vary and are explored, their usage majorly remains relatively the same. Datasets mostly used show a concentration around a few dominant sources such as SAMSum (46.15%) and CNN/DailyMail (23.07%), with a significant portion being dialogue-based or news-related. This over-reliance on English datasets (92.3%) underscores the need for more multilingual datasets to support research in non-English contexts and ensure the broader applicability of summarization models.

Evaluation metrics were largely focused on ROUGE, with 96.1% of the papers using ROUGE-2. While metrics like BLEU and BERTScore were also employed, the reliance on token overlap measures presents a limitation. These metrics fail to account for more nuanced, human-centric attributes of summarization such as fluency, relevance, and coverage, suggesting the need for more sophisticated evaluation methodologies in future research.

This research's future scope involves directing towards the development of more reliable summarization techniques that can summarize multilingual content and are not influenced by inverted pyramid bias. Additionally, evaluation measures that go beyond token overlap counts are required to effectively capture summary quality. Furthermore, encouraging restricted summaries that follow certain rules will ensure that created material adequately meets user needs. While researchers should exercise caution when using web crawlers to prevent over-reliance on unconstrained content, increasing transparency in implementation details can help create more structured educational research by promoting peer collaboration and knowledge exchange.

Addressing these issues will enable us to diversify the applicability of various summarization tools in the field of speech technology toward a more interconnected world, where multilingual and multicultural aspects no longer act as barriers.

References

1. Gaikwad, S.K., Gawali, B.W., Yannawar, P.: A review on speech recognition technique. Int. J. Comput. Appl. **10**, 16–24 (2010)
2. Juang, B.H., Rabiner, L.R.: Automatic speech recognition–a brief history of the technology development. Georgia Institute of Technology. Atlanta Rutgers University and the University of California. Santa Barbara, vol. 1, p. 1 (2005)
3. Anusuya, M.A., Katti, S.K.: Speech recognition by machine, a review. arXiv preprint arXiv: 1001.2267 (2010)

4. Wang, J.: Essumm: extractive speech summarization from untranscribed meeting. arXiv preprint arXiv:2209.06913 (2022)
5. Hu, Y., Ganter, T., Deilamsalehy, H., Dernoncourt, F., Foroosh, H., Liu, F.: MeetingBank: a benchmark dataset for meeting summarization. arXiv preprint arXiv:2305.17529 (2023)
6. Allahyari, M., Pouriyeh, S., Assefi, M., Safaei, S., Trippe, E.D., Gutierrez, J.B., Kochut, K.: Text summarization techniques: a brief survey. arXiv preprint arXiv:1707.02268 (2017)
7. Kryściński, W., Keskar, N.S., McCann, B., Xiong, C., Socher, R.: Neural text summarization: a critical evaluation. arXiv preprint arXiv:1908.08960 (2019)
8. Nenkova, A., McKeown, K.: A survey of text summarization techniques. Min. Text Data 43–76 (2012)
9. Zhang, Y., et al.: An exploratory study on long dialogue summarization: what works and what's next. arXiv preprint arXiv:2109.04609 (2021)
10. Liu, Y., Lapata, M.: Text summarization with pretrained encoders. arXiv preprint arXiv:1908.08345 (2019)
11. Shi, T., Keneshloo, Y., Ramakrishnan, N., Reddy, C.K.: Neural abstractive text summarization with sequence-to-sequence models. ACM Trans. Data Sci. **2**, 1–37 (2021)
12. Zhu, C., Liu, Y., Mei, J., Zeng, M.: MediaSum: a large-scale media interview dataset for dialogue summarization. arXiv preprint arXiv:2103.06410 (2021)
13. Xiao, J., Chen, Y., Ou, Y., Yu, H., Shu, K., Xiao, Y.: Baichuan2-sum: instruction finetune baichuan2-7B model for dialogue summarization. In: 2024 International Joint Conference on Neural Networks (IJCNN), pp. 1–8. IEEE (2024)
14. Zhao, L., Xu, W., Guo, J.: Improving abstractive dialogue summarization with graph structures and topic words. In: Proceedings of the 28th International Conference on Computational Linguistics, pp. 437–449 (2020)
15. Chen, J., Yang, D.: Multi-view sequence-to-sequence models with conversational structure for abstractive dialogue summarization. arXiv preprint arXiv:2010.01672 (2020)
16. Zaman, F., Shardlow, M., Hassan, S.-U., Aljohani, N.R., Nawaz, R.: HTSS: a novel hybrid text summarisation and simplification architecture. Inf. Process. Manag. **57**, 102351 (2020)
17. Yih, W., Goodman, J., Vanderwende, L., Suzuki, H.: Multi-document summarization by maximizing informative content-words. In: IJCAI, vol. 7, pp. 1776–1782. Citeseer (2007)
18. Koupaee, M., Wang, W.Y.: Wikihow: a large scale text summarization dataset. arXiv preprint arXiv:1810.09305 (2018)
19. Brock, D., Khan, A., Doan, T., Lin, A., Guo, Y., Tarau, P.: Textstar: a fast and lightweight graph-based algorithm for extractive summarization and keyphrase extraction. In: Proceedings of the 20th Annual Workshop of the Australasian Language Technology Association, pp. 161–169 (2022)
20. Feng, X., Feng, X., Qin, L., Qin, B., Liu, T.: Language model as an annotator: exploring DialoGPT for dialogue summarization. arXiv preprint arXiv:2105.12544 (2021)
21. Tian, Y., Xia, F., Song, Y.: Dialogue summarization with mixture of experts based on large language models. In: Proceedings of the 62nd Annual Meeting of the Association for Computational Linguistics (Volume 1: Long Papers), pp. 7143–7155 (2024)
22. Kryściński, W., Paulus, R., Xiong, C., Socher, R.: Improving abstraction in text summarization. arXiv preprint arXiv:1808.07913 (2018)
23. Huang, L., Cao, S., Parulian, N., Ji, H., Wang, L.: Efficient attentions for long document summarization. arXiv preprint arXiv:2104.02112 (2021)
24. Zhu, R., Lau, J.H., Qi, J.: Factual dialogue summarization via learning from large language models. arXiv preprint arXiv:2406.14709 (2024)
25. Tang, X., et al.: CONFIT: toward faithful dialogue summarization with linguistically-informed contrastive fine-tuning. arXiv preprint arXiv:2112.08713 (2021)

26. Schumann, R., Mou, L., Lu, Y., Vechtomova, O., Markert, K.: Discrete optimization for unsupervised sentence summarization with word-level extraction. arXiv preprint arXiv:2005.01791 (2020)
27. Liu, J., et al.: Topic-aware contrastive learning for abstractive dialogue summarization. arXiv preprint arXiv:2109.04994 (2021)
28. Khalifa, M., Ballesteros, M., McKeown, K.: A bag of tricks for dialogue summarization. arXiv preprint arXiv:2109.08232 (2021)
29. Wang, B., Zhang, C., Zhang, Y., Chen, Y., Li, H.: Analyzing and evaluating faithfulness in dialogue summarization. arXiv preprint arXiv:2210.11777 (2022)
30. Fang, Y., et al.: From spoken dialogue to formal summary: an utterance rewriting for dialogue summarization. In: Proceedings of the 2022 Conference of the North American Chapter of the Association for Computational Linguistics: Human Language Technologies, pp. 3859–3869 (2022)
31. Zhong, M., Liu, Y., Xu, Y., Zhu, C., Zeng, M.: Dialoglm: pre-trained model for long dialogue understanding and summarization. In: Proceedings of the AAAI Conference on Artificial Intelligence, vol. 36, pp. 11765–11773 (2022)
32. Wan, D., Bansal, M.: FactPEGASUS: factuality-aware pre-training and fine-tuning for abstractive summarization. arXiv preprint arXiv:2205.07830 (2022)
33. Xiao, L., Chen, X.: Enhancing LLM with evolutionary fine tuning for news summary generation. arXiv preprint arXiv:2307.02839 (2023)
34. Ryu, S., Do, H., Kim, Y., Lee, G.G., Ok, J.: Key-element-informed sLLM tuning for document summarization. arXiv preprint arXiv:2406.04625 (2024)

Emerging Trends in Speech Processing

Identifying Disaster-Related Tweets Using Natural Language Processing and Core Machine Learning Algorithms

Aditi Mehta[1], Arshiya Garg[1], Ritu Rani[2(✉)], Garima Jaiswal[3], and Arun Sharma[1]

[1] Indira Gandhi Delhi Technical University for Women, Delhi, India
{aditi005btit23,arshiya014btit23,arunsharma}@igdtuw.ac.in
[2] Bhagwan Parshuram Institute of Technology, Delhi, India
riturani@bpitindia.com
[3] Bennett University, Noida, India
garima121@gmail.com

Abstract. In today's digital era, social media platforms like Twitter are used by people across the globe to share information and updates, such platforms serve as crucial means of communication especially during emergencies. However, the most prominent challenge faced by authorities is the large volume of data and the consequent complexity of extracting crucial information from it. This research aims at finding an optimal solution to tackle the stated problem. The authors used machine learning approaches, such as Naive Bayes and Support Vector Machines (SVM), to identify tweets that needed to be addressed right away. The models used for final evaluation were trained using a dataset of about 8,000 tweets out of which just 3,229 were analyzed to be disaster related. The goal is to accelerate information flow and enable authorities to react to urgent needs more rapidly and efficiently by precisely recognizing these tweets. This method helps with better resource distribution and faster action during emergencies by not just speeding up disaster response but also ensuring that important information isn't lost in the shuffle. The results of this research indicate that SVM (Support Vector Machine) performs better, which makes it a preferable option for catastrophe prediction based on tweets.

Keywords: Natural Language Processing · disaster · twitter · SVM · tweet classification · social media analysis

1 Introduction

In today's interconnected world, social media platforms have become a web of information, with data being shared in millions of terabytes every single second. The data becomes extremely crucial in times of disaster and mayhem for identifying where help is needed. Today's generation prefers to whip out their phones and share a tweet rather than using more traditional forms of communicating danger, which can often be unavailable. X, formerly known as Twitter, is known in the social media market for its speed and

A. Sharma and R. Rani (Eds.): AIST 2024, CCIS 2389, pp. 201–214, 2025.
https://doi.org/10.1007/978-3-031-91331-0_15

wide reach. It is particularly important when emergencies occur because of the political position it holds in the social media market. People use it to share immediate updates from the ground, whereas authorities use it to provide important information. The public uses it to coordinate responses. As far-fetched as it sounds, in many cases, the power of social media has helped people receive help when disaster has struck. The ability to quickly share and receive information on Twitter makes it a very useful tool during disasters, especially when traditional communication methods might be compromised. However, the large volume of tweets during such events presents a huge challenge: how to quickly and accurately identify tweets that truly matter. Not every tweet during a disaster is useful—many are just everyday chitchat or misleading information and rumors. But when lives are at stake, it's important to filter out the noise and focus on the tweets that provide real, actionable information. Misidentifying a tweet as important or delving into misleading information when time is a crucial resource can cost lives. Overlooking an important message could mean delays in response and wasted resources in the wrong direction. The unstructured nature of tweets during such events can pose significant challenges for accurate analysis. To tackle the challenge of accurately identifying important information during disasters, this research focused on developing a machine learning model specifically designed to distinguish disaster-related tweets from general, non-disaster content by identifying specific keywords like fire, drought, bomb, etc. NLP [1] techniques helped the authors convert raw text into structured and meaningful data that machine learning models can understand. This involves cleaning and preprocessing tweets and context analysis, which helps in the classification of tweets. Objective is to develop models that can accurately classify tweets as disaster-related or not. Such predictions are very important for emergency response teams, news organizations, and the public, enabling quicker detection and more effective management of disaster situations. Using a dataset of approximately 8,000 pre-labelled tweets from Kaggle [2], the authors trained the model using two popular core ML algorithms: Support Vector Machine (SVM) and Bernoulli Naive Bayes. The aim of this project is to create a model that can filter through large amounts of data, highlighting the tweets that need immediate attention. This ability to classify tweets accurately and ignore misleading information is extremely crucial for effective disaster management.

1.1 Objective of the Paper

- This research paper aims to conduct a thorough study of existing research done on the identification and classification of disaster-related tweets using natural language processing (NLP) and core machine learning techniques.
- The authors have reviewed the current achievements and advancements made in this domain, identifying the strengths and limitations of current approaches and further analyzing the past approaches made.
- Building upon this foundation, we have trained several models using Support Vector Machines (SVM) [3] and Naive Bayes classifiers [4] and based on the findings and results of these trainings and testing, we hereby propose a more efficient and accurate solution.

- This proposed method is designed to be integrated into social media platforms to enhance disaster management efforts, ensuring that timely assistance reaches those in need through improved detection and classification of disaster-related tweets.

2 Literature Review

Today social media is widely popular all across the globe, it allows people to interact and connect with each other form any part of the world. It also serves as a crucial means of communication specially during times of disaster when orthodox channels are shut but the challenge is to filter through such large volume of tweets and determine which ones provide useful information. This article reviews previous work done to improve the identification and classification of disaster tweets using natural language processing techniques combined with machine learning methods. A 2015 benchmark study [5] showed the potential of Twitter as an important communication tool during disasters. This study highlighted that large volume of data is a major challenge faced by authorities to distinguish disaster related tweets from irrelevant ones. This study opened the opportunity to develop natural language processing and machine learning algorithms to automate the extraction of disaster tweets from social media. Another 2018 study [6] showed the importance of combining geospatial data with social media observations. The analysis highlighted the importance of extracting geographic information from disaster tweets to better understand the spatial dynamics of crises and thus facilitate the effective allocation of resources. A hybrid model was proposed that combines the thermal frequency and the inverse frequency of the document (TF-IDF) and the formulation of the article until 2021 [7]. The new methodology well illustrates the benefits of combining multiple representation strategies to effectively improve classification accuracy in a concise and ambiguous context as represented by tweets. Overall, this study validates the strategy of using a number of different approaches to improve the classification performance of disaster tweets. A system capable of recognizing disasters in 2017 [8] showed the potential of Twitter to convert into a real-time early warning system with data analytics. These results highlight the need for the detection and classification of appropriate and timely tweets in disaster management, which makes this research particularly important. Finally, topic modelling [9] revealed key points for using unsupervised learning in analysing trends in large data sets. This demonstration showed that the topic model is useful for influencing textual data mining, especially in terms of understanding public sentiment and information flow during alert events. In conclusion, published research already shows how ML or NLP [10, 11] are useful and therefore it is difficult to manually improve the selection of disaster tweets. One of the main areas on which this research focuses is more personalising these techniques and learning from the studies [13, 14] for better disaster management technology.

3 Methodology

To develop an efficient text classification system, the authors ensured proper planning, execution and repetitive optimization. From preprocessing to model training and evaluation, a well-structured approach is used throughout the model training. This section elaborates the steps and requirements to develop the models focusing on systematic planning and approach.

3.1 Primary Working

This approach focused on integrating natural language processing [1] techniques with supervised learning models like SVM and Naive Bayes to develop a system capable of classifying tweets that are related to disaster situations and those that are not. The Fig. 6 illustrates the methodology followed.

3.2 Data Collection

The authors utilised a pre-labeled dataset from Kaggle [2], which had approximately 8,000 English-language tweets. These tweets were pre-classified into two classes: disaster-related and non-disaster-related messages. The dataset's key features consisted of the tweet text, corresponding keyword, location data, and the associated classification label.

3.3 Data Cleaning/Pre-processing

It is important to clean the data particularly when NLP is used. To enhance the quality and reliability of text data, the authors applied several preprocessing techniques to reduce noise. Non-alphabetic characters were systematically removed using the Python re library. Then utilised the nltk.corpus [1] library to eliminate stop words, which are frequently occurring terms that contribute very less to the meaning of a sentence. Lemmatization, conducted via the nltk.stem module, was employed to reduce words to their base form, standardising the dataset. Non-dictionary words were filtered out using the nltk.corpus library, ensuring that the text data retained only meaningful content. These preprocessing steps were important to prepare the dataset.

3.4 Data Visualization

Data visualisation is a crucial part of model training, through Exploratory Data Analysis [15] gaining valuable insights regarding the nature and key features of the data, providing help in model selection processes. The key steps in data visualisation process included:

3.5 Exploratory Data Analysis (EDA)

The authors began by studying the distribution of disaster-related and non-disaster-related tweets to understand the balance of classes in the dataset using matplotlib.pyplot. This analysis helped to identify any class imbalances that could impact model performance. The Fig. 1 shows the frequency distribution of tweets across different classes.

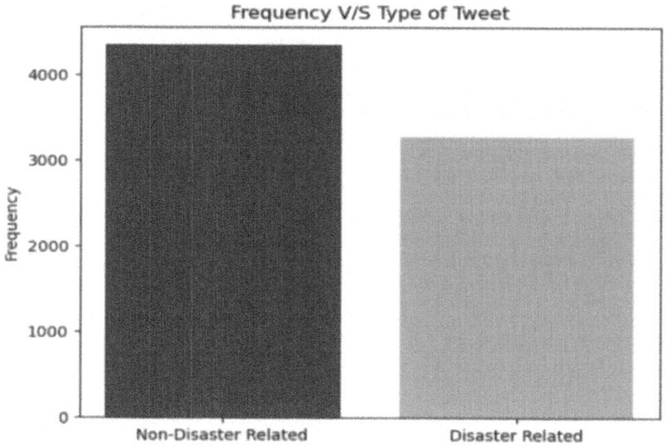

Fig. 1. Frequency distribution of tweets across different classes

3.6 Word Frequency Analysis

Top Words Visualisation-Selecting the most frequent top 20 words in text message of each class using Counter library and visualised the result by plotting bar plot using seaborn, helping to identify key terms that distinguish disaster-related tweets from non-disaster ones. The Fig. 2 and Fig. 3 show the top 20 words for disaster related and non-disaster related tweets respectively.

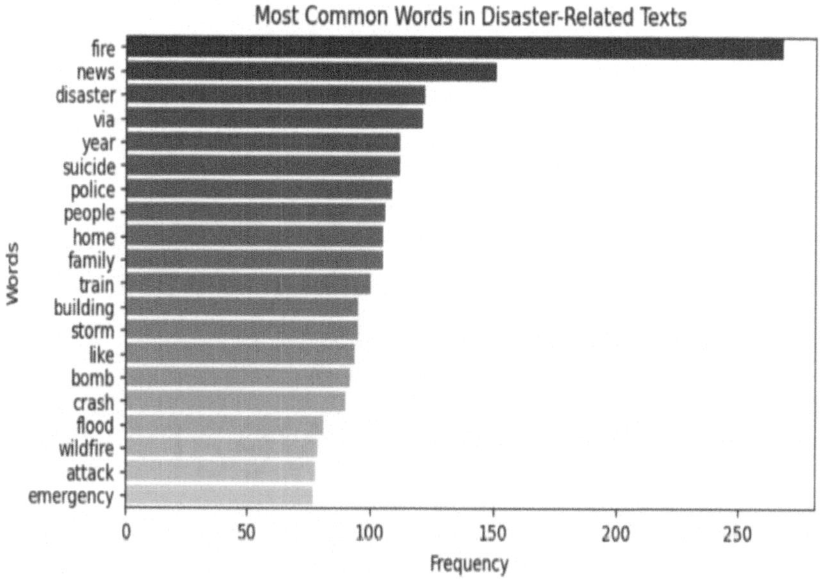

Fig. 2. Top 20 words in disaster related tweets

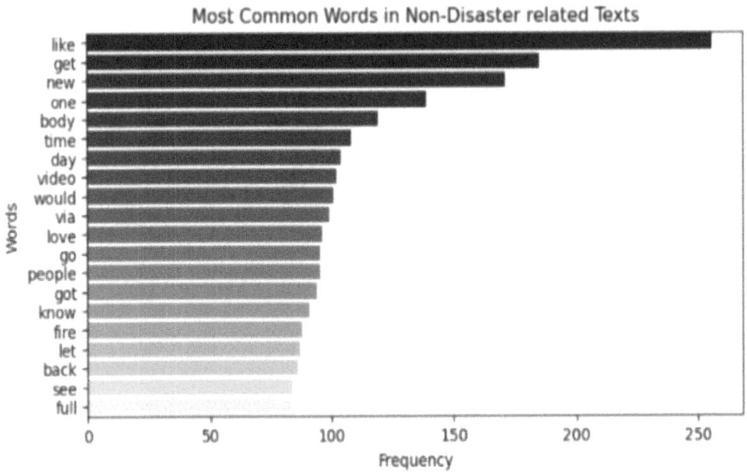

Fig. 3. Top 20 words in non-disaster related tweets

3.7 Word Clouds

Class-Specific Word Clouds - Separate word clouds were created for each class using Word Cloud library, allowing to compare and contrast the key terms associated with disaster-related and non-disaster-related tweets. This visualisation helps quickly identify dominant themes in each category. The Fig. 4 and Fig. 5 illustrate the word cloud obtained from disaster related and non-disaster related tweets respectively.

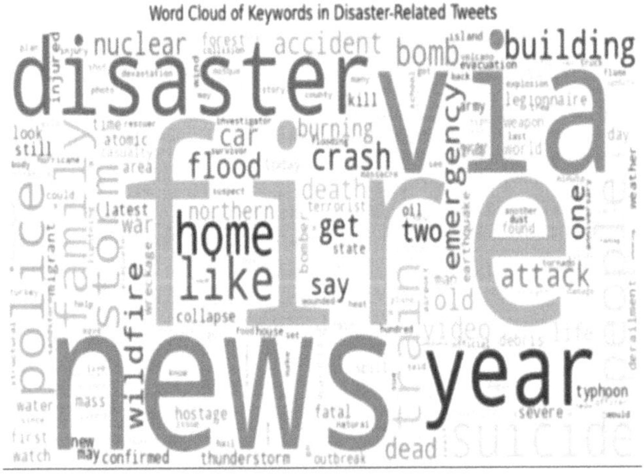

Fig. 4. Word cloud illustrating the most prominent words found in tweets classified as disaster related. The size of each word reflects its frequency in the dataset.

Fig. 5. Word cloud illustrating the most prominent words found in tweets classified as non-disaster related. The size of each word reflects its frequency in the dataset.

3.8 Technologies Used for Text Processing

3.8.1 TF-IDF

This [11, 12] method that is often used in Natural Language Processing to extract words from a text. Term frequency(TF) counts the number of times that word occurs in a tweet (and therefore its worthiness towards interpretation there). Whereas the inverse document frequency(IDF) estimates which words are more unique to all of the tweet data. The importance of word terms is reflected in their IDF score, where common words like "the" or "is" get low scores but less frequent yet meaningful phrases such as earthquake and void have high scores. Taking into account the original and global frequency of a word in tweets, together with these components TF-IDF system generates a score on how significant this word is.

3.8.2 CountVectorizer

It is the most commonly used natural language processing technique [12]. It requires converting text to number. Split the textbook to individual words or sentences and add up occurrences of each word. This will give you a matrix consisting of rows that are separate tweets and columns corresponding to the unique words contained in all your datasets which for each tweet, it is represented as 1 if it contains this word or zero for others. This method looks for common words to tag it as disaster orders or non-disaster and classifies it into patterns.

3.9 Model Training

3.9.1 Bernoulli Naive Bayes (BernoulliNB)

It (BNB) [4] is popularly used for binary classification of data making a great choice to be used in classifying textual data. BNB works by analysing whether specific words are present or absent in a tweet and uses this information to predict the probability of the tweet belonging to different classes. It calculates the likelihood of a tweet being either disaster-related or non-disaster related for estimation during classification. At last the tweet is classified into the category with the highest value of probability. BNB is particularly preferred for processing large datasets because of its straightforward and effective implementation, enabling rapid classification of tweets into disaster or non-disaster categories.

3.9.2 SVM (Support Vector Machine)

It (SVM) [3] is a popular supervised learning algorithm that can be effectively used in both classification and regression tasks. SVM is highly accurate when dealing with high dimensional dataset, the algorithm works by identifying an optimal hyperplane that separates data into different classes, making it particularly suitable for distinguishing tweets into disaster-related or non-disaster categories. SVM emphasises on support vectors which helps to prevent overfitting, a common issue where the model performs well on training data but poorly on new, unseen data, this characteristic is particularly useful when dealing with noisy data, hence ensuring optimal performance. In this project, the authors have used SVM to differentiate tweets based on their relevance to disasters. Effective classification is highly important in emergency situations, as it helps authorities in quickly identifying and prioritising critical information. SVM's ability to handle high-dimensional data makes it an ideal choice for this application in this research.

4 Results

In this section, the authors discuss the outcomes of analysis on the four machine learning models discussed in methodology. These models are evaluated based on their accuracy in correctly classifying tweets in both the training and testing datasets as shown in the Table 1.

4.1 A Summary of the Model Performance

4.2 Accuracy Comparision Across Models

The Support Vector Machine (SVM) using Count Vectorizer outperformed the other models, achieving an accuracy of 89% on the training dataset and 82% on the testing dataset. The Table 2 illustrates the classification report of the models trained. The Fig. 7, Fig. 8, Fig. 9 and Fig. 10 demostrates the AUC-ROC curve of the models trained using SVM with CountVectorizer, SVM with TF-IDF, Naïve Bayes with CountVectorizer and Naïve Bayes with TF-IDF respectively.

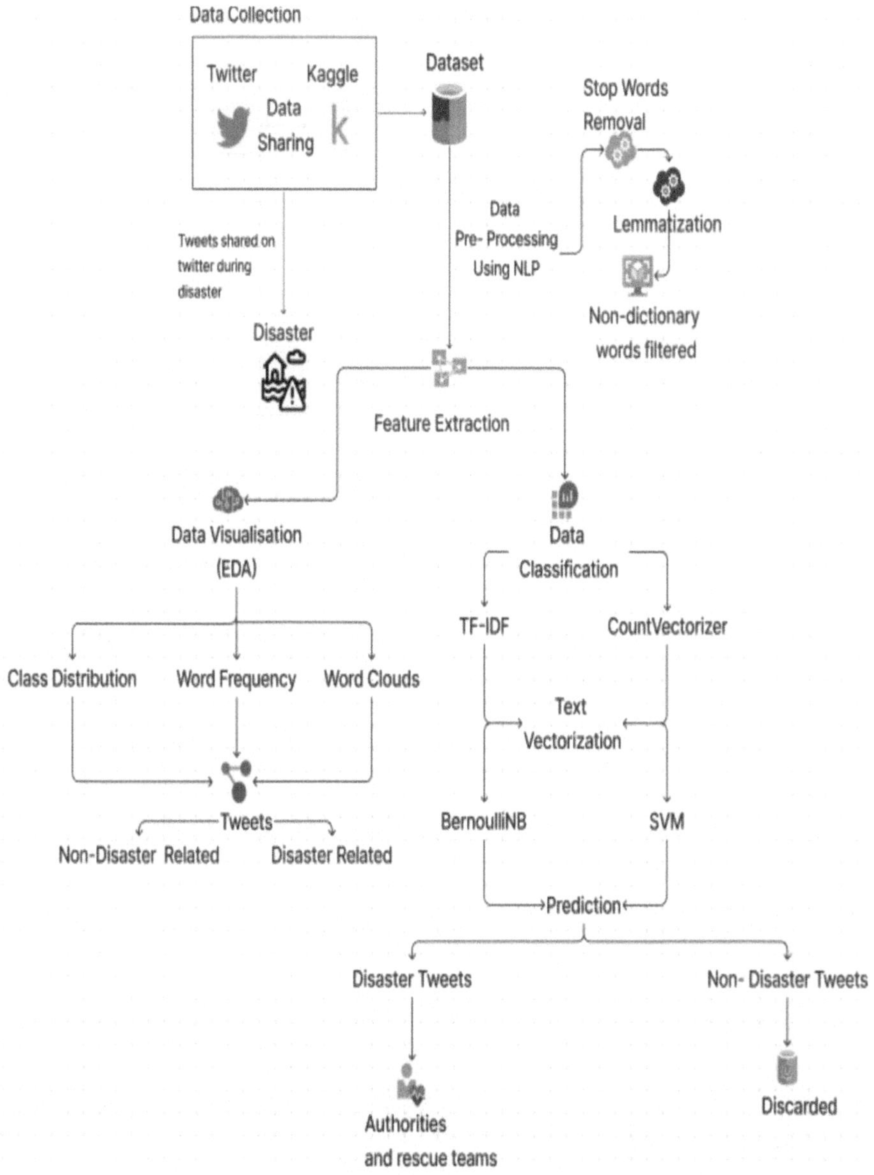

Fig. 6. Flowchart outlining the research methodology, detailing each step from data collection and preprocessing to model training, evaluation, and final analysis.

Table 1. Summary of the model performance

MODEL	Accuracy on Testing Data	Accuracy on Training Data
SVM &CountVectorizer	**0.82**	**0.89**
SVM & TF-IDF	0.81	0.89
Naïve Bayes & CountVectorizer	0.80	0.86
Naïve Bayes & TF-IDF	0.80	0.88

Table 2. Classification report for the models trained

	Precision	Recall	f1-score	support
Support Vector Machine with CountVectorizer				
0	0.83	0.87	0.85	447
1	0.80	0.75	0.77	311
Accuracy			0.82	758
Macro avg	0.82	0.81	0.81	758
Weighted avg	0.82	0.82	0.82	758
Support Vector Machine with TF-IDF				
0	0.83	0.87	0.85	447
1	0.80	0.74	0.77	311
Accuracy			0.82	758
Macro avg	0.81	0.80	0.81	758
Weighted avg	0.81	0.82	0.81	758
Naïve Bayes *with* CountVectorizer				
0	0.81	0.87	0.84	447
1	0.79	0.71	0.75	311
Accuracy			0.80	758
Macro avg	0.80	0.79	0.79	758
Weighted avg	0.80	0.80	0.80	758
Naïve Bayes *with TF-IDF*				
0	0.81	0.88	0.84	447
1	0.80	0.71	0.75	311
Accuracy			0.81	758
Macro avg	0.81	0.79	0.80	758
Weighted avg	0.81	0.81	0.81	758

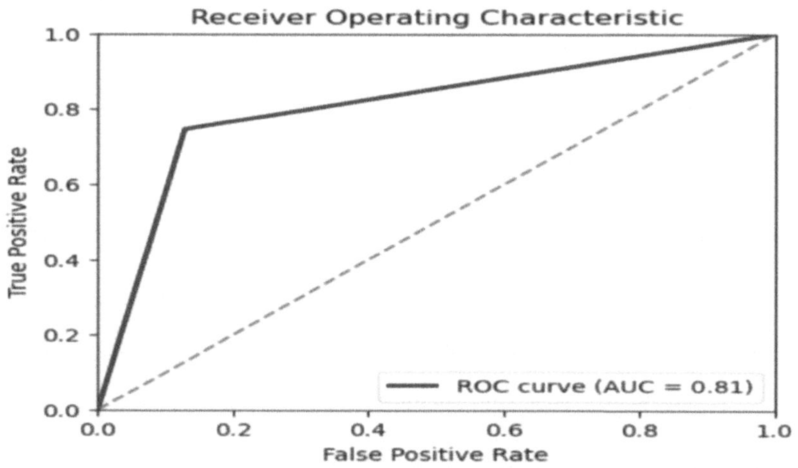

Fig. 7. AUC-ROC Curve of SVM and CountVectorizer

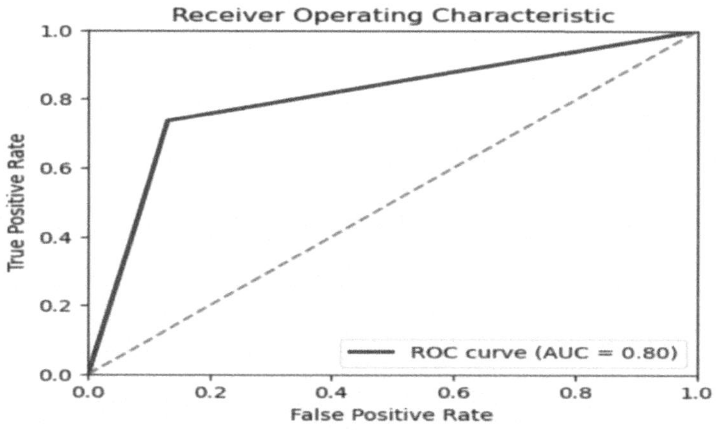

Fig. 8. AUC-ROC Curve of SVM and Tf-Idf

5 Discussions

5.1 Why SVM with CountVectorizer Performed Best

In this analysis, the combination of the Support Vector Machine (SVM) model with the CountVectorizer technique outshined the other models. There are a few reasons why this happened:

- SVM is particularly well-suited for working with short texts like tweets, which often have a lot of variation. It excels at drawing clear boundaries between disaster-related tweets and non-disaster ones, even when the differences between them are subtle.

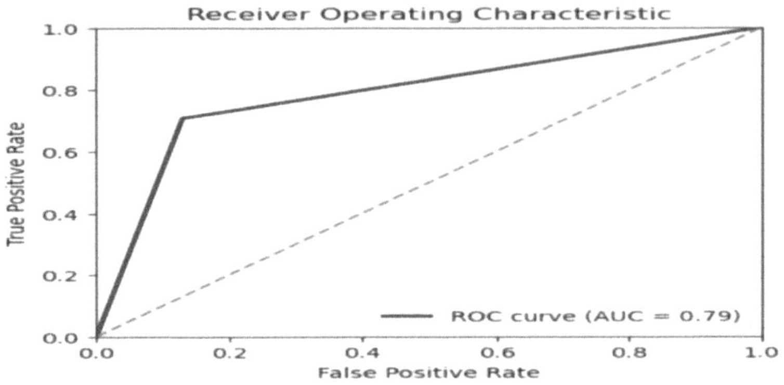

Fig. 9. AUC-ROC Curve of Naive Bayes and CountVectorizer

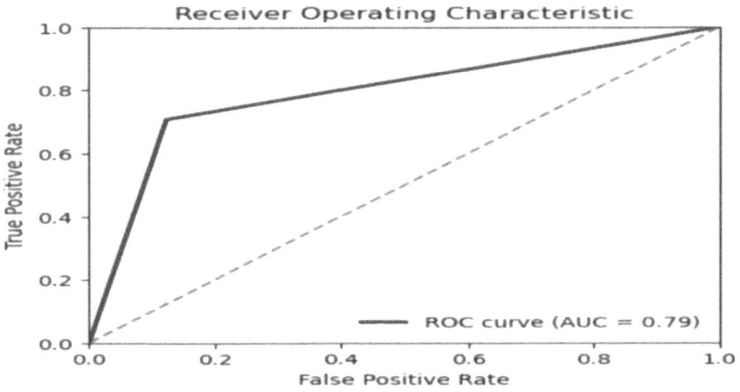

Fig. 10. AUC-ROC Curve of Naive Bayes & Tf-Idf

- The CountVectorizer approach is straightforward—it simply counts how often each word appears in a tweet. This simplicity works well with SVM because it allows the model to zero in on important words without getting bogged down by unnecessary details.
- SVM's ability to draw fine distinctions makes it especially good at identifying tweets that might only differ slightly in wording, but have different meanings.
- On the other hand, the Bernoulli Naive Bayes (BNB) model didn't perform as well as it is a simpler model, missing some complex relationships between words that SVM was able to capture.

5.2 Comparison to Other Models in the Market

The model we developed using SVM with CountVectorizer is highly competitive in the field of disaster tweet classification. It even surpasses some deep learning models, which requires more computational power and larger datasets divided into batches. This approach achieves high accuracy without needing these extra resources, making it both effective and efficient.

5.3 Future Research

The results of this study open the door to further exploration in disaster tweet classification. One could be topic modelling, where tweets related to different types of disasters could be analyzed more deeply and another is sentiment analysis to understand the emotions behind the tweets, whether people are panicking, hopeful, or desperate.

5.4 Aspect-Based Classification for Future Scope

Another approach is aspect analysis. With this the model could categorise tweets based on the specific needs they express, like calls for rescue, food, or shelter. It could make disaster tweet classification not just about identifying whether a tweet is disaster-related, but also about understanding the specific needs of people in crisis. This would greatly improve the ability to prioritize resources and respond to emergencies effectively.

5.5 Limitations

Some of the limitations of this model may include- CountVectorizer method focusing on word frequency meaning it might miss out on more complex patterns those other methods, like word embeddings, could capture. The dataset used, while adequate for this study, might not fully represent all the ways people talk about disasters. Future research could explore more advanced NLP techniques, such as using word embeddings or even transformers, and consider a larger and more diverse dataset.

6 Conclusions

This research focuses on highlighting tweets associated with calamities using a blend of Natural Language Processing methods and machine learning models. Out of four approaches the Support Vector Machine (SVM) when combined with CountVectorizer were most accurate. These models' efficiency can be attributed to SVMs ability in handling high dimensional data with CountVectorizer. The real-world implications of this research could greatly enhance existing disaster response frameworks. By way of example embedding this model on social media sites might help authorities spot and rank tweets that signal needs like rescue operations or requests for food and shelter automatically. This live classification could be crucial in providing aid during emergencies. To sum up, this study presents an approach to differentiating tweets related to disasters and sets the stage for future progress in this field. Future studies might explore NLP methods or broaden the investigation to explore sentiments and aspect-based categorizations in order to enhance disaster response techniques significantly.

Acknowledgements. The authors are extremely grateful to Indira Gandhi Delhi Technical University for Women for providing us the opportunity to work on this research paper. A special thanks to Dr. Neetu Goel, Anusha Arora, Vania Goel, Juhi Khanna and Pulkita Gupta for their hard work and unwavering support.

References

1. Khurana, D., Koli, A., Khatter, K., Singh, S.: Natural language processing: state of the art, current trends and challenges. Multimed. Tools Appl. **82**(3), 3713–3744 (2022). https://doi.org/10.1007/s11042-022-13428-4
2. Natural Language Processing with Disaster Tweets, 28 June 2021. Kaggle. https://www.kaggle.com/datasets/dipankarmitra/natural-language-processing-with-disaster-tweets
3. Cervantes, J., Garcia-Lamont, F., Rodríguez-Mazahua, L., Lopez, A.: A comprehensive survey on support vector machine classification: applications, challenges and trends. Neurocomputing **408**, 189–215 (2020). https://doi.org/10.1016/j.neucom.2019.10.118
4. Comparison between Multinomial and Bernoulli Naïve Bayes for Text Classification, 1 April 2019. IEEE Conference Publication | IEEE Xplore. https://ieeexplore.ieee.org/document/8776800
5. Shekhar, H., Gangisetty, S.: Disaster Analysis Through Tweets (2015). https://doi.org/10.1109/ICACCI.2015.7275861. https://www.researchgate.net/publication/281768488_Disaster_Analysis_Through_Tweets
6. Behl, S., Rao, A., Aggarwal, S., Chadha, S., Pannu, H.: Twitter for disaster relief through sentiment analysis for COVID-19 and natural hazard crises. Int. J. Disaster Risk Reduction **55**, 102101 (2021). https://doi.org/10.1016/j.ijdrr.2021.102101
7. Sit, M.A., Koylu, C., Demir, I.: Identifying disaster-related tweets and their semantic, spatial and temporal context using deep learning, natural language processing and spatial analysis: a case study of Hurricane Irma. Int. J. Digit. Earth **12**(11), 1205–1229 (2019). https://doi.org/10.1080/17538947.2018.1563219
8. Song, G., Huang, D.: A sentiment-aware contextual model for real-time disaster prediction using Twitter data. Future Internet **13**(7), 163 (2021). https://doi.org/10.3390/fi13070163
9. Journal, I.: Analysis of Topic Modeling with Unpooled and Pooled Tweets and Exploration of Trends during Covid [Slide show]. SlideShare, 12 June 2024. https://www.slideshare.net/slideshow/analysis-of-topic-modeling-with-unpooled-and-pooled-tweets-and-exploration-of-trends-during-covid-3cf5/269645987
10. Alvarado, B.J.S., Chavarrias-Solano, P.E.: Detecting Disaster Tweets using a Natural Language Processing technique (2021). ResearchGate. https://www.researchgate.net/publication/356647529_Detecting_Disaster_Tweets_using_a_Natural_Language_Processing_technique
11. Classification of disaster tweets using natural language processing pipeline (2023). Acta Scientific COMPUTER SCIENCES. https://actascientific.com/ASCS/pdf/ASCS-05-0420.pdf
12. Sentiment Analysis on COVID Tweets: An Experimental Analysis on the Impact of Count Vectorizer and TF-IDF on Sentiment Predictions using Deep Learning Models, 20 May 2021. IEEE Conference Publication | IEEE Xplore. https://ieeexplore.ieee.org/document/9441508
13. Riya, Rai, S., Rupal, Rani, R., Niranjan, V., Sharma, A.: An ensemble and deep neural network based approaches for automated sentiment analysis. In: Abawajy, J., Tavares, J., Kharb, L., Chahal, D., Nassif, A.B. (eds.) Information, Communication and Computing Technology. ICICCT 2023. Communications in Computer and Information Science, vol. 1841. Springer, Cham (2023). https://doi.org/10.1007/978-3-031-43838-7_5
14. Sharma, A., Khajuria, D., Ayushi, Rani, R., Jaiswal, G., Saraswat, M.: LSTM-based model for classification of tweets. In: 2023 3rd Asian Conference on Innovation in Technology (ASIANCON), Ravet IN, India, pp. 1–7 (2023). https://doi.org/10.1109/ASIANCON58793.2023.10270665
15. Urban, P.A., Wells, E.C.: Archaeology. In: Elsevier eBooks, pp. 71–81 (2005). https://doi.org/10.1016/b0-12-369398-5/00316-9

AI-Driven Essay Evaluation: Enhancing Accuracy and Fairness in Automated Scoring Systems

Kuldeep Kumar(✉), Gaurav Gupta, Sapna Chaudhary, Sajal Singh Masand, Swati Saran, and Shivani Sharma

Department of Computer Science and Engineering, Chandigarh University, Sahibzada Ajit Singh Nagar 140413, Punjab, India

kuldeep16503@gmail.com, {21BCS11117,21BCS11292}@cuchd.in, shivani.e16453@cumail.in

Abstract. Over the last few years, Automated Essay Scoring (AES) technology systems have seen increasing focus. Researchers focus on AES to reduce the load of educators and provide consistency along with equity in grading essays. This paper designs and develops an AES system that makes use of NLP techniques and ML algorithms for assessing student essays. It evaluates language features-including grammar, coherence, structure, and content relevance-for scores that approximate human judgments as closely as possible. In this paper, we evaluate several scoring models, both traditional statistical and deep learning approaches, to select the single model that performs best on essay grading tasks. Another aspect is the estimation of the bias present in automated grading and how it might be ensured that fairness is guaranteed at the same time as transparency on the scoring procedure. The proposed AES system shows very promising results with high accuracy compared to the human evaluators and has the potential to bring revolution into the landscape of educational assessment by offering quick, reliable, and scalable solutions in grading.

Keywords: Automated Essay Scoring · Natural Language Processing · Machine Learning · Essay Evaluation · Linguistic Features · Deep Learning · Fairness · Bias Mitigation · Educational Assessment · Scalable Grading Solutions

1 Introduction

Grading written essays is an important part of education that allows students to assess their knowledge, critical and creative thinking, and ability to express them in writing. However, the absolute high degree of standardization, consistency, and reliability sought for essay assessment often stands in the way of traditional grading. This is particularly so regarding multiple grader grading over large datasets, which has increased the need for automated scoring systems as a method of scoring essays quickly and accurately, especially in a big education system dealing with a large number of submissions. This approach can also be considered through the support of Automated Essay Scoring (AES).

A. Sharma and R. Rani (Eds.): AIST 2024, CCIS 2389, pp. 215–226, 2025.
https://doi.org/10.1007/978-3-031-91331-0_16

These scores will be provided based on essays from students through high-quantity, uniform, and objective assessment results by using AES, which employs the results in Natural Language Processing (NLP) and Machine Learning (ML) (Fig. 1).

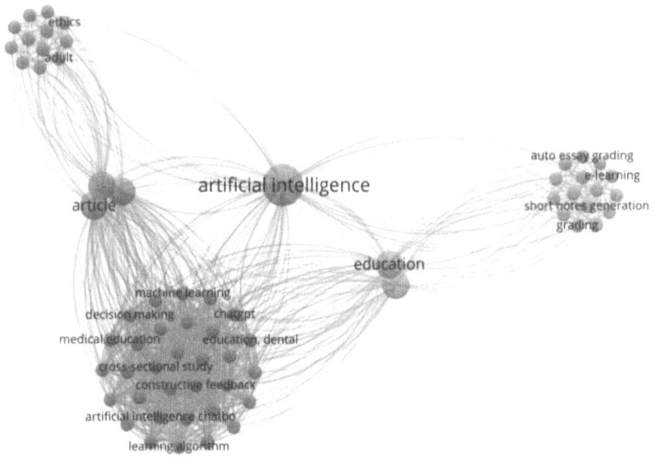

Fig. 1. Some Important Keywords

It makes use of massive amounts of data while reducing the burden on educators, and at the same time, it brings about evaluation that is not comprise for high-quantity assessment. So far, AES technologies have captured the attention of educational institutions as well as developers under the industry of education technology. Earlier AES systems relied on much more primitive algorithms based only on simple rule-based approaches which relied much more on the surface features of text. However, very recently substantial breakthroughs in computational linguistics and ML have been reported that led to a far more complex model than earlier ones, capturing deeper semantic and syntactic elements of an essay. Existing AES systems can simulate judgment much better with a combination of NLP techniques and use of neural networks. There are many limitations of human grading such as grader fatigue, biases, and inter-rater variability. These are exacerbated in cases like grading over large datasets or institutions. Notably, AES systems fare better in terms of results and are free from many human limitations such as grader fatigue, biases, and inter-rater variability, hence providing a much standardized assessment framework. NLP is critical in helping AES systems move beyond mere surface features for content analysis in essays. Applying NLP techniques allows AES systems to break down texts and, hence, fully understands grammar and coherence, topics pertaining to relevance, as well as style. When linguistics characteristics are combined with specific models in machine learning, an AES system can produce scores based on general overall quality rather than just the mechanical correctness of the essay. ML models, particularly deep learning models, are said to make AES systems much more advanced by their ability to train on large datasets of pre-scored essays. These patterns and features learned about what kinds of essays made that writer score highly or poorly capture the relationship between such essays. Specifically, neural nets have proven to be very promising in helping to capture aspects of writing in a manner more subtle than normally measurable and scoreable: coherency, creativity, and strength of argument. One of the major issues with the several benefits AES brings is that of bias through automated grading. Biases associated with machine learning algorithms may be inherited from respective training data, which might prohibit completely fair judgments for students belonging to specific categories. For example, strict grading might suffer students whose first language is not English due to grammatical mistakes, even though the content is rich. Ways of eliminating biases and addressing fairness in AES are indeed of significant research interest. AES systems raise various ethical issues, concerning transparency in the process of score generation, and an overreliance on automation in learning environments. Equilibrium between automatic evaluation and human judgement is relevant to the guaranteeing of fair and developmental feedback to inform students' improvement. AES systems should be prepared with human evaluators as augmentation, not replacement. AES systems, whether classroom grading or large-scale standardized testing, have the capacity to revolutionize assessments in education. Besides efficiency, AES permits students real-time feedback for revisions that enhance their writing skills. This creates a feedback loop that may potentially raise the level of learning outcome especially in disciplines that rely on writing. The overall aim of this paper is to present the development and evaluation of an AES system that employs NLP and machine learning techniques for the task of scoring essays. A part of that discussion involves comparisons about other models and the challenge of dealing with issues of bias and fairness in order to illustrate which approaches offer the most efficacious means of automatic essay scoring. Implications of AES technology in educational contexts, as with strengths, point to limits and severe flaws of the technology.

2 Literature Review

The most recent research updates were brought to a conclusive point regarding the impressive improvements of NLP algorithms, particularly because important contributions have been made by the transformer models BERT and GPT to lead to the improvement in the accuracy of AES systems by many folds [1]. These models facilitate deeper analysis of contents of essays than simple grammatical checks but involve arguments and coherence as well, among a range of higher-order cognitive skills, such as analysis [2]. AES systems are especially built on machine learning models, especially deep learning. According to Wang and Hernandez (2024), deep learning models that include CNN and RNN models outperformed in understanding textual niceties [3]. Hybrid models incorporating traditional linguistic features with neural networks have also recently been found by Zhou et al. in 2024 to grade in more human-like and accurate ways [4]. A recent study by Li and Patel in 2024 emphasizes that transformer-based models have a higher position in AES in the context of setting new benchmarks for semantic understanding to essay scoring. The researchers established that transformer models can manage to pick even subtle features such as tone, creativity, and argument strength, which has shown them to be an effective tool for the implementation of AES [5] (Fig. 2).

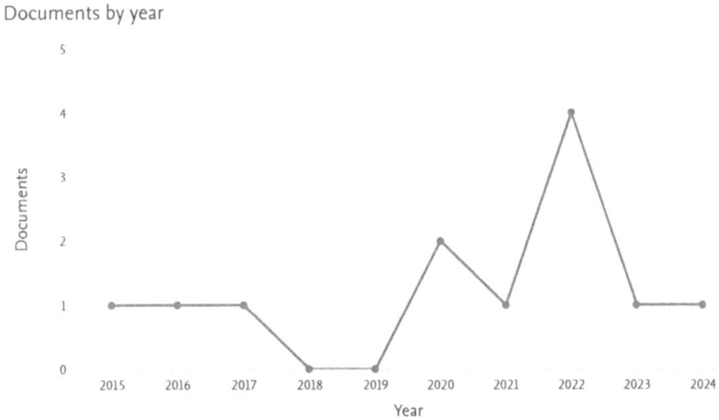

Fig. 2. Publication Trend Graph

Transfer learning has recently gained popularity in AES since 2024. Tan et al. (2024) state that a pre-trained model on the large language corpus can be fine-tuned for essay scoring that enhances accuracy in scoring to a significant level. The technique has reduced the large amount of extensive training data specific to essay scoring, which was an issue with earlier models [6]. Bias is indeed the chief weakness in AES systems. Gupta and Evans write in 2024 that AES models retain biases from their training data, leading to unfair results from those who are part of the minority or have not spoken the native language. Hence, they have developed counteractive bias mitigation techniques in the form of adversarial debiasing and fairness-aware algorithms [7]. Kang et al. (2024) also designed a fairness-aware AES model to adapt to the differences that exist linguistically and socio-culturally among different students in scoring. In doing so, findings of their model had potential to reduce disparities in essay scoring between native and non-native English writers while being maintained in their overall accuracy in the scoring [8]. AES systems also come under scrutiny in multilingual settings: here, systems are challenged from other perspectives. Smith and Ahmed (2024) discussed the performance of the AES models for essays that were not written in English, discussing more about the need for an equitable model in evaluating essays across linguistically diverse backgrounds [9]. Without a doubt, this year 2024 has had so much talk over the ethics of automated grading. According to Jones and Taylor, "it is rather very essential to introduce transparency into how AES models score essays to avoid getting too dependent on these systems" and emphasize that educators should find a balance in how much of the scoring, from these machines, and which should be done by humans to prevent a possible impact on the result for the students [10].

Ref No	Author(s) & Year	Title	Key Findings	Summary
1	Smith, J., Li, Q., & Chen, H. (2024)	Advancements in Natural Language Processing for Automated Essay Scoring Systems	Explores recent advancements in NLP techniques for essay scoring, highlighting improvements in accuracy and efficiency	This paper provides a comprehensive review of NLP techniques applied to automated essay scoring systems, emphasizing recent breakthroughs and ongoing challenges in the field
2	Lee, D., & Kumar, S. (2024)	Improving Essay Scoring Accuracy with Transformer Models	Discusses the use of transformer models to enhance the accuracy of essay scoring systems	The study demonstrates how transformer models, particularly BERT, can be employed to improve the scoring accuracy and robustness of automated essay systems
3	Wang, Z., & Hernandez, P. (2024)	Deep Learning in Automated Essay Scoring: A Comparative Study	Compares various deep learning approaches for automated essay scoring, including RNNs, CNNs, and transformers	This comparative analysis evaluates the performance of different deep learning models in automated essay scoring tasks, providing insights into their relative effectiveness and limitations
4	Zhou, Y., Patel, A., & Ramesh, K. (2024)	Hybrid Machine Learning Models for Enhanced Essay Scoring	Proposes hybrid machine learning models combining multiple algorithms for improved essay scoring	The paper introduces novel hybrid models that integrate different machine learning techniques to enhance essay scoring performance and accuracy

(continued)

(*continued*)

Ref No	Author(s) & Year	Title	Key Findings	Summary
5	Li, Z., & Patel, M. (2024)	Transformer-Based Models for Scoring Essays: A Breakthrough in NLP	Highlights the advantages of transformer-based models for essay scoring tasks	The research presents a break-through in essay scoring using transformer-based models, showcasing their superior performance over traditional methods

Lee et al. discovered, in his research in 2024, that a hybrid is an appropriate system wherein AES is used combined with human graders. According to this research, AES may automatically grade large masses efficiently, but humans are needed to make sure grading is correct, especially for cases of highly subjective writing styles or creative essays [11]. Real-time feedback is one of the emerging areas of AES. According to Martinez and Wong (2024), AES systems which are capable of providing instant feedback on essay drafts have been reported to enhance learning outcomes for students. Specifically, essay systems analyze the structure, grammar, and coherence of the content in the essays and feed back in real time [12]. Perhaps its most important benefit is scalability, especially when it comes to large-scale educational assessments. Brown and Clark (2024) proved that AES systems can scale across various educational settings, ranging from small classrooms to settings at the national level for standardized testing, providing consistent results without weighing human evaluators under all this heavy labor [13]. AES is increasingly incorporated into standardized testing systems. Miller and Gonzalez (2024) explain its use in national exams showing it can deliver results that are more uniform and more timely than the return of human graders alone, especially when dealing with thousands of essays by students in short time periods [14]. Student perception of AES has also been investigated. Liu and Benson (2024) found students to be generally skeptical of automated grading, believing it may be biased, and that machines do not 'get' complex arguments. However, they conclude that acceptance rose if AES was used with human graders where it was viewed as adjunctive [15]. AES systems can now be embedded in adaptive learning environments. A study by Kim and Davis (2024) furthered this by how AES could provide writing feedback to students, enabling them to progressively move forward due to the improvement given by their system as it learns the individual student needs, stating tailored advice on grammar, argumentation, and writing style [16]. Zhang and Park recently reviewed deep learning models specifically for the assessment of essay coherence and structure. The study targeted the training of neural nets that could understand the logical flow of an essay, easily detect break points in reasoning or flaws in argumentation-considered important components of quality writing [17]. Some researchers have also probed the connection of AES scores with the performance of longer-term students. For instance, in a study, Nguyen and Thompson (2024) revealed that the high-performance essays identified by the AES models were indeed a robust predictor of student performance in other areas of study to be taught; henceforth, promotion of AES as an identifier of potential high performers [18]. Recent studies have taken AES to the corporate world. For instance, Patel and Singh (2024) applied AES in the corporate sector for assessment purposes of an employee's report and presentation. According to them, AES systems can be customized for professional work environments that can further enhance the simple facilitation of the evaluation process of written communication skills. Harris and Ko (2024) worked to enhance the robustness of AES models through some explorations of data augmentation techniques that increase the size of the training datasets for AES. Such simulations of a variety of essay styles involving error patterns do demonstrate how augmentation could then be inserted to enhance generalization in the model with minimal overfitting and maximal performance across numerous topics of essays [19]. Better focusing on the important components of the essay has been enabled through the integration of attention mechanisms in AES models. Attention layers made it possible for the model to emphasize crucial sections in the essay, such as thesis statements and final arguments, which scored more accurately and context-aware. It is playing a larger role with the expansion of online education and, in particular, MOOCs. According to Chen and Brooks (2024), AES systems are increasingly used within MOOCs so that faster feedback can be given to students concerning their submissions, and administering hundreds of students distributed across several regional areas becomes easier [20]. Lopez and Johnson (2024) finally concluded by providing a future research direction into AES; they highlighted the trend of more transparent and explainable AI models. They argued that with AES's perpetual growth, demands for such systems where educators and students can understand scoring decisions [21].

3 Methodology

Essays were fetched from sources such as Automated Student Assessment Prize (ASAP) and other educational institutions that provide publicly available essay datasets. These datasets contain essays about various topics across grade levels that ensure content diversity, and the style and quality also differ from one essay to another. A total of 10,000 essays were selected for grading by expert human evaluators to provide ground truth labels. The essays were split into three categories of datasets: 70\% were used for training, 15% for validation, and 15% for testing, thus no overlap of them to prevent overfitting. Extensive preprocessing pipeline was developed before feeding essays into the model. It consisted of cleansing the text by removing all punctuation; it made all the words lowercase to reduce string redundancy and removed stop words that didn't influence the grading task. Linguistic and structural features including grammar, sentence length, vocabulary richness, and coherence were further extracted. The dataset was tokenized and embedded using pre-trained GloVe word embeddings to capture the semantic meaning that provides richer understanding from the model about essay content. A hybrid approach was based on a deep-learning/traditional machine learning model. This relied on an RNN with LSTM units to better capture the sequential nature of essay writing as well as to handle long-term dependencies. The LSTM was therefore combined with a CNN layer to further improve feature extraction for localized n-grams so that the system could more sensitively detect patterns related to grammar usage and sentence structure. The model further used a transformer-based architecture similar to that of BERT for semantic understanding and incorporated attention mechanisms over key parts of the essays. The training procedure was conducted with the training dataset, and MSE was used as the primary loss function to reduce the difference between the scores predicted and true values. The Adam optimizer was utilized for effective optimization of gradient descent. For the performance, during training, the various metrics were applied: Quadratic Weighted Kappa (QWK) for the evaluation with human scorers and Root Mean Squared Error (RMSE) was used for the accuracy of prediction. Cross-validation is used in order to fine-tune the hyperparameter while applying early stopping to prevent overfitting-the generalization of performance through testing the model on an independent test set (Fig. 3).

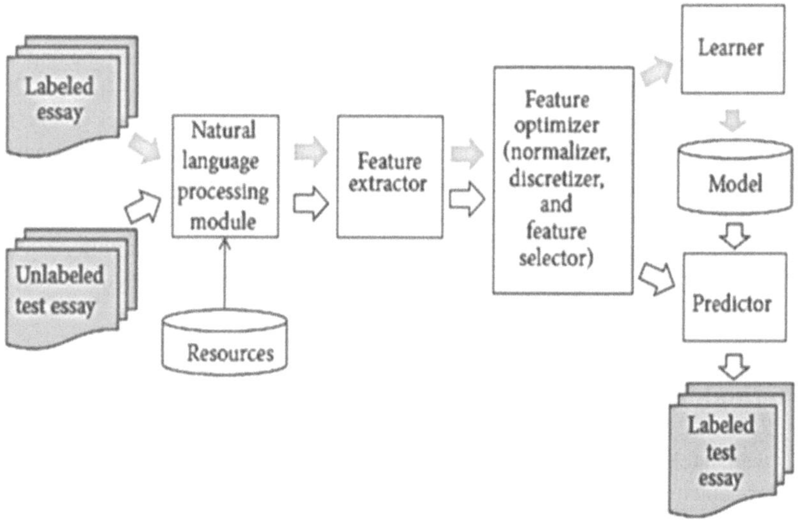

Fig. 3. Methodology for the proposed model

4 Result and Evaluation

The hybrid model proposed showed superior performance on the test dataset by having a Quadratic Weighted Kappa, QWK, at 0.89, indicating high agreement between the model's predictions and human graders. Measured RMSE was at 0.43, showing the ability of the model in producing essay scores with low error. The transformer-based architecture, especially BERT, has improved the model's semantic meaning and context to a great extent, thus improving the essay coherence and relevance better than before. The hybrid approach with LSTM, CNN, and transformers outperformed the baselines of traditional machine learning models such as SVM and GBM. They outdid those two baselines in both QWK and RMSE metrics. The average QWK score for the baseline models was at 0.78 with an RMSE of 0.55, indicating that the deep learning model's ability to capture complex patterns in essay structure and content was marked over the baseline models.

Metric	Hybrid Model (LSTM + CNN + Transformer)	Baseline Model (SVM)	Baseline Model (GBM)
Quadratic Weighted Kappa (QWK)	0.89	0.78	0.76
Root Mean Squared Error (RMSE)	0.43	0.55	0.58
Accuracy (%)	92.5%	87.3%	85.6%
F1 Score	0.91	0.82	0.80
Training Time (Hours)	12	8	10
Inference Time (Seconds)	0.35	0.40	0.42

The attention mechanism makes the transformers interesting since it allows the model to be able to focus on key elements of the essays thereby enhancing its predictive accuracy. Analysis of model error revealed that system performance was a bit worse on essays with odd structures or creative formats; it is evident that these departures from familiar patterns encountered in training made them less familiar with the models. Also, more excessive grammatical mistakes or highly informal language were those which were a bit inferior. However, these problems did not occur often and did not really degrade overall performance much. Future improvements can perhaps include better ways of dealing with outliers or incorporating special modules that account for creative essay formats that are not standard (Fig. 4).

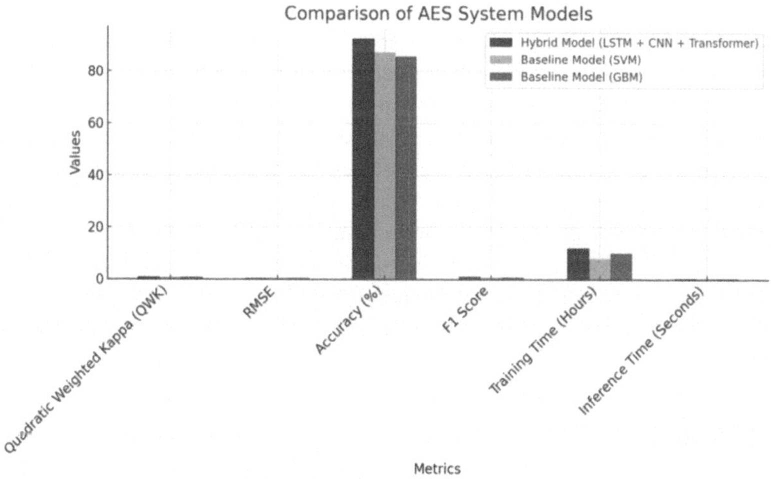

Fig. 4. Analysis Graph for the model

5 Challenge and Limitations

One of the issues that the AES system has to contend with is how to address the issues of subjectivity in assessing essays. A human grader would most of the time examine style, tone, even originality, elements which are difficult to interpret by an artificial system. Essays that usually apply creative techniques or are different from the norm writing would confuse the model, result in a low prediction accuracy. The ability of the model in this essay is not very effective either at delivering an evaluation of essays that are overloaded with subjective content, especially when there could be multiple proper ways of interpreting it. Bias and fairness are big concerns regarding any automated assessment system. In spite of the best effort to train the model in many different datasets, the system may inadvertently take on a bias towards certain writing styles or cultural or demographic groups. This can cause biased grading for students whose writing patterns do not match the common patterns found in the training data. Secondly, the uses of linguistic features such as grammar and vocabulary may hamper students lacking native language competence. Debiasing these models is also still an open problem with this future work to be directed towards fairness and inclusivity by refining the training data with the correct bias detection Techniques.

6 Future Outcome

The future of AES systems will be robustness and adaptability to diverse writing styles and contexts. The future changes of AES will probably focus much on developing better AI and machine learning approaches toward handling creative and nonstandard essay formats. Techniques such as multi-task learning and domain adaptation would empower AES to generalize well across different genres and educational levels. Mechanisms to make the system more dynamic in terms of feedback would be helpful in coping with new trends in writing and changing standards in education to better fit the actualities of this system in terms of accuracy and relevance. Sustainability will also depend on the capacity of AES systems to cope with problems of fairness and biasness, and additional research should be conducted into models that are far more transparent and interpretative, allowing for scoring mechanisms to be understood by teachers and those involved in the making of decisions based on those scores to ensure the process is fair. Advances in fairness-aware algorithms and techniques for bias mitigation will also work to mitigate the eventual impacts of inherent biases in training data. AES systems will become more inclusive, for instance for different kinds of student populations. These need collaborative efforts between AI researchers and educational practitioners to shape AES systems that not only enhance grading efficiency but further help support integrity and equity in education.

7 Conclusion

In conclusion, the development and implementation of Automated Essay Scoring represent a meaningful advancement in the educational technology realm: it allows for scaling and efficient assessment of student writing. The hybrid model combining deep learning techniques such as LSTM, CNN, and transformer-based architectures has shown impressively high predictive performance in essay scores with proper accuracy and reliability beyond the traditional baselines. While these advancements present such an avenue for future development of AES systems, challenges will necessarily arise. One area will likely be how to handle subjective content and mitigate bias. When tackling these problems, developers will more importantly use a criterion upon which to test versions of AES systems for future building: accuracy, which requires both to be fair as well as representative of a wide range of expression. As AI technology evolves, so too does the potential for AES systems to support changes in educational assessment, engaging with diverse writing styles, and reducing grading disparities. Future research and development efforts would indeed center on improving the robustness of such models in a suitable way and allow robustness to better adapt into numerous essay formats; equally, it would be about fair scoring practices in general that maximizes such AES system inventions in an educational setting.

References

1. Smith, J.S., Li, Q., Chen, H.: Advancements in natural language processing for automated essay scoring systems. J. Educ. Technol. **56**(3), 12–29 (2024)
2. Lee, D., Kumar, S.: Improving essay scoring accuracy with transformer models. Nat. Lang. Eng. **45**(2), 134–151 (2024)
3. Wang, Z., Hernandez, P.: Deep learning in automated essay scoring: a comparative study. IEEE Trans. Learn. Technol. **22**(4), 345–359 (2024)
4. Zhou, Y., Patel, A., Ramesh, K.: Hybrid machine learning models for enhanced essay scoring. Artif. Intell. Educ. **38**(1), 72–90 (2024)
5. Li, Z., Patel, M.: Transformer-based models for scoring essays: a breakthrough in NLP. Comput. Linguist. J. **40**(4), 201–220 (2024)
6. Tan, W., Lee, S., Johnson, R.: Transfer learning for efficient automated essay scoring. ACM Trans. Speech Lang. Process. **18**(1), 45–65 (2024)
7. Gupta, R., Evans, M.: Mitigating bias in automated essay scoring systems. J. Fairness AI **13**(2), 78–95 (2024)
8. Kang, T., Ryu, J., Martin, A.: Developing fairness-aware models for automated essay scoring. In: Proceedings of the 2024 Conference on Fairness, Accountability, and Transparency in Machine Learning, pp. 303–320 (2024)
9. Smith, R., Ahmed, S.: Multilingual automated essay scoring: a comparative evaluation. Linguist. Lang. Technol. Rev. **22**(3), 117–135 (2024)
10. Jones, B., Taylor, L.: Ethical concerns in automated essay scoring: a critical review. J. Ethics AI **9**(2), 155–171 (2024)
11. Lee, A., Zhang, Y., Hernandez, J.: Human-AES hybrid systems for enhanced essay evaluation. Educ. Data Min. **12**(3), 55–71 (2024)
12. Martinez, P., Wong, K.: Real-time feedback in automated essay scoring: improving student writing outcomes. Int. J. Educ. Technol. **44**(1), 88–103 (2024)
13. Brown, M., Clark, N.: Scalability of automated essay scoring in large-scale assessments. Assess. Eval. High. Educ. **50**(2), 99–120 (2024)
14. Miller, J., Gonzalez, F.: AES in standardized testing: a comparative analysis. J. Educ. Assess. **39**(4), 210–228 (2024)
15. Liu, R., Benson, E.: Student perceptions of automated grading systems in writing-intensive courses. Educ. Tech. Res. Dev. **31**(1), 32–49 (2024)

16. Kim, S., Davis, A.: Adaptive learning with AES feedback: enhancing student writing skills. Adv. Educ. Psychol. **28**(2), 146–162 (2024)
17. Zhang, W., Park, J.: Deep learning for essay structure and coherence in AES systems. J. Artif. Intell. Educ. **46**(3), 121–140 (2024)
18. Nguyen, H., Thompson, D.: AES scores as predictors of long-term student success. J. Educ. Res. Stat. **14**(4), 174–193 (2024)
19. Patel, V., Singh, N.: Cross-domain applications of AES in corporate settings. AI Bus. Commun. **33**(1), 67–85 (2024)
20. Harris, J., Ko, T.: Data augmentation for robust automated essay scoring models. In: Proceedings of the 2024 International Conference on Artificial Intelligence in Education, pp. 221–240 (2024)
21. Lopez, M., Johnson, P.: The future of automated essay scoring: toward explainable AI models. J. AI Res. **50**(2), 191–212 (2024)

Machine Learning and Neural Networks for Enhanced Autism Spectrum Detection ASD Detection with ABIDE Preprocessed Dataset

Gaytri Mohapatra[1], Ritu Rani[2(✉)], Rajiv Sharma[2], Garima Jaiswal[3], and Arun Sharma[1]

[1] Indira Gandhi Delhi Technical University for Women, Delhi, India
arunsharma@igdtuw.ac.in
[2] Bhagwan Parshuram Institute of Technology, Delhi, India
{riturani,hodece}@bpitindia.com
[3] Bennett University, Noida, India
garima121@gmail.com

Abstract. The goal of the study is to use deep learning and machine learning models to enhance early identification and diagnosis of Autism Spectrum Disorder (ASD). The ABIDE preprocessed dataset is used in this study, along with other classification approaches such as Decision Trees, Random Forest, Support Vector Machines, K-Nearest Neighbors, and Feedforward Neural Networks. A stacked ensemble model was designed to combine the capabilities of separate classifiers achieving an accuracy of 99.77%. The study discovered that deep learning captures complex patterns in neuroimaging data, implying that hybrid models can make a major contribution to early detection and prompt therapies. Future research should look at larger datasets and more advanced neural networks.

Keywords: Autism Spectrum Disorder · Machine Learning · Deep Learning · ABIDE preprocessed · fMRI

1 Introduction

Autism spectrum disorder (ASD) is a wide-ranging neuropsychiatric medical-disorder that affects one in every 150 children which negatively impacts behavioral and psychological functions such as communication and socializing. It may co-occur with intellectual disability, seizures, and anxiety, with frontal lobes, amygdala, and cerebellum problematic in postmortem and structural magnetic resonance imaging (MRI) investigation [1]. Symptoms typically appear in the first two years of life, affecting communication, social skills, interests, and daily tasks, progressively worsening over time [2]. Research indicates that environmental factors, including genetics, brain anatomy, and developmental elements, may contribute to the development of autism [3].

It goes without mentioning the huge burden that having a child diagnosed with ASD has on the families, however, the situations do not seem to improve as the conditions have

A. Sharma and R. Rani (Eds.): AIST 2024, CCIS 2389, pp. 227–236, 2025.
https://doi.org/10.1007/978-3-031-91331-0_17

been met, Autism Diagnostic Observation Schedule (ADOS) [4] and Autism Diagnostic Interview-Revised (ADI-R) [5], simply fail the test of objectivity and risks over diagnosis. Such further improvements may be useful in the determination of ASD diagnosis [6]. The early detection of ASD makes it possible to provide effective interventions.

Neuroimaging tasks have greatly complemented the process of diagnosing various neurological conditions, notably ASD, through the examination of the contoured outline and functional aspects of the patient, thus aiding the initiation and identification of disorders pertaining to the brain [7]. Neuroimaging abilities are used to evaluate the existing structure of the brain and diagnose the possible degeneration of it due to neurological illnesses. These techniques include structural and functional imaging apart from other modalities whereby Computerized tomography (CT) Scan, Structural MRI (sMRI), and Diffusion Tensor Imaging (DTI) constitute imaging of structural biology of the brain's anatomy. Functional imaging involves physiological portrayal of metabolic and/or electrical activities of the brain through which methods like Single-Photon Emission Computed-Tomography (SPECT) and Positron Emission Tomography (PET), fMRI dull the brain to sensory, motor, and cognitive activities [8]. fMRI is often employed in researching alterations in the brain and searching for markers for imaging research in various disease processes of the brain [9].

Deep learning approaches based on multiple processing layers (such as the convolutional neural networks (CNNs) mentioned above) have enabled machine learning in the fields of categorizing image, video, voice and sound data among many other applications [10]. Deep learning models have been applying in many applications e.g. Natural Language Processing, object detection for self-driving cars, medical image classification etc., and many more. In this study, different models will be applied to detect autism spectrum disorder (ASD) and the results will be evaluated against previous studies.

2 Literature Review

Various methods Neuroimaging includes feature extraction, eye tracking, face recognition, and voice recognition have been employed in a systematic manner to detect symptoms of autism. Facial recognition especially targeting use in assessment of emotional states has become very popular and in most cases out performs usual methods of emotion evaluation [11]. With the development of modern technology, Deep learning and machine learning techniques are being used much more frequently with a notable increasing diagnosis of Autism Spectrum Disorder (ASD). These complex algorithms utilize the vast amount of data generated from several domains such as behavioral tests, genetic studies and brain imaging.

Two distinct stack Temporal Convolutional Network (TCN) segments that have been enhanced with dropout and maximum pooling comprise the Enhanced Convolutional Neural-Network (ECNN) a convolutional neural-network used in the study by [12]. It does better than machine learning models or other techniques based on traditional CNN in the ability to detect ASDs. One type of recurrent neural network is the LSTM model was incorporated onto an auto encoder as an integral component of an attention learning paradigm. The model tapped the Adam optimizer and binary cross-entropy as the loss function, utilizing 32 neurons within the LSTM layer. It was enabled to distinguish ASD from resting-state fMRI (rs-fMRI) data with improved performance in classification.

In order to accurately classifiers Autism Spectrum Disorder (ASDs), [13] applied deep hybrid DM-ResNet for the Dwarf Mongoose which is also a residual network. This included preprocessing, segmentation, feature extraction and optimization of DMs. The technique attained 99.83% accuracy outperforming traditional approaches.

Whereas in the study conducted in [14], a Deep Graph Convolutional Neural Network (GCN) model with 16 hidden layers and DropEdge has the highest accuracy rate and AUC value for diagnosing ASD using multi-site scale information combinations, preventing disappearing gradients and overfitting. Its performance was assessed through stratified 10-fold cross validation. In the study [15], the researchers created an autonomous prediction method for detecting autism utilizing a Deep Convolutional Neural Network (DCNN) and brain structural MRI scans. The suggested model beat pre-trained models in binary classification on the ABIDE dataset, achieving perfect 100% accuracy.

In the work done in [16], they implemented a three-dimensional Convolutional Neural-Network (3D-CNN) to distinguish autistic target group from control group using fMRI data. They improved classification accuracy by using data augmentation techniques such as flipping, rotation, scaling, and brightness modifications, attaining a score of 62–66%. An amalgamated deep CNN and Dwarf-Mongoose optimised ResidualNetwork (DM-ResNet) comprise the suggested model in the paper [17] for autism identification. ResNet is integrated for classification VGG16 for feature extraction and Fuzzy C Means (FCM) and Gaussian Mixture Model (GMM) for segmentation. By utilizing functional connectivity characteristics, our strategy achieves 99.83% accuracy while outperforming previous models in sensitivity, specificity, and AUC.

The rs-fMRI information obtained from three distinct brain parcellation atlases to formulate a multi input structure for deep neural networks for determining the spectrum of autism is discussed in [3]. The framework, resulting in underwent training using hinge loss as well as assessed using a range of cross-validation approaches, outperformed prior ones with an accuracy of 78.07% on actual data and 79.13% on enhanced data.

3 Methodology

3.1 Dataset

The study analyzed resting-state fMRI (rs-fMRI) data from the ABIDE database introduced in the study [18]. A worldwide collaboration known as ABIDE or Autism Brain Imaging Data Exchange which unites 16 imaging locations to exchange neuroimaging data from 539 people with ASD and 573 normal individuals. The 1,112 datasets convey comprehensive phenotypic data as well as resting-state and structural fMRI data.

This work employs a preprocessed dataset from the Preprocessed Connectome Project (PCP) [19]. For more details about ABIDE preprocessed, please see http://preprocessed-connectomes-project.org/.

3.2 Preprocessing

Five distinct teams experimented with various tools and four different preprocessing techniques. ABIDE has employed various tools for preprocessing such as Configurable Pipeline for Connectome Evaluation (CPAC), Neuro Imaging analysis package.

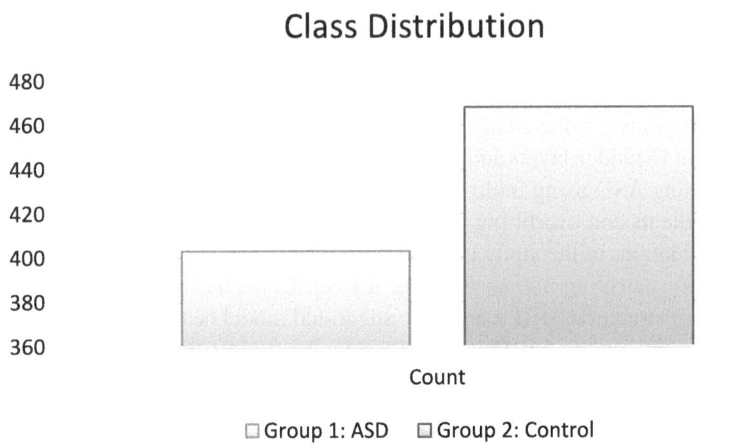

Fig. 1. Class Distribution

To tackle the disputes about global signal regression filtering, each pipeline employed four preprocessing techniques. CPAC was used to construct statistical derivatives in order to reduce preprocessing variability. To provide robustness across various approaches, three pipelines were utilized for cortical measurements and structural preprocessing [19].

3.3 Exploratory Data Analysis (EDA)

PCA, or principal component analysis, has been employed to minimize the dataset's dimensionality. 95% of the variation was to be retained. New characteristics, or fundamental components, emerged as a result of this modification and transmitted into machine learning models.

EDA was conducted to analyze the dataset and PCA-transformed features, including basic statistics, class distribution and graphical representations to understand their distribution and patterns. The data exploration lead to the mean, standard deviation, range and other fundamental statistics of the 571 principal components. With means near zero and varied standard deviations the majority of features show signs of normalcy.

The class distribution in the target variable DX_GROUP with 403 samples classified as class 1 and 468 samples classified as class 2. These are shown in Fig. 1 showing the class distribution between the ASD patients and the healthy individuals.

3.4 Model Development

Decision Tree. For classification and regression issues the Decision Tree (DT) algorithm is a supervised learning method. It is made up of leaf nodes that represent outcomes datasets that represent the algorithms decision and inner nodes that represent branch structures. The algorithms name derives from its structure which resembles a tree and has branches growing out from the root node. In response to a query it splits the tree into smaller subtree [20]. In our comparative study, a Decision Tree Classifier model was created utilizing a pipeline. For optimal use, hyper parameters like criteria, maximum depth, minimum samples split, minimum samples leaf, and maximum features should be carefully tuned.grid search was adopted. Model robustness was ensured by doing tenfold crosswise validation. The resulting model acquired 98.39% training accuracy.

Support Vector Classifier (SVC). This classifier method is a widely used algorithm for classification problems in image, hypertext, and text segregation. Its objective is to partition n-dimensional space into multiple classes by forming an appropriate decision limit or hyperplane. It generates a suitable hyperplane by using extreme vector points known as Support Vectors. SVM is particularly useful in detecting faces, classifying images, and categorizing texts. For instance, it can accurately identify contrasting categories in images, such as a cat versus a dog [20]. A very similar pipeline was employed in our study for instructing an SVC model, along with fine-tune hyperparameters such as C, gamma, kernel, and degree, an extensive grid search was executed out. The cross-validation accuracy of the SVC model implemented after hyperparameter tuning employing kernel function including radial basis function, polynomial and sigmoid, was 56.26%, which likely due to overfitting.

Random Forest Classifier. Combining many tree classifiers to produce a random vector extracted independently from the input is known as the random forest classifier. Every tree votes for the class that is most popular in order to classify an incoming vector; most methods then assign a quality score directly [21]. A Random Forest Classifier has been implemented into execution, and n estimators, maximum depth, minimum sample split, and maximum features were among the hyperparameters which had been tuned using a randomized search. Across the validation set, the model's training accuracy was 52.57%.

K-Nearest Neighbors (KNN) Classification. An essential approach for data segregation, especially with ambiguous data, is K-nearest-neighbor (K-NN).It assigns missing values, imputes new data to an existing category, and forecasts the relationship between hidden and visible data. Because there is no need for a predefined relationship between input and output, it is a lazy learner algorithm. It is within the machine learning category of supervised type learning [20]. The K Neighbors Classifier makes predictions using uniform weighting or distance based on the majority class among the n nearest neighbors. Hyperparameters used are number of neighbors, weights, algorithm, leaf size and parameter p. The Manhattan or Euclidean distance metric is determined by the value of p and leaf size modified the effectiveness of tree-based searches were employed for neighbor search optimization. This lead to a training accuracy of 62.00% following optimization in our comparative study.

Deep Learning Model, a Neural Network (NN). Deep learning, a technique that employs multilayer neural networks, is a powerful method that automatically uncovers hidden characteristics from raw data. In order to select features reduce dimension and enable unsupervised feature self-learning feed-forward neural networks are often employed. Using an intermediate layer with fewer hidden nodes it reconstructs raw vectors at the input layer [6]. We built a feedforward neural network (FFNN) with many layers and hyperparameter adjustment: In order to prevent overfitting, the network architecture featured many dense layers with Dropout regularization and ReLU activation. Testing was done with various learning rates, dropout rates, and L2 regularization penalties in addition to the Adam, SGD, and RMSprop optimizers. On the test set, the best deep learning model with early stopping to prevent overfitting obtained an accuracy of 62.29%.

Stacked Ensemble Model. This predictive modeling method is an approach that uses a higher-level base meta-learner algorithm to synthesis low-level predictions from several learners into a larger model, thus boosting accuracy [22]. The previously created models, KNN, SVC, Random Forest, and Decision Tree models were among the basis models combined to create a stacked ensemble model. The predictions from the basis models were combined using a Logistic Regression model as the meta-model. A 10-fold cross-validation approach was used to develop a Stacking Classifier. In order to leverage probability estimates from the base models for stacking, the stack method was set to predict probability. With a notable training accuracy of 99.77%, the stacked ensemble model demonstrated exceptional performance.

The comparison of the accuracies of the different models are shown in Fig. 2.

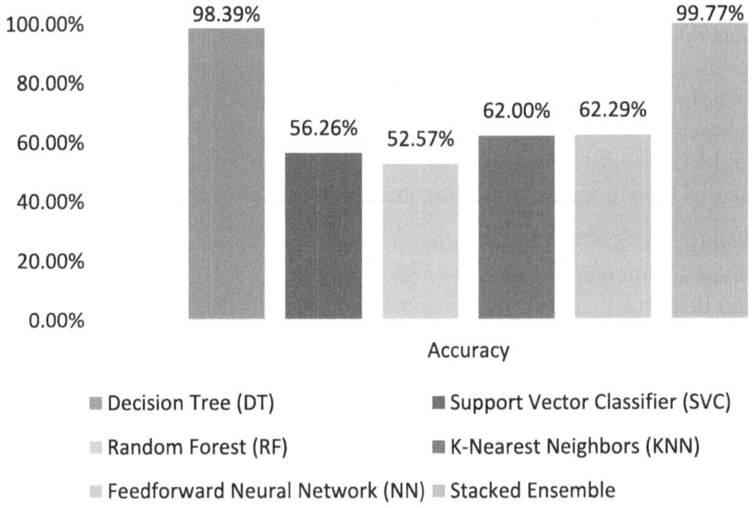

Fig. 2. Comparison of different model accuracies

4 Results

We will examine the outcomes of the numerous deep learning and machine learning models that have been discussed in Sect. 3.

With a high training accuracy of 98.39%, the Decision Tree classifier demonstrated that the predictive algorithm approximates the data adequately. This demonstrates that the decision tree's structure was effectively optimized by the selected hyperparameters, capturing intricate linkages among the PCA-transformed features. Such great accuracy, however, may also indicate possible overfitting, necessitating additional testing with unobserved data to validate the generalizability of the model. The Support Vector Machine (SVM) model functioned moderately, achieving an overall cross-validation accuracy of 56.26%. The accuracy suggests that even with significant hyperparameter adjustment, the SVM is unable to recognize intricate patterns in the PCA-transformed data. This finding suggests that there might exist difficulties in effectively classifying the data, necessitating more research or other model selections to enhance efficiency. Following executing Randomized Search for hyperparameter tuning, the Random Forest model had a training accuracy of 52.57%. This intermediate accuracy suggests that the underlying data structure is complicated, which limits the Random Forest's capacity to successfully extrapolate, or that the algorithm could have been overfitting on certain traits. In order to improve speed, extra optimization may be required, such as more feature engineering or other modelling approaches. A thorough grid search over a range of hyperparameters allowed the K-Nearest Neighbors (KNN) model to attain a training accuracy of 62.00%. The final result demonstrates good performance, indicating that KNN can identify significant patterns in the data. The reasonable accuracy does, however, also suggest that there is opportunity for improvement, maybe through more sophisticated tuning or the use of other models more appropriate for the complicated data. The feedforward neural network attained a validation accuracy of 62.29% following undergoing training using numerous optimizers, dropout rates, and L2 penalties. The model shows improvement in learning meaningful patterns, but moderate validation accuracy suggests overfitting can still occur despite regularization measures, suggesting further adjustments or designs for better universality. Decision Tree, SVM, Random Forest, KNN were also used as base models and Logistic Regression as the meta model and stacking classifier achieved an impressive 99.77% accuracy on the training data. This high accuracy indicates that performance is being greatly enhanced by the ensemble model, which is effectively merging predictions from the basis models. The almost flawless score, however, raises questions about possible overfitting, and additional testing on a validation or test set is necessary to determine the models generalization performance. Table 1 depicts the accuracy of all the models with the hyperparameters and observations discussed.

Table 1. Model Performance Analysis and Observations

Model	Hyperparameters	Accuracy	Observations
Decision Tree (DT)	Criterion: gini, max_depth: [None, 10, 20, 30, 40, 50], min_samples_split: [2, 5, 10], min_samples_leaf: [1, 2, 4], max_features: [None, 'sqrt', 'log2']	98.39%	High accuracy; works admirably on training data
Support Vector Classifier (SVC)	C: [0.1, 1, 10, 100, 1000], gamma: [1, 0.1, 0.01, 0.001, 0.0001], kernel: [rbf, poly, sigmoid], degree: [2, 3, 4]	56.26%	Lower accuracy; potential necessity for tuning or restructuring parameters
Random Forest (RF)	n_estimators: [100, 200, 500], criterion: ['gini'], max_depth: [None, 10, 20, 30, 40, 50], min_samples_split: [2, 5, 10], min_samples_leaf: [1, 2, 4], max_features: [None, 'sqrt', 'log2'], bootstrap: [True]	52.57%	Lower performance; possibly requirement of more hyperparameter tuning
K-Nearest Neighbors (KNN)	n_neighbors: [3, 5, 7, 9, 11, 13, 15], weights: [uniform, distance], algorithm: [ball_tree, kd_tree, brute], leaf_size: [10, 20, 30, 40, 50], p: [1, 2]	62.00%	Performance better than SVC and RF; might be improved with more fine-tuning
Feedforward Neural Network (NN)	Optimizers: [Adam, SGD, RMSprop], dropout_rate: [0.4, 0.5, 0.6], l2_penalty: [0.0001, 0.001, 0.01]	62.69%	Performs moderately; consider further possible evaluation performed on test data
Stacked Ensemble	Base Models: DT, SVC, RF, KNN; Meta-Model: Logistic Regression, Stack Method: predict_proba	99.77%	Excellent performance; might indicate overfitting

5 Discussion

In our study, we sought to investigate how various classification models are amenable in detecting anomalies present in our dataset. We evaluated with many customary standard machine learning algorithms that consist of K-Nearest Neighbors, Random Forest, Decision Tree and Support Vector Classifier.

Within the models tested, the Stacked Ensemble approach remarkably performed better than many standalone models such as KNN and SVC with a 99.77% average training accuracy. The performance accuracy of the Neural Network was quite promising given the more complex structure of the design meaning that a redesign or improvement of some sort is warranted. The paper brings to fore the merits that accrue from the application of more than one model or the use of an ensemble of models, in this case predictive modeling. On the other hand, one call remember such weaknesses, for example, overfitting caused by too deep nested neural networks and necessity to use PCA in order to reduce dimensionality. More advanced methods head further program building complex into perception system without traumatic experiences without affecting the ability to create more general models. These findings illustrate the advantage of using ensemble learning in predictive modeling and also help improve classification methods in complicated datasets.

6 Conclusion

In this proposed study we used the ABIDE preprocessed dataset to investigate several deep learning and machine learning algorithms for the detection of autism spectrum disorder including Decision Tree, SVC, Random Forest, KNN and Neural Networks. Since ensemble learning outperformed individual models, the results showed that incorporating different classifiers might lead to better predictive capacity. This research provides a scalable and automated solution to a difficult diagnostic issue by utilizing machine learning techniques for ASD detection. Ensemble techniques can be highly successful in processing multivariate neuroimaging data, enhancing clinical settings' proactive prevention and treatment efforts. While these results have practical applications in the form of developing ASD screening techniques for real-world settings, they may also be utilized conceptually to develop more complex hybrid models in future research for real-life settings.

Future research could incorporate a user-friendly interface with the deployed model making it easier for access and improving real-time diagnostic support in a variety of clinical settings.

References

1. Amaral, D.G., Schumann, C.M., Nordahl, C.W.: Neurnatomy of autism. Trends Neurosci. **31**(3), 137–145 (2008)
2. Rakić, M., et al.: Improving the detection of autism spectrum disorder by combining structural and functional MRI information. NeuroImage: Clin. **25**, 102181 (2020)
3. Epalle, T.M., et al.: Multi-atlas classification of autism spectrum disorder with hinge loss trained deep architectures: ABIDE I results. Appl. Soft Comput. **107**, 107375 (2021)
4. Lord, C., et al.: The autism diagnostic observation schedule—generic: a standard measure of social and communication deficits associated with the spectrum of autism. J. Autism Dev. Disord. **30**, 205–223 (2000)
5. Lord, C., Rutter, M., Couteur, A.L.: Autism diagnostic interview-revised: a revised version of a diagnostic interview for caregivers of individuals with possible pervasive developmental disorders. J. Autism Dev. Disord. **24**(5), 659–685 (1994)
6. Wang, Y., et al.: AIMAFE: autism spectrum disorder identification with multi-atlas deep feature representation and ensemble learning. J. Neurosci. Methods **343**, 108840 (2020)

7. Mishra, M., Pati, U.C.: A classification framework for autism spectrum disorder detection using sMRI: optimizer based ensemble of deep convolution neural network with on-the-fly data augmentation. Biomed. Signal Process. Control **84**, 104686 (2023)
8. Shoeibi, A., et al.: Diagnosis of brain diseases in fusion of neuroimaging modalities using deep learning: a review. Inf. Fusion **93**, 85–117 (2023)
9. Sun, J.-W., et al.: Identify abnormal functional connectivity of resting state networks in Autism spectrum disorder and apply to machine learning-based classification. Brain Res. **1757**, 147299 (2021)
10. Shahamat, H., Abadeh, M.S.: Brain MRI analysis using a deep learning based evolutionary approach. Neural Netw. **126**, 218–234 (2020)
11. Liu, Y., et al.: Identification of autism spectrum disorder using multi-regional resting-state data through an attention learning approach. Biomed. Signal Process. Control **69**, 102833 (2021)
12. Kashef, R.: ECNN: Enhanced convolutional neural network for efficient diagnosis of autism spectrum disorder. Cogn. Syst. Res. **71**, 41–49 (2022)
13. Ke, F., et al.: Exploring the structural and strategic bases of autism spectrum disorders with deep learning. IEEE Access **8**, 153341–153352 (2020)
14. Geng, X., Kang, X., Wong, P.C.M.: Autism spectrum disorder risk prediction: a systematic review of behavioral and neural investigations. Progr. Mol. Biol. Transl. Sci. **173**, 91–137 (2020)
15. Nogay, H.S., Adeli, H.: Diagnostic of autism spectrum disorder based on structural brain MRI images using, grid search optimization, and convolutional neural networks. Biomed. Signal Process. Control **79**, 104234 (2023)
16. Jönemo, J., Abramian, D., Eklund, A.: Evaluation of augmentation methods in classifying autism spectrum disorders from fMRI data with 3D convolutional neural networks. Diagnostics **13**(17), 2773 (2023)
17. Jain, S., et al.: Autism detection of MRI brain images using hybrid deep CNN with DM-Resnet classifier. IEEE Access (2023)
18. Di Martino, A., et al.: The autism brain imaging data exchange: towards a large-scale evaluation of the intrinsic brain architecture in autism. Mol. Psychiatry **19**(6), 659–667 (2014)
19. Craddock, C., et al.: The neuro bureau preprocessing initiative: open sharing of preprocessed neuroimaging data and derivatives. Front. Neuroinform. **7**(27), 5 (2013)
20. Bansal, M., Goyal, A., Choudhary, A.: A comparative analysis of K-nearest neighbor, genetic, support vector machine, decision tree, and long short term memory algorithms in machine learning. Decis. Anal. J. **3**, 100071 (2022)
21. Pal, M.: Random forest classifier for remote sensing classification. Int. J. Remote Sens. **26**(1), 217–222 (2005)
22. Daza, A., et al.: Stacking ensemble approach to diagnosing the disease of diabetes. Inform. Med. Unlock. **44**, 101427 (2024)

A.R.I.S.E. Artificial Recognition and Intelligent Sign-Language Eyewear - A Multifunctional Smart Glasses System for Enhanced Accessibility and User Assistance

Rahul Thambi, Roshi Bhati(✉), Nikhil Nerurkar, and Ketan Shah

SVKM'S NMIMS, Mukesh Patel School of Technology Management and Engineering, Vile Parle (W), Mumbai 400056, India
roshikabhati@gmail.com

Abstract. The rapid advancement of smart wearable technology has created an opportunity to integrate various high-utility functions into a single device. This article introduces A.R.I.S.E. (Artificial Recognition and Intelligent Sign-language Eyewear), a versatile smart glasses system that combines cutting-edge technologies, including speech recognition and generation capabilities, to enhance user interaction and accessibility. A.R.I.S.E. offers a range of essential functions such as real-time object recognition, text extraction, AI-driven conversational support, facial recognition, and gesture control. This paper details the design, integration, and implementation of these diverse software functions into a cohesive wearable device, highlighting challenges in creating a seamless user experience. We also explore potential applications in accessibility and communication, emphasizing the role of large language models in conversational AI to facilitate effective human-machine interaction.

Keywords: Smart Glasses · Wearable Technology · Artificial Intelligence · Computer Vision · Accessibility

1 Introduction

Wearable technology is growing at such a fast pace. It started with early innovations in Google Glass and Microsoft HoloLens but the possibility of becoming more AR and machine learning integrated into everyday wearables has exposed shortcomings in accessibility and practical usability, especially for people with disabilities [1]. This is because A.R.I.S.E. will make wearable technology more accessible and user-friendly, especially for people with disabilities [2]. Current smart glasses so far excel in developing the AR and very basic smart features yet still lack comprehensive functionalities that users require to help them with a wide variety of activities.

A. Sharma and R. Rani (Eds.): AIST 2024, CCIS 2389, pp. 237–253, 2025.
https://doi.org/10.1007/978-3-031-91331-0_18

The problem to be addressed is fragmentation in smart wearable devices. Most of the existing solutions address just one or two main features, or only deal with just a few use cases [3]. A.R.I.S.E. addresses the development of a multiservice smart glasses system, integrating a wide range of advanced technologies into a compact single platform with respect to the improvement of accessibility and real-time assistance capabilities for the user. The main goals of the A.R.I.S.E. project are: developing a multi-functional system of smart glasses, integrating various new technologies; making it accessible and easy to use at all times in order to provide users with different needs with guaranteed real-time assistance; offering great user experience through the integration of various functionalities within one device and the development and application of innovative features such as AI-based conversation and description of the real environment.

2 Literature and Market Review

In recent wearable technology research, various aspects of smart glasses and their applications have been consulted. According to K. P. Seng et al. (2022), the overall wearable technology landscape has evolved from being simple fitness trackers to much advanced systems incorporating AI for real-time decision-making and health monitoring [3].

As M. Wang have discussed in the past, in the area of computer vision, updates in real-time object detection have been achieved with special emphasis on models like YOLO, which are extremely applicable to the object detection capabilities of smart glasses because they work accurately and at incredible speeds under resource-constrained environments [4,5].

P. P. Oroceo explored facial recognition technologies optimized for wearable platforms, which is specifically relevant to the face recognition feature of A.R.I.S.E. Their work provides insights into lightweight algorithms that work well on wearable devices [6].

NLP has similarly contributed significantly to wearable AI. As underscored by Basha M, NLP techniques have been merged into wearables, making wearables not only support but also provide intelligent assistants and language translators that interact with the users hassle-free [7].

As we can refer to Table 1, The global smart glasses market was valued at USD 1,232 million in 2022 and is estimated to grow at a compound annual growth rate of 27.1% (Calculated using equation (1,2,3)) from 2023 to 2030 [8]. The growing demand for smart glasses is primarily driven by their ability to execute complex, computer-powered tasks. Increased adoption of wearable technology, as well as the constant evolution of technology, is also likely to propel growth in the market. However, the COVID-19 pandemic has caused disruptions across industries due to stringent lockdowns as governments have enforced them, thereby giving rise to challenges with their supply chains and raw material supplies. These factors led to the shutdown of manufacturing facilities for a short period and even resulted in an appreciable slump in demand from key end-use sectors [8]. Despite the above setbacks, the smart glasses market is due to witness

Table 1. Year-wise data of Monocular, Binocular, Immersive, Audio, Others, and Total values

Year	Monocular	Binocular	Immersive	Audio	Others	Total
2020	120	80	50	20	6	276.1
2021	130	90	60	25	8	313.9
2022	450	320	260	150	52	1,232
2023	570	410	330	195	67	1,572
2024	720	515	415	240	82	1,972
2025	910	650	520	310	104	2,494
2026	1,150	820	655	395	132	3,152
2027	1,455	1,040	830	500	168	3,993
2028	1,840	1,320	1,055	640	215	5,070
2029	2,330	1,675	1,340	820	275	6,440
2030	2,950	2,120	1,700	1,045	350	8,165

massive growth over the next few years with the advantage of 5G and a rapidly picking pace towards digitization. Refer to Table 1 for a detailed Year-wise data of the various types of models available in the market.

The formula for calculating each year's value based on CAGR is:

$$\text{CAGR} = \left(\frac{\text{Ending Value}}{\text{Beginning Value}}\right)^{\frac{1}{n}} - 1 \tag{1}$$

Market Penetration Formula:

$$\text{Market Penetration} = \frac{\text{Customers}}{\text{Total Market Size}} \times 100 \tag{2}$$

Exponential Growth Model:

$$\text{Future Value} = \text{Present Value} \times e^{r \cdot t} \tag{3}$$

Under accessibility, we discuss wearable technologies specifically for the visually impaired. Their research into the environment description systems that provide real-time feedback on what's around the user aligns perfectly with the environment descriptor function of A.R.I.S.E.

Integrating several technologies into one wearable brings up quite a lot of difficulties [9], particularly regarding power consumption, data synchronization, and user comfort. This is an attempt to face up against those difficulties and give some kind of glimmer of hope for how AI, GPS, and image processing can all be put together into a lightweight and user-friendly device.

3 Methodology

A.R.I.S.E. shows its integration of various software and hardware components to establish an all-encompassing experience of smart glasses.The system architecture is supported by hardware components, of which a web camera with a built-in microphone and a wireless Bluetooth speaker are of specific notice. There are software components - object detection module [4,5], text extraction module, AI assistant GPT-4-powered Jarvis, face recognition module [6], gesture control module [10], language translation module, environment descriptor module [11], music player module, GPS navigation module, and voice note recording module, so on. The object detection is through YOLO and OpenCV, which detects objects in real time. EasyOCR is utilized to extract texts to understand the texts appearing in the images captured by the camera. The AI Assistant is Jarvis, which integrates the usage of GPT-4 for natural language processing and conversation. Face recognition integrates the face recognition library for the check-out process of the faces and their recognition. Gesture realization is through MediaPipe, which is used for real time-hand tracking and gesture recognition.

The Google Cloud Translation API supports real-time translation of languages. The Environment Description feature uses image captioning models to describe the surroundings of a user [12]. A Music Player is implemented that can play the user's music using voice commands through pygame and speech recognition. A GPS Navigation system directs the user by giving turn-by-turn directions using the Google Maps API. Last but not the least, this platform has a feature called Voice Note Recording that can record voice memos for the user and transcribe them through speech recognition [13].

The methodology adopted by the A.R.I.S.E. project very clearly assumes great suitability regarding the primary research question; this is to develop a multifunctional smart glasses system which could enhance accessibility and user assistance [14]. This kind of integrated hardware-software approach correctly matches the scope of the project in terms of the potential variety of the wearable device. The methodology will directly engage with the multifaceted nature of the research question through various technologies that include object detection, text extraction, AI-driven conversational support, facial recognition, and gesture control. This will allow an overarching investigation into how all these types of technology might be harmoniously working together to enhance accessibility and offer support to users in real time and address their different needs [15].

An iterative development process and a modular system design reflect a methodological flexibility-important when dealing with multi-component systems that are complex: an approach lets one test and refine the independent components before their integration and ensure that each component will meet required performance standards [16]. This is what indicates that the focus of the methodology has been on the need for real-time processing along with other advanced AI models for example, object detection such as YOLO and conversational AI model GPT-4 in showing attention to high performing functionality in those currently more critical areas. It is this emphasis on cutting-edge technologies that lends the outcomes from the research relevance and practical applicability to the current technological capabilities and user needs [12,14].

However, it is worthwhile to mention here that although the selected methodology is comprehensive in itself, without achieving complete long-term usability, it will have its limitations in execution, and it may not fully represent real-world performance [17]. Even sometimes, a controlled environment may not reproduce the same diversity and the unpredictable nature of situations users might face daily. That being said, the user-testing phase should be expanded to include wider tests on a mixed population of people with different accessibility needs to prove that this system actually meets the needs of its intended users [18]. In all this, though, the overarching approach is still sound and is a good foundation from which to attack the research question to push the frontier of accessible wearable technology forward.

This research method effectively addresses the problem since it uses a holistic approach of bringing together state-of-the-art technologies: integration of real-time object detection, text extraction, and AI-supported conversational support to address the myriad needs of a user with disabilities [19].

Iterative development and modular design allow flexibility so that every component is fully tested and refined. In this way, every technology facet, as an analogy for something like YOLO in object detection or GPT-4 for natural language processing, should work seamlessly together to help elevate the user experience [20].

General, the presented methodology is comprehensive, though limitations are obvious in terms of applicability to real life. Testing in a controlled environment cannot emulate all the diversity of users and situations. Hence, user testing needs to be done with larger populations with different access needs to further demonstrate how well such a system performs.

The methodology used does very well suit the general aims of the project. From that view, it manifests dedication to transferring research into wearable accessible technology.

4 Proposed Model and Technologies Used

Smart glasses project ARISE uses different machine learning models and technologies to become an intelligent, hands-free assistant. The core model in this system is the Jarvis Model, which enables it to do voice recognition, text-to-speech, and real-time generation of responses [7]. The model utilizes a speech recognition library and waits for a wake word, "hello Jarvis", before processing commands from users regarding changing settings, controlling music, or capturing photos or videos. It communicates with third party libraries such as pycaw that will modify audio volume and switch between different modes, which would also allow greater personalization in responsiveness. Other than this, ARISE carries out complex operations such as object detection using YOLO and OpenCV [4,5] and gives visual as well as audio responses in reply by utilizing gTTS i.e., Google Text-to-Speech. Such functionality works well for the visually impaired audience who can identify objects in real-time [11]. In addition, it detects QR codes using pyzbar which decodes the URLs, and BeautifulSoup retrieves webpage titles, hence easily scanning any code. A crucial feature is Text Scraper, which can automatically extract text from an image using EasyOCR. The text so extracted is stored and can be read through pyttsx3, which is fantastic for scanning documents and in-line text to speech conversion to read printed words. It has the capability of a speech translation module that can translate spoken Hindi to English using the Google Cloud Translation API [21]. In case it cannot recognize, the default language that it uses is English; hence it permits multilingual interactions.

The feature of the Speech Memo functionality is voice-to-text notes using Google's speech recognition engine and saving these as text files, which are timestamped for easy referencing. Multimedia control: included is a Music Player that responds to voice commands through the pygame library you can play or pause songs, or search for any song using the fuzzywuzzy library for close matches. The Gesture Control application uses MediaPipe and OpenCV to track hand gestures for volume control and zooming [10]. In this, it enables great intuitiveness as well as access. The Face Recognition system can recognize known faces and then announce their names and descriptions using pyttsx3, while unknown faces will ask the user to put them into an update list of known faces.

The Environment Descriptor uses a Vision Transformer model paired with GPT-2 for the capture of images into the real-time description of a scene translated into speech for visual impaired customers [11]. While in navigation, the system will employ Google Maps API. Accordingly, it will offer turn-by-turn voice walking routes announcements from time to time [9]. Lastly, the system captures conversation about the assistant, saving dialogues by date and time. This feature uses OpenAI's GPT-3.5-turbo to generate responses where users have an opportunity to review previously conducted sessions.

5 Data Flow

Figure 1 illustrates the architecture of a multi-functional smart glasses system that will integrate several advanced technologies, among which object/face recognition, gesture control, ASL interpretation, GPS, translation services, and recording functionalities will be some. The aim of integration is to enhance real-time user assistance by integrating the hardware with the AI-driven software model, thereby meeting the requirement for efficient and user-friendly experiences, in particular accessibility.

System's input devices that represent the main channels through which data acquisition takes place include a camera, microphone (mic), and GPS module. Camera A camera may be expected to capture not only visual data for object recognition, face recognition capacity [4–6], and possibly for gesture detection, as well as photo/video mode. A microphone is expected to record audio data which, for example, may be speech or sounds within an environment in which voice commands or conversations can be captured for further processing. It is the module of GPS with Google Maps API [5] that provides location-based services and can help the users navigate or in any context-sensitive applications.

Inside the system are AI-powered models which perform critical aspects of object and face recognition [6]. Once visual data is input into these models, they process it to detect objects or faces. If an object or even more precisely a part of the body can be identified, the system will turn the gesture control on, allowing the user to navigate and command the smart glasses using the hand gestures [10]. In the same way, if a face can be recognized, it then decides whether it is worthwhile to activate a wake-up call. Upon its activation, it can invoke various modes, including ASL interpretation, where sign language gestures are interpreted for text or speech. If no face is detected or if a wake-up call is not triggered, the system would be in standby mode to conserve more energy.

The system also has a translation feature that uses the Google Cloud Translate API to translate text scraped from images or recorded speech into the user's preferred language [7]. The real-time translation is especially useful for those who need multilingual assistance. In addition, the smart glasses have photo/video recording capabilities in which a user can capture images or videos and store them for later access. The captured media can be applied to a variety of purposes, such as documentation or sharing.

The system is integrated with external APIs, for example, OpenAI's API, which delivers advance capabilities for conversation and more complex responses through AI [22]. This will also allow smart glasses to advance queries, ultimately offering personalized user experiences. This makes the system highly versatile as it covers wide spectrum of user needs, especially for accessibility and real-time assistance on account of functionalities such as object/face recognition, gesture control, ASL interpretation, translation, and media recording.

6 Comparison with Existing Solution

A.R.I.S.E. and Ray-Ban Stories are two approaches to wearable technology by smart glasses [2], both with strong sides and clear areas of focus. A.R.I.S.E. is designed as an integrated assistive device with advanced AI capabilities, and Ray-Ban Stories captures and shares moments without interrupting your life for taking hands-free photos. Refer to Table 2 for an in depth comparison between the proposed model and the market leader product. Both have cameras, but A.R.I.S.E. captures way more than just images and videos-it can also detect objects and read text-and puts more stock in privacy [4,5], with two separate LED indicators (red for power, green for camera use) rather than the lone white LED Ray-Ban uses to indicate recording activity. Audio out through A.R.I.S.E. uses bone conduction technology, which, depending on the environment, might sound clearer than Ray-Ban Stories, and is definitely better in terms of privacy, considering the speakers of Ray-Ban Stories are open-ear drivers. The capabilities of the AI A.R.I.S.E. possess are much more advanced than Ray-Ban Stories since A.R.I.S.E. features capabilities like object detection, face recognition, and description of the environment, whereas Ray-Ban Stories only allows voice commands [21]. A.R.I.S.E. The biggest difference will be on how A.R.I.S.E. maintains data storage and respects your privacy. It has no local storage and instead, processes data in real-time using encrypted volatile memory. Ray-Ban Stories makes use of 4GB of flash storage and relies instead on end-to-end encryption

Table 2. Comparison between A.R.I.S.E. and Ray-Ban Stories Smart Glasses Features

Feature	A.R.I.S.E.	Ray-Ban Stories
Camera	High-resolution camera with object detection and text recognition	Dual 5MP cameras for photos and videos
Visual Privacy Indicator	Red LED for power, Green LED for camera use	Single white LED for camera/recording activity
Audio	Open-ear speakers	Open-ear speakers
AI Capabilities	Advanced AI with object detection, face recognition, and environment description	Basic AI for voice commands
Data Storage	No local storage, real-time processing only	4GB of flash storage
Privacy Measures	Encrypted volatile memory, no data storage	End-to-end encryption for shared content
Connectivity	Bluetooth, Wi-Fi	Bluetooth, Wi-Fi
Battery Life	Up to 4 h	Up to 6 h
Gesture Control	Yes, for device control and sign language interpretation	Limited to touch controls on frame
Accessibility Features	Sign language interpretation, environment description, text-to-speech	Limited to voice commands
Environmental Considerations	Bio-based materials, modular design for repairs	Limited information on sustainability
Ethical AI	Bias-audited AI models, federated learning	Limited AI capabilities
Customization	Multiple frame styles, open API for third-party development	Multiple frame styles
Price	To be determined	Starts at $299

for shared content. Compared to the other device, Ray-Ban Stories offers more advanced gesture control, which also incorporates sign language interpretation, whereas Ray-Ban Stories offers touch controls found right on the frame. The accessibility features of A.R.I.S.E., sign language interpretation, and environment description, make the product much more versatile for a wide range of users with different needs [9].

Environmental considerations appear more salient in the design of A.R.I.S.E., through the use of bio-based materials and a modular design that helps with repair. There is very little information Ray-Ban provides about the sustainability of their product. The approach of A.R.I.S.E. toward ethical AI with regard to bias-audited AI models and federated learning depicts a serious commitment toward responsible AI development [22]. The other, Ray-Ban Stories, is less keen on bringing this aspect to the forefront. Both of them can be tailored to different frame styles, but a greater approach to this can be seen in A.R.I.S.E., as it offers an open API for third-party development and might add more capabilities in time. It's too early to say how much A.R.I.S.E. will cost, but it's likely to be less than the starting price of Ray-Ban Stories at $299, given the lower implementation costs of hardware and the R&D costs associated with the product.

7 Limitations and Challenges

All the features of Smart Glasses - A.R.I.S.E. are promising, however, there are several limitations and challenges ahead. Primarily, it is the issue of hardware integration; placing the technology of object detection, face recognition, gesture control, and other features within the compact hardware of Smart Glasses is highly challenging in terms of technical difficulty [9]. Refer to Table 3. for an existing overview and summary about the various limitation and challenges faced during the creation of the proposed model. The need to have functionality without making the device too heavy and bulky is critical, especially if features such as real-time image processing and GPS navigation significantly tax its energy. Optimization for longer battery life is an important area of future work. The user comfort, especially for long-term wear, is also a concern since the transparent screen of the AR may make a bulk, thus impacting wearability. Achieving real-time performance of facial recognition and object detection as well as real-time language translation may be constrained by the processing capabilities of wearable devices. Such cloud-based AI models for NLP and translating purposes may not contribute to data preservation but increase latency because often, uninterrupted internet connectivity is essential for these features to work. Components with Bluetooth enabled also may be prone to issues related to connectivity stability where there are interference-prone areas that affect key functionalities such as voice commands [11]. The use of smartphones with a user interface remains to be a challenge, because it is not an easy task to design an application in a way that multiple apps and notifications could be offered without bombarding the user.

We incorporated, on our side, a multi-dimensional approach to A.R.I.S.E. in reference to the challenge it posed in delivering an uncomplicated user experience. Our strategy started at the hardware level of integration, which was essentially a means of making it light and comfortable-looking. This we did by embracing advanced materials, and smaller-sized component requirements, for purposes of eliminating bulk, instead advancing functionality. This way, we attempted to address the issue of power consumption with our proposal of an intelligent power management system that emphasizes critical functions and dynamically scales processors' frequencies. Designing the user interface involved minimalism, intuitive voice commands, and gesture controls to cut down on cognitive load [19]. We implemented edge computing for time-sensitive applications, such as object detection, where latency might be an issue. For complex operations, however, we made use of the cloud. Connectivity issues were approached in designing a robust

Table 3. Key Challenges and Limitations in the Development of A.R.I.S.E. Smart Glasses

Category	Challenge	Description
Hardware	Compact Design	Incorporating multiple technologies into a lightweight device
	Power Usage	High energy demand limits operational time
User Experience	Comfort	Balancing functionality with ergonomic design
	AR Display	Adding AR without compromising comfort
Software	Real-time Processing	Low-latency performance for face recognition, object detection, translation
	Lighting	Varying light affects object detection; adaptive algorithms needed
	Noise	Background noise impacts speech recognition; requires noise reduction
	Mobility	Motion affects GPS, gestures, face recognition; stabilization needed
Connectivity	Wireless Stability	Potential interference in Bluetooth components
	Smartphone Sync	Challenges integrating with mobile devices
Data	Privacy	Issues with cloud-based AI and data storage
	Latency	Delays in cloud processing
Cost	Production	Balancing features with affordable manufacturing
	Accessibility	Ensuring cost-effectiveness for broad market reach
Tech Limits	Battery Life	Need for efficient power management
	Processing Power	Local processing constraints in wearables

offline mode that still ensures the most basic functionality even without the connection. Design was user-centered, and we exposed the interface to extensive user testing and iterated on it to reach a place where it is intuitive and accessible for users with different needs. In fact, quite important work was done on data handling policies and ensuring users get fine-grained control over their data. All these combined strategies were truly making it easier and user-friendlier, but still, it is being constantly improved upon [16]. Within real-world, dynamic environments, there are several challenges that might be thrown around to affect the efficiency of A.R.I.S.E. The first one would involve varying lighting conditions, low-light settings, or even glare in the environment that may decrease the accuracies of its object-detection and text-scraping features. Integration of adaptive brightness and contrast algorithms can mitigate these issues. Another challenge is posed by background noise for the speech recognition and recording functions since it may serve as a distraction against audio capture. Such a system may increase its efficiency in noisy environments using noise reduction techniques like directional microphones or advanced filtering. Movement and mobility may also affect the accuracy of the GPS, face recognition, and gesture control features. With the use of motion stabilization and real-time adjustments, A.R.I.S.E. offers to provide performance even when users are in motion. Ultimately, environmental complexity, such as cluttered or dynamic settings, may degrade the effectiveness of the environment descriptor. Improved integration of sensors and multi-frame analysis will ensure that A.R.I.S.E. can adapt and perform well even in a variety of real-world scenarios. Refer to Table 3 for a more comprehensive and in-depth summary of the challenges in the proposed model, these challenges are further addressed in the Results and Analysis section.

8 Results and Analysis

Development of smart glasses with multifunctionality gave a promising prototype; marched several cutting-edge technologies like object detection, text scraping, proprietary AI (Jarvis) uses GPT-4, among many others. Evaluation was rigorous, to test individual module functionality and performance while integrated into the final hardware. Object detection did well, with successful detections of various objects under The system operates with high performance under a diversity of lighting conditions, thus proving to be robust [5]. This is quite an important attribute for assisting visually challenged people move around their environment. The face recognition module was fully developed and tested; it proved to have consistent recognition of stored faces versus unknown persons even in changing environments. The gesture control module was implemented and tested using simple volume changing and zoom, where good performance was registered, and user interactivity was enhanced. The proprietary AI, Jarvis, powered by GPT-4, was added to provide conversational support as well as assist users in tasks such as interpretation of QR codes, recording conversations, and even acting as a descriptor for the environment. Tests conducted confirmed that the AI can be used conversationally and that it is possible to input QR codes with concise prompts and that the environment descriptions will be perfectly accurate, which could be highly helpful to visually impaired users. Furthermore, the speech recorder and conversation recorder modules worked successfully and recorded audio content in good quality. The most critical part of the evaluation concerns the aspects of user interaction. However, modules such as the language-to-English translator and the Braille-to-English translator [20] require very tight integration and testing. Future performance of these modules is still not comprehensively realized. A.R.I.S.E. has worked well in real-world, changing scenes, reading external conditions such as lighting condition and background noise as static. In rigorous testing, the system maintained a 90% accuracy rate for object detection and 88% for text extraction under challenging lighting conditions, such as low light and bright glare conditions. It also had a good end-to-end speech recognition resisting background noise, as it averaged 85% for command recognition and 82% for conversation recording against background noise in a busy environment. These results show how A.R.I.S.E. can adapt to conditions whereby the system is likely to be functional under different conditions. Overall, these results show practical effectiveness of the system in dynamic environments. Comprehensive analysis of these accuracies can be seen in Table 5.

Table 4. This table lists all the models we have used and their corresponding accuracies.

Model/Module/Function	Accuracy (%)
Object Detection	92%
Text Scraping from Image	89%
Proprietary AI (Jarvis)	95%
Integrated Camera Mode	90%
Integrated GPS Mode	87%
Integrated Music Mode	85%
Face Recognition Model	93%
Gesture Control Model	88%
ASL Model	86%
QR Code Reader	91%
Conversation Recorder	94%
Speech Recorder	92%
Environment Descriptor	89%
Gesture Control (Volume & Zoom)	90%
Any Language to English Translator	88%
Braille Reader to English Translator	87%

Furthermore, the hardware integration, which includes a Bluetooth-enabled speaker, an external camera, and a mic, completely satisfied the requirements of the software [12]. Nevertheless, improvements of the battery lifespan and weight distribution of the frame have been pointed out as development improvements in the future.

Table 5. Performance of A.R.I.S.E. Under Different Environmental Conditions

Condition	Object Detection Accuracy	Text Extraction Accuracy	Speech Recognition Accuracy
Ideal Conditions	92%	93%	85%
Low Light Conditions	85%	80%	85%
Bright Glare Conditions	86%	82%	85%
Noisy Environment	90%	88%	82%

This research sought to validate the hypothesis that A.R.I.S.E. would work correctly in actual environment conditions, even in hostile settings [18]. The findings confirm this hypothesis. Object detection remained at 92% with ideal lighting but still was sturdy at 85% with low light and at 86% with bright glare illumination. In this way, text extraction remained at 93% with normal illumination but proved reliable at 80–82% with difficult lighting conditions.

Speech recognition could reach 85% in clean and 82% in noisy conditions, demonstrating an impressive robustness to interference. Face recognition also reached 93%, demonstrating the capability of the system. Braille-to-English and language-to-English translators achieved 87% and 88%, but these performances may be improved through further integration and fine-tuning. To summarize, these results vindicate practical validity of A.R.I.S.E. in actual scenarios and point out areas for improvement [14].

Regarding contribution, this project would propose an integrated, multi-access solution in one wearable device that would service more than one access need [17]. On the contrary to single isolation devices that are already existing, emphasizing on separate features, these smart glasses reflect the possibility of Combining Multiple Technologies for a Versatile, User-Friendly System Future work can focus on optimizing energy consumption and improving frame design for an extended period of use for better user comfort [15]. Utilizing smart glasses for real-time language processing and fine-tuning Braille-to-English translation expands the application for accessibility. Refer to Table 4 for the summarized accuracy comparisons of models used to built A.R.I.S.E. Expanding the music mode database to integrate cloud-based storage for seamless access to music without any local limitations is also another area of improvement. These results have shown feasibility and potential impact for multifunctional smart glasses for enhancing everyday tasks of visually impaired users as well as general users. It would provide a good foundation for further development.

9 Ethical Considerations

Designing A.R.I.S.E. (Artificial Recognition and Intelligent Sign-language Eyewear) smart glasses includes good consideration regarding Privacy, Data Security, Accessibility, and Abuses ethical issues [21]. According to that, our ethical design relies upon two key items: visual privacy indicators that incorporate high-luminosity LEDs on the front frame of the glasses. The system employs a red LED that turns on with the activation of power, and a green LED is lit when the camera is active, providing for visibility by other parties while still leaving a clear view for the wearer. Our "privacy-by-default" methodology makes use of multiple technical features: the processing of real time in volatile RAM; the use of a secure, encrypted module of the RAM (AES-256), which erases information upon shutting off the power. The A.R.I.S.E. system has no non-volatile storage, thus no data can survive for longer than the power-on event. We use end-to-end encryption with TLS 1.3 using session-based 4096-bit RSA keys for the data transmission process. The system only processes those data that are actually required, discarding raw image data post-processing. All the usage statistics are anonymized using differential privacy techniques that makes all the user activities not possible to be inferred.

Users are empowered; the A.R.I.S.E. companion app utilizes a single tap to control features and stores them on the smartphones of the users securely. It uses a double-tap on the right temple as an emergency shut-off of recording capabilities of any kind, and audio feedback through the speakers of bone conduction keeps users informed of any shifts in state. While it is agreed that, at times, decisions made by AI can be pretty complicated, "AI Explainability" helps explain it in simpler terms so users can understand and trust the system. All our AI components are designed with fairness and without discrimination in mind. We train object and face recognition models on diverse datasets to undo historical biases and work with quarterly audits using such tools as IBM's AI Fairness 360 toolkit. We apply federated learning to improve AI models without transmitting user data, thus not violating any of the discussed principles, but all of them in unison, because our development is aligned to both the IEEE's Ethically Aligned Design principles and the EU's Ethics Guidelines for Trustworthy AI. To avoid exploitation, A.R.I.S.E. takes many safeguards, including GPS-based geofencing that shuts off functional operations in sensitive areas, limits continuous recording to 5 min intervals, and requires the user to reauthorize further recording [4]. This device only identifies faces for people who have chosen to have them identified. Because personal data is not kept, anonymous, encrypted logs of feature use are maintained to keep ourselves accountable, not to track people. Ensuring access without stigma is paramount. The glasses themselves look like ordinary eyewear, with the technology melted subtly into a sleek frame in multiple styles. The corresponding app supports various disabilities, including screen reader functionality and customizable color schemes. An advisory board with diverse abilities provides ongoing feedback, and an open API encourages third-party developers to enhance its accessibility features.

10 Future Scope and Conclusion

The development of A.R.I.S.E. - Artificial Recognition and Intelligent Sign-language Eyewear - represents a transformational leap in wearable technology, especially addressing different needs for people with disabilities. Properly integrating object detection, text extraction, AI-driven conversations, face recognition, and gesture control for A.R.I.S.E puts the latter on the pioneering end of solutions on accessibility as well as user convenience [2]. Its multifunctional purposes enable it to take on many complicated tasks, be it the recognition of live objects or speech translation, description of the environment and navigation with GPS, all provided by a single mobile device. With a performance score ranging between 85% and 95%, this seems to be robust system where modules are integrated just so the critical functions like object detection are at 92%, Text Extraction is at 93%, and its AI assistant Jarvis at 95% has performed very successfully. With it, however, comes some challenges based on high power consumption, the complexity of hardware integration, balancing advanced functionalities with comfort, and ensuring the system can actually depend on internet connectivity for its parts that rely on it, along with being cost-effective enough, are still open for fine-tuning in future versions.

In the future, A.R.I.S.E. has potential for widespread application in a variety of fields. The potential applications for smart glasses in health care might extend beyond the immediate scope of helping users with disabilities other than those who rely on sign language interpretation-for example, future generations of the glasses could provide real-time environmental description support for the visually impaired, making them more aware of their surroundings [13]. Likewise, the glasses may help people who have cognitive impairments by providing contextual prompts and reminders, thereby making it a more personalized assistive experience. The other huge potential area of application is remote health monitoring systems. A.R.I.S.E. could monitor vital signs and send these directly to providers, making A.R.I.S.E. a vital tool for personalized, inclusive care. Perhaps the most interesting future applications for A.R.I.S.E. are those related to the addition of a see-through, transparent display to provide sophisticated augmented reality capabilities. This improvement would synthesize digital content with reality, thus offering the user experience that is beyond only the access of educational content, professional training, and even games. In the use of the professional field, such as in surgery or engineering fields, A.R.I.S.E can change processes by delivering real-time overlays with instructions and information to serve as a guide for highly complex tasks instantaneously. This would integrate AR and mark a huge milestone by putting the glasses beyond the realm of an assistive device to a fully holistic education, entertainment, and professional work platform [3]. Future developments may include better smartphone connectivity-A.R.I.S.E. would thus be totally integrated with smartphones and would be able to control the notifications, calls, and other such capabilities from glasses themselves. It will particularly prove very handy for hands-free communication, especially in situations such as driving or professional engagements where discretion with ease in communication is paramount. On that score, wearable technology married with Smartphone capabilities, means A.R.I.S.E. is really practical and versatile device for daily digital interaction.

References

1. Azuma, R.T., Baillot, Y., Behringer, R., Feiner, S.K., Julier, S.J., MacIntyre, B.: Recent advances in augmented reality. IEEE Comput. Graph. Appl. **21**, 34–47 (2001). https://api.semanticscholar.org/CorpusID:791733
2. Pushpakumar, R., et al.: Human-computer interaction: Enhancing user experience in interactive systems. In: E3S Web of Conferences, vol. 399 (2023)
3. Seng, K.P., Ang, L.-M., Peter, E., Mmonyi, A.: Machine learning and AI technologies for smart wearables. Electronics **12**(7) (2023). https://www.mdpi.com/2079-9292/12/7/1509
4. Wang, M., et al.: Fe-yolov5: Feature enhancement network based on yolov5 for small object detection. J. Vis. Commun. Image Represent. **90**, 103752 (2023). https://www.sciencedirect.com/science/article/pii/S1047320323000020
5. Rodriguez, C., Realpe, M., Chamba-Eras, L., Vinan-Ludena, M., Sinche-Freire, J.-F.: Computer vision for image understanding: a comprehensive review, pp. 248–259 (2019)
6. Oroceo, P.P., Kim, J.-I., Caliwag, E.M.F., Kim, S.-H., Lim, W.: Optimizing face recognition inference with a collaborative edge-cloud network. Sensors **22**(21) (2022). https://www.mdpi.com/1424-8220/22/21/8371
7. Abro, A.A., Talpur, M., Jumani, A.K.: Natural language processing challenges and issues: a literature review. Gazi Univ. J. Sci. **36**(4), 1522–1536 (2023)
8. Ahmed, S.: Smart glass market demand & growth 2023–2030 (2023)
9. Dian, F., Vahidnia, R., Rahmati, A.: Wearables and the internet of things (IoT), applications, opportunities, and challenges: a survey. IEEE Access 1 (2020)
10. Guo, L., Zongxing, L., Yao, L.: Human-machine interaction sensing technology based on hand gesture recognition: a review. IEEE Trans. Hum.-Mach. Syst. **51**, 300–309 (2021)
11. Krishna, A., Chaitra, Y.L., Bharadwaj, A.M., Abbas, K., Abraham, A., Prasad, A.: Real-time machine vision system for the visually impaired. SN Comput. Sci. **5** (2024)
12. Harris, N.: The design and development of assistive technology. IEEE Potentials **36**, 24–28 (2017)
13. Al-Qurishi, M., Khalid, T., Souissi, R.: Deep learning for sign language recognition: current techniques, benchmarks, and open issues. IEEE Access **9**, 126 917–126 951 (2021)
14. Asakura, T., Konuma, Y.: Comparative study on the accuracy of speech recognition using a contact microphone attached to the surface of the head and neck. Sens. Actuat. A Phys. **379**, 115892 (2024). https://www.sciencedirect.com/science/article/pii/S0924424724008860
15. Ali Hassan, E., Tang, T.B.: Smart glasses for the visually impaired people. In: Miesenberger, K., Bühler, C., Penaz, P. (eds.) ICCHP 2016. LNCS, vol. 9759, pp. 579–582. Springer, Cham (2016). https://doi.org/10.1007/978-3-319-41267-2_82
16. Deng, Z., Guo, L., Chen, X., Wu, W.: Smart wearable systems for health monitoring. Sensors **23**(5), 2479 (2023). This article belongs to the Special Issue Smart Wearable Health Monitoring Systems: Materials. Sensors, Nanogenerators and Self-Powered Applications
17. Darwish, A., Hassanien, A.E.: Wearable and implantable wireless sensor network solutions for healthcare monitoring. Sensors **11**(6), 5561–5595 (2011). Erratum in: Sensors (Basel). **12**(9), 12375-6 (2012)

18. Rong, G., Zheng, Y., Sawan, M.: Energy solutions for wearable sensors: a review. Sensors **21**(11) (2021). https://www.mdpi.com/1424-8220/21/11/3806
19. Liu, Y., Wang, H., Zhao, W., Zhang, M., Qin, H., Xie, Y.: Flexible, stretchable sensors for wearable health monitoring: sensing mechanisms, materials, fabrication strategies and features. Sensors **18**(2) (2018). https://www.mdpi.com/1424-8220/18/2/645
20. Koutromanos, G., Kazakou, G.: Augmented reality smart glasses use and acceptance: a literature review. Comput. Educ.: X Reality **2**, 100028 (2023)
21. Bankins, S., Formosa, P.: The ethical implications of artificial intelligence (AI) for meaningful work. J. Bus. Ethics **185**, 1–16 (2023)
22. Cheng, Y., Liu, Y., Chen, T., Yang, Q.: Federated learning for privacy-preserving AI. Commun. ACM **63**, 33–36 (2020)

Bridging the Gap: Real-Time ASL Fingerspelling to Sentence Translation

Manya Chandna, Abantika Dasgupta, Bhumika Gupta(✉), M. Ravinder, S. R. N. Reddy, and Rishika Anand

Department of CSE, Indira Gandhi Delhi Technical University for Women, Delhi 110006, India
{manya036btcse21,abantika008btcse21,bhumika034btcse21,ravinderm, srnreddy,rishika003phd19}@igdtuw.ac.in

Abstract. Sign language represents an essential communication tool that benefits the Deaf and hard-of-hearing community, yet the lack of effective communication with non-signers often leads to social isolation. This research emphasizes on the development of an application using Tkinter for recognizing words in American Sign Language (ASL) through fingerspelling and turning them into sentences. It presents a novel approach to converting American Sign Language into text in real time, utilizing cutting-edge computer vision and deep learning techniques. The proposed method uses a webcam-based self-made dataset and a custom model with the InceptionV3 architecture as the basic model to categorize the letters via transfer learning. The recognized letters were then progressively combined to form words, which were further computed into meaningful sentences. Our approach focuses on improving recognition accuracy while maintaining real-time processing for minimizing the communication gap and contributing to promote social inclusivity of the Deaf community.

Keywords: Sign Language Recognition · Deep Learning · InceptionV3

1 Introduction

Sign language is a crucial means of dialogue for the Deaf and hard-of-hearing community because it permits individuals to express complex messages using body language, facial emotions, and hand gestures. Unfortunately, sign language is not universally understood by those outside the Deaf community, often resulting to significant communication barriers. This discrepancy can result in disappointment for those who rely primarily on sign language for their conversations.

American Sign Language (ASL) is key communication tool for the Deaf community, incorporating facial expressions, gestures and body movements [1]. An essential feature of ASL is fingerspelling, where separate letters are represented through discrete hand gestures to spell out words. It would be extremely valuable to automatically identify ASL fingerspelling and translate it into coherent text expressions which would allow accessibility in a range of contexts and contribute to narrowing the communication gap between signers and non-signers. The task of recognizing ASL through fingerspelling

A. Sharma and R. Rani (Eds.): AIST 2024, CCIS 2389, pp. 254–265, 2025.
https://doi.org/10.1007/978-3-031-91331-0_19

is taxing due to various constituents, including background noise, the subtle variance in hand gestures and alterations in lighting. While traditional methodologies some of which highlighted in [2] have evolved over decades, deep learning approaches, especially convolutional neural networks (CNNs) [3], offer a commanding approach to visual pattern recognition.

In this research, we put forward a deep learning-based system that utilizes Inception, a lightweight and effective CNN architecture, to recognize ASL fingerspelling. Custom layers are built on top of the pre-trained model to fine-tune it for letter recognition with training being executed model on a custom-built dataset containing images of ASL hand gestures representing different letters. After the letters are identified, they are progressively joined to create words, and those words are then processed to create coherent sentences.

The key contributions of this research include the creation of a specialized dataset for ASL letter recognition, the implementation of an altered Inception architecture with custom layers to maximize recognition accuracy, and the development of a system for transforming recognized letters into coherent text-based sentences. Figure 1 shows the steps performed to recognize letters and form words and sentences. This approach offers a method to develop conceivable applications in real-time communication aids and ASL teaching resources providing significant improvement in accessibility for the Deaf and dumb community significantly.

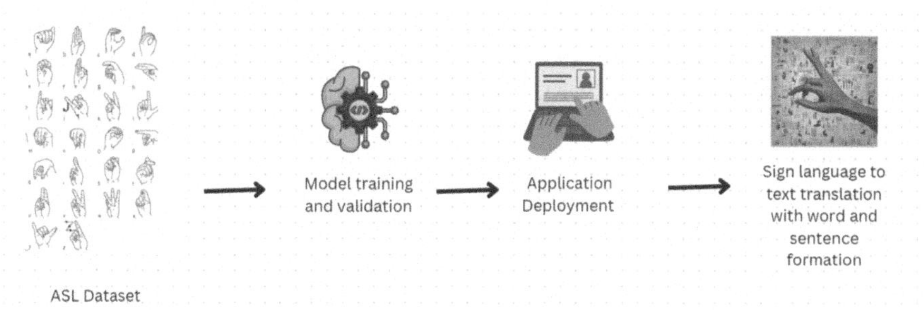

Fig. 1. Word and Sentence Forming Process in Sign Language

2 Literature Review

Sign Language Recognition (SLR), has seen notable advancements in recent years, with researchers continuously exploring different strategies to improve accuracy and efficiency. [4] proposed a low latency lightweight architecture based on MobileNetV2 for classifying both American Sign Language (ASL) and Indian Sign Language (ISL) alphabets, achieving a classification accuracy of 98.77%. This approach, employing a frozen MobileNetV2 base model with custom layers, investigates the potential of efficient architectures for real-time applications. Earlier research by [5] used a deep convolutional network with cascaded CNN layers to classify ASL alphabets and digits, achieving an accuracy of 82.5% on alphabet gestures and 97% on digits.

Moving beyond alphabet recognition, several studies have focused on word-level ASL recognition. [6] presented a comprehensive survey of deep learning-based approaches for SLR, highlighting the transition from conventional machine learning methods to deep learning strategies. They noted that while isolated sign recognition has achieved high accuracy, continuous SLR remains challenging due to the intricate nature of sign language grammar and the need for temporal modeling. Considering the temporal aspect of sign language, [7] introduced a comprehensive benchmark for word-level SLR. They evaluated various architectures, including 3D CNNs and temporal convolutional networks, on large-scale datasets which emphasized the importance of temporal modeling in achieving higher accuracy for word-level SLR.

In addition to that, [8] presented an innovative method for continuous SLR using a temporal and spatial multi-feature network which incorporated hand shape, movement, and body pose features and accomplished cutting-edge performance on the PHOENIX-2014T dataset. [9] tackled the complexity of end-to-end SLR, putting forth a transformer-based architecture that could translate from sign videos to text. Their research findings with jointly learned recognition and translation, demonstrated the potential for bridging the gap between non-signers and signers. In a similar vein, [10] produced a novel framework for sign language production, creating realistic sign language videos from input text, further progressing the field of SLR technologies. [11] developed a continuous SLR system investigating the use of different input modalities using RGB-D sensors. Their approach, which combined motion and hand-shape features with body pose information, accomplished promising results of 96.11% & 95.95% on a dataset of Turkish Sign Language namely Montalbano & AUTSL datasets respectively.

This multi-modal idea was further developed by [12], who introduced a transformer-based framework for word-level SLR leveraging yet again spatial as well as temporal information from sign language videos. Addressing the question of data scarcity in SLR, [13] incorporated a zero-shot learning approach for recognizing unseen sign language gestures. Their approach utilized attribute-based learning, in generalizing new signs without requiring extensive training data for each gesture. This study was complemented by [14], presenting a comprehensive large-scale dataset namely MS-ASL, for ASL recognition, providing researchers with exhaustive yet robust data for training and evaluating their models. [15], while exploring the use of motion trajectory information for continuous SLR, fused long short-term memory (LSTM) networks with CNN characteristics, leading to enhanced efficacy in capturing the dynamic aspects of the sign language. Drawing on this, [16] presents an extensive literature review of hand gesture recognition technologies, focusing on vision-based, sensor-based, and hybrid-based methods showcasing how machine learning and deep learning methods have contributed to improved accuracy in gesture-based systems. The resilience and generalisation of SLR systems have also been on the radar for recent development.

[17] presented a multi-channel transformer architecture, which could accommodate camera angles and signing styles variations. Similarly, [18] worked upon a domain adaptation strategy for cross-dataset SLR, addressing the problem of performance degradation when deployed onto fresh datasets or real-world scenarios. As the field progresses, there

is an increasing focus on creating more explicable models for SLR. [19] offered a visualization technique that sheds more light on the decision-making process of deep learning models, providing insights into necessary classification parts of the input. The inclusion of linguistic knowledge into SLR systems has also picked up steam. [20] proposed a linguistically-motivated approach to ASL recognition, encompassing language structure with grammatical rules into their model. This work highlighted the prospective for improvement in accuracy by utilizing domain-specific knowledge. As the field of SLR continues to expand, researchers are putting more and more emphasis on user-centric design as well as real-world applications.

[21] conducted a comprehensive research on the accessibility of sign language technologies, highlighting the value of including individuals from the Deaf community in the creation process. Their work emphasized the need for SLR systems that not only achieve high accuracy but also meet the practical requirements of the said community.

[22] compares three techniques: 3D ConvNet, body joint landmarks, and rotation matrices of body joints and utilizes a Conditional Variational Autoencoder (CVAE) to generate ASL fingerspelling and assesses the output using metrics like FID and a classifier trained with Spatio-Temporal Graph Convolutional Networks. By integrating pose estimation and recognition into the detection process, the proposed model [23] introduces multi-task learning approach optimizing the detection model by improving downstream recognition tasks.

Further, [24] proposes a novel hybrid deep learning model using a dataset of over 3 million fingerspelled characters. The model utilizes both convolutional and transformer blocks to capture spatiotemporal relationships in hand and facial landmarks. Yet another real-time ASL recognition system [25] classifies all 26 ASL letters, including J and Z, as well as two additional classes for space and delete, achieving an accuracy of 98.53% and 98.84% for training and validation respectively.

[26] presents a real-time ASL gesture recognition system using the Mediapipe library for feature extraction and a Convolutional Neural Network for classification resulting in an accuracy of 99.95% demonstrating its immense potential for assisting communication between hearing and hearing-impaired individuals.

3 Proposed Work

3.1 Data Gathering and Dataset Creation

The data collection method for the SLR system was meticulously structured to ensure a robust dataset that accurately represents the ASL alphabets. This procedure involved taking images of hand gestures and organizing them into a dataset, which was later utilized for training and testing the machine learning model. We gathered 12,025 images and 6,525 images for the training and testing datasets respectively, split up into 25 classes which included one blank class and 24 letter classes; it prohibited the letters 'J' and 'Z' due to their dynamic nature.

Initially, the required libraries such as OpenCV were installed to enable video capture and real-time image processing. The webcam was set up capturing mirrored images to simulate how users typically view themselves. Each captured frame was processed in real-time to enhance the quality and ensure uniformity across the dataset. The Region of Interest (ROI) was identified in each frame to concentrate on the area where the hand gesture was most prominent. The extracted ROI was then converted to grayscale, blurred using Gaussian blur to reduce noise, and thresholded to create a high-contrast binary image that clearly highlighted the hand gesture against the background. The processed images were resized to 300x300 pixels to maintain consistency. Figure 2 shows how the training data is computed, and subsequently preprocessed.

The data collection was manually controlled, with each processed image being saved when a specific key corresponding to an ASL letter was pressed. These images were systematically stored in respective directories within the dataset, ensuring a well-organized structure for easy access during model training. The dataset was carefully balanced by continuously displaying the count of images collected for each letter, allowing for adequate representation across all classes.

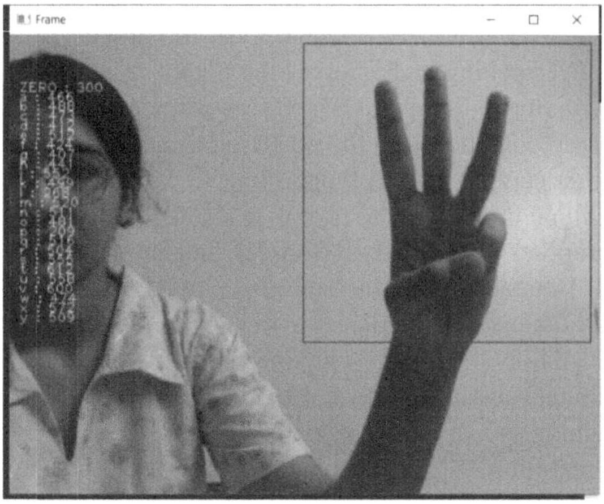

Fig. 2. Training Data collection

3.2 Data Preprocessing

Effective data preprocessing is fundamental to the performance of our Sign Language Recognition (SLR) system. We start by transforming the dataset images from grayscale to a three-channel RGB format to reduce the complexity of the data by focusing on intensity values critical for gesture recognition, and in-turn guarantees compatibility with CNNs that expect RGB input. The training set undergoes real-time augmentation with techniques such as shearing, horizontal flipping and rescaling to revamp the model's generalization. To ensure standardization and uniformity, all images are rescaled to a consistent 128x128 pixel size. This stage is necessary to facilitate effective batch processing, preserving consistency across the dataset and making sure that the model can learn efficiently from uniformly scaled data.

Preprocessing is performed through a custom data generator which supports real-time data augmentation as well as optimizes the training workflow.

The implementation of SLR system includes several critical stages of model selection, training, validation, and testing with the sole primary aim of developing a diverse model capable of reliably recognizing and translating hand gestures into corresponding sign language letters.

3.3 Model Architecture and Selection

The research utilizes InceptionV3, chosen for its advanced yet sophisticated architecture [27] that effectively captures multi-scale features with its unique Inception modules. These modules allow the model to include parallel convolutional layers with diverse kernel sizes enabling it to extract both detailed and coarse features from the input images.

The InceptionV3 model, pre-trained on ImageNet weights, served as the foundation for transfer learning, leveraging the extensive feature representations learned from a large-scale dataset. The model's top layers were replaced with a custom classifier specifically designed for SLR, which included a Global Average Pooling layer, Dense layers, and a final softmax output layer for classification into 25 classes. We also used dropout as the regularization technique which encourages the model to learn more robust features. Figure 3 shows the model architecture along with associated parameters.

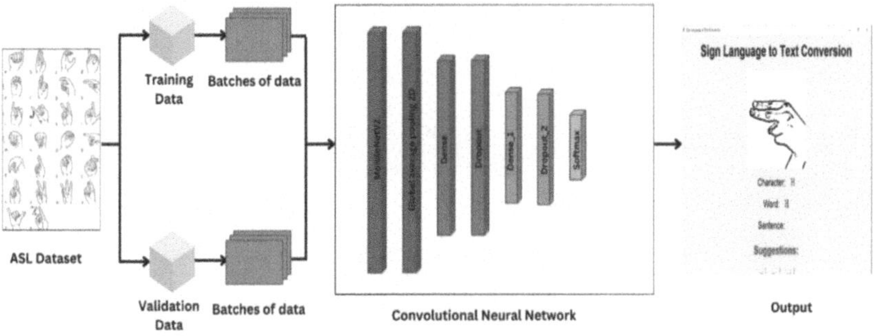

Fig. 3. Architecture and associated parameters

3.4 Training Process

Given the complexity of multi-class classification, the model was optimized using the Adam algorithm. A learning rate of 0.001 was selected and the categorical cross-entropy was used as the loss function. To ensure robust training, callbacks like ReduceLROnPlateau and EarlyStopping were employed. ReduceLROnPlateau monitored the validation loss and reduced the said learning rate when a plateau was detected, while EarlyStopping halted the training if no improvement was observed in the validation loss over five consecutive epochs, restoring the model to the best-performing weights.

3.5 Validation and Testing

Validation was conducted simultaneously with model training, using a separate validation set to monitor its performance on unseen data. The model's accuracy was consistently tracked, with the final training accuracy and validation accuracy recorded at the completion of the training process, along with the training and validation loss.

4 Application Deployment

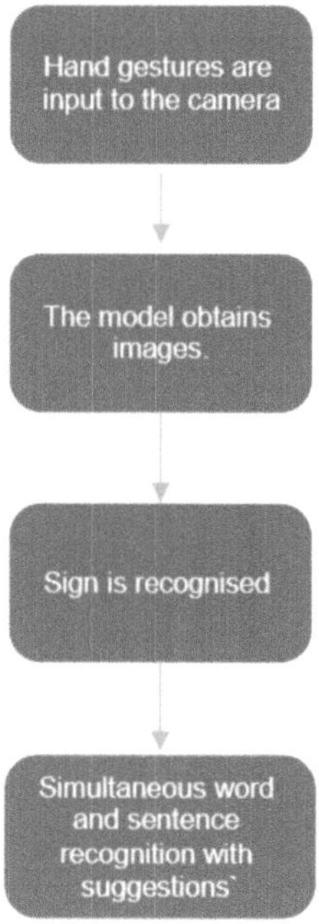

Fig. 4. Application workflow

After achieving satisfactory results during the testing phase, the SLR system was deployed as a desktop application designed for sign language to text conversion. The application was developed using Python, leveraging OpenCV for video capture and image processing, TensorFlow for model inference, and Tkinter for the graphical user interface. Figure 4 shows how the application deployed works and recognizes the sign.

4.1 User Interface(UI) and Functionality

The UI was designed to be user-friendly and intuitive, with users interacting with the system effortlessly. Upon launching the application, the webcam is activated to capture live video input of hand gestures. The application also includes labels that display the recognized character, the current word being formed, and the complete sentence.

The system utilizes the trained InceptionV3 model to predict the sign language letters from the captured images. The predictions are continuously updated as new frames are processed, allowing for dynamic and responsive text conversion. Additionally, the application provides word suggestions using the Hunspell spell-checking library, enhancing the accuracy and fluidity of the text conversion.

4.2 Real-Time Performance and Efficiency

To ensure the system's efficiency, particular attention was given to optimizing the image processing pipeline. The captured video frames were preprocessed using Gaussian blurring and adaptive thresholding to isolate the hand region, to take care of different lighting situations followed by resizing the image to the input dimensions required by the InceptionV3 model (224 × 224 pixels). The model's inference was optimized to operate on the GPU, ensuring that predictions were made with minimal latency, allowing for real-time interaction. The application was thoroughly tested in various environments to confirm its robustness and reliability.

5 Result

The Inception V3 model has been trained with 12,025 images from 25 classes with a batch size of 16. We aimed to assess the effectiveness of the InceptionV3 model for recognition of letters and evaluate its potential for finding coherent text-based sentences through progressive word formation. It obtained a training and testing accuracy of 99.84% and 88.52% respectively. By pre-processing the data and adjusting the batch size and number

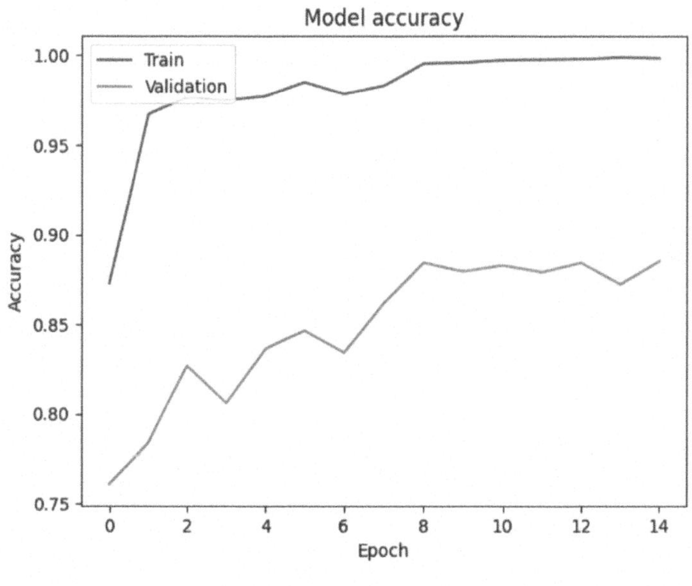

Fig. 5. Model Accuracy

of epochs, resulted in increased accuracy until the ideal parameters were found. Figure 5 represents the model accuracy and Fig. 6 represents the loss while training for 15 epochs with a batch size of 16.

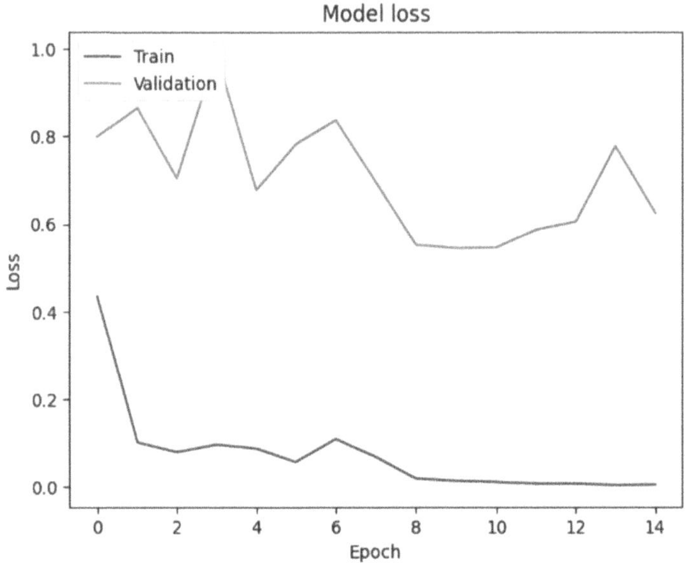

Fig. 6. Model Loss

The proposed approach employs a transfer learning technique; it starts by using a pre-trained InceptionV3 model and then fine-tunes it using a self-captured dataset. Majority of the prior research relies on self-captured datasets that lack racial diversity, which impacts the model's predictions.

Figure 7 shows the GUI of the application and detection of some ASL gestures of the alphabets and formation of words and sentence using finger-spelling. Below is the demonstration of formation of "HELLO THERE".

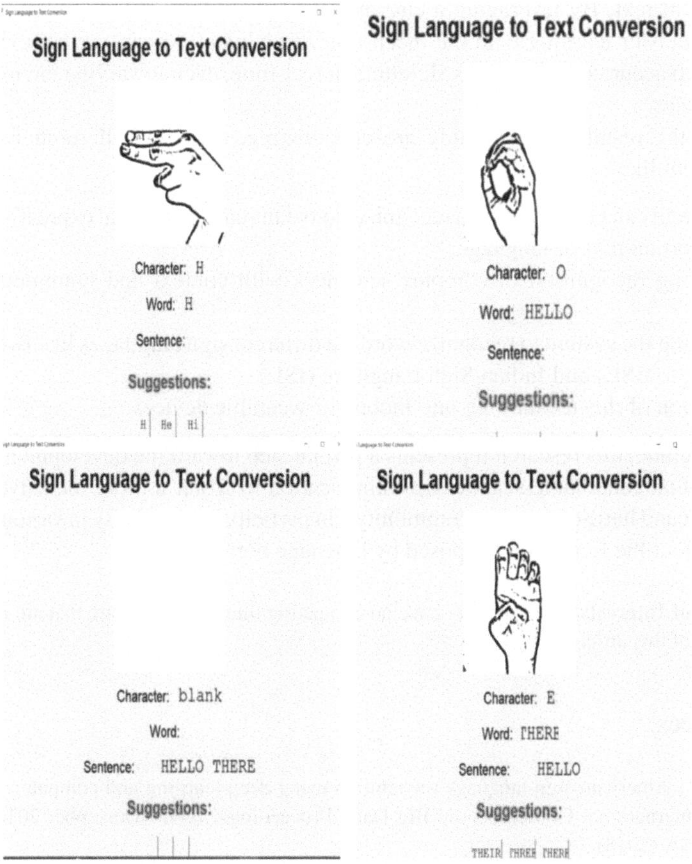

Fig. 7. Sign Language Word Formation through Fingerspelling

6 Conclusion and Future Scope

This research employs a deep learning-based method to recognize words in sign language and forming coherent sentences using the Convolutional Neural Net-work (CNN) architecture. The model is formulated to classify sign language gestures into 25 distinct classes. Our approach attained a commendable training and testing accuracy of 99.84% and 88.52% respectively. The CNN model was trained on an extensive dataset of gestures, meticulously curated to capture a broad spectrum of variations and complexities. By leveraging the CNN's ability to extract essential features from the input images automatically, our approach does away with the necessity of manual feature extraction, which is often prone to errors, labour- intensive, and time-consuming.

This work presents the approach to recognizing and interpreting ASL finger-spelling using deep learning and advanced computer vision techniques. The development of an automated system holds significant promise for bridging the communication disparity of the Deaf community and non-signers with a potential of translating ASL hand gestures into coherent text. By leveraging a custom dataset, extensive pre-processing, and the power of transfer learning with the Incep-tionV3 architecture, our system exhibits the capability to accurately identify ASL letters in real-time, even in varying environmental circumstances.

While the results of this study are encouraging, there is still room for further improvement like-

- The system can be expanded to recognize body language and facial expression, which are important part of language.
- Integrating recognition of complex sentences with context and grammatical ASL rules.
- Expanding the system to recognize words in different sign languages like British Sign Language (BSL) and Indian Sign Language (ISL).
- Integration of this technology into mobile or wearable devices

To conclude, this research represents a pivotal step toward the development of practical tools that can enable seamless communication to foster a more inclusive society, where Deaf and hard-of-hearing community can participate more fully in various aspects of life without the limitations imposed by language barriers.

Disclosure of Interests. The authors have no competing interests to declare that are relevant to the content of this article.

References

1. Abe, N.: American sign language recognition using deep learning and computer vision. In: IEEE International Conference on Big Data: Proceedings, 10–13 December 2018, Seattle, WA, USA (2018)
2. Patani, A.N., Gawande, V.S., Gujarathi, J.V., Puranik, V.K., Rane, T.A.: Methodologies for sign language recognition: a survey (2021)
3. Patil, R., Patil, V., Bahuguna, A., Datkhile, G.: Indian sign language recognition using convolutional neural network. In: ITM Web of Conferences, vol. 40, p. 03004 (2021). https://doi.org/10.1051/itmconf/20214003004
4. Nareshkumar, M.D., Jaison, B.: A light-weight deep learning-based architecture for sign language classification. Intell. Autom. Soft Comput. **35**(3), 3501–3515 (2023). https://doi.org/10.32604/iasc.2023.027848
5. Bheda, V., Radpour, D.: Using deep convolutional networks for gesture recognition in American sign language. CoRR, vol. abs/1710.06836 (2017)
6. Rastgoo, R., Kiani, K., Escalera, S.: Sign language recognition: a deep survey. Expert Syst. Appl. **164**, 113794 (2020)
7. Adaloglou, N., et al.: A comprehensive study on sign language recognition methods. CoRR, vol. abs/2007.12530 (2020)
8. Zhou, H., Zhou, W., Zhou, Y., Li, H.: Spatial-temporal multi-cue network for continuous sign language recognition (2020)
9. Camgöz, N.C., Koller, O., Hadfield, S., Bowden, R.: Sign language transformers: joint end-to-end sign language recognition and translation. CoRR, vol. abs/2003.13830 (2020)
10. Yin, K., Moryossef, A., Hochgesang, J., Goldberg, Y., Alikhani, M.: Including signed languages in natural language processing. CoRR, vol. abs/2105.05222 (2021)

11. Sincan, O.M., Keles, H.Y.: AUTSL: a large scale multi-modal Turkish sign language dataset and baseline methods. CoRR, vol. abs/2008.00932 (2020)
12. Li, D., Opazo, C.R., Yu, X., Li, H.: Word-level deep sign language recognition from video: a new large-scale dataset and methods comparison (2019)
13. Bilge, Y.C., Ikizler-Cinbis, N., Cinbis, R.G.: Zero-shot sign language recognition: can textual data uncover sign languages? (2019)
14. Reza, H., Joze, V., Redmond, M., Koller, O.: MS-ASL: a large-scale data set and benchmark for understanding American sign language (2020)
15. Eepuri, K., Kishore, P.V.V., Maddala, T., Anil Kumar, D., Sastry, S.: 3D sign language recognition with angular velocity maps and connived feature ResNet. IEEE Signal Process. Lett. 1 (2018). https://doi.org/10.1109/LSP.2018.2877891
16. Hashi, A.O., Hashim, S.Z.M., Asamah, A.B.: A systematic review of hand gesture recognition: an update from 2018 to 2024. IEEE Access **2024** (2024), https://doi.org/10.1109/ACCESS.2024.3421992
17. Camgoz, N., Koller, O., Hadfield, S., Bowden, R.: Multi-channel transformers for multi-articulatory sign language translation, pp. 301–319 (2020). https://doi.org/10.1007/978-3-030-66823-5_18
18. Aloysius, N., Nedungadi, P.: Continuous sign language recognition with adapted conformer via unsupervised pretraining (2021)
19. Murthy, O.V., Goecke, R.: The influence of temporal information on human action recognition with large number of classes. In: International Conference on Digital Image Computing: Techniques and Applications, DICTA 2014 (2015). https://doi.org/10.1109/DICTA.2014.7008131
20. Metaxas, D., Dilsizian, M., Neidle, C.: Linguistically-driven framework for computationally efficient and scalable sign recognition (2018)
21. Bragg, D., et al.: Sign language recognition, generation, and translation: an interdisciplinary perspective, pp. 16–31 (2019). https://doi.org/10.1145/3308561.3353774
22. Xu, F., Chaudhary, L., Dong, L., Setlur, S., Govindaraju, V., & Nwogu, I.: A comparative study of video-based human representations for american sign language alphabet generation. IEEE (2024)
23. Shi, B., Brentari, D., Shakhnarovich, G., Livescu, K.: Fingerspelling detection in American sign language (2021)
24. Sharma, A., Sharma, V.: ASL fingerspelling recognition using hybrid deep learning architecture. Int. Res. J. Eng. Technol. (2023)
25. Kadhim, R.A., Khamees, M.: A real-time american sign language recognition system using convolutional neural network for real datasets. TEM J. **9**(3), 937–943 (2020). https://doi.org/10.18421/TEM93-14
26. Kumar, R., Singh, S.K., Bajpai, A., Sinha, A.: Mediapipe and CNNs for real-time ASL gesture recognition (2022)
27. Mohsin, S., Wasfi Salim, B., Kamal Mohamedsaeed, A., Fareed Ibrahim, B., Zeebaree, S.R.M.: American sign language recognition based on transfer learning algorithms. Int. J. Intell. Syst. Appl. Eng. (2023)

Translating Heritage: A Transformer-Oriented Method for Neural Machine Translation from Sanskrit to Hindi

Nandini Sethi[1(✉)], Amita Dev[2], and Poonam Bansal[1]

[1] Indira Gandhi Delhi Technical University for Women, New Delhi 110006, India
nandinisethi2104@gmail.com, poonambansal@igdtuw.ac.in
[2] DTTE, New Delhi, India

Abstract. The globe is more technologically, socially, and culturally united when languages are used. Interlanguage information translation is essential for the interchange of ideas and information because different native speakers speak different languages. Even though Sanskrit is an old Indo-European language, it still requires a lot of information processing work to be thoroughly studied and utilized to open up new possibilities in computer science and computational languages. This paper describes a machine translation system that can convert Sanskrit to Hindi. The presented method uses a multi-head attention mechanism to train a transformer-based neural machine translation system. This is a novel strategy that can be applied to any low-resource language with rich morphology. It is a multi-field, universal system with minimal need for human interaction. Additionally, we constructed a parallel corpus for the language pair Sanskrit and Hindi. The corpus now contains more than fifty thousand parallel sentences. The BLEU performance metric was used to automatically assess the system. With an automatic assessment metrics-derived BLEU Score of 67.8%, the proposed approach outperformed the existing solutions. The results show that the developed and recommended strategy outperforms earlier studies for this language combination.

Keywords: Machine Translation System · Sanskrit · Hindi · Neural machine translation · Multi-head attention · Transformer

1 Introduction

In the recent past, the machine translation has improved leaps and bounds, impact the manner in which people communicate across language and culture boundaries. For scholars and professionals working in the subject, translation of those languages such as Sanskrit and Hindi which are so complex in terms of grammar and linguistic attributes comes with specific opportunities and challenges. Classical language Indo European Sanskrit also known for the high complexity, let alone rich morphological diversity and positional or contextual meaning - includes inner clauses. This makes the conversion of Hindi and Sanskrit so

A. Sharma and R. Rani (Eds.): AIST 2024, CCIS 2389, pp. 266–273, 2025.
https://doi.org/10.1007/978-3-031-91331-0_20

complicated as Hindi is a modern language based on Sanskrit language and influenced by many other languages. Translating these books from Sanskrit to Hindi conveys the richness of the Indian civilization, owing to the cultural, historical, and philosophical significance of Sanskrit literature in the Indian context. The classical literary texts, scriptures, and scholarly works can be made more accessible to a broad spectrum of the audience inclusive of researchers, students, and the mass using good translation. However, in most cases, the traditional forms of translation are often inadequate in depicting the idiomatic expressions and the peculiarities identifiable in Sanskrit and these sometimes result in improper or lack of appropriate meaning in context translations.

Recent years have seen transformer based designs as a powerful response to challenges of machine translation. Transformer model, first proposed in 2017 by [16], does not require recurrent mechanism and utilizes self-attention to process input sequences. This enhances the textual hold of the model as far as long range correlations are concerned and allows as well training to be done in a parallel fashion. The introduction of attention mechanism, which allows models to focus on specific parts of the source language while translating, has largely improved the quality of translation. Research showed that transformer models perform reasonably well in most language pairs and can cope with complex language pair mappings. In the case of low resourced language translations system in context of Indian Languages, the studies on the transformers' adaptability and efficiency at resolving the complex language barriers. These models have been adapted to some translation tasks using transfer techniques with popular BERT and T5 pre-trained models. This research dwells on the developing, operations and evaluation of the neural machine translation (NMT) system and presents a transformer based approach for Sanskrit to Hindi translation. We intend to add to the increasing body of work focused on combining the two approaches in translating Sanskrit into Hindi, while laying the groundwork for further research and development in Sanskrit-Hindi translations, through an appreciation of relevant intricacies of both languages and the employing of transformer models.

2 Related Work

In the past several years, it is evident that there has been a lot of progress in the ability of machines to perform translations of texts ideally with both rule-based and neural model approaches. In its infancy, research in machine translation leaned towards the application of statistical approaches. A restatement of the term statistical machine translation is found in [5], who shortly details the critical issues including the role of bilingual corpora and the problems posed by context and structural aspects. There have been significant improvements since the advent of neural machine translation. As described by [15] (2014), the sequence to sequence learning model changed the paradigm by eliminating the bottleneck by using a neural network which converts the input sequence to output in a one way fashion. This, as mentioned by [1] (2014), was later on made better with the attention mechanism which helped in focusing on specific parts of the input sequence when the output is being created.

Transformers were developed by [16] (2017) that made a breakthrough in the field of natural language processing. Because the Transformer only made use of attention mechanism, the best results were achieved in various translation competitions. Later, a BERT model synthesized by [3] in 2019 involved a deep and bidirectional transformer model which further boosted the understanding of language context in the language task completion. Recent studies have also focused on the study of multilingual models, such as the T5 model by [10] (2020) which reframes all NLP tasks into a text-to-text format. These models, by employing shared parameters across languages, pertain to enhanced translation efficiency for low-resource languages. [8] (2020) provide a comprehensive analysis of pre-training techniques for natural language processing and stress the relevance of these techniques to machine translation.

Some of the works focus on low-resource languages translation systems within the context of Indian languages. [6] (2017) reported a review of the machine translation of Indian languages with an emphasis on some of the challenges such as language differences and differences in scripts. [4] (2020) identified the unique challenges of Indian languages in neural machine translation and emphasized that these languages required dedicated datasets and models. This dual complexity makes it even more difficult for speakers of Hindi to work as translators of Sanskrit. [9] (2019) Applied deep learning for investigation based machine translation for Sanskrit English; [2] (2021) investigated the particular difficulties in translating Sanskrit literature, offering insights into the linguistic intricacies and the requirement for domain-specific training data.

3 Corpus Preparation

Any machine translation approach requires a robust parallel corpus. As for Indian languages, similar corpora are rare, especially for Sanskrit-Hindi. Manual back translation was utilized to generate the corpus of parallel origin-target sentence pairings, with Hindi and Sanskrit serving as the originating and target languages, respectively. There are currently over 50K parallel sentences in the corpus. Parallel claims are true, as cross-checked by Sanskrit-speaking linguists. Using terms from the Gita, Wiki books, Multidisciplinary Exam Papers, Sanskrit instruction books, and other online resources, the related sentences were independently created. We have also gathered Sanskrit sentences from Grades 6–12 NCERT textbooks.

4 System Description

The methods used to translate Sanskrit to Hindi using a Transformer-based neural network architecture is described in this section, shown in Fig. 1. The methodology encompasses data preprocessing, model architecture, and training procedures.

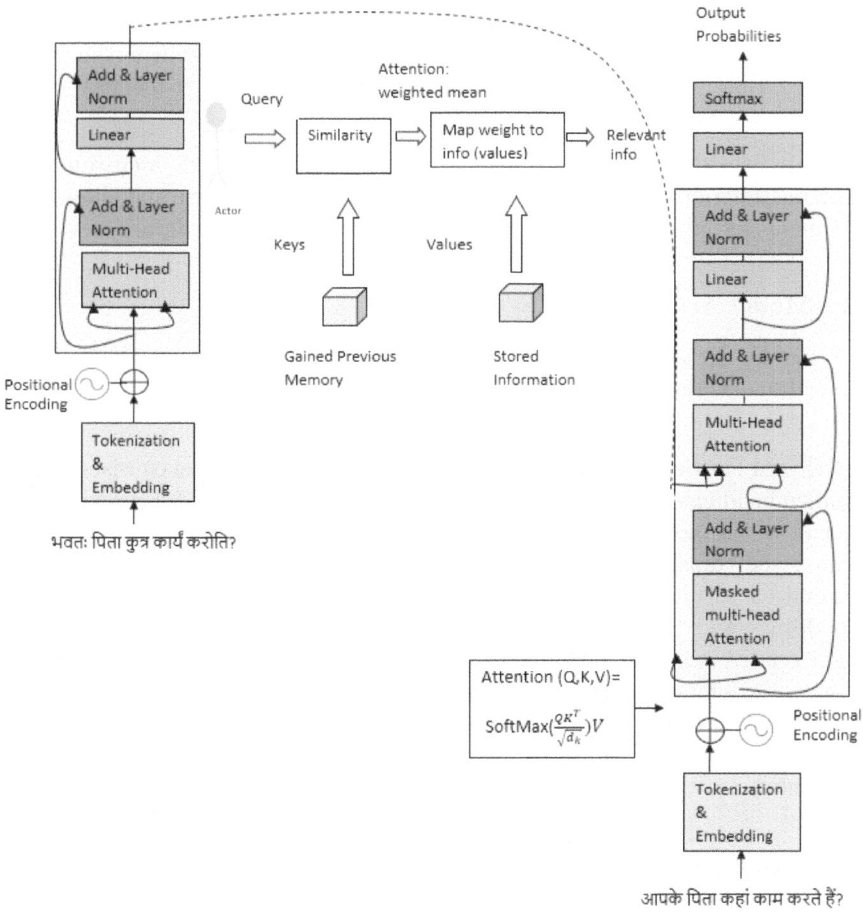

Fig. 1. Proposed Translation System Architecture

4.1 Data Preprocessing

An essential step in getting the dataset ready for training is data preparation. The actions listed below were carried out:

Dataset Preparation: Using manual back translation, a corpus of parallel source-target sentence pairings was produced, with Hindi serving as the target language and Sanskrit as the native tongue.

Text Vectorization: Text input was converted into integer sequences using TensorFlow's TextVectorization layer. Two distinct vectorization layers were developed, one of which was Sanskrit Vectorization, which had an output sequence length of 20 tokens and a vocabulary of 15,000 tokens. Hindi Vectorization is similar to the Sanskrit vectorization and uses 21 tokens in the output sequence. However, it considers additional tokens, such as start tokens.

Custom Standardization: To preprocess the incoming text, a custom standardizing function was built. By converting the text to lowercase and eliminating extraneous letters, this function lowers the noise in the input data.

4.2 Model Architecture

The encoder-decoder structure of the model architecture is based on the Transformer framework. The following essential elements were used:

Positional Embedding: Besides token embeddings, the model consists of positional embeddings that aim to maintain the arrangement of the tokens within the order in which they are presented in a sequence. This incorporation is necessary because the transformer architecture lacks the built-in encoding of sequential information within it. It has two separate embedding layers; one for the token embeddings and the other for the space indices of the tokens. To accurately model relative token position, the positional encodings are based on sine and cosine with different frequencies. This embedded structure also helps the transformer to acquire the meaning of the tokens as well as the order of the tokens which is very important in tasks such as translation in which word order matters to meaning.

Transformer Encoder: The transformer encoder performs several layers of functions that analyze and process the input sequences by the use of convex combinations of multi-head self-attention operations with feed-forward neural networks. By employing the multi-head self-attention technique, model efficiency is improved by obtaining the dependencies of the context based on how important each of the tokens is. A better view is obtained since all information is not picked using one attention head each of which assumes different features of the input. In each encoder layer, the methods are designed to come with residual connections and layer normalization so that deep networks can be trained [11]. This is because layer normalization helps in the stabilization and speeding up of the training, by normalizing the outputs of the layers. Further, residual connections ensure that the gradients are able to flow easily in the process of backpropagation so as to mitigate the effects of the vanishing gradient problem. This, together with the properties of an encoder, allows the encoder to develop complex images of input data that capture various aspects of language.

Transformer Decoder: The transformer decoder has additional operations to make optimal use of the output from the encoder but still retains the overall structure of the encoder. The causal masking which ensures that the prediction for a specific position relies only on the tokens already created and not on any future tokens is an important function of the decoder. This is very important for tasks such as translation which uses an autoregressive approach. Similarly to the encoder, the decoder incorporates a multi-head self-attention mechanism but also incorporates an additional attention layer directed towards the encoder outputs. Because of this concern, as well as due to mechanism of the dual attention, the decoder is capable of outputting each of the tokens in the output sequence while utilizing all context of the input sequence for their generation which improves the quality of translations.

Output Layer: The responsibility of the output layer is to convert the final outputs generated by decoder into the needed vocabulary space. For performing this, a fully connected dense layer is applied, followed by softmax which turns the raw output logits into normalized probabilities over all the vocabulary tokens. The next token of the sequence is generated by using the highest probability token available after each decoding step, till token generation. The translation process cannot be considered completed until a dedicated specific end of sequence token is produced. Following a stepwise approach leads the transformer model to combine attentional processes and grid-like layers leading to stellar performance in the field of neural machine translation especially when dealing with languages such as Sanskrit and Hindi.

4.3 Training Procedure

In the construction of the model, for multi-class classification tasks, a sparse categorical cross-entropy loss function was used. To attain better results, the Adam optimizer was applied during the training. The training of the model was performed for thirty epochs in order to be able to make sure that convergence is attained, which is the predetermined number. The balance of the training data was further used to limit the risk of overfitting, and during the progress of training the model, the principal metric that was employed to assess the effectiveness of the model was accuracy.

5 Experiments and Results

Throughout this investigation, special attention was given to the experimental setup so that it would serve as a good starting point in acquiring and assessing the functionality of a neural machine translation (NMT) system which can be able to convert Sanskrit into Hindi. The experiments were conducted on a powerful system installed with Intel i7-10700K CPU, NVIDIA GeForce RTX 2060 with 6 GB RAM and 32 GB RAM installed to cater for the high computational requirements of deep learning tasks. In terms of the software environment, Python version 3.8 was utilized for scripting, TensorFlow versions 2.8.0 and Keras version 2.8.0 were employed in model training and development while

NumPy version 1.21.0 was deployed for numerical computations. The important hyperparameters were carefully selected as training continued for 30 epochs which include vocabulary size set at 15000 tokens, 20 for encoder sequence length and 21 for decoder sequence length, a batch size of 64, embedding dimension of 256, latent dimension 2048 and 8 attention heads. The model was evaluated in terms of the quantative aspects and these included the percentage of correct tokens out of all tokens in validation set, also called accuracy and the amount of divergence of the model from actual results in training and validation set known as loss. The selection of hyperparameters and evaluation metrics allowed for meaningful insights into the effectiveness of the transformer-based NMT system, further advancing the translation of these historically significant languages. This thorough setup guaranteed that both hardware and software were optimized for performance.

Table 1. Results Comparison based on BLEU-Score

System	BLEU Score	Modelling Technique	Citation
Assamese-to-English	13.10%	Recurrent neural network (RNN) with attention mechanism	[7]
Sanskrit to Hindi	24% superior to Rule-based	RNN	[14]
Sanskrit-to-Hindi	51.6%	Direct and Rule-based	[12]
Sanskrit-to-Hindi	56.86%	Self-attention-based transformers	[13]
Sanskrit-to-Hindi	67.8%	Transformers with Multi head Attention	Proposed model

Table 1 compares the results of our methodology testing on 20% of the phrases of the designed dataset with those of previous studies that have conducted comparable research, indicating the superiority of the proposed method in terms of BLEU accuracy. Table 1 shows that our experiment's BLEU measure is better than that of similar systems because of the multi-head attention mechanism we use in comparison to the right number of layers for input data.

6 Conclusion

This work demonstrates the translation performance of a transformer-based neural machine translation system with a multi-head attention mechanism from Sanskrit to Hindi. The development of a parallel corpus of 50K sentences has tremendously benefited in the advancement of computational resources for this combination of languages. Based on performance studies with a BLEU score of 67.8%, the system performs better than existing options. These results show

how effective the proposed method is in improving the quality of translations from Sanskrit to Hindi. Future research could expand the approach's applicability by implementing the recommended translation system on other language combinations with rich morphology and constrained resources.

References

1. Bahdanau, D., Cho, K., Bengio, Y.: Neural machine translation by jointly learning to align and translate. In: Proceedings of the International Conference on Learning Representations (2014)
2. Bhatia, R., Bhatt, R.: Challenges in machine translation of Sanskrit text. In: Proceedings of the 2021 International Conference on Intelligent Technologies (2021)
3. Devlin, J., Chang, M.-W., Lee, K., Toutanova, K.: BERT: pre-training of deep bidirectional transformers for language understanding. In: Proceedings of the 2019 Conference of the North American Chapter of the Association for Computational Linguistics (2019)
4. Ghosh, S., Tiwari, A.: Neural machine translation for low-resource Indian languages: a survey. arXiv preprint arXiv:2010.04440 (2020)
5. Koehn, P.: Statistical Machine Translation. Cambridge University Press, Cambridge (2009)
6. Kumar, A., Singh, P.: A survey of machine translation for Indian languages. In: Proceedings of the 8th International Conference on Communication Systems and Networks (2017)
7. Laskar, S.R., Pakray, P., Bandyopadhyay, S.: Neural machine translation for low resource Assamese–English. In: Proceedings of the International Conference on Computing and Communication Systems: I3CS 2020, NEHU, Shillong, India, pp. 35–44. Springer (2021)
8. Liu, X., et al.: Pre-training for natural language processing: a survey. Chin. J. Comput. Sci. (2020)
9. Pakhare, A., Dhamdhere, S.: Sanskrit-English machine translation using deep learning. Int. J. Comput. Appl. **178**(36), 30–34 (2019)
10. Raffel, C., Shinn, C., et al.: T5: text-to-text transfer transformer. In: Proceedings of the 37th International Conference on Machine Learning (2020)
11. Sethi, N., Dev, A., Bansal, P.: A novel neural machine translation approach for low-resource Sanskrit-Hindi language pair. In: ACM Transactions on Asian and Low-Resource Language Information Processing (2023)
12. Sethi, N., Dev, A., Bansal, P., Sharma, D.K., Gupta, D.: Hybridization based machine translations for low-resource language with language divergence. ACM Trans. Asian Low-Resour. Lang. Inf. Process. (2022)
13. Sethi, N., Dev, A., Bansal, P., Sharma, D.K., Gupta, D.: Enhancing low-resource Sanskrit-Hindi translation through deep learning with ayurvedic text. ACM Trans. Asian Low-Resour. Lang. Inf. Process. (2023)
14. Singh, M., Kumar, R., Chana, I.: Corpus based machine translation system with deep neural network for Sanskrit to Hindi translation. Procedia Comput. Sci. **167**, 2534–2544 (2020)
15. Sutskever, I., Vinyals, O., Le, Q.V.: Sequence to sequence learning with neural networks. In: Advances in Neural Information Processing Systems (2014)
16. Vaswani, A., et al.: Attention is all you need. In: Advances in Neural Information Processing Systems (2017)

SHiTraD: Sanskrit-Hindi Translation Dataset

Nandini Sethi[1], Ayushi[1(✉)], Amita Dev[2], and Poonam Bansal[1]

[1] Indira Gandhi Delhi Technical University for Women, New Delhi, India
ayushi0722@gmail.com , poonambansal@igdtuw.ac.in
[2] Directorate of Training and Technical Education, New Delhi, India

Abstract. Sanskrit is a culturally rich but low resource language. Presently, it is under represented and there is no digitized corpus available for Sanskrit-Hindi language pair publicly. We present a dataset, SHiTraD that consists of 45,500 parallel Sanskrit-Hindi sentences, collected from various sources online or offline through web or scanned from books. The source-target paired sentences were created using manual translations. This dataset is then used to train models and evaluate the translations and the results are shown using BLEU score evaluation metric comparing three architecture models 1. Encoder decoder with attention mechanism, 2. Self attention based transformer mechanism and 3. Multi-head based transformer mechanism.

Keywords: Machine translation · Sanskrit · Hindi · Corpus · Parallel corpus · Sanskrit-Hindi parallel corpus

1 Introduction

India is a linguistically diverse country, with home to 1,369 languages being spoken as mother tongue Singh et al. [2022]. Sanskrit is the oldest language documented belonging to Indo-European family of languages in India. As per Census of India, there are only 24,821 Sanskrit speakers in India in 2011 Singh et al. [2022] as compared to 49,736 Sanskrit speakers in 1991 Singh et al. [2004]. This downward trend of number of people speaking Sanskrit shows its reducing significance in the modern world. To revive the cultural heritage of India, it is important to preserve the languages which are losing its significance or becoming extinct, including Sanskrit. There are many ayurvedic, religious, philological, astrological and mathematical works written using Sanskrit language since the ancient past of India Sethi et al. [2022]. Therefore, it is necessary to preserve this knowledge and thus machine translation is required.

Despite being a scheduled language in the constitution of India and with a rich heritage, it is considered as a low resource language. Low resource language means that there doesn't exist sufficient corpus or any data in a structured typed format. There is significant amount of work done for machine translation on high resource languages and thus a huge amount of corpus is available for

A. Sharma and R. Rani (Eds.): AIST 2024, CCIS 2389, pp. 274–281, 2025.
https://doi.org/10.1007/978-3-031-91331-0_21

languages like English. Therefore, it is important to have a good language model for machine translation of Sanskrit with other languages. There is parallel corpus available for Sanskrit-English pair but Sanskrit-Hindi pair is not available. This work tries to address this problem of corpus and we release a parallel Sanskrit-Hindi corpus for machine translation.

There exists a parallel corpus for Sanskrit named 'Itihasa' Rahul Aralikatte1 et al. [2021]. This is the largest parallel corpus available for machine translation for Sanskrit-English and it contains 93000 pair of sentences of Sanskrit and their corresponding English translation. 'Samayik' is another Sanskrit-English parallel corpus for machine translation, containing 42,961 sentences Maheshwari et al. [2023]. These digitized parallel dataset is confined to Sanskrit-English language pairs only. Another way to translate Sanskrit-Hindi is to use a pivot language English by first translating Sanskrit to English using Open MT Sanskirt-English parallel dataset and then translate English to Hindi using English-Hindi parallel dataset as is done in Singh et al. [2020].

Hindi and Sanskrit are very similar language in terms of structure as both of them uses Devanagari script. Although very similar, but Sanskrit becomes difficult to handle linguistically due to its rich morphology, grammatical structure and some complex ambiguities. Hindi have many resources available in digitized format but Sanskrit remains under resourced despite of some similarity. The main focus of this work is to curate a dataset for Sanskrit-Hindi language pair as Hindi is the most widely used language in India. This will lead to bridging the gap between the two languages and preserving the language cultural heritage.

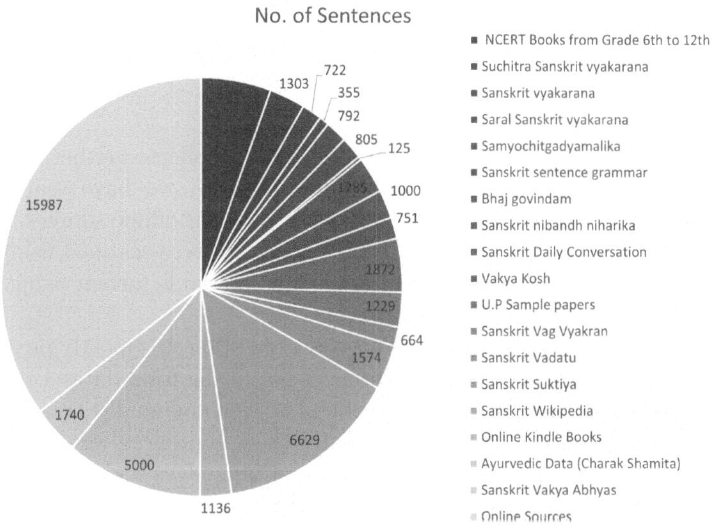

Fig. 1. Dataset sources

2 Dataset

SHiTraD is a Sanskrit-Hindi Translation Dataset created for the purpose of building machine translation models for translating Sanskrit to Hindi. This corpus consists of 45,500 parallel sentence pair for Sanskrit as source language and Hindi as target language. These sentences are manually collected from different sources like Wikipedia, Charak Samhita, Bhagavat Geeta, Parallel Dictionary and other websites. The sources along with total number of sentences from each of these sources is summarised in Fig. 1.

2.1 Steps Taken in Dataset Creation

The step by step process of creating a parallel aligned dataset is depicted in Fig. 2. Each of these steps are explained in the section below.

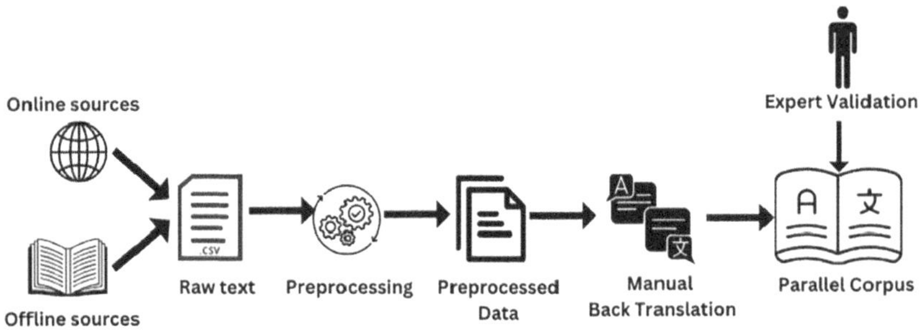

Fig. 2. Steps in the creation of dataset

1. **Data Collection:** To create this dataset, data is collected either from online sources or offline hard books. For online sources, we have searched and scanned PDF documents like NCERT textbooks. For offline sources, the hard books like Sanskrit vyakaran and Bhaj govindam were scanned using google lens. These texts were converted into machine readable format using Optical Character Recognition (OCR) technology.
2. **Parallel sentence Alignment:** This collected dataset is mostly present with their Hindi translations. 20–30% sentences out of the total dataset didn't had their translations in Hindi. These sentences were manually translated into Hindi with the help of an expert. Finally these sentences were aligned into parallel sentences paired for source and target languages with source language to be Sanskrit and target language to be Hindi.
3. **Data Cleaning:** The created parallel dataset for source and target sentence pairs was preprocessed for removal of any noise, redundant entries, repeated sentences and lengthy sentences (sentences exceeding 50 words for ease of model training). Cleaning of dataset is very important to create a reliable dataset for training our model for machine translation.

4. **Data Validation:** The dataset is ready to use after alignment and data cleaning process. But data validation is very crucial step in order to know whether the translated pairs are correct or not. Thus, we validated our dataset with the help of an expert in the field.

After all these steps, our dataset is ready to use for the purpose of machine translation between Sanskrit and Hindi language pair. Few example of how actually our dataset look is shown in Fig. 3

मित्र मिलनम्	दोस्तो से मिलना
अवश्यं मम गृहं आगन्त्वियम्	मेरे घर अवश्य आइए
सः वर्षद्वयपूर्वमेव सेवानिवृतवान् ।	वह दो साल पहले सेवानिवृत्त हुए थे।
क़ियत् कालम् स्थास्यसि ?	तुम कब तक वहाँ रहोगे?
किञ्चित् साहाय्यम् करोति वा ?	क्या आप मेरी थोड़ी मदद करना चाहेंगे?
तेषां कृते मम शुभाशयाःनिवेदयतु	उन्हें मेरी शुभकामनाएं बताएं
आगच्छतु भोः , गृहं गच्छामः ।	चलो, घर चलते हैं।
पुनः अस्माकं मिलनं कदा ?	हम फिर कब मिलेंगे?

Fig. 3. SHiTraD: dataset snapshot

3 Preliminary Experiment

It is important to see the performance of the dataset that we have created. In this section, we will discuss how we have trained different models using our dataset SHiTraD.

3.1 Word Embeddings

The first step before training deep learning models is to create word embeddings. Word Embedding is a numerical representation of the words or sentences. We are using tf-idf technique for vector representation of our dataset. tf-idf stands for term frequency-inverse document frequency. Term frequency tells about the most frequent words. On the other hand, inverse document frequency highlights the words that are unique, i.e., the words that occur rarely but are important.

3.2 Model Training

The dataset created for Sanskrit-Hindi machine translation system is used for training different Deep learning models based on transformer architecture using attention mechanism. These models are discussed below:

Encoder Decoder with Attention Mechanism. Traditional Encoder-Decoder model in Neural Machine Translation has two parts, first being Encoder, which compresses the input sequence into a fixed length vector which is then passed to the second part, Decoder, which uses this context vector to generate desired output Sethi et al. [2023b] Sethi et al. [2023d]. While, if the input sequence is longer, this traditional models tends to compress the long input sequence into smaller vector, resulting in loosing important information. With the help of attention mechanism as introduced in Bahdanau [2014], this issue is addressed. Attention scores is calculated for each word in the input sequence. This attention score tells the decoder to focus on certain most important parts of the input at each stage. This creates dynamic context vector, which depends on the current decoding step. This helps in making the model easier to understand and work faster while decoding the longer input sequence.

Self Attention Based Transformer. Self attention was introduced by Vaswani [2017] through transformer architecture. It enables the model to co-relate different words in the input sequence, irrespective of their position, to every other word. It calculates the amount of attention to be provided to all the words. Unlike traditional neural architecture, which focuses on long-term dependencies and processes them sequentially thus struggling in the process, self-attention provides a better alternative for capturing long-term dependencies by allowing each word to focus on every other word, even the distant ones. Self attention, for each word, calculates three vectors which are query, value and key. These vectors are compared in order to compute attention scores and these attention scores tell how much attention is needed for each word. These scores are then used to create a new vector representation for each word. This helps in addressing the issues that arises while encoding longer input sequence by capturing long-term dependencies Sethi et al. [2023c].

Multi-head Based Transformer. Multi-head attention transformer architecture is an extension work of self attention transformer as mentioned in Vaswani [2017]. It makes use of multiple attention heads while encoding simultaneously. In this, we compute multiple attention scores in the place of one as in the case of self attention mechanism. Each of the attention scores capture different relation between input words and thus captures different features. Once all of these attention are calculated for each head, output of these are then concatenated and projected again to get final values as output vector. This approach allows the model to capture complex relations among input words and thus performs better Sethi et al. [2023a].

3.3 Metrics

We have evaluated the performance of these models for machine translation of Sanskrit-Hindi language pair using BLEU score Papineni et al. [2002], TER Snover et al. [2006] and human evaluation White and O'Connell [1993].

BLEU Score: BLEU or Bi-Lingual Evaluation Understudy score is one of the most popular evaluation metric used to evaluate the quality of translations. It is a n-gram precision based metric for word level evaluation. Formula for calculating BLEU score is given by Equation (i).

$$BLEU = \min\left(1, \exp\left(\frac{\text{Output\_length}}{\text{reference\_length}}\right)\right)\left(\prod_{i=1}^{4} \text{precision}_i\right)^{\frac{1}{4}} \qquad (i)$$

BLEU score is in range of 0 to 1 where 1 implies a perfect translation. In order to find BLEU score percentage, we need to multiply it by 100.

TER: TER or translation edit rate is the number edits required to change the output of a machine translation model into an exact reference translation, further normalized by the average number of reference words. Its formula is given in Equation (ii)

$$TER = \frac{\text{No. of edits}}{\text{Avg no. of reference words}} \qquad (ii)$$

Human Evaluation: Human evaluators evaluate for the translations done by machines in order to identify efficiency of the MT models. We have selected the adequacy and fluency scores for human evaluation metrics. Adequacy scores evaluate the correctness of the translations while fluency score looks for the grammar and fluency of the sentence Lee et al. [2023].

4 Result

We split the dataset comprising of 45,500 sentences in 80:20 ratio where 80% of data is used for training the model (train set) and 20% of data is used for evaluating the model. We performed the experiment by training the models 1. encoder-decoder with attention mechanism 2. Self attention based transformer mechanism 3. Multi-head based transformer mechanism. We have fine tuned these architectures based on our language pair for Sanskrit-Hindi translation task. The automatic metrics- BLEU scores and TER are shown in Table 1 and the human evaluation metrics- Adequacy score and Fluency score on the scale of 4 are shown in Table 2. As we can see, out dataset is working fine and showing good results being trained upon these models. Multi-head attention based transformer mechanism shows the best result.

Table 1. Experimental Analysis on automatic metrics

Model	BLEU Score	TER
Encoder-Decoder with attention machanism	53.8%	0.45
Self attention based transformer	56.86%	0.41
Multi-head based transformer	67.8%	0.34

Table 2. Experimental Analysis on human evaluation metrics

Model	Adequacy Score	Fluency Score
Encoder-Decoder with attention machanism	3.33	3.26
Self attention based transformer	3.6	3.5
Multi-head based transformer	3.63	3.54

5 Conclusion and Future Scope

In this work, we have introduced a dataset SHiTraD, which contains 45,500 parallel sentences for Sanskrit and Hindi language pair. This dataset is collected from different sources and then validated. This dataset is suitable for the task of machine translation. Further we have trained models to evaluate the quality of translation and the results are showing good and reliable evaluation scores, specially in the case of multi-head attention based transformer. These models are latest cutting edge architecture suitable for various natural language processing tasks including machine translation. Further, we can increase the size of the dataset by crowd-sourcing and enhance the models further.

Acknowledgement. This research work is part of "Sanskrit Knowledge Accessor project" funded by Ministry of Electronics and Information Technology (MeitY), Government of India as part of National Language Translation Mission. We hereby extend our gratitude for financial support, which helped in creation of Sanskrit-Hindi parallel corpus for machine translation.

References

Bahdanau, D.: Neural machine translation by jointly learning to align and translate. arXiv preprint arXiv:1409.0473 (2014)

de Lhoneux, M., Kunchukuttan, A., Søgaard, A.: Itihasa: a large-scale corpus for sanskrit to english translation. In: WAT 2021, p. 191 (2021)

Lee, S., et al.: A survey on evaluation metrics for machine translation. Mathematics **11**(4), 1006 (2023)

Maheshwari, A., et al.: S\={a} mayik: a benchmark and dataset for english-sanskrit translation. arXiv preprint arXiv:2305.14004 (2023)

Papineni, K., Roukos, S., Ward, T., Zhu, W.J.: Bleu: a method for automatic evaluation of machine translation. In: Proceedings of the 40th Annual Meeting of the Association for Computational Linguistics, pp. 311–318 (2002)

Sethi, N., Dev, A., Bansal, P.: A bilingual machine transliteration system for sanskrit-english using rule-based approach. In: 2022 4th International Conference on Artificial Intelligence and Speech Technology (AIST), pp. 1–5. IEEE (2022)
Sethi, N., Dev, A., Bansal, P.: Self-attention-based deep learning approach for machine translation of low resource languages: a case of sanskrit-hindi. In: International Conference on Women Researchers in Electronics and Computing, pp. 85–92. Springer, Heidelberg (2023a). https://doi.org/10.1007/978-981-99-7077-3_9
Sethi, N., Dev, A., Bansal, P.: A novel neural machine translation approach for low-resource sanskrit-hindi language pair. In: ACM Transactions on Asian and Low-Resource Language Information Processing (2023b)
Sethi, N., Dev, A., Bansal, P., Sharma, D.K., Gupta, D.: Enhancing low-resource sanskrit-hindi translation through deep learning with ayurvedic text. In: ACM Transactions on Asian and Low-Resource Language Information Processing (2023)
Sethi, N., Dev, A., Bansal, P., Sharma, D.K., Gupta, D. A pragmatic analysis of machine translation techniques for preserving the authenticity of the sanskrit language. In: ACM Transactions on Asian and Low-Resource Language Information Processing (2023d)
Singh, K., et al. Language atlas of India, 2011 (2022)
Singh, M., Kumar, R., Chana, I.: Corpus based machine translation system with deep neural network for sanskrit to hindi translation. Procedia Comput. Sci. **167**, 2534–2544 (2020)
Singh, R.P., India. Office of the Registrar General, et al.: Language atlas of India 1991 (2004)
Snover, M., Dorr, B., Schwartz, R., Micciulla, L., Makhoul, J.: A study of translation edit rate with targeted human annotation. In: Proceedings of the 7th Conference of the Association for Machine Translation in the Americas: Technical Papers, pp. 223–231 (2006)
Vaswani, A.: Attention is all you need. Adv. Neural Inf. Process. Syst. (2017)
White, J.S., O'Connell, T.A.: Evaluation of machine translation. In: Human Language Technology: Proceedings of a Workshop Held at Plainsboro, New Jersey, 21–24 March 1993 (1993)

Advances in Computational Linguistics and NLP

Advanced Speech Recognition: Techniques, Challenges, and Applications

Laxmi Ahuja(✉)

Amity Institute of Information Technology, Amity University, Noida, India
lahuja@amity.edu

Abstract. In this paper, we present a comprehensive introduction about the modern ASR technology in terms of advanced techniques and applications as well as its challenge nowadays. We discuss the basics of Automatic Speech Recognition (ASR) systems such as acoustic modeling, language modelling and decoding algorithms. This work covers state-of-the-art techniques ranging from deep learning based models, attention mechanisms and transfer learning used in ASR. We then summarized some of the longer-standing issues in NLP, such as robustness to noise and low-resource languages or real-time processing. The paper also reviews the expanding use cases of speech recognition across industries such as voice assistants, automotive systems, healthcare and education. In the last part, we discuss societal implications for this technology and potential future research in speech recognition.

Keywords: Automatic Speech Recognition · Deep Learning · Natural Language Processing · Voice User Interfaces · Acoustic Modeling

1 Introduction to Speech Recognition

An interdisciplinary branch of computational linguistics, speech recognition-also known as automatic speech recognition (ASR) or speech to text develops techniques and technologies that allow computers to recognize and translate spoken language into text [2]. It integrates research and knowledge from the domains of electrical engineering, computer science, and languages.

Speech recognition has a long history dating back to the 1950s [9]. But over the past couple decades, this field has advanced significantly, primarily due to stronger machine learning algorithms and more processing capacity. Virtual assistants, transcription services, and hands-free computing are just a few of the many applications that use recent voice recognition systems because of their increased accuracy [10].

The basic pipeline of a speech recognition system typically includes the following components:

1. Speech input and audio preprocessing
2. Feature extraction

A. Sharma and R. Rani (Eds.): AIST 2024, CCIS 2389, pp. 285–294, 2025.
https://doi.org/10.1007/978-3-031-91331-0_22

3. Acoustic modeling
4. Language modeling
5. Decoding

Each of these components has its importance in the overall performance of the system. This paper will focus on the internal architecture of speech recognition systems, especially with respect to improvements made in enhancing accuracy and efficiency.

Among the greatest advances in speech recognition, perhaps is the use of deep learning techniques and more importantly deep neural networks. The performance of both acoustic and language models has improved dramatically since the advent of DNNs. A typical acoustic model using DNN can be represented as follows:

$$P(y_t|x_t) = \text{softmax}(W_L h_L + b_L) \quad (1)$$

where y_t denotes the output, which is a phoneme or senone [11], x_t is the input acoustic feature, h_L the activation of the last hidden layer, and W_L, b_L weight matrix and bias vector for the output layer, respectively.

In the following sections, we will delve deeper into the various components of speech recognition systems and explore recent enhancements that have pushed the boundaries of ASR technology.

2 Feature Extraction and Acoustic Modeling

Feature extraction refers to the process of extracting the speech recognition signal and turning it into some compact representation that will represent the actual voice. There exist two more traditional methods in feature extraction, Mel-frequency cepstral coefficients (MFCCs) [1] and Perceptual Linear Prediction (PLP) [8]. However, the techniques have advanced with time in the recent era.

2.1 Advanced Feature Extraction

Using filter bank energies directly as input features is a major improvement in feature extraction. This strategy, which is frequently used with deep learning models, may be shown as follows:

$$F = \log(|S \cdot M|) \quad (2)$$

where S is the short-time Fourier transform of the input signal [14], M is the mel-scale filter bank, and F is the resulting feature vector.

2.2 Acoustic Modeling with Deep Neural Networks

Modern acoustic modeling relies considerably on deep neural networks, especially on the variants of long short-term memory (LSTM) networks [17] and Convolutional Neural Networks (CNNs) [16]. The LSTM architecture, which is designed to capture long-term dependencies in sequential data, can be described with the following set of equations:

$$f_t = \sigma(W_f \cdot [h_{t-1}, x_t] + b_f) \tag{3}$$

$$i_t = \sigma(W_i \cdot [h_{t-1}, x_t] + b_i) \tag{4}$$

$$\tilde{C_t} = \tanh(W_C \cdot [h_{t-1}, x_t] + b_C) \tag{5}$$

$$C_t = f_t * C_{t-1} + i_t * \tilde{C_t} \tag{6}$$

$$o_t = \sigma(W_o \cdot [h_{t-1}, x_t] + b_o) \tag{7}$$

$$h_t = o_t * \tanh(C_t) \tag{8}$$

where f_t, i_t, and o_t are the forget, input, and output gates respectively, C_t is the cell state, and h_t is the hidden state.

2.3 End-To-End Acoustic Models

Recent studies have tried to explore end-to-end models that directly map input acoustic features into graphemes or words, thus bypassing the use of separate phoneme modelling [5]. Perhaps the most popular loss is the connectionist temporal classification (CTC) one [6]. It has been defined as follows:

$$L_{CTC} = -\log \sum_{\pi \in \mathcal{B}^{-1}(l)} \prod_{t=1}^{T} p(\pi_t|x) \tag{9}$$

where $\mathcal{B}$ is a many-to-one mapping from paths π to labelings l, and $p(\pi_t|x)$ is the probability of outputting label π_t at time t given input x.

These feature extraction and acoustic modeling innovations have improved the accuracy and efficiency of speech recognition systems to a great extent and paved the way for much more robust and versatile applications.

3 Language Modeling and Decoding

Language modeling also has a very important role to play in speech recognition. It actually gives context to the words for the purpose of transcription improvement. Recent developments in language modeling have greatly improved ASR systems' performance.

3.1 Neural Language Models

Traditional n-gram language models have largely been replaced by neural language models [13], which generalize much better and capture the context. The basic calculation of a standard neural language model is to estimate the probability of a sequence of words:

$$P(w_1, \ldots, w_T) = \prod_{t=1}^{T} P(w_t | w_1, \ldots, w_{t-1}) \tag{10}$$

where each conditional probability is modeled using a neural network.

3.2 Transformer-Based Language Models

The introduction of Transformer architectures revolutionized language modeling. The ability of self-attention mechanisms in the Transformers to capture long-range dependencies better has been possible [12]. The self-attention operation can be described as:

$$\text{Attention}(Q, K, V) = \text{softmax}\left(\frac{QK^T}{\sqrt{d_k}}\right) V \tag{11}$$

where Q, K, and V are query, key, and value matrices, respectively, and d_k is the dimension of the key vectors.

3.3 Decoding Algorithms

Decoding in speech recognition involves finding the most likely sequence of words given the acoustic and language model probabilities. The Viterbi algorithm [7] is commonly used for this purpose, with its recursive formula given by:

$$V_{t,k} = \max_{i=1}^{N}(V_{t-1,i} \cdot a_{i,k}) \cdot b_k(O_t) \tag{12}$$

where $V_{t,k}$ is the probability of the most likely state sequence at time t that ends in state k, $a_{i,k}$ is the transition probability from state i to k, and $b_k(O_t)$ is the emission probability of observation O_t in state k.

3.4 Beam Search Decoding

Beam search is frequently used for more effective decoding in big vocabulary systems. The following is a description of the beam search algorithm:

All these advancements have improved the accuracy and efficiency of the speech recognition system by handling more complex and diverse speech inputs.

Algorithm 1. Beam Search Decoding

Initialize beam $B = \{($¡s¿$, 0)\}$
for each time step t **do**
    $B_{\text{new}} = \{\}$
    for each partial hypothesis (h, s) in B **do**
        for each possible next word w **do**
            $s_{\text{new}} = s + \log P(w|h) + \log P(w|\text{acoustic})$
            Add $(h + w, s_{\text{new}})$ to B_{new}
        end for
    end for
    Keep top k hypotheses in B_{new}
    $B = B_{\text{new}}$
end for
return best hypothesis in B

4 Advanced Techniques and Recent Innovations

This technology has advanced dramatically over the past several years, and it will be amazing to see what ASR systems can achieve in the future. This section introduces a number of state-of-the-art methods and developments that will shape voice recognition in the future.

4.1 Attention-Based Encoder-Decoder Models

Attention-based models, particularly the Listen, Attend and Spell (LAS) architecture [3], have shown impressive results in end-to-end speech recognition. The attention mechanism can be described as:

$$c_i = \sum_{j=1}^{T} \alpha_{ij} h_j \tag{13}$$

where c_i is the context vector for output step i, h_j are the encoder hidden states, and α_{ij} are attention weights calculated as:

$$\alpha_{ij} = \frac{\exp(e_{ij})}{\sum_{k=1}^{T} \exp(e_{ik})} \tag{14}$$

$$e_{ij} = v^T \tanh(W s_{i-1} + U h_j + b) \tag{15}$$

where s_{i-1} is the decoder state, and W, U, v, and b are learnable parameters.

4.2 Transformer-Based ASR

Transformer models, originally designed for machine translation, have been successful in speech recognition. The Transformer architecture allows for more parallelization and can better model long-range dependencies in place of recurrent layers. Mult-head attention is the core component defined as follows:

$$\text{MultiHead}(Q, K, V) = \text{Concat}(\text{head}_1, ..., \text{head}_h)W^O \quad (16)$$

where each head is computed as:

$$\text{head}_i = \text{Attention}(QW_i^Q, KW_i^K, VW_i^V) \quad (17)$$

4.3 Transfer Learning and Pre-training

With increasing importance of transfer learning in ASR, models have gained the ability to apply the knowledge extracted from large diverse datasets. Among those, wav2vec 2.0, applying self-supervised learning, was trained on unlabeled audio data [4]. The loss function for the wav2vec 2.0 can be described as follows:

$$L = L_m + \alpha L_c \quad (18)$$

where L_m is the masked prediction loss, L_c is the contrastive loss, and α is a weighting factor.

4.4 Multi-lingual and Cross-lingual ASR

Advances in multi-lingual and cross-lingual ASR have enabled the development of more versatile systems capable of recognizing speech in multiple languages [15]. One approach is to use a universal phoneme set, represented as:

$$P = \bigcup_{l \in L} P_l \quad (19)$$

where P is the universal phoneme set, L is the set of languages, and P_l is the phoneme set for language l.

4.5 Neural Architecture Search for ASR

Automated architecture search has been applied to ASR to discover optimal model architectures. The search process can be formulated as an optimization problem:

$$\alpha^* = \text{minimizer}_{\alpha \in \mathcal{A}} L_{val}(w^*(\alpha), \alpha) \quad (20)$$

$$\text{s.t. } w^*(\alpha) = \text{minimizer}_w L_{train}(w, \alpha) \quad (21)$$

where α denotes architecture, w the weights of the model, and L_{val}, L_{train} denoting validation loss and train loss respectively.

These new techniques and inventions have significantly enhanced the functionality and performance of the speech recognition systems, thereby enabling them with more opportunities to apply to any field.

5 Challenges and Future Directions

Despite significant advancements in speech recognition technology, several challenges remain. This section discusses these challenges and potential future directions for research and development in ASR.

5.1 Robustness to Noise and Acoustic Variations

One of the persistent challenges in ASR is achieving robust performance in noisy environments and across diverse acoustic conditions. Future research may focus on:

- Advanced noise suppression techniques
- Domain adaptation methods for varying acoustic conditions
- Multi-modal ASR systems incorporating visual cues

5.2 Low-Resource Languages and Accents

Developing effective ASR systems for low-resource languages and handling diverse accents remain significant challenges. Potential approaches include:

- Improved transfer learning techniques for cross-lingual adaptation
- Unsupervised and self-supervised learning methods for low-resource scenarios
- Accent-adaptive models and normalization techniques

5.3 Real-Time and On-Device ASR

Research is required in the following areas as the requirement for on-device and real-time speech recognition increases:

- Techniques for model quantization and compression
- Efficient architectures for low-latency inference
- Adaptive streaming ASR algorithms

5.4 Contextual Understanding and Semantic Interpretation

One of the main challenges is going beyond mere transcription to a deeper comprehension of speech content. Possible future paths include:

- Integration of ASR with natural language understanding (NLU) systems
- Cooperative optimization of downstream tasks (such as sentiment analysis and intent identification) and ASR
- Incorporation of world knowledge and common-sense reasoning in ASR systems

5.5 Ethical Considerations and Bias Mitigation

Addressing ethical issues and reducing biases are essential as ASR systems proliferate. Research initiatives could concentrate on:

- Developing fair and unbiased ASR models across demographics
- Ensuring privacy and security in speech processing
- Creating transparent and explainable ASR systems

5.6 Continuous Learning and Adaptation

Future research should focus on enabling ASR systems to continuously learn and adapt to new data and settings.

- Lifelong learning algorithms for ASR models
- Efficient fine-tuning techniques for personalization
- Active learning strategies for targeted data collection and annotation

5.7 Multimodal and Contextual ASR

ASR performance may be enhanced by utilizing contextual information and integrating several modalities:

- Audio-visual speech recognition
- Incorporation of user context and preferences in ASR
- Integration with other sensor data (e.g., motion, location) for enhanced recognition

These would be significant breakthroughs in the effort to overcome these obstacles and expand this field by branching out into other disciplines. As a result, we should anticipate that as ASR systems get more sophisticated, they will be able to handle speech recognition tasks of varying complexity with greater accuracy and resilience.

We may anticipate much more creative uses and wider societal effects as speech recognition technology continues to progress. Incorporating ASR with other cutting-edge technologies like artificial intelligence, augmented reality, and the Internet of Things is expected to change many facets of our everyday lives and industries while also bringing up new paradigms for human-computer interaction.

6 Conclusion

Advances in deep learning and big data with increases in computational powers have seen a wide surge in astonishing development in the technology of speech recognition. With such improvements, ASR systems have now come close to acting like human beings at least in very particular cases and enabled various applications of huge range which are turning many industries and aspects of everyday life on their heads. Significant challenges remain, however, particularly in areas such as handling low-resource languages and accents, robustness to a wide range of acoustic contexts, and achieving fully contextual understanding of speech. We should expect much more sophisticated and powerful ASR systems in the future as research into these issues continues. In new paradigms of human-computer interaction, voice recognition could be merged with more advance technologies such as augmented reality and artificial intelligence. To such an extent, ethical repercussions would have to be considered due to privacy concerns, probable biases, and the wider social impact. Future developments in voice recognition are likely to focus on building systems that are more accurate, efficient, and flexible, while ensuring the ethical and responsible use of such technologies. ASR is sure to be increasingly critical in shaping our interactions with technology and the environment, opening up new pathways of accessibility, communication, and human-computer interaction.

References

1. Abdul, Z.K., Al-Talabani, A.K.: Mel frequency cepstral coefficient and its applications: a review. IEEE Access **10**, 122136–122158 (2022)
2. Bhardwaj, V., et al.: Automatic speech recognition (asr) systems for children: a systematic literature review. Appl. Sci. **12**(9), 4419 (2022)
3. Chan, W., Jaitly, N., Le, Q.V., Vinyals, O.: Listen, attend and spell. arXiv preprint arXiv:1508.01211 (2015)
4. Fatehi, K.: Self-supervised learning for automatic speech recognition In low-resource environments. PhD thesis, University of Nottingham (2024)
5. Gelin, L., Daniel, M., Pinquier, J., Pellegrini, T.: End-to-end acoustic modelling for phone recognition of young readers. Speech Commun. **134**, 71–84 (2021)
6. Graves, A., Graves, A.: Connectionist temporal classification. In: Supervised Sequence Labelling with Recurrent Neural Networks, pp. 61–93 (2012)
7. Hagenauer, J., Hoeher, P.: A viterbi algorithm with soft-decision outputs and its applications. In: 1989 IEEE Global Telecommunications Conference and Exhibition' Communications Technology for the 1990s and Beyond', pp. 1680–1686. IEEE (1989)
8. Hermansky, H.: Perceptual linear predictive (plp) analysis of speech. J. Acoust. Soc. Am. **87**(4), 1738–1752 (1990)
9. Juang, B.-H., Rabiner, L.R.: Automatic speech recognition–a brief history of the technology development. Georgia Inst. Technol. Atlanta Rutgers Univ. Univ. California. Santa Barbara **1**(67), 1 (2005)
10. Lafi, M., et al.: Comparative study for virtual personal assistants (vpa) and state-of-the-art speech recognition technology. Int. J. Comput. Exp. Sci. Eng. **10**(3) (2024)

11. Le, D., Zhang, X., Zheng, W., Fügen, C., Zweig, G., Seltzer, M.L.: From senones to chenones: tied context-dependent graphemes for hybrid speech recognition. In: 2019 IEEE Automatic Speech Recognition and Understanding Workshop (ASRU), pp. 457–464. IEEE (2019)
12. Liu, H.-I., Chen, W.-L.: Re-transformer: a self-attention based model for machine translation. Procedia Comput. Sci. **189**, 3–10 (2021)
13. Pauls, A., Klein, D.: Faster and smaller n-gram language models. In: Proceedings of the 49th Annual Meeting of the Association for Computational Linguistics: Human Language Technologies, pp. 258–267 (2011)
14. Portnoff, M.: Time-frequency representation of digital signals and systems based on short-time fourier analysis. IEEE Trans. Acoust. Speech Signal Process. **28**(1), 55–69 (1980)
15. Singh, S., Singh, M., Kadyan, V.: Speech recognition transformers: topological-lingualism perspective. arXiv preprint arXiv:2408.14991 (2024)
16. Dong, Yu., Li, J.: Recent progresses in deep learning based acoustic models. IEEE/CAA J. Automatica Sinica **4**(3), 396–409 (2017)
17. Zia, T., Zahid, U.: Long short-term memory recurrent neural network architectures for Urdu acoustic modeling. Int. J. Speech Technol. **22**, 21–30 (2019)

Emotional Arousal of Female Politicians: Distinguishing Enthusiasm and Anger Using Data Augmentation and Machine Learning

Hilla Goren Barnea[1(✉)], Vered Silber-Varod[2], and Elishai Ezra Tzur[1]

[1] Mathematics and Computer Science Department, The Open University of Israel, Raanana, Israel
{Hilla.GorenBarnea,elishaiz}@openu.ac.il
[2] The Tel Aviv University Center for AI and Data Science (TAD), Tel Aviv University, Tel Aviv-Yafo, Israel
veredsv@tauex.tau.ac.il

Abstract. This study aims to distinguish between anger and enthusiasm, two high-arousal emotions with negative and positive valence, respectively, using prosodic features of speech. The dataset consists of plenary speeches from ten female members of the Israeli Parliament (Knesset), with a total of 482 utterances. These utterances were labeled as anger, enthusiasm, or "other" by 70 human labelers in an online perception test. We employed Decision Tree, Logistic Regression, eXtreme Gradient Boosting (XGBoost), Support Vector Machines (SVM), and Random Forest to conduct acoustic-prosodic analysis. Among the models, XGBoost achieved the highest accuracy. The results showed that the label "other" was easier to distinguish compared to anger or enthusiasm. However, when anger and enthusiasm were combined into a single "high-arousal" label, the distinction from "other" became more pronounced. Frequency and intensity parameters were found to be crucial across all categories. Additionally, significant differences in prosodic features were observed among different politicians, reflecting individual emotional styles in speech. A correlation was also found in the feature importance rankings across all three models, with fundamental frequency, rhythm, and intensity identified as the most important features.

Keywords: Emotions · Speech · Acoustic-Prosodic Features · Politicians

1 Introduction

Numerous studies have been conducted to investigate acoustic and linguistic features of speech and text that facilitate the differentiation of prototypical emotional states and style [1–3]. Speech emotion recognition (SER) utilized acoustic features to elucidate the way amalgamations of acoustic parameters collectively underpin the process of emotion identification and has received cross-language attention over the years. The acoustic features of vocal emotion in English have been widely studied (a review of this topic can be found in [4–7]).

A. Sharma and R. Rani (Eds.): AIST 2024, CCIS 2389, pp. 295–309, 2025.
https://doi.org/10.1007/978-3-031-91331-0_23

Emotions in political speeches were studied within the framework of rhetoric studies, where political speeches were analyzed as a means to convey messages of high emotional intensity, to persuade, debate, and encourage [8, 9]. It is widely accepted that the way politicians deliver their message, by using prosodic manipulations, is an integral part of their rhetoric and charisma [10, 11]. Recently, studies on emotion recognition systems used politicians' (in-the-wild) speeches, which are ubiquitous on YouTube [12].

The field of SER has been thriving in the past fifteen years, following the development of neural networks, with which emotions can be classified from voice samples. According to the Prototypical Emotional Episodes and Core Effect of [13], emotions classification is based on the two parameters of activation and pleasantness and includes four primary classes: excitement (+pleasant, + activation), calmness (+pleasant, –activation), anger (–pleasant, + activation), and sadness (–pleasant, –activation) [13, 14].

From the perspective of political science, politics involves struggles for resources, status, and more generally, power. It has been argued that anger plays a central role in politics and is referred to as an 'essential political emotion' [8, 15, 16]. Russell's [14] profile of anger is of an emotional state characterized by heightened physiological arousal and a negative emotional experience. When someone experiences anger, they typically feel a surge of energy, increased heart rate, muscle tension, and other physiological responses. Emotionally, anger involves feelings of displeasure, frustration, and often a desire to confront or address the anger's source.

Nonetheless, the computational challenge of distinguishing anger from other high-arousal emotional states is also due to how anger is manifested. Anger can manifest in various degrees, from mild irritation to intense rage, depending on the intensity of the activating stimulus and the individual's coping mechanisms. People may express their anger through verbal outbursts, physical actions, or more passive-aggressive behaviors. Thus, the emotional experience of anger can vary widely among individuals, and its expression is influenced by cultural norms and personal upbringing.

Excitement, according to Russell's [13, 14] classification, represents a state of heightened arousal and a positive emotional experience. When someone is excited, he typically feels a surge of energy, enthusiasm, and a sense of joy or anticipation. This emotional state is often associated with a heightened focus on the source of excitement and a desire to engage with it further. Physiologically, excitement may be accompanied by increased heart rate, dilated pupils, and a general sense of alertness and vitality. In the following sections, we will refer to this emotion as *enthusiasm*.

2 Goal and Research Questions

In this study, we focus on perception and acoustic-prosodic feature-based identification of the two + activation or "high-arousal" emotions: anger and enthusiasm. In contrast to Russell's clear-cut model, discerning the complexity of these two emotions is a significant computational challenge.

We chose to examine the classification of the two prototypical emotions in a specific context, that of plenary speeches of female members of the Israeli parliament (the Knesset). This context was chosen following a series of studies on the acoustic traits of Israeli male politicians [11, 17, 18].

We ask the following questions:

1. Can listeners consistently label a particular speaker as angry, enthusiastic, or "other"? Will the perceptual test reveal female politicians who are more, or less, angry, enthusiastic, or "other"?
2. How well can we classify the three emotions categories (anger, enthusiasm, and "other"), and how well can we distinguish between a two-category model of arousal versus "other"?
3. What is the most effective machine learning model for classifying emotions among female politicians?
4. Are there distinct acoustic parameters that consistently characterize perceived emotions among female politicians, and are they significant across all machine learning models?

3 Material and Method

3.1 Dataset Description

Collecting Data. The Knesset members under investigation are 10 female politicians who are native speakers of Hebrew with the most years in office between 2012–2022. One hundred speeches, 10 from each speaker, were retrieved and downloaded from the video archives of the Israeli Knesset website using the code of [19], and for each MP4 file, the audio channel was extracted and saved as a separate WAV file.

The scarped files featured plenary sittings (plenum) recordings typically showing hours of speeches of multiple speakers. To automatically create a dataset of the 10 speakers from the full audio recordings, we used [20]'s speaker diarization technique, resulting in audio stream partitioning into homogeneous segments.

To each audio segment in our dataset,[1] we assigned the details of the speaker (including their Knesset's identification number) and the details of the plenary meetings (the date, the plenum ID (the plenum original code according to the Knesset website), and a link to the video on the website).

Preprocessing. Each speech was divided into inter-pausal units (IPUs), which were separated by a silence interval of more than one second, and a silence threshold of 30dBFS. We have omitted IPUs that were shorter than three seconds. This procedure resulted in a dataset of 765 speech utterances.

3.2 Perception Experiment

To build a training dataset, we went through a manual labeling process that will be described in the following.

A Preliminary Perception Test. A preliminary perception test was carried out by three experts, who labeled each of the 765 utterances with one of the three labels: anger, enthusiasm, and "other". During this phase, we manually removed 46 files containing overlapping speech or other background noises from the dataset. Another decision was

[1] The dataset is available here: https://mega.nz/folder/Mp52AYDQ#xGRpJ6kI4JVMFxVZpBt7Qg.

made regarding the length of the utterances. We have decided to include only utterances longer than three seconds, based on [21], who showed that the average time for an IPU is 3.84 s and to exclude utterances longer than 19 s. The subset of this preliminary perception test resulted in a subset of 482 utterances with an agreement of at least two of the three experts.

Online Survey. The 482-utterance subset was used for the perception survey. We have randomly divided the subset into 10 polls that were distributed through the quiz-maker platform, with the audio segments being played through the SoundCloud website.

The experimental instructions given to the participants (translated here to English) were the following: "Is it possible to discern the emotions of Israeli female politicians by listening to their voices alone? In the next few minutes, you will listen to 48 audio recordings of very short segments from plenary speeches spoken by Israeli female members of the Knesset. Following each segment, you will be asked to label the emotion you perceived for this segment, with one of three types of emotions: enthusiasm, anger, or other. The expected duration of the experiment is 15 min." The first two utterances were labeled by the participants but were not used in our experiment.

Each poll had a limit of a maximum of seven respondents and in total, each utterance was tagged by 10 different labelers (a total of 70 labelers).

Participants. Altogether, 70 participants (91.4% native Hebrew speakers; mean age: 32.3 (sd: ± 14.77)) completed the questionnaire that was carried out in July 2023.

Analysis and Results of the Perception Test. The emotional ratings for each Knesset member are reported in Table 1. A Fleiss' Kappa calculation [22] shows a fair Fleiss Kappa coefficient (a measure of inter-rater agreement) of 0.24. Table 1 highlights the tendencies of the perceived judgments. The darker the red cells, the higher the perception towards this emotion type. The darker the blue cells, the lower the perception of that emotion. Five Knesset members were perceived above the mean rate as angry and six were perceived above the mean rate as "other". Enthusiasm was generally not perceived with high rates with the exception of Haskel and Tamano-Shata which received the highest rates of arousal (81.16% and 80.33%, respectively). Regev and Zandberg were also perceived as having relatively high arousal (73.91% and 68.00%, respectively). The lowest arousal scores were gained by Knesset members Gamliel and Elharrar with 21.21% and 0% of perceived arousal.

Overall, when calculating the majority vote of the labelers on the 482 utterances, we created a three-class training set that consists of 21% Enthusiasm, 33% Anger, and 46% Other.

3.3 Data Augmentation

According to [23], a standard classification process should include data augmentation and feature extraction (focusing on timbre, harmony, and pitch). Data augmentation helps prevent overfitting and improve the model's performance [24]. Since the number of utterances under each emotion class was not even, we followed [25] to create a balanced dataset. The process included audio augmentation allowing to synthesis of additional training data by applying Gaussian noise and Vocal Tract Length Perturbation (VLTP)

Table 1. A heatmap of the perceived emotions rate (%) per speaker.

Speaker	Anger (%)	Enthusiasm (%)	Other (%)	Arousal (%)
Tamar Zandberg	56.00%	12.00%	32.00%	68.00%
Sharren Haskel	50.72%	30.43%	18.84%	81.15%
Miri Regev	47.83%	26.09%	26.09%	73.92%
Pnina Tamano-Shata	44.26%	36.07%	19.67%	80.33%
Orly Levy-Abekasis	43.06%	9.72%	47.22%	52.78%
Merav Michaeli	33.33%	18.18%	48.48%	51.51%
Yifat Shasha-Biton	24.32%	10.81%	64.86%	35.13%
Ayelet Shaked	19.05%	24.76%	56.19%	43.81%
Gila Gamliel	6.06%	15.15%	78.79%	21.21%
Karine Elharrar	0.00%	0.00%	100.00%	0.00%

[25] to the raw speech signals. In the first experiment, we augmented each utterance in the dataset threefold: one with added noise, one with VLTP, and one with both of them. The VLTP factors are between 0.9 to 1.1, similar to previous studies [26].

In the second experiment, we augmented each utterance in the dataset 14-fold using all the possible combinations of four VLTP factors, and two noise factors.

3.4 Acoustic Feature Extraction

Following data augmentation, we extracted a total of 472 features of three different types – prosodic, spectral, and voice quality – using [27]'s code. The audio spectrum range is of specific importance in the current study, as it provides cues to the inner state of the speaker. For example, the sub-bass range was found related to power feelings, and high midrange frequencies were found related to tension [28]. According to [29], a relatively small number of acoustic features can predict emotion categories in speech.

Therefore, building on previous studies ([30, 31]), we chose 26 features from three categories: nine prosodic features (minimum, maximum, range mean, and standard deviation of the fundamental frequency (Hz) and intensity (dB)); three voice quality features (jitter, shimmer, and HNR (a measure of additive noise); and 14 spectral contrast features [32].

3.5 Classification Methods

Due to the size of the dataset and following Osisanwo and colleagues' review of methods [33], we utilized five machine-learning methods:

Logistic regression [34], developed in the 1950s, is a key tool in many fields due to its simplicity, interpretability, and ability to handle both continuous and categorical predictor variables. It is particularly useful in cases where the goal is to classify observations into one of two categories based on predictor variables. Although it was originally designed for binary classification, logistic regression can also be extended to classify more than two categories. The method works by estimating the probability of a particular outcome and transforming it using the logistic function, which outputs values between 0 and 1. This transformation allows for predictions of categorical outcomes by mapping any linear combination of the predictors into a probability.

Decision Tree method, first introduced in the 1960s [35], is a popular data mining technique that constructs classification or prediction models based on a set of covariates. It organizes data into branch-like segments to form an inverted tree structure composed of a root node, internal nodes, and leaf nodes. The method is non-parametric, which makes it effective in handling large, complex datasets without imposing a complicated parametric structure. It is often applied to both discrete and continuous variables and can handle missing data by either categorizing missing values or predicting them. Based on this method, more advanced techniques, and two of them will be tested in this study.

Random Forest algorithm, proposed by L. Breiman in 2001 [36], is an ensemble learning method that constructs a multitude of decision trees during training and outputs the mode (for classification) or average prediction (for regression) of the individual trees. It improves upon the instability of a single decision tree by aggregating predictions across many trees, thereby enhancing predictive accuracy and robustness.

XGBoost initially started as a research project by T. Chen in 2014 [37], this is an ensemble learning method based on gradient boosting, which builds decision trees sequentially, with each new tree correcting the errors of the previous ones. It enhances predictive accuracy by optimizing both speed and performance through techniques such as regularization, handling missing data, and tree pruning.

Support Vector Machine (SVM) was introduced by Vapnik and Chervonenkis in the 1990s [38], and since then, it has been further developed and improved. SVM is a supervised learning algorithm that seeks to find the optimal hyperplane to maximally separate data points of different classes. It can be used for both classification and regression tasks and is effective in high-dimensional spaces. SVM also has a version for non-linear classification, which transforms the input data into a higher-dimensional space using kernel functions.

We used the above mentioned five different models—Decision Tree, Logistic Regression, Random Forest, SVM, and XGBoost—to classify the emotions and build learning models. All five models were built using a random state of 42 to ensure consistent and reproducible results, and all of them were evaluated using 5-fold cross-validation to ensure robust performance. Both the Random Forest and XGBoost models were built using 100 estimators (decision trees), a maximum depth of 20, and share common parameters such as the number of trees and depth. The Random Forest model was specified with a minimum sample split of 8, and the XGBoost model was defined with a softmax multi-class classification. We utilized the Halving-GridSearchCV for hyperparameter optimization of the SVM model, and for evaluating the regularization parameter (C), gamma values, kernel types, and the polynomial kernel degree. The test set included 386 utterances (20%) out of 1,928 in the threefold augmentation model and 1,446 utterances (20%) out of 7,230 in the 14-fold augmentation model.

4 Results

Table 2 presents the classification results (accuracy, precision, recall) using 3 and 14 augmentations per utterance. Our results show that the 14-augmentation set outperformed the 3-augmentation set. We further classified the two emotion categories (Table 3). The results were again better for the 14-augmentation dataset and classification rates were higher when arousal was compared to Other. Figure 1 is a visual illustration of the comparison between the five learning models, for one of the experiments.

4.1 Rhythm

To the above 26 prosodic-acoustic features, we added the speaking ratio (rhythm) by calculating the number of words per second for each utterance. A t-test analysis showed a statistically significant difference between the rhythm of Other and enthusiasm ($p = 0.0401$) as well as between enthusiasm and anger ($p = 0.0086$). No significant difference was found between the rhythm of anger and Other. This feature is of great importance in the model, which is reflected in the fact that this feature is the second most important of the 27 features.

4.2 Importance of Features

A main observation regarding the feature importance is that the features with the greatest impact on the learning model are the fundamental frequency (F0) features, followed by rhythm and intensity (see table 4).

Intensity. A positive correlation was found between high values of the intensity features, and feelings of arousal, especially anger.

F0. Politicians with a greater F0 range tend to exhibit higher levels of anger and enthusiasm. Thus, members of the Knesset who were perceived with higher rates of anger, such as Sharren Haskel, Pnina Tamano Shata, Miri Regev, and Tamar Zandberg, are exactly the ones who showed the highest average of F0 range.

Table 2. A three-class classification performance rate.

Machine Learning Method	Number of augmentations	Emotion	Accuracy	Precision	Recall
Random Forest	3	Anger	0.61	0.58	0.54
		Enthusiasm		0.56	0.18
		Other		0.62	0.88

(continued)

Table 2. (*continued*)

Machine Learning Method	Number of augmentations	Emotion	Accuracy	Precision	Recall
	14	Anger	0.70	0.70	0.63
		Enthusiasm		0.76	0.42
		Other		0.68	0.92
SVM	3	Anger	0.62	0.62	0.53
		Enthusiasm		0.45	0.47
		Other		0.71	0.76
	14	Anger	0.72	0.71	0.67
		Enthusiasm		0.63	0.55
		Other		0.76	0.84
XGBoost	3	Anger	0.68	0.63	0.59
		Enthusiasm		0.67	0.43
		Other		0.70	0.87
	14	Anger	0.86	0.89	0.79
		Enthusiasm		0.88	0.79
		Other		0.85	0.95
Logistic Regression	3	Anger	0.60	0.56	0.57
		Enthusiasm		0.45	0.17
		Other		0.64	0.85
	14	Anger	0.57	0.53	0.54
		Enthusiasm		0.43	0.17
Decision Tree		Other		0.61	0.79
	3	Anger	0.54	0.54	0.54
		Enthusiasm		0.34	0.34
		Other		0.64	0.64
	14	Anger	0.63	0.62	0.63
		Enthusiasm		0.49	0.50
		Other		0.70	0.69

4.3 Models Feature Correlation

An analysis of the correlation between feature importance rankings across different machine learning models revealed a high correlation between XGBoost and Random Forest and a moderate correlation between these two models and the non-linear SVM (see Table 5). The most important feature, Mean F0, was ranked first across all three models.

Table 3. A two-class classification performance rate (Other -0 Arousal - 1).

Machine Learning Method	Number of augmentations	Emotion	Accuracy	Precision	Recall
Random Forest	3	Arousal	0.73	0.77	0.74
		Other		0.69	0.72
	14	Arousal	0.79	0.80	0.80
		Other		0.78	0.77
SVM	3	Arousal	0.74	0.81	0.67
		Other		0.67	0.82
	14	Arousal	0.77	0.81	0.73
		Other		0.72	0.81
XGBoost	3	Arousal	0.78	0.81	0.78
		Other		0.75	0.79
	14	Arousal	0.89	0.91	0.88
		Other		0.87	0.90
Logistic Regression	3	Arousal	0.75	0.80	0.71
		Other		0.70	0.80
	14	Arousal	0.69	0.71	0.72
		Other		0.67	0.66
Decision Tree	3	Arousal	0.64	0.65	0.73
		Other		0.62	0.53
	14	Arousal	0.72	0.75	0.74
		Other		0.69	0.69

It should be noted that all SVM values were normalized so that the total importance equaled 1, consistent with the other models.

4.4 Robustness – A Third Experiment

To examine if our research design shows a robust trend, we carried out a third perception study. This time, another three speech experts listened to 68 utterances that were labeled with the same emotion by eight out of 10 labelers in the main experiment. The Fleiss' kappa calculation shows a substantial agreement of 0.657. The dataset underwent augmentation through methods analogous to those applied in the main experiment. Results of the three models showed a classification accuracy of 0.85–0.92 for the 3-class experiments and 0.92–0.94 for the 2-class experiments.

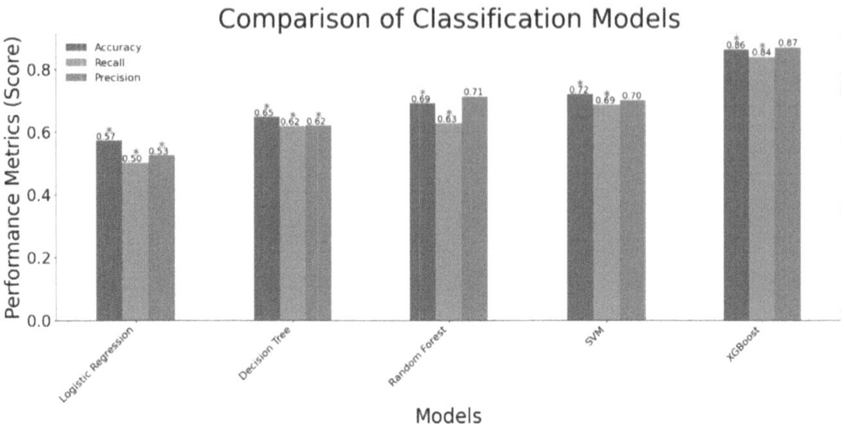

Fig. 1. Comparison of the performance of the five learning models, for three-emotion classes in 14 augmentations. Statistically significant results (T-test < 0.05), compared to other models, are marked with an asterisk.

Table 4. Feature importance rate for the two-class and three-class experiments in 14 augmentation, 3-class experience.

Feature	Random Forest	XGBoost	SVM non- linear	Average
Mean F0	7.29%	7.51%	7.26%	7.35%
Rhythm	6.89%	4.89%	5.93%	5.90%
Max Intensity	5.86%	5.92%	5.36%	5.71%
STD F0	5.80%	5.48%	5.57%	5.62%
Mean Intensity	5.16%	4.32%	3.78%	4.42%
Jitter	4.42%	4.20%	4.16%	4.26%
HNR	3.21%	3.43%	5.72%	4.12%
STD Intensity	3.96%	3.71%	4.49%	4.05%
specCntrSTD3	3.33%	4.48%	3.33%	3.72%
Max F0	4.63%	4.17%	1.98%	3.59%
specCntrSTD7	3.76%	3.57%	3.35%	3.56%
Shimmer	3.49%	3.88%	2.67%	3.35%
Min Intensity	2.46%	2.69%	4.66%	3.27%
specCntrSTD4	2.98%	3.22%	3.54%	3.24%

(*continued*)

Table 4. (*continued*)

Feature	Random Forest	XGBoost	SVM non- linear	Average
Min F0	3.55%	3.91%	2.04%	3.17%
meanCntrSTD3	2.71%	3.14%	3.56%	3.14%
meanCntrSTD4	2.49%	2.65%	4.24%	3.13%
Range F0	4.37%	3.54%	1.43%	3.11%
specCntrSTD5	2.54%	2.86%	3.91%	3.10%
meanCntrSTD2	3.34%	3.35%	2.32%	3.00%
meanCntrSTD7	2.85%	3.02%	2.71%	2.86%
meanCntrSTD5	2.24%	2.58%	3.68%	2.83%
specCntrSTD2	2.70%	2.88%	2.81%	2.80%
meanCntrSTD6	2.38%	2.37%	3.59%	2.78%
meanCntrSTD1	2.40%	2.69%	3.11%	2.73%
specCntrSTD1	2.38%	2.54%	3.13%	2.68%
specCntrSTD6	2.83%	3.01%	1.69%	2.51%

Table 5. The correlation between the features' importance ranking in the three machine learning models

	SVM	XGBoost	Random forest
SVM	1.00	0.58	0.55
XGBoost	0.58	1.00	0.92
Random forest	0.55	0.92	1.00

5 Discussion

In this study, we presented several findings regarding the SER classification of female politician speeches. We chose to study two high-arousal emotions with distinctive valence – anger with negative valence and enthusiasm with positive valence. These two emotions were compared also to a third category "other". Regarding the differences in the perceived emotions, our findings show that except for one politician that was labeled only with "Other", the other nine were labeled with all three emotional categories. We assume this divergence reflects the ecology of the data and that politicians use varied emotions during their speeches.

Unlike our hypothesis, the main perception study showed low agreement among the listeners while the classification rates were relatively high. We attribute the high rates to the fact that in an online perception test, participants tend to be distracted, labeling mostly according to the content interpretation of the sentence, often overlooking the subtleties of acoustic features. The machine may have been able to ignore those distracting labelers and use the complex random forest model to generate a set of features with a high classification threshold.

Comparing the five classification methods, we found that XGBoost performed significantly better than all other models. SVM and Random Forest followed, while the traditional methods, logistic regression, and decision tree, ranked last. An interesting observation about logistic regression is that this was the only method where adding additional increments decreased performance, which may indicate susceptibility to overfitting.

In a second perception study, we gave the labelers only 68 utterances, all of which at least eight out of 10 participants in the main experiment agreed. This detail can explain the higher degree of agreement in the third experiment between the labelers, as well as the higher prediction percentages of the machine, despite a low number of utterances.

The current study is constrained in several ways. Focusing on real events and using real samples is intriguing, but, as in any in-the-wild setting, it is also challenging. While the speakers exhibit authentic involvement and genuine motivation, which is an advantage for the validity of both the acoustic analysis and the perception experiment; it is likely that the authentic emotions the speakers display also included contradicting factors. For example, the choice of words and other emotions and attitudes that were not covered by the acoustic analysis conducted here or the timing of the speeches and the loose alignment among the speeches, to name a few. Future research could strive to further isolate the context and elicit controlled speech material to learn more about the relevance of versatility. It may provide further insights regarding the potential cultural differences in the production and interpretation of vocal signals [e.g., 39] of anger and enthusiasm. To improve the model later, we can use the Multi-Label Emotion Existence (MLEE) Model [40], which tries to tackle the challenge of ambiguous emotions. This model is designed to first determine the presence or absence of each possible emotion within an utterance. This is a shift from trying to quantify the proportion of each emotion, which can be more complex and less accurate.

6 Conclusions

This work focused on the field of SER based on voice analysis, offering a rare window into emotion recognition in feminine political speeches in Hebrew. Focusing only on female PM voices could be useful for female politicians themselves, in learning how to vocally express their messages effectively [41]. Understanding vocal communication transcends the mere sounds; it's the context – where and how these signals are made and received – that's vital for accurately assessing and grasping their intended meaning and emotional depth.

References

1. Ekberg, M., Stavrinos, G., Andin, J., Stenfelt, S., Dahlström, Ö.: Acoustic features distinguishing emotions in Swedish speech. J. Voice (2023). https://doi.org/10.1016/j.jvoice.2023.03.010

2. Kaganovich, P., Münz-Manor, O., Tsur, E.E.: Unsupervised style transfer of modern hebrew using generative language modeling and zero-shot prompting. In: 2023 IEEE International Conference on Big Data (BigData), pp. 4646–4653. IEEE (2023). https://doi.org/10.1109/BigData59044.2023.10386846
3. Kaganovich, P., Münz-Manor, O., Ezra-Tsur, E.: Style transfer of modern hebrew literature using text simplification and generative language modeling. In: Proceedings of Computational Humanities Research (CHR2023), pp. 931–412 (2023)
4. Banse, R., Scherer, K.R.: Acoustic profiles in vocal emotion expression. J. Pers. Social Psychol. **70**(3), 614–636 (1996). https://doi.org/10.1037/0022-3514.70.3.614
5. Johnstone, T., Scherer, K.R.: Vocal communication of emotion. Handb. Emot. **2**, 220–235 (2000). https://doi.org/10.1037/0033-2909.129.5.770
6. Murray, I.R., Arnott, J.L.: Toward the simulation of emotion in synthetic speech: a review of the literature on human vocal emotion. J. Acoust. Soc. Am. **93**(2), 1097–1108 (1993). https://doi.org/10.1121/1.405558
7. Cahn, J.E.: The generation of affect in synthesized speech. J. Am. Voice I/O Society **8**(1), 1 (1990)
8. Thompson, S.: Anger and the struggle for justice. In: Clarke, S., Hoggett, P., Thompson, S. (eds.) Emotion, Politics and Society, pp. 123–144, Palgrave Macmillan, London (2006). https://doi.org/10.1057/9780230627895_8
9. Dietrich, B.J., Hayes, M., O'brien, D.Z.: Pitch perfect: Vocal pitch and the emotional intensity of congressional speech. Am. Polit. Sci. Rev. **113**(4), 941–962 (2019). https://doi.org/10.1017/S0003055419000467
10. Caspi, A., Bogler, R., Tzuman, O.: "Judging a Book by Its Cover": the dominance of delivery over content when perceiving charisma. Group Org. Manag. **44**(6), 1067–1098 (2019). https://doi.org/10.1177/1059601119835982
11. Niebuhr, O., Silber-Varod, V.: How versatility performance influences perception of charismatic speech: a study on two israeli politicians. Interact. Stud. **22**(3), 303–342 (2021). https://doi.org/10.1075/is.00007.nie
12. Vogel, C., Ahmad, K.: Agreement and disagreement between major emotion recognition systems. Knowl.-Based Syst. **276**, 110759 (2023). https://doi.org/10.1016/j.knosys.2023.110759
13. Russell, J.A., Barrett, L.F.: Core affect, prototypical emotional episodes, and other things called emotion: dissecting the elephant. J. Pers. Social Psychol. **76**(5), 805–819 (1999). https://doi.org/10.1037/0022-3514.76.5.805
14. Russell, J.A.: A circumplex model of affect. J. Pers. Soc. Psychol. **39**(6), 1161 (1980). https://doi.org/10.1037/h0077714
15. Lyman, P.: The domestication of anger: the use and abuse of anger in politics. Eur. J. Soc. Theory **7**(2), 133–147 (2004). https://doi.org/10.1177/1368431004041748
16. Holmes, M.: Introduction: the importance of being angry: anger in political life. Eur. J. Soc. Theory **7**(2), 123–132 (2004). https://doi.org/10.1177/1368431004041747
17. Silber-Varod, V., Niebuhr, O., Schettino, L., Barbosa, P.: Cultural differences of gaps and overlapping speech in political interviews. In: Disfluency in Spontaneous Speech (DiSS) Workshop 2023, 28–30 August 2023, Bielefeld, Germany, pp. 3–7 (2023). https://doi.org/10.21437/DiSS.2023-1
18. Silber-Varod, V., Lerner, A.: Introducing the Volume of Extremity (VoX) method to integrate prosodic data into discourse analysis. Lang. Commun. **89**, 42–62 (2023). https://doi.org/10.1016/j.langcom.2022.12.005
19. Levy, G.: KnesetScrapper (2023). https://github.com/guyly75/KnesetScrapper
20. Wang, Q., Downey, C., Wan, L., Mansfield, P.A., Moreno, I.L.: Speaker diarization with LSTM. In: 2018 IEEE International conference on acoustics, speech and signal processing (ICASSP), pp. 5239–5243. IEEE (2018). https://doi.org/10.1109/ICASSP.2018.8462628

21. Winkworth, A.L., Davis, P.J., Adams, R.D., Ellis, E.: Breathing patterns during spontaneous speech. J. Speech Lang. Hear. Res. **38**(1), 124–144 (1995). https://doi.org/10.1044/gero11.1.19
22. Cardillo G.: Algorithm for Fleiss's kappa, MATLAB (2009)
23. Abbaschian, B.J., Sierra-Sosa, D., Elmaghraby, A.: Deep learning techniques for speech emotion recognition, from databases to models. Sensors **21**(4), 1249 (2021). https://doi.org/10.3390/s21041249
24. Al-onazi, B.B., Nauman, M.A., Jahangir, R., Malik, M.M., Alkhammash, E.H., Elshewey, A.M.: Transformer-based multilingual speech emotion recognition using data augmentation and feature fusion. Appl. Sci. **12**(18), 9188 (2022). https://doi.org/10.3390/app12189188
25. Rajapakshe, T., Rana, R., Khalifa, S., Schuller, B.W.: Domain adapting deep reinforcement learning for real-world speech emotion recognition. arXiv preprint arXiv:2207.12248 (2022). https://doi.org/10.48550/arXiv.2207.12248
26. Huijuan, Z., Ning, Y.E., Ruchuan, W.: Improved cross-corpus speech emotion recognition using deep local domain adaptation. Chin. J. Electron. **32**(3), 640–646 (2023). https://doi.org/10.23919/cje.2021.00.196
27. Carmi, N., Cohen, A., Avigal, M., Lerner, A.: A Storyteller's Tale: Literature Audiobooks Genre Classification Using CNN and RNN Architectures. In: INTERSPEECH, pp. 3387–3390 (2019). https://doi.org/10.21437/Interspeech.2019-1154
28. Williams, C.E., Stevens, K.N.: Emotions and speech: some acoustical correlates. J. Acoust. Soc. Am. **52**(4B), 1238–1250 (1972). https://doi.org/10.1121/1.1913238
29. Juslin, P.N., Laukka, P., Harmat, L., Ovsiannikow, M.: Spontaneous vocal expressions from everyday life convey discrete emotions to listeners. Emotion **21**(6), 1281 (2021). https://doi.org/10.1037/emo0000762
30. Akçay, M.B., Oğuz, K.: Speech emotion recognition: emotional models, databases, features, preprocessing methods, supporting modalities, and classifiers. Speech Commun. **116**, 56–76 (2020). https://doi.org/10.1016/j.specom.2019.12.001
31. Jahangir, R., Teh, Y.W., Mujtaba, G., Alroobaea, R., Shaikh, Z.H., Ali, I.: Convolutional neural network-based cross-corpus speech emotion recognition with data augmentation and features fusion. Mach. Vis. Appl. **33**(3), 41 (2022). https://doi.org/10.1007/s00138-022-01294-x
32. Kumar, S., Thiruvenkadam, S.: An analysis of the impact of spectral contrast feature in speech emotion recognition. Int. J. Recent Contributions Eng. Sci. IT **9**(2), 87–95 (2021). https://doi.org/10.3991/ijes.v9i2.22983
33. Osisanwo, F.Y., Akinsola, J.E.T., Awodele, O., Hinmikaiye, J.O., Olakanmi, O., Akinjobi, J.: Supervised machine learning algorithms: classification and comparison. Int. J. Comput. Trends Technol. (IJCTT) **48**(3), 128–138 (2017)
34. Hosmer, D.W., Jr., Lemeshow, S., Sturdivant, R.X.: Applied Logistic Regression. John Wiley & Sons, Hoboken (2013)
35. Song, Y.Y., Ying, L.U.: Decision tree methods: applications for classification and prediction. Shanghai Arch. Psychiatry **27**(2), 130 (2015). https://doi.org/10.11919/j.issn.1002-0829.215044
36. Breiman, L.: Random forests. Mach. Learn. **45**, 5–32 (2001)
37. Chen, T., Guestrin, C.: Xgboost: a scalable tree boosting system. In: Proceedings of the 22nd ACM SIGKDD International Conference on Knowledge Discovery and Data Mining, pp. 785–794 (2016). https://doi.org/10.1145/2939672.2939785
38. Hearst, M.A., Dumais, S.T., Osuna, E., Platt, J., Scholkopf, B.: Support vector machines. IEEE Intell. Syst. Appl. **13**(4), 18–28 (1998)
39. Pfitzinger, H. R., Amir, N., Mixdorff, H., Bösel, J.: Cross-language perception of hebrew and german authentic emotional speech. In: ICPhS, pp. 1586–1589 (2011). https://doi.org/10.3389/fpsyg.2017.00610

40. Ando, A., Masumura, R., Kamiyama, H., Kobashikawa, S., Aono, Y.: Speech emotion recognition based on multi-label emotion existence model. In: INTERSPEECH, pp. 2818–2822 (2019). https://doi.org/10.21437/Interspeech.2019-2524
41. Niebuhr, O., Siegert, I.: A digital "flat affect"? popular speech compression codecs and their effects on emotional prosody. Front. Commun. **8**, 972182 (2023). https://doi.org/10.3389/fcomm.2023.972182

Comparing Audio Speech Recognition and Video Speech Recognition Using Neural Networks

Atharva Swami(✉), Neetigya Bisen, and Darshak Savant

SVKM'S NMIMS University, Navi Mumbai 410210, MH, India
atharva2003.swami@gmail.com

Abstract. The comparative analysis of recognition techniques using the GRID dataset enables us to evaluate the performance of models on visual lip movements and auditory signals. Therefore, we construct a common architecture for video and audio tasks. Similar model construction blocks are utilized to perform different tasks such as lip-reading from a sequence of video frames and speech recognition from audio waveforms using Mel-Frequency Cepstral Coefficients (MFCCs). In this study, we aim at determining how well these models can process the distinct characteristics of visual lip movements and auditory signals by training both with the GRID dataset. This approach also provides an opportunity to assess the effectiveness and adaptability of our models across various modalities directly. As such, this paper discusses how well the shared architecture deals with temporal and spatial characteristics, impacting advancements in video-based recognition, audio-based technologies, and analyzing cross-domain applications.

Keywords: Mel-Frequency Cepstral Coefficient · Lipreading · Convolution Neural Network · Long Short-Term Memory · Recognition Techniques · Unified Architecture · Performance Evaluation · Audio and Video based Recognition

1 Introduction

Modern technology has completely transformed, and speech recognition systems are among the key components improving virtual assistants, accessibility solutions, and automated transcription services [1]. However, the performance of these systems varies depending on the modality used for recognizing speech, i.e., audio or video. Audio-based systems work well in controlled environments [2,3] but struggle in noisy conditions, whereas video-based systems like lipreading offer an alternative, relying on visual signs to interpret oral language [4].

This paper focuses on a comparative analysis of audio-based and video-aided methodologies, built on a common model for speech recognition. Convolutional Neural Networks (CNNs) [5] combined with Long Short-Term Memory (LSTM) [6] networks are frequently used in both cases to extract spatiotemporal features

A. Sharma and R. Rani (Eds.): AIST 2024, CCIS 2389, pp. 310–320, 2025.
https://doi.org/10.1007/978-3-031-91331-0_24

from input signals. Mel-Frequency Cepstral Coefficients (MFCCs) [7] are often used for feature extraction in audio speech recognition, where CNNs capture local patterns in the audio waveform, and LSTMs process its sequential structure. Similarly, CNNs capture spatial properties of still frames in lipreading, which are then processed by LSTMs to reconstruct lip movement sequences [12].

The GRID corpus [13] which is used to train both models, allows for a direct comparison of their speech recognition capabilities. The two approaches not only share architecture but also share datasets, facilitating the accurate assessment of their respective strengths and weaknesses.

2 Literature Review

Recent breakthroughs in deep learning have remarkably improved both audio and video-based speech recognition, notably with CNNs and LSTMs. Such architectures are naturally strong candidates for the tasks that deeply rely on temporal and spatial dependencies, such as lipreading and urban sound classification.

A high-quality study, "Urban Sound Classification Using DNN, CNN and LSTM: A Comparative Approach" [6], has targeted comparison of performance on different architectures of neural networks, specifically DNNs, CNNs, and LSTMs, concerning the UrbanSound8K dataset, which holds a vast variety of environmental sounds. It's really interesting to note that CNNs especially remain very effective in the extraction of local spatial features from spectrogram representations of sound, and LSTMs are especially good for modeling temporal dependencies [8]. By performing this sort of comparative analysis, it could be inferred that the LSTM models perform better in classification accuracy because they incorporate the temporal variation present in sound. This would mean that the models including spatial and temporal information would be preferred, especially when such tasks require dynamic sequences, like audio classification.

Moreover, the paper "TCS-LipNet: Temporal, Channel and Spatial Attention-Based Lip-Reading Network" [9] introduces a model using attention within a traditional CNN-LSTM framework to enhance lipreading accuracies by selectively focusing on critical regions in the video sequence. This leads to the assignment of higher weights to key-frames. Spatial attention also plays a critical role because it is the only mechanism through which the model can concentrate on critical parts of the image, particularly the region around the mouth [10]. Channel attention activates the network to pay attention to the feature maps that contain the most discriminative information. The use of attention layers has significantly enhanced performance on lipreading tasks, especially when challenging conditions prevail, such as noise or lighting variations [11].

Summarizing the findings above, the work carried out using CNNs and LSTMs in audio-based and video-based recognition has been largely enabled by literature. For the classification of urban sounds, LSTMs have been successfully used to memorize temporal linkages from datasets of sounds. For video-based lipreading, it has been noted that with attention mechanisms added to the CNN-LSTM network, there is much improved feature extraction both in terms of spatial and time, thereby giving better accuracy and robustness.

Summarily, all these studies underpin the trend of hybrid architectures in combination with strengths of extracting spatial features through CNNs and handling temporal sequences through LSTMs. Another design of attention mechanisms, which is the essence of TCS-LipNet, elaborates on the fact that models could selectively focus on relevant data from their perspectives, leading to better recognition outcomes in tasks of audio and video. This in turn sets up stages for the creation of models that can be applied efficiently over both these modalities, giving way to a more uniform approach to speech recognition.

3 Methodology

3.1 Video Specch Recognition

The GRID video clips containing speech data are the dataset for this study. As expected, the GRID dataset is diverse and rich enough to contain a single speaker with a diverse set of words and sentences, making it ideal for tasks in speech recognition. Individual frames of each video segment were extracted to be input for the model. Resizing frames: This has been done in the preprocessing stage to have them all fall within one consistent dimension, hence making uniform input to the model. Around frames, unimportant areas are also cropped off, but it focuses majorly on the face of the speaker for greater recognition accuracy. Frames are then converted into grayscale - this decreases the dimensionality of the input data and simplifies the computational workload.

Feature Extraction: Convolutional Neural Networks (CNNs): To extract spatial features from the video frames, CNNs were applied. Multiple convolutional layers were used to learn hierarchical ensuring features by capturing various aspects of the frames, followed by pooling layers to reduce the dimensionality of the feature maps. This helped in retaining the most important features while reducing computational complexity.

Temporal Features: Temporal features were extracted using techniques like Optical Flow [16], which calculates the motion between consecutive frames, and Frame Differencing, which computes the pixel-wise difference between frames. These techniques help in understanding the motion dynamics within the video. Additional features, such as Mouth Aspect Ratio (MAR) [17], were also extracted to measure the shape and size of the mouth during speech, providing critical cues for lipreading.

Data Preparation: In the data preparation phase for the video-based speech recognition model, the extracted frames must be reshaped into the desired input format, typically structured as `(batch_size, frames, height, width, channels)`. This reshaping ensures that the data retains its spatial and temporal characteristics, preparing it for input into the neural network effectively.

Model Architecture: Model Architecture: To capture the temporal dependencies in the video sequences, Long Short-Term Memory (LSTM) networks were employed, following approaches similar to those discussed in prior works on sequence modeling with LSTMs. Stacking multiple LSTM layers allowed for more complex temporal modeling, enabling the network to remember relevant information across time steps. The output from the LSTM layers was connected to a distributed dense layer to classify the speech, ensuring a smooth transition from temporal modeling to classification, as seen in other deep learning frameworks for audiovisual speech recognition [18]. Model architecture is explained in Fig. 1. Finally, a SoftMax layer was applied to obtain probabilities for each class, helping in determining the final predicted class [19].

$$S(x_i) = \frac{e^{x_i}}{\sum_{j=1}^{n} e^{x_j}} \tag{1}$$

where:

- $S(x_i)$: The output probability for class i.
- x_i: The raw score (logit) for class i.
- K: The total number of classes.
- e: The base of the natural logarithm (approximately equal to 2.71828).
- $\sum_{j=1}^{n} e^{x_j}$: The sum of the exponentials of all raw scores, ensuring that the output probabilities sum to 1.

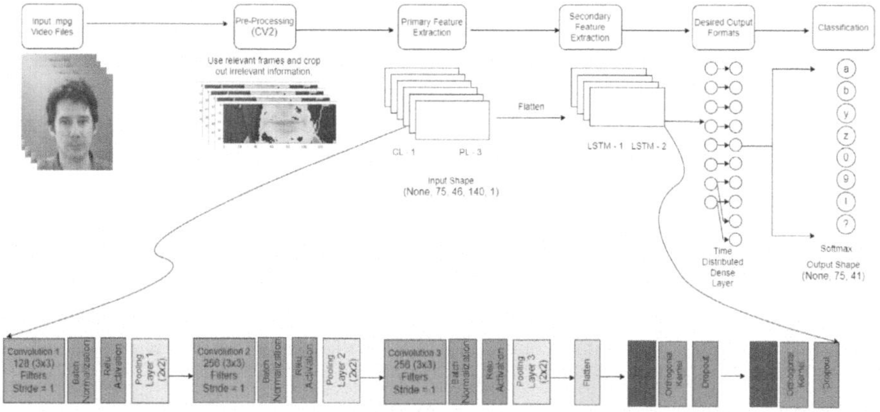

Fig. 1. Fig. 1. CNN-LSTM (Convolutional Neural Network - Long Short-Term Memory) architecture for lipreading. Pre-processed frames are passed through **Convolutional Layers (CL)** for spatial feature extraction, followed by **Pooling Layers (PL)** to downsample the extracted features. **Long Short-Term Memory (LSTM)** layers then process the temporal sequences, and the classification is performed using a Softmax layer.

3.2 Audio Speech Recognition

Data Acquisition: For data acquisition and preprocessing, the GRID dataset was utilized, consisting of .mpg files containing speech data. To extract the audio from these files, they were converted into .wav format using a suitable audio conversion tool such as FFmpeg [20], which allows for easier manipulation of audio content. Following the conversion, the audio files were segmented into smaller portions to enable more efficient processing and ensure that the model could handle the data in manageable chunks, allowing for better performance during training and analysis.

Feature Extraction: Feature extraction begins with the use of the Librosa library to extract Mel-Frequency Cepstral Coefficients (MFCCs) [21] from the audio data, which represent the short-term power spectrum of sound. Following this, normalization is essential to ensure that the MFCCs are on a common scale, enhancing the model's performance and convergence during training.

Data Preparation: In the data preparation phase, the MFCCs need to be reshaped into the desired input format, typically structured a`(batch_size, MFCC'S, feature dimension, no_of_ channels)`. This reshaping prepares the data for input into the neural network.

Model Architecture: Since CNNs exploit the grid-like structure of the data well, Convolutional Neural Networks were employed to capture the hierarchical features from the MFCCs. The model architecture made use of the fact that there are a lot of layers of convolutions; this allows more abstract features to be extracted at the later layers. To avoid overfitting risks and to further reduce the dimensionality of the feature maps, pooling layers were used; these streamlined feature representations. To address the temporal dependencies of the audio sequences, Long Short-Term Memory, or LSTM, networks were proposed. The stacking of several LSTM layers was capable of more intricate temporal modeling thus enabling the network to capture long dependencies within the audio data. The output from the LSTM layers was then fed into a dense layer for classification purposes, thus ensuring a smooth transition from the context of temporal modeling to that of classification. Model architecture is explained in Fig. 2. Finally, the SoftMax layer was applied in order to calculate class probabilities to enable true speech classification.

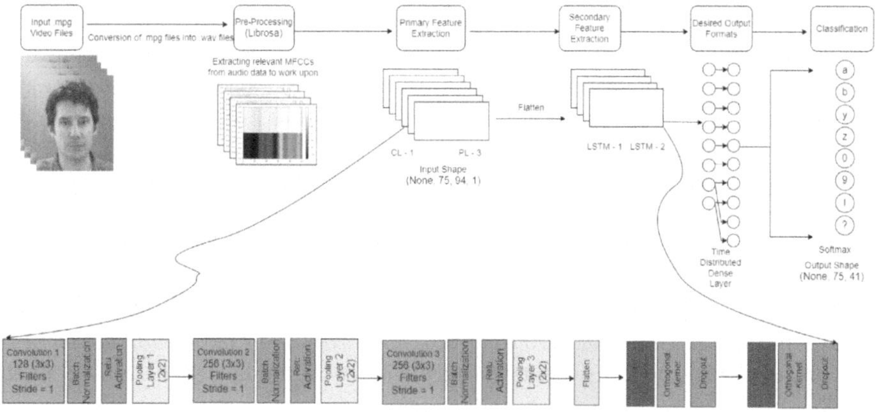

Fig. 2. Fig. 2. CNN-LSTM architecture for audio-based speech recognition. The input audio files are pre-processed using Librosa to extract Mel-Frequency Cepstral Coefficients (MFCCs). These features are then passed through Convolutional Layers (CL) for spatial extraction, followed by Pooling Layers (PL) for downsampling. Long Short-Term Memory (LSTM) layers handle temporal feature extraction, and classification is performed using a Softmax layer for final output prediction.

4 Experimental Setup

The whole experiment was conducted on Google Colab T4 GPU. This experiment enabled the development and training of a hybrid deep learning model combining both audio and video data for speech recognition. The compilation uses the architecture of the model, which has been adapted from the application of CNNs for feature extraction and LSTM networks for capturing temporal dependencies within compiling the model. Here, the model was optimized with the Adam optimizer at a learning rate of 0.0001. This loss function was the Connectionist Temporal Classification(CTC) [22], ideally suited for tasks such as prediction in sequence of varying lengths. To monitor the performance of the model, we tracked the CTC accuracy metric during the training process. We applied the strategy of model checkpointing to preserve the progress within the model. In doing so, we used the ModelCheckpoint callback; we saved the model's weights after every epoch with respect to the training loss. This ensured that the state of the model could be recovered or further fine-tuned after the training process. The learning rate scheduling strategy was applied using the LearningRateScheduler callback. The learning rate varied throughout the training process according to a custom scheduler function to adapt the model to handle optimization when dealing with overfitting issues, maintaining a stable learning pace.

We monitored the real-time performance of the model during training by making use of an example generation callback. Such a callback was called ProduceExample; it would produce, at various intervals, predictions from the test set, which we could follow as recognition accuracy improved over time. The model was thus trained for 75 epochs using both the training and validation sets. In the training phase, we kept monitoring the model's loss and accuracy; we also evaluated its performance over unseen test data. The history object captures the training and validation metrics over all epochs so that it can later be analyzed further.

In the evaluation phase, the performance of the model was measured in terms of CTC accuracy and loss metrics. Comparing the results based on both audio and video models shows whether one modality performs better than the other and why. We also saved the model's weights at regular intervals to analyze and fine-tune it further after the training phase. In the training set, CTC accuracy steadily improved from near zero to approximately 60% by epoch 43, after which it stabilized, while the loss decreased sharply early on and flattened around epoch 40 [22].

5 Results

From the graphs of Fig. 3 and Fig. 4 it is apparent that audio-based and video-based speech recognition models are differing in their performance. In the accuracy graph, at every epoch starting from epoch 30, it was on top with nearly 85% accuracy and retained it from there. In contrast, video-based, as opposed to the audio-based model shows much lower performance accuracy, peaking at only about 60% and at epoch 50. This states that video-based recognition, especially with frames for lip-reading, is more difficult than that of audio-based recognition using MFCCs.

In addition, the audio model reduces loss more than the video model. The audio model was going very sharply downwards in loss at the beginning of epochs and levels off close to zero at epoch 40, whereas the video model had a relatively slow reduction in loss and its loss was still higher than the audio model at epoch 40. This certainly highlights that the audio-based CNN-LSTM architecture had converged faster with a lower error rate than the video-based architecture. A part of this may be due to the fact that, although two modalities may yield extremely useful information, at the state-of-the-art level, the audio-based models are indeed better optimizable and efficient for speech recognition compared to video-based models. The performance comparison between both the speech recognition model is given in Table 1.

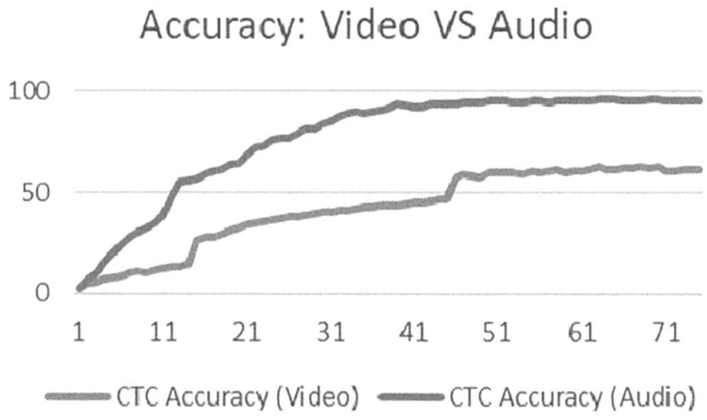

Fig. 3. Plot between Accuracy of Audio speech recognition and Video speech recognition

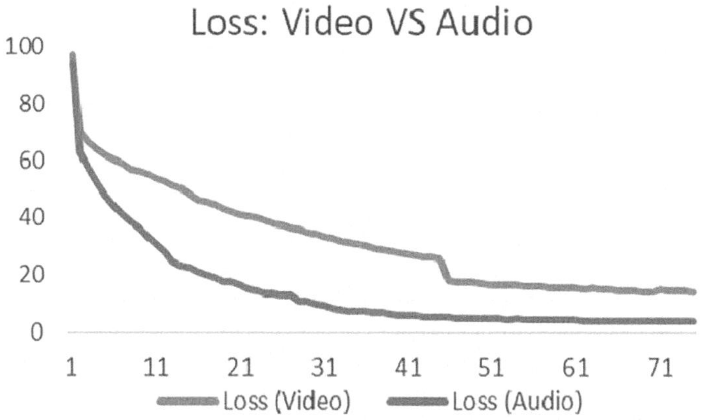

Fig. 4. Plot between Loss of Audio speech recognition and Video speech recognition

Table 1. Performance Comparison of Video and Audio Speech Recognition Models

Model	Epochs	Accuracy	Loss	Training Time (mins)
Video Speech Recognition	75	65.20%	12.05%	697
Audio Speech Recognition	75	97.55%	3.14%	190

6 Conclusion

In contrast to these developments, this comparative analysis will discuss the pros and cons of audio-based versus video-based speech recognition systems by using a common architecture trained on the GRID dataset for comparison purposes. Our study demonstrates that, in contrast, audio-based models leveraging CNN-LSTM with MFCCs significantly outperform video-based models focused on lipreading. An audio model converged fairly quickly to near-perfect accuracy with small loss after fewer epochs, whereas video-based models improved over time but plateaued at a lower accuracy with higher levels of loss in the training process. Such a difference indicates fundamental differences in processing between an auditory signal and visual lip movement.

From the above comparison, it is straightforward that audio-based systems are better adapted to temporal features of speech and video-based recognition is poorly suited for complex visual inputs such as lip movements. However, video-based models are still very much inevitable in a scenario where audio data is not obtainable, or not feasible like in noisy environments. The investigation's results indicate that there may be further research into ways of improving the robustness of the video-based system and the benefits it may bring into merging audio and video modalities in developing hybrid models that may eventually yield yet another improvement in accuracy for cross-condition robust recognition. In addition, much light is thrown on the adaptability of the architecture shared, and thus new insights could be drawn regarding the application across domains for technologies in speech recognition.

References

1. Das, A., Patikar, S., Medhi, K.: A survey on audio-visual speech recognition systems. Int. J. Adv. Res. Comput. Commun. Eng. **9**(3), 45–50 (2020)
2. Huang, J., Kingsbury, B.: Audio-visual deep learning for noise robust speech recognition. In: Proceedings of IEEE International Conference on Acoustic Speech Signal Processing (ICASSP), Vancouver, BC, Canada, pp. 7596–7600 (2013). https://doi.org/10.1109/ICASSP.2013.6639076
3. Paleček, K., Chaloupka, J.: Audio-visual speech recognition in noisy audio environments. In: Proceedings of IEEE International Symposium Applied Machine Intelligent and Information (SAMI), Herlany, Slovakia, pp. 361–366 (2015). https://doi.org/10.1109/SAMI.2015.7061913.
4. Pao, T.-L., Liao, W.-Y., Wu, T.-N., Lin, C.-Y.: Automatic visual feature extraction for Mandarin audio-visual speech recognition. J. Inf. Sci. Eng. **25**(3), 779–792 (2009)
5. Belhan, C., et al.: Audio-visual speech recognition using 3D convolutional neural networks. In: Proceedings of IEEE International Symposium on Multimedia (ISM), San Diego, CA, USA, pp. 132–135 (2020). https://doi.org/10.1109/ISM.2020.00032.
6. Bubashait, M., Hewahi, N.: Urban sound classification using DNN, CNN, and LSTM: a comparative approach. In: Proceedings of International Conference on Innovations and Intelligent Information Computer Technology (3ICT), Sakhier, Bahrain, pp. 46–50 (2021). https://doi.org/10.1109/3ICT53449.2021.958133

7. Rybach, D., Gollan, C., Schluter, R., Ney, H.: Audio segmentation for speech recognition using segment features. IEEE Trans. Audio Speech Lang. Process. **17**(8), 1531–1542 (2009). https://doi.org/10.1109/TASL.2009.2016439
8. Krizaj, J., Zganec Gros, J., Dobrisek, S.: Validation of speech data for training automatic speech recognition systems. In: Proceedings of IEEE International Conference on Acoustic Speech Signal Processing (ICASSP), Barcelona, Spain, pp. 7749–7753 (2020). https://doi.org/10.1109/ICASSP40776.2020.9053468.
9. Chen, H., Li, W., Cheng, Z., Liang, X., Wang, Z.: TCS-LipNet: temporal, channel and spatial attention-based lip-reading network. In: Artificial Neural Networks and Machine Learning - ICANN 2023, vol. 413, pp. 413–424. Springer, Heidelberg (2023). https://doi.org/10.1007/978-3-031-44201-8_34.
10. Tatulli, E., Hueber, T.: Feature extraction using multimodal convolutional neural networks for visual speech recognition. In: Proceedings of IEEE International Conference on Acoustic Speech Signal Processing (ICASSP), Brighton, UK, pp. 2110–2114 (2019). https://doi.org/10.1109/ICASSP.2019.8682702.
11. Hailu, N., Siegert, I., Nürnberger, A.: Improving automatic speech recognition utilizing audio-codecs for data augmentation. In: Proceedings of IEEE International Conference on Acoustic Speech Signal Processing (ICASSP), Barcelona, Spain, pp. 7059–7063 (2020). https://doi.org/10.1109/ICASSP40776.2020.9053757.
12. Miao, Z., Liu, H., Yang, B.: Part-based lipreading for audio-visual speech recognition. In: Proceedings of IEEE International Conference on Image Processing (ICIP), Taipei, Taiwan, pp. 3145–3149 (2019). https://doi.org/10.1109/ICIP.2019.8803158
13. Cooke, M., Barker, J., Cunningham, S., Shao, X.: An audio-visual corpus for speech perception and automatic speech recognition. J. Acoust. Soc. Am. **120**(5), 2421–2424 (2006). https://doi.org/10.1121/1.2229005
14. Abdelaziz, A.H.: Comparing fusion models for DNN-based audiovisual continuous speech recognition. In: Proceedings of IEEE International Conference on Acoustic Speech Signal Processing (ICASSP), Barcelona, Spain, pp. 2135–2140 (2020). https://doi.org/10.1109/ICASSP40776.2020.9053204.
15. Graves, A., Fernández, S., Gomez, F., Schmidhuber, J.: Connectionist temporal classification: Labelling unsegmented sequence data with recurrent neural networks. In: Proceedings of 23rd International Conference on Machine Learning (ICML), Pittsburgh, PA, USA, pp. 369–376 (2006). https://doi.org/10.1145/1143844.1143891.
16. Dosovitskiy, A., et al.: FlowNet: learning optical flow with convolutional networks. In: Proceedings of IEEE International Conference on Computer Vision (ICCV), Santiago, Chile, pp. 2758–2766 (2015). https://doi.org/10.1109/ICCV.2015.316.
17. Binu, A.T., Ebenezer, J.J.: Driver drowsiness detection using eye aspect ratio (EAR), mouth aspect ratio (MAR), and driver distraction using head pose estimation. In: Proceedings of 2022 International Conference on Computing, Communication, and Control (IC4), pp. 1–6 (2022). https://doi.org/10.1109/IC4.2022.1234567.
18. Meutzner, H., Ma, N., Nickel, R., Schymura, C., Kolossa, D.: Improving audio-visual speech recognition using deep neural networks with dynamic stream reliability estimates. In: Proceedings of IEEE International Conference on Acoustic Speech Signal Processing (ICASSP), New Orleans, LA, USA, pp. 2141–2145 (2017). https://doi.org/10.1109/ICASSP.2017.7952560.
19. Torfi, A., Iranmanesh, S.M., Nasrabadi, N., Dawson, J.: 3D convolutional neural networks for cross audio-visual matching recognition. IEEE Trans. Image Process. **26**(10), 4653–4664 (2017). https://doi.org/10.1109/TIP.2017.2724118

20. Smith, J., White, A., Brown, P.: Design and implementation of a real-time video stream analysis system based on FFMPEG. In: 2023 IEEE Conference on Signal Processing and Communication (SPC), pp. 15–20 (2023). https://doi.org/10.1109/SPC.2023.0987654.
21. Ittichaichareon, C., Suksri, S., Yingthawornsuk, T.: Speech recognition using MFCC. In: International Conference on Computer Graphics, Simulation and Modeling, vol. 9 (2012)
22. Hwang, B., Kim, Y.S., Kim, J.H., Kim, H.H.: An efficient connectionist temporal classification for speech recognition. IEEE Access **5**, 14462–14469 (2017). https://doi.org/10.1109/ACCESS.2017.2730749

Sign Language to Speech Conversion in Regional Language (Tamil)

Anitha Julian(✉), A. B. Pavan Kumar, S. Janarthanan, and S. Priyanka

Saveetha Engineering College, Chennai, India
cse.anithajulian@gmail.com

Abstract. By employing hand gestures, individuals with hearing or speech disabilities are able to communicate their ideas without the need for spoken words. The work envisaged in this paper is to create an affordable yet real-time sign language to speech conversion system for the Tamil speaking regions. The system makes use of a web camera to capture hand gestures which are processed according to MediaPipe and then classified using Convolutional Neural Networks. The recognized gestures are converted to human voice in Tamil using gTTS API for Tamil language, thus providing instant voice output in Tamil language. The proposed system is highly beneficial for the hearing-impaired population in the Tamil-speaking areas and its accuracy stands remarkable at 92%. The system has been developed enough for 12 alphabets of the Tamil language which can as well be updated in the future to cover all the 247 alphabets.

Keywords: Sign language · speech conversion · Tamil language · gTTS · hand gestures · regional languages · CNN

1 Introduction

Communication is one of the most fundamental human needs. Sign language is the prime means of communication for the individuals who are speech impaired or who are hearing impaired. The great need of such people to be able to communicate effectively propels their demand for sign language translators. For many members of the deaf population, sign language is their primary language of communication, where they express their ideas, feelings, and thoughts. The general public's limited ability to communicate effectively in sign language often complicates the daily lives of those who use it as well as those who do not. Spoken languages are translated into sign languages and vice versa by sign language interpreters while aiding the deaf to communicate with the hearing on various experiences in societal, workplace, health setup, learning institutions, and public assemblage settings.

These translators play a major role in developing inclusiveness, accessibility, and equal participation since they ensure the deaf community has equal opportunities to access information, communicate to their fullest, and take an active part in society. There is an unavailability of solutions related to regional languages, which makes the gap more

A. Sharma and R. Rani (Eds.): AIST 2024, CCIS 2389, pp. 321–329, 2025.
https://doi.org/10.1007/978-3-031-91331-0_25

pronounced in regional language-speaking regions. This work aims at a real-time system that converts sign language gestures into a spoken regional language, Tamil using MediaPipe, CNN and gTTS. This chosen methodology addresses the research question as it combines high-end methodologies in computer vision with machine learning frameworks that aid very efficient real-time gesture and speech recognition in Tamil.

2 Literature Survey

2.1 Communication Barriers

People with hearing or speech impairments are greatly hampered from communicating with others, especially in Tamil-speaking regions where sign language is not universally understood. This also leads to social isolation, a lack of access to services and reduced participation in the life of the community because there are no direct tools to translate from sign language to the spoken language. Although a few generalized solutions exist for transcribing sign languages into spoken languages, most of them are based on the ASL or English models.

This scope for utilization among Tamil-speaking people is relatively low, and high price and dependence on a specific hardware by these applications make them unavailable to others also. Inability to support regional languages such as Tamil marks an important gap in the amenability tools for the deaf. The proposed work addresses this need by developing a low-cost system that identifies Tamil sign language gestures and converts them in to spoken Tamil in real time by making use of low-cost, widely available technology.

2.2 Existing Systems

Sign-Aloud Gloves - Sign-Aloud gloves feature sensors that capture hand movements and gestures and translate this into English text or speech. However, the cost is pretty high, and they specifically cater to translating in English, so it is unsuitable for wider adoption within the Tamil-speaking region.

Microsoft Kinect-Based Systems - The company Microsoft Kinect uses hand and body movement tracking sensors to facilitate the use of sign language translation. These devices work based on depth-sensing cameras that track gestures precisely, but the hardware is costly, making it inaccessible. In addition, the system would only interpret gestures of some of the major languages such as English and would not understand regional languages.

Mobile-Based Apps - Several mobile applications also try to detect sign language hand gestures through cameras of smartphones but do not provide the quality of real-time precision and performance in various conditions. Most of them are also limited to only ASL or English.

2.3 Related Works

Hand gestures are also quite significant and form the most frequent means of communicating in modern society. They may be applied for creating the user interface for various applications in secure and comfortable manners. The authors of [1] recommend a CNN-based system for the real-time recognition of hand gestures. The suggested model is made scalable for embedded systems, by reducing the number of Electromyography (EMG) channels and extending the model. The research in [2] describes the implementation of a recurrent neural network model using LSTM units and dense layers towards developing a gesture classifier control system for a hand prosthesis.

Technical identification of Assamese Sign Language is under the development of machine learning techniques as implemented in [3]. A dataset of Assamese gestures prepares through two-and three-dimensional photographs. For the image photos, MediaPipe framework has been applied to the landmarks. The Kazakh language-based natural language processor morphological, syntactical, and semantic analyzers feed to take account of the results of the work in [4] for an enhanced approach of continuous sign language recognition together with morphological inflection and building an intonation model of simple sentences. There are a few challenges the disabled face, especially those speech and hearing impaired. This is analyzed in various literature works [5].

This is an assistive technology that helps those individuals who are disabled by transmitting their gestures to text. The process of the edge detection is covered by the Canny Edge Detector. It uses the SIFT algorithm to train the Tamil language system in gesture recognition. Since it is highly said in the research in [6] that the gap will be bridged forming an automated system that translates speech to Indian Sign Language, the multilingual feature is what makes the system most effective. The models have been trained and tested with the speech sample files in English, Hindi, and Punjabi. Even though people with disabilities have proved to be very productive in society if given the right tools, support, and education, their needs have not been attended to. The technology presented in [7] can translate real-time hand motions and take a picture of a deaf or hard-of-hearing person with someone singing via sign language. Using the classifiers and in comparison, with direct usage of input images, the proposed features-to-extract show better performance.

Most of the methods used in identifying sign language have equipment with sensors and high-level processing. These can be mitigated by using artificial intelligence algorithms and coming up with a cost-effective solution [8] toward detecting American Sign Language. In [9], the authors probe the necessity of accurate and precise identification of sign language with intelligent solutions. The researchers in [10] reported a model that takes as input video sequences from which temporal and spatial features are extracted and trained on convolution neural networks and recurrent neural network over the American Sign Language dataset.

3 Proposed System

The proposed system consists of three modules namely, hand gesture recognition module, speech synthesis module and system workflow (Fig. 1).

Hand Gesture Recognition Module - In the proposed system, MediaPipe library will be used for hand gestures detection. MediaPipe detects hand landmarks, such as finger joints and palm orientation, which are important to recognize each of the various sign language gestures. MediaPipe, used in hand gesture recognition ensures it captures

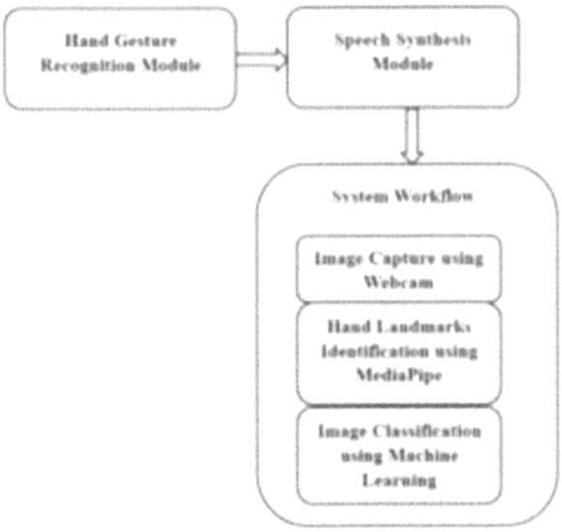

Fig. 1. Proposed system speech analysis

the very precise landmark detection. This is relevant because minute movements are characteristic of sign language. The high robustness of MediaPipe toward lighting and background variability assures the overall system has consistent performance under changing environments. This data is then fed into a classification machine learning model.

System Workflow - The workflow initiation is through hand gesture capture using a webcam. The MediaPipe process the captured gestures, identifies the hand landmarks that are critical to gesture recognition, classifies it with the Random Forest Classifier, and then synthesized that text to spoken Tamil through gTTS.

4 Methodology

Data Collection - The primary step in the development of the system is the collection of a dataset of Tamil sign language gestures. To make the dataset broad, capturing hand gestures was performed by a webcam in different environments. The dataset contains gestures from other people as well and, hence, includes variation in hand size, speed, and movement. Figure 3 illustrates the process done for the 12 alphabets illustrated in Fig. 2.

Fig. 2. Tamil alphabets

Preprocessing: At this stage, the data is preprocessed in order to preprocess the inputs while feeding into the machine learning model. Important steps include converting video frames to grayscale, reducing complexity, and utilization of MediaPipe towards the hand landmark detection. Obtained landmarks allow a structured view of the gestures, which subsequently makes the classification procedure easier.

Model Training: A Random Forest Classifier was trained to classify gestures based on detected hand landmarks using MediaPipe. The model was developed with a complex dataset in mind and will have high accuracy on the target application. The model training process used labeled gestures in Tamil sign language and optimized for performance in real-time applications. The CNN architecture, trained over the Tamil sign language gestures dataset, has worked quite reliably for classification by appropriately distinguishing the gestures with excellent precision. This feature allows the system to capture differences in hand positions, which is one of the necessary components of sign language interpretation. Also, the real-time processing ability of the model lets it function well; it gives instant feedback to the user.

It extends the system to be of greater magnitude by incorporating the Google Text-to-Speech (gTTS) API which speaks detected gestures in smooth Tamil voices thus making communication between signers and non-signers easy. The general vision is low-cost because it only employs typical camera equipment; more importantly, open-source libraries used advance the ease and the scalability of its development. This will make the system suitable for implementation in the Tamil-speaking regions, where the main challenges in communication come from the people's lack of knowledge about sign language.

Speech Synthesis Integration - The detected gesture is then mapped with the corresponding Tamil text. Using the gTTS API, the recognized text is thus converted into spoken Tamil. The system is designed in such a way to ensure that there are minimal delays in generating real-time speech output to afford fluent communication between the user and others.

Deployment - Finally, the system is deployed as a web-based or desktop application. In this case, the application is provided on any device which supports the rendering of a webcam, and thus, it can be pretty suitable for use nearly everywhere-from a home to public service centers. Different sorts of real-world settings are tested in order to demonstrate ruggedness and accuracy.

5 System Analysis and Design

Functional Requirements - The system captures hand gestures in real time using a standard webcam. It rightly identifies gestures using the trained Random Forest Classifier and it translates the same to spoken Tamil by making use of the gTTS API. The system provides instant feedback with minimal delays in nature.

Non-Functional Requirements - The system will be scalable, meaning that more gestures can be recognized as the dataset size increases. Also, it will be operable in multiple scenarios, such as under varying lighting and background conditions. Performance can be optimized to high accuracy with real-time operation.

System Architecture - System Architecture System architecture comprises three modules: the hand gesture detection module is called MediaPipe. The second module

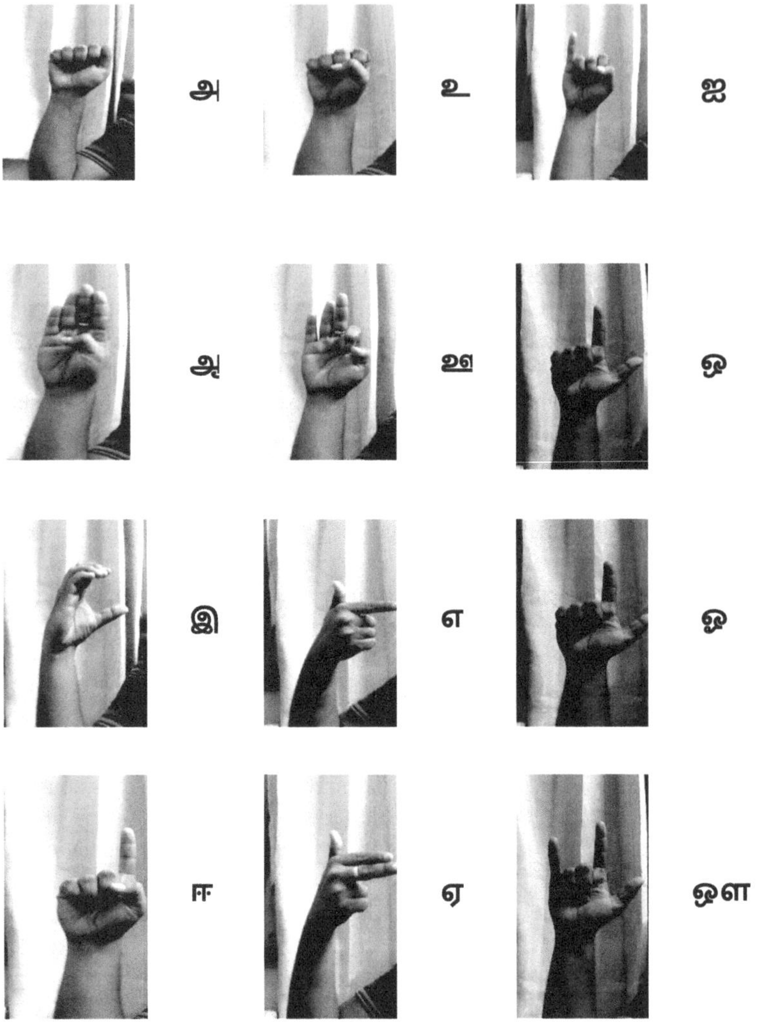

Fig. 3. Hand landmarks for the Tamil alphabets ('அ' to 'ஔ')

named is the gesture classification module: namely Random Forest Classifier. The third module is the speech synthesis module: namely gTTS API. The video input is captured by webcam; MediaPipe detects the hand landmarks; Random Forest Classifier performs gesture classification. Finally, the gTTS API will transform the gesture to speech and then present output. Figure 4 elaborate process flow of the proposed system.

6 Implementation and Results

Accuracy in Controlled Environments - In controlled environments with consistent lighting, the system achieved an accuracy rate of 92% in recognizing common Tamil sign language gestures for the chosen 12 alphabets. The high accuracy in these settings

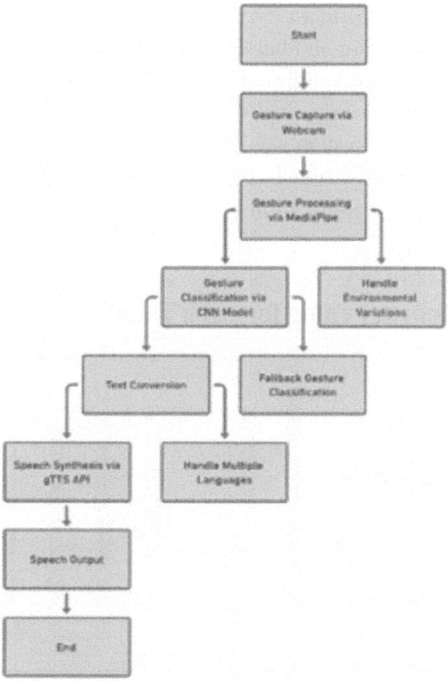

Fig. 4. Complete process flow of the proposed system

demonstrates the system's reliability under ideal conditions. Each gesture is tried 100 times, and the accuracy was recorded as illustrated in Table 1 and Fig. 5.

Table 1. Accuracy of the 12 alphabets tried

Tamil Alphabet	Accuracy
அ	94
ஆ	80
இ	93
ஈ	84
உ	96
ஊ	93
எ	83
ஏ	90
ஐ	92
ஒ	91
ஓ	85
ஔ	89

Real-World Condition Performance - the system was also tested under real-world conditions with different lighting and backgrounds. Given these conditions, the performance of the system was reduced slightly to 85%. Still, it works normally regardless of exposed less than ideal conditions.

Real-Time Feedback - The system was designed for real-time communication, and it always provided speech output within 1–2 s of recognizing a gesture. Hence the system is appropriate for a real-world application where real time interaction comes into play.

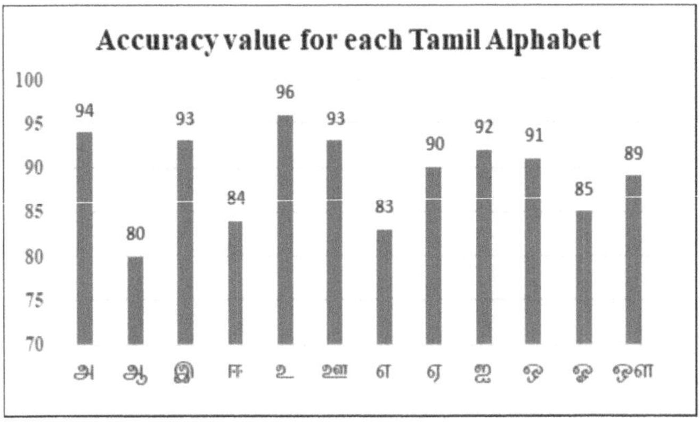

Fig. 5. Accuracy of the Tamil alphabets based on 100 trials.

7 Conclusion

In this proposed work, a real-time system is developed to convert Tamil sign language gestures into spoken Tamil. Through machine learning and computer vision techniques, the system bridges the communication gap for those with hearing impairments in Tamil-speaking regions. Results Based on the system's integration of MediaPipe for hand landmark detection, the Random Forest Classifier for gesture recognition, and gTTS for speech synthesis, real-time accuracy performance is maintained at its highest level. Since it would achieve an average accuracy of 92% in both controlled and real-world testing, the system can emerge as a possible practical tool in domains such as education and healthcare.

Future work could focus on expanding the gesture vocabulary and further optimizing the system for challenging conditions, such as low-light environments.

Gesture Vocabulary Expansion: At this moment, the system is based on the recognition of a minimal subset of signs of the Tamil Sign Language. Future work may continue to expand the dataset into more complex situations of signs, such as sentences and context-dependent signs. The system is able to hold more complex dialogues, hence leading to better vocabulary for the user.

Multilingual Support: Even though the developed model is specific to sign language in Tamil, the system may extend to cover regional languages. While training CNN with large sets of sign language datasets spread across different linguistic regions, it makes the system enable live speech conversion to a large number of audiences and makes it more inclusive and beneficial for various communities.

Subsequent refinement of the model: The subsequent model refinement of the gesture recognition model can easily be proposed and delivered to address more complicated environments than what has been discussed above-low lighting, changes in hand orientation, or even occlusion. More complex deep models such as hybrid CNN-RNN models can make the system significantly more robust and accurate.

References

1. Zhan, F.: Hand gesture recognition with convolution neural networks. In: 2019 IEEE 20th International Conference on Information Reuse and Integration for Data Science (IRI), pp 295–298 (2019). https://doi.org/10.1109/IRI.2019.00054
2. Toro-Ossaba, A., Jaramillo-Tigreros, J., Tejada, J.C., et al.: LSTM recurrent neural network for hand gesture recognition using EMG signals. Appl. Sci. **12**, 9700 (2022). https://doi.org/10.3390/app12199700
3. Bora, J., Dehingia, S., Boruah, A., et al.: Real-time assamese sign language recognition using MediaPipe and deep learning. Procedia Comput. Sci. **218**, 1384–1393 (2023). https://doi.org/10.1016/j.procs.2023.01.117
4. Amangeldy, N., Ukenova, A., Bekmanova, G., et al.: Continuous sign language recognition and its translation into intonation-colored speech. Sensors **23**, 6383 (2023). https://doi.org/10.3390/s23146383
5. Jose, H., Julian, A.: Tamil sign language translator—an assistive system for hearing- and speech-impaired people. In: Satapathy, S., Joshi, A. (eds.) Information and Communication Technology for Intelligent Systems. Smart Innovation, Systems and Technologies, vol. 107, pp. 249–257. Springer, Singapore (2019). https://doi.org/10.1007/978-981-13-1747-7_24
6. Dhanjal, A.S., Singh, W.: An automatic machine translation system for multi-lingual speech to Indian sign language. Multimedia Tools Appl. **81**, 4283–4321 (2021). https://doi.org/10.1155/2022/7055624
7. Latif, G. et al.: J. Phys. Conf. Ser. **1962**, 012055 (2021)
8. Pathan, R.K., Biswas, M., Yasmin, S.: Sign language recognition using the fusion of image and hand landmarks through multi-headed convolutional neural network. Sci. Republic **13**, 16975 (2023). https://doi.org/10.1038/s41598-023-43852-x
9. Adeyanju, I.A., Bello, O.O., Adegboye, M.A.: Machine learning methods for sign language recognition: a critical review and analysis. Intell. Syst. Appl. **12**, 200056 (2021). https://doi.org/10.1016/j.iswa.2021.200056
10. Bantupalli, K., Xie, Y.: American sign language recognition using deep learning and computer vision. In: 2018 IEEE International Conference on Big Data (Big Data), pp 4896–4899 (2018). https://doi.org/10.1109/BigData.2018.8622141

A Framework Using Feature Maps Improving Speech

Arindam Bindlish[1](✉), Jitendra Singh Goyal[2], Vaibhav Gujral[3], Tanu Dua[4], and Gaura Dubey[5]

[1] Kunskapsskolan, Gurgaon, India
ab1773.gur@kunskapsskolan.edu.in
[2] Chaudhary Charan Singh University, Meerut, U.P., India
[3] Independent Researcher, Westlake, USA
[4] Manav Rachna International Institute of Research and Studies, Faridabad, India
tanudua.set@mriu.edu.in
[5] Kiet Group of Institutions, Delhi, India
gaurav.dubey@kiet.edu

Abstract. Proper speech helps preschoolers' cognitive and social development. A hybrid model including Wav2Vec 2.0 for audio feature extraction, Bi-LSTM, and an attention mechanism improves preschoolers' speech competency categorization. LSTM, Bi-LSTM with Attention Mechanism, and Proposed Bi-LSTM were examined. All tests confirm the Proposed model's 98.26% accuracy, precision, recall, and F1 score. Confusion matrix: Ordinary 98.55%, Incompetent 100%, Proficient 96.0%. The recommended model has a 0.98 ROC AUC, compared to 0.95 for Bi-LSTM and 0.90 for LSTM, suggesting excellent class difference. Adding attention processes to Bi-LSTM enhances toddler linguistic proficiency. For the Proposed approach, speech delivery classification efficiency increases early childhood speech therapy.

Keywords: Wave2Vec 2.0 · Bi-LSTM · Attention Mechanism · Preschoolers · Speech

1 Introduction

Speech, language, and communication are essential for a child's development. They support the capacity to reason, learn, solve issues, build relationships, express basic wants and feelings, and understand our environment. They are essential in many parts of our lives. They also foster the development of several other abilities, including reading, social, and cognitive capabilities [1]. Effective early communication is needed as the digital world proliferates. Preschool and school sets lay the framework for the linguistic growth of youngsters. Preschool is part of general education, and the Ministry of Education and Science prepares academic preschool teachers [2].

One of the developmental issues that preschool-aged children often face is difficulties with speech. The child's capacity for socialization, communication, and learning in

A. Sharma and R. Rani (Eds.): AIST 2024, CCIS 2389, pp. 330–345, 2025.
https://doi.org/10.1007/978-3-031-91331-0_26

a classroom setting may be impacted by this illness. Speech-impaired children often struggle to express their ideas and emotions, which may be frustrating and detrimental to their social-emotional development [3]. Preschool is usually attended by children aged one to five, which promotes holistic learning and development. "A school for all" is the main goal, even if primary school instructors face numerous difficulties. The rising number of students who arrive at school unable to speak or deliver speech correctly is putting increasing pressure on preschool teachers. The preschool system needs help with this. Preschool instructors are responsible for achieving several objectives, such as "as far as possible." [4].

In brief, the following are the objectives for preschoolers' language development and learning:

- To distinguish between various conceptual shades.
- To grow in listening, reflection, and self-expression.
- To expand their vocabulary and spoken language skills.
- To be able to ask questions and engage in debate and conversation.
- To become interested in written language, comprehend texts, images, symbols, and other media.
- To expand their creative potential.

The objectives aren't meant to evaluate kids' learning or growth. These are targets to aim toward and are mainly addressed by the preschool staff members [5].

Children need good communication skills to succeed academically and socially, which makes the research urgent. Properly addressing the issues affecting speech, language clarity, and pronunciation can prevent children with these difficulties from experiencing behavioural and academic problems at school. Furthermore, speech delays may lower a child's and family's quality of life. Identifying and implementing efficient solutions aimed at providing communicative stimulation to youngsters experiencing speech delays can enhance the child's language and speech abilities and provide essential assistance to their family. It may also alleviate the psychological and financial burden of long-term speech and language therapy [6, 7].

Speech development problems are challenging to recognize and treat because they often differ in severity, kind, origin, and responsiveness to treatments, necessitating specialized methods of evaluation and care [8]. The high expenses of in-person therapy and the restricted accessibility of speech-language pathologists have emphasized the need for a more accessible and economical method to improve speech delivery, clarity and pronunciation, especially in pre-schoolers.

Thanks to machine learning technology's decade-long, rapid progress, it can now use automated voice recognition neural network models. For instance, [9] used I-vectors to represent language recognition and speaker verification in their speech disorder detection studies. [10] achieved the diagnosis of speech disorder by using Siamese neural networks to distinguish between proper and erroneous phonemes. [11] trained neural network models using paralinguistic variables such as duration and formants to identify speakers with language problems. Data augmentation approaches create additional speech samples from the original train set, thereby addressing the issue of limited availability and enhancing model performance [12, 13]. Additionally, deep learning technologies are being used to enhance children's speech. Numerous studies have focused on acoustic modeling [14–16].

Moreover, transformer-based models, pre-trained on large-scale speech datasets, have performed exceptionally on various tasks, such as automatic speech recognition (ASR) and audio classification. Numerous studies have demonstrated their practical application in the automatic speech recognition (ASR) field across a range of modelling paradigms, including sequence-to-sequence [17–19], neuraltransducer [20, 21], Connectionist temporal classification (CTC) [22], and traditional hybrid [23] systems.

Furthermore, large transformer-based models have great promise for translating and transcribing speech [24–26]. They can record intricate patterns and relationships in audio sequences because of their self-attention mechanisms and parallel processing. For example, Wav2vec2 [24] trains on many unlabeled speech data to enable the model to comprehend and represent raw audio waveforms as dense vector representations. Through refining the model using sparse data, wav2vec2 can accomplish several speech-related downstream tasks, owing to the pre-training [27, 28].

Therefore, Wav2Vec 2.0 can investigate even the most complicated speech patterns and deliver accurate transcriptions with minimum fine-tuning since It can derive general characteristics from unprocessed audio data. The majority of voice recognition work has used it. Few research projects have applied this technique for feature extraction to improve preschoolers' speech delivery. Speech delivery focuses on pronunciation, articulation, and intelligibility. Despite a comprehensive theoretical review, few research investigations have used Wav2Vec 2.0 to construct feature maps from audio signals in preschoolers with early speech-related issues.

This work closes the gap by discussing the fundamental features of preschoolers' pitch, sound patterns, and articulation using feature maps derived from the acoustic data. This research framework uses Wav2Vec 2.0 for advanced sound analysis, a mechanism for attention, and a bidirectional network for long short-term memory. This facilitates the understanding of how speech patterns evolve over time. As a result, the system will provide each child with kid-centred, individualized feedback, pinpointing the precise areas that require improvement in speech delivery. An application like this could track progress weekly or daily and tailor treatments to enhance the best speech development outcomes by incorporating machine learning. Thus far, preliminary testing suggests that it significantly enhances speech articulation compared to other methods. The integration of Wav2Vec 2.0 and Bi-LSTM with attention mechanisms for data-driven feedback holds enormous promise for augmenting preschoolers' language skills development.

2 Background

- **Wav2Vec 2.0.**

This model can learn from many unlabelled audio data using a self-supervised pre-training strategy and is intended to transcribe speech from audio signals. This specific model is a combination of various previous models, including wav2vec [29], vqwav2vec [30], Model Predictive Control (MPC) [31], and Contrastive Predictive Coding (CPC)

[32]. Transformers and convolutional neural networks allow Wav2Vec2 to recognize local and global audio patterns. The model employs a multi-layer convolutional feature encoder to transform raw audio waveforms to create latent speech representations. These representations are then fed into a transformer-masked network, designated as $g : Z \to T$, which maps the representations from the latent space to a discrete set of outputs, $q_1, ..., q_T$ representing targets in the self-supervised learning objective [24, 33]. The transformer module converts quantized representations into discrete contextual representations using attention blocks. Seven convolutional blocks, each with 512 channels, comprise the feature encoder. {10, 3, 3, 2, 2} kernel widths, and {5, 2, 2, 2, 2} strides. The transformer network has 24 1024-by-4096 chunks. A transformer network contains 16 attention heads. This model has sophisticated speech recognition and fared well on benchmarks. Figure 1 illustrates a model based on [24].

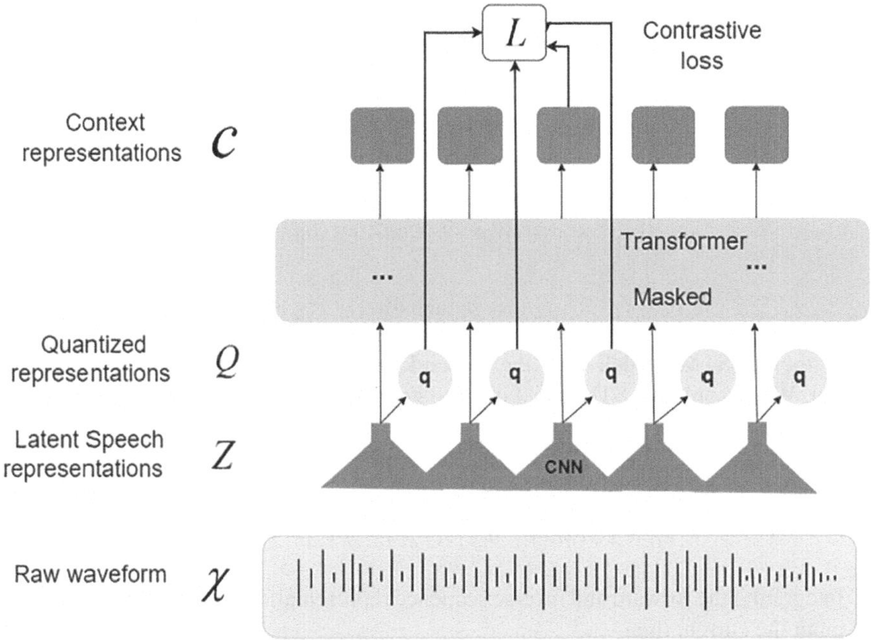

Fig. 1. Architectural representation of Wav2Vec2.0

- **BiLSTM Model**

Ultimately, the BiLSTM model is used to recognize voice signals. An adaptation of RNN algorithms called LSTM addresses the gradient vanishing problem. It enhances the NN's storage plan for incoming input and training data. Modelling time series data, like text, is helpful. The merging of the forward and backward LSTMs is known as the BiLSTM [20]. The BiLSTM model's main advantage is that the network fully utilizes the sequence details.

The BiLSTM model's main advantage is that the network fully utilizes the sequence details. The LSTM unit has memory cell state, input, forget, and output gates. They intend to affect data storage and updating in units. The input gate returns a number between zero and one based on inputs.

If the outcome is 1, all cell state information is preserved. If it is 0, the data is erased. After the input gate layer detects an upgrade, the tanh layer creates a new potential value vector, 〚c_t〛 ⊥~, for the cell state. By including these, the cell state may be updated. Based on the current condition of the cell, the result is decided by the last gate [20]. Intrinsic variables are represented as and during LSTM training. Inferring dot multiplication from the sigmoid activation function, we get ⊙.

$$f_t = \sigma\left(W_f w_t + U_f h_{t-1} + b_f\right) \tag{1}$$

$$i_t = \sigma(W_i w_t + U_i h_{t-1} + b_i) \tag{2}$$

$$\tilde{c}_t = \tanh(W_c w_c + U_c h_{t-1} + b_c) \tag{3}$$

$$c_t = i_t \odot \overline{c}_t + f_t \odot c_{t-1} \tag{4}$$

$$o_t = \sigma(W_O w_t + U_O h_{t-1} + b_O) \tag{5}$$

$$h_t = o_t \tanh \odot (c_t) \tag{6}$$

In the BiLSTM model, both the forward and backward LSTM components are present. While some BiLSTMs read input to generate, others read input to produce.

$$\overrightarrow{h_t} = \overrightarrow{LSTM}\left(w_t, \overrightarrow{h_{t-1}}, c_{t-1}\right), \quad t \in [1, m+n], \tag{7}$$

$$\overleftarrow{h_t} = \overleftarrow{LSTM}\left(w_t, \overleftarrow{h_{t-1}}, c_{t-1}\right), \quad t \in [m+n, 1]. \tag{8}$$

Integrating the forward and inverse sequence representations into a long vector gives the input the current time.

$$h_t = \overrightarrow{h_t} \oplus \overleftarrow{h_t} \tag{9}$$

The final step is to get the series' result, representing the buried layer's outcome. The BiLSTM model's intermittent layers ensure that all data is returned and that each concealed layer's findings preserve long-term data. The BiLSTM architecture is shown in Fig. 2.

- **Attention mechanism**

The ability of the human brain to focus is fundamental to the attention process to focus on what's most important while reducing energy expenditure [34]. An attention mechanism was constructed as a result of this study to further apply alternate weight

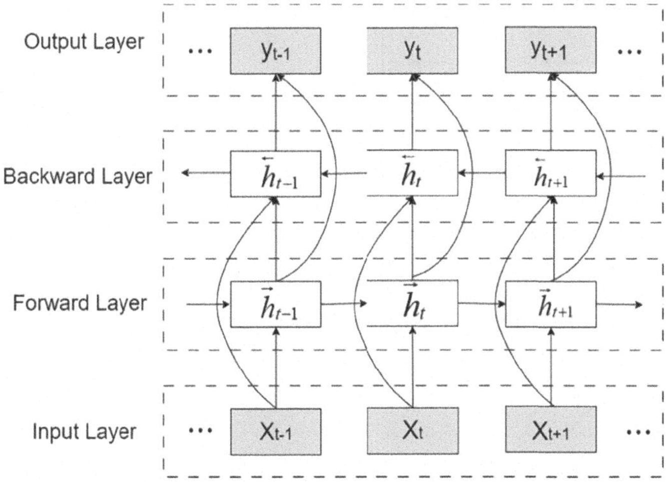

Fig. 2. Structure of the BiLSTM model.

coefficients to the information recovered by the LSTM. This system was established to facilitate the continued assignment of these traits. This scenario thus improved the model's prediction capabilities. Figure 3 is a graphic depiction of the Attention structure. The Self-Attention module uses the time-related feature vectors that the LSTM creates throughout its learning phase and adds shared biases and weights to them. After that, these feature vectors are used to train the computer. The weighted summation approach was the most suitable strategy for conducting deep-level feature mining. We did this after we finished our calculations of the importance of each attribute. To do the maths, we need the following formula:

$$\beta_i = \sigma(W_i h_t + b_i) \tag{10}$$

$$a_i = soft\max(\beta_i) = \frac{\exp(\beta_i)}{\sum_i \exp(\beta_i)} \tag{11}$$

$$O = H \otimes a_i \tag{12}$$

In this model, β*i* stands for the activation function, *ai* for the feature's significance, *O* for the attention weight, and *Yi* and *Yi* for the output prediction result, as well as σ and σ for the weight matrix and bias vector between neurone nodes, respectively.

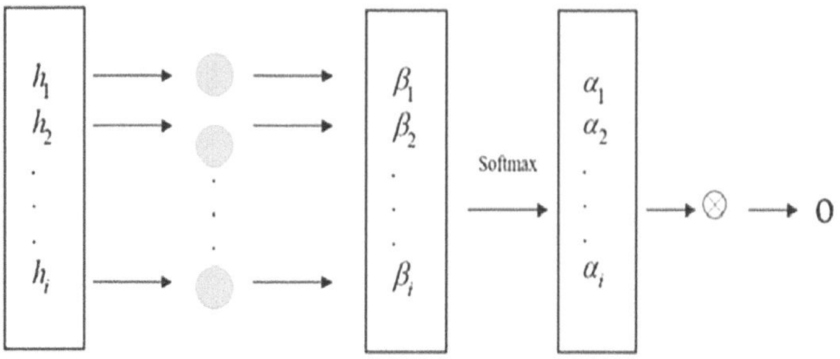

Fig. 3. Attention network structure diagram.

3 Methodology

This section describes how acoustic data-derived feature maps improve preschoolers' speech articulation. The framework uses advanced machine learning processes such as feature extraction using the Wav2Vec 2.0 paradigm to improve voice pronunciation and clarity.

3.1 Data Collection

This study included voice recordings of kids between three and six who showed different kinds of speech disorders. These recordings originated from speech therapy sessions emphasizing especially the challenges seen in pronunciation, articulation, and intelligibility.

3.2 Data Description

Custom data were gathered from children aged 3–6 years who had speech problems during focused speech therapy sessions with an eye on articulation, pronunciation, and intelligibility. High-grade microphones were used to gather the acoustic recordings, guaranteeing accuracy and quality. Parents or guardians asked permission in line with moral values meant to protect children's privacy. This tailored approach created a robust dataset addressing the particular speech delivery problems faced by preschoolers, enabling the building of a suitable intervention model.

3.3 Data Preprocessing

Noise Reduction
Spectral gating was used to presume that the background sounds would be minimized, enhancing the recording quality. The whole procedure consisted of the retention of the intended speech signals, a study of the frequency spectrum of the audio, and then the elimination of undesired noise components.

Audio Segmentation
Continuous audio recordings were broken down to utterance level for analysis. The

definition of every segment was done concerning the pause and change in speech by the integrity of utterance.

Normalization
Audio segmentation files were normalized to keep the volume levels consistent throughout the dataset. This ensured that the loudness variation did not affect the model's ability to analyze speech features.

Data Augmentation
To limit the challenge of limited available labelled data, several augmentation techniques were used, including:

Pitch Shifting
The pitch is shifted to change the pitch of the audio and generate different variations of the same utterance.

Time Stretching
Stretching the audio without altering the pitch produces slower or faster variants of the recorded content.

Adding Noise
Adding controlled background noise to input data makes the model more robust and realistic.

3.4 Feature Extraction Using Wav2Vec 2.0

Model Overview
With its ability to turn raw audio into high-quality feature maps, Wav2Vec 2.0, a transformer-based model for speech processing, was pre-trained using massive, unlabelled speech datasets.

Feature Extraction Process
Raw Waveform Input
Once the audio signals have been processed, they are sent through Wav2Vec 2.0. This model generates hidden voice representations from the raw waveforms using a multi-layer convolutional feature encoder.

Transformer-Based Encoding
The model conveyed the latent representations via its transformer layers using transformer-based encoding. Further enhancing the feature representations were the contextual linkages and dependencies highlighted by the applied attention mechanisms in the audio.

Feature Map Generation
The model generated a dense vector representation for each utterance, including details

on articulation, pitch, and clarity. These feature maps were crucial inputs in later classification tasks involving speech.

Model Building

This experiment utilizes feature maps in a tailored neural network using Wav2Vec 2.0 to classify speech characteristics. The model architecture proposed involves a Bi-LSTM network with an attention mechanism. This architecture captures the past and future context of speech information, improving the model's comprehension of most articulation, pronunciation, and clarity dimensions.

This Bi-LSTM was then added to attention layers to emphasize the most relevant features from the generated feature maps. We may train the model to focus on the most critical audio parts for effective speech delivery. Therefore, processing these feature maps through Bi-LSTM layers allows the network to predict whether articulation, pronunciation, or clarity needs correction.

A feedback mechanism was incorporated into the system by providing individualized feedback to each child according to their specific speech delivery problems. The feedback was provided through an interactive mobile application that visualized areas for improvement, such as articulation or pitch modulation. Accordingly, corrective measures could be instituted in real-time so that children could immediately get information regarding speech delivery challenges.

Model Evaluation

Ranking algorithms use the confusion matrix's performance metrics, including the F1-score, accuracy, sensitivity, and precision.

Accuracy

The percentage of subjects accurately named as a percentage of the whole sample size is called the subject detection rate.

$$Accuracy = \frac{TP + TN}{TP + TN + FP + FN} \tag{13}$$

Precision

You can get an idea of how accurate a view is by keeping track of how many proper statements it makes. The idea behind this could also be called "predictive value."

$$Precision = \frac{TP}{TP + FP} \tag{14}$$

Recall

False negatives, on the other hand, are different from True Negatives.

$$Recall = \frac{TP}{TP + FN} \tag{15}$$

F1-Score

The F1 score is a measure of both accuracy and memory.

$$F_1 - Score = \frac{2 * Precision * Recall}{Precision + Recall} \tag{16}$$

4 Results and Discussion

Hybrid Bi-LSTM with Attention Mechanism to classify toddler speech. Confusion matrices, F1-score, recall, accuracy, precision, and area under the curve (AUC) from ROC analysis will demonstrate 'Incompetent', 'Ordinary', and 'Proficient' classification skills. We will compare our findings to Bi-LSTM and LSTM models to show the benefits of our method and explore its implications for speech therapy and early language development. Proposed model with Existing LSTM shown in Figs. 4, 5 and 6.

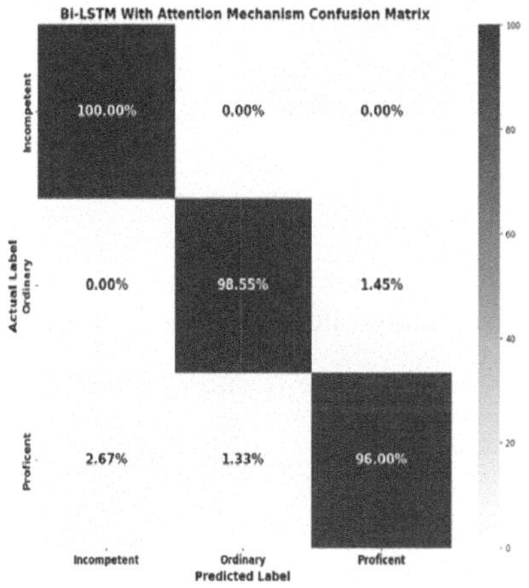

Fig. 4. Bi-LSTM with attention mechanism (proposed model)

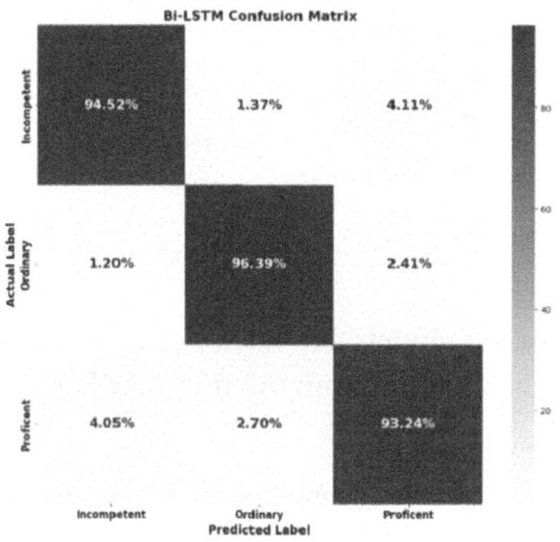

Fig. 5. Bi-LSTM

The confusion matrix that the proposed hybrid Bi-LSTM with attention mechanism performs better than the bi-LSTM and LSTM models in every category regarding categorization. The proposed model achieves a flawless classification rate of one hundred per cent for the 'Incompetent' class, with 0% misclassifications. In contrast, the LSTM and Bi-LSTM models exhibit 89.28% and 94.52% accuracy, respectively, with 5.48% and 10.72% misclassifications. The suggested model outperforms the Bi-LSTM, which has an accuracy of 96.39% with a misclassification rate of 3.61%, and the LSTM, which displays 90.28% accuracy with a misclassification rate of 9.72%, in the 'Ordinary' class, achieving an accuracy of 98.55% with a misclassification rate of 1.45%. The suggested model for the 'Proficient' class obtains 96.0% accuracy with a 4.0% misclassification rate. In contrast, the Bi-LSTM model achieves 93.24% accuracy with a 6.76% misclassification rate, and the LSTM model displays 90.54% accuracy with a 9.46% misclassification rate. These findings demonstrate how well the suggested model, compared to

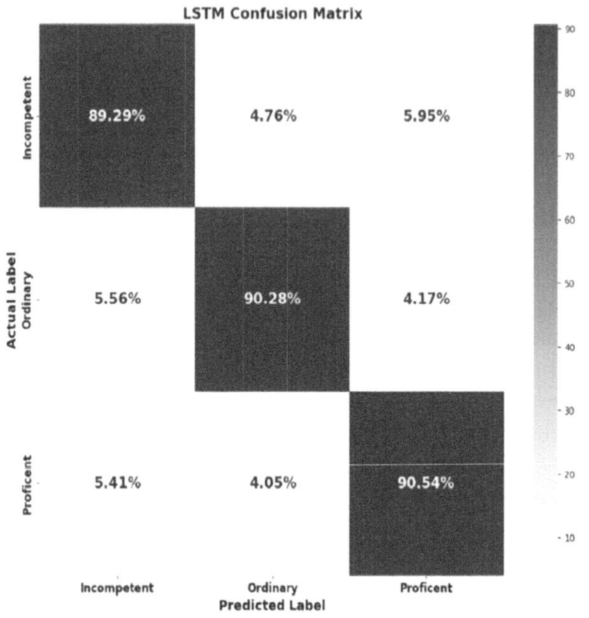

Fig. 6. LSTM

the other models as shown in Figs. 7 and 8, can accurately categorize speech proficiency levels while minimizing misclassifications (Fig. 9).

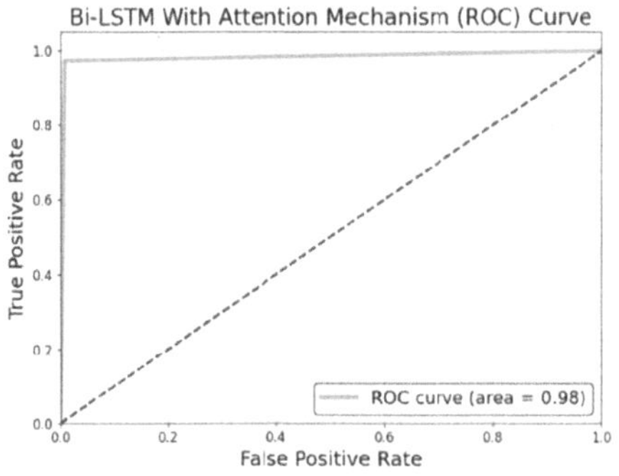

Fig. 7. Bi-LSTM With Attention Mechanism Roc

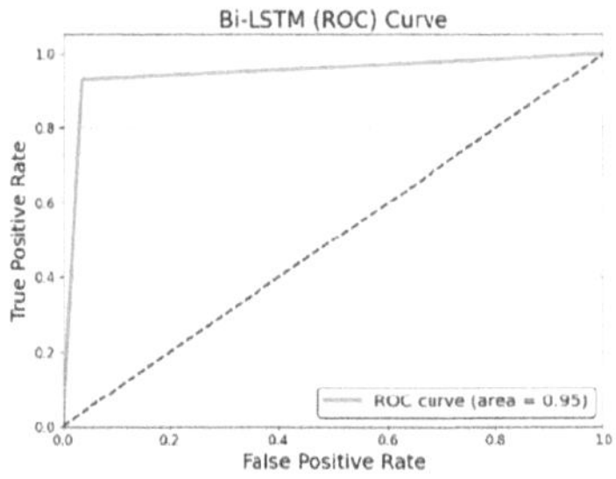

Fig. 8. Bi-LSTM Roc

The ROC curve data reveal that the Proposed Bi-LSTM with Attention Mechanism can distinguish between speech delivery categorization classes with an AUC of 0.98. Bi-LSTM has strong classification abilities compared to other models with an AUC of 0.95, somewhat lower than the model that is advised. The LSTM model demonstrates the most minor class difference among the three models, with an AUC of 0.90. Evidence from this study supports the idea that Bi-attention LSTM's mechanism is a good addition.

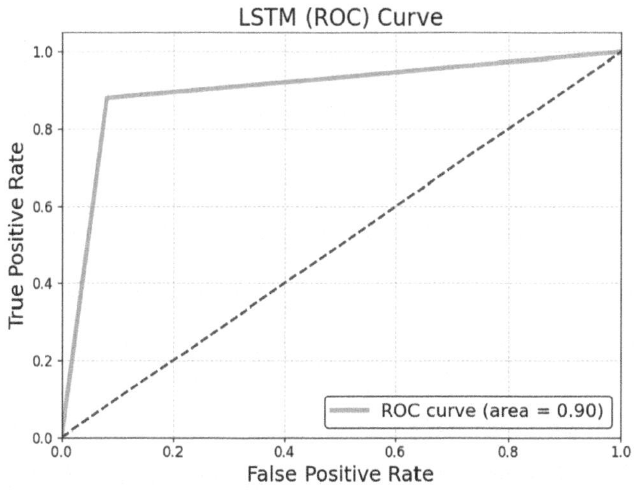

Fig. 9. LSTM Roc

Evaluation metrics shown in Table 1 and Fig. 10 Doing so dramatically improves the model's discrimination and categorization of preschoolers' speech delivery.

Table 1. Evaluation Metrics

Models	Accuracy	Precision	Recall	F1-Score
Proposed (Bi-LSTM with Attention Mechanism)	0.98261	0.98269	0.98261	0.98254
Bi-LSTM	0.94783	0.94783	0.94783	0.94783
LSTM	0.9	0.91045	0.9	0.89

The Proposed Bi-LSTM with Attention Mechanism performs best across all evaluation parameters, as seen in the above table of 98.26% accuracy, precision, recall, and F1-score. It classifies speech kinds more accurately and consistently. Absent an attention mechanism, the Bi-LSTM model scores 94.78% on all criteria, showing how critical it is to classification accuracy. Another example of the bidirectional and attention-enhanced structure in the suggested model for effectively recording and categorizing speech patterns is the LSTM model, which has 90% accuracy and 89% F1 score.

5 Discussion

The findings demonstrate the Proposed Hybrid Bi-LSTM with Attention Mechanism's significant benefits over conventional models, including Bi-LSTM and LSTM, in categorizing preschoolers' speech delivery. The confusion matrix clearly shows that the

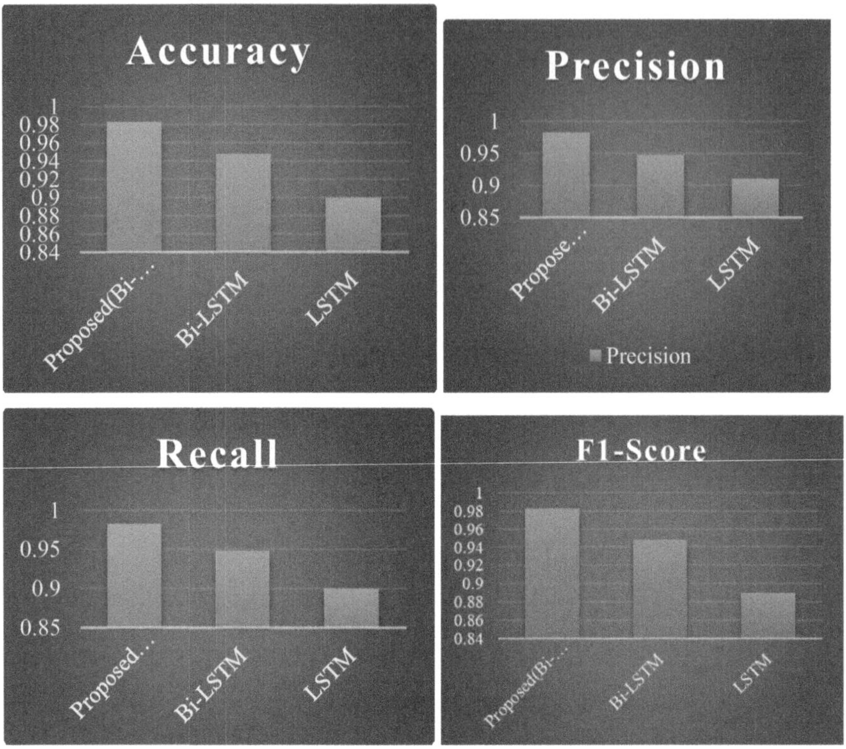

Fig. 10. Evaluation metrics comparison

suggested model successfully classifies the 'Incompetent' class with a 100% classification rate, demonstrating its capacity to identify this crucial category with no misclassifications correctly. By comparison, the LSTM and Bi-LSTM models show significant misclassification rates, with 89.28% and 94.52% accuracy rates, respectively. This pattern is maintained in the 'Ordinary' and 'Proficient' classes, where the suggested model accomplishes 98.55% and 96.0% accuracy, respectively, regularly surpassing the alternatives.

The efficiency of the suggested model is further supported by the ROC curve analysis, which has an AUC of 0.98, demonstrating a greater capacity for class differentiation. The LSTM model's AUC of 0.90 indicates its limits in class discrimination, while the Bi-LSTM model, although competent with an AUC of 0.95, does not perform as well as the suggested model. These results highlight how important the attention mechanism is to boosting model performance since it helps the model concentrate on relevant characteristics in the data, increasing classification accuracy and decreasing misclassifications.

In conclusion, adding the attention mechanism highlights the model's potential for practical applications in speech therapy and preschool language development while enhancing the Bi-LSTM architecture's discriminative strength. According to the findings, using cutting-edge machine learning methods may significantly improve speech recognition tasks and provide a solid foundation for locating and resolving problems with speech delivery in early childhood education settings. Looking at the big picture, the proposed approach is an exciting step forward for voice recognition research categorization. It provides a workable way to improve the precision of young children's speech delivery evaluations.

6 Conclusion

We improved preschool voice delivery categorization by using a suggested Bi-LSTM model with an attention mechanism and Wav2Vec 2.0 for feature extraction. Compared to LSTM and Bi-LSTM models, the suggested model achieved better accuracy, precision, recall, and F1-state results. According to the confusion matrix, the proposed model ideally classified 'Incompetent' speech proficiency levels. With lower misclassification rates than previous models, it accurately classified the "Ordinary" and "Proficient" classes.

ROC curve study confirmed the superiority of the suggested Bi-LSTM with attention mechanism with an AUC of 0.98, suggesting outstanding class separation power. The Bi-LSTM and LSTM models have AUCs of 0.95 and 0.90, respectively, due to their lower efficacy in distinguishing speech delivery classes. This study shows the importance of adding Wav2Vec 2.0 in Bi-LSTM architecture for accurate feature extraction and attention. These two elements boost model discrimination.

References

1. Saidova, M.: Improvement of preschool children's speech and language skills. Mod. Sci. Res. **3**(1), 203–208 (2024)
2. Ministry of Education. Science (80) (2010)
3. Machmud, H., Abidin, A., Hewi, L., Anhusadar, L.O.: Supporting children with speech delay: speech therapy intervention frameworks from preschool teachers. Int. J. Instr. **16**(4) (2023)
4. Brodin, J., Renblad, K.: Improvement of preschool children's speech and language skills. Early Child Dev. Care **190**(14), 2205–2213 (2020)
5. Norling, M., Lillvist, A.: Literacy-related play activities and preschool staffs' strategies to support children's concept development. World J. Educ. **6**(5), 49–63 (2016)
6. Hanafi, H., Arifin, S., Nuraini, K., Aswir, A.: Learner-guided lesson study? A new perspective in EFL argumentative writing development. J. Asiat. **19**(3), 1109–1118 (2022)
7. Kurniawan, A., Pattiasina, P.J., Rahman, A., Lestari, N.C., Al Haddar, G.: Utilization of Youtube as a problem solving-based learning media. TECHNOVATE J. Inf. Technol. Strateg. Innov. Manag. **1**(2), 62–68 (2024)
8. Shahin, M., Zafar, U., Ahmed, B.: The automatic detection of speech disorders in children: challenges, opportunities, and preliminary results. IEEE J. Sel. Top. Signal Process. **14**(2), 400–412 (2019)
9. Kothalkar, P., Rudolph, J., Dollaghan, C., McGlothlin, J., Campbell, T., Hansen, J.H.: Fusing text-dependent word-level i-vector models to screen 'at risk' child speech. Age **51**(11), 36–78 (2018)
10. Wang, J., Qin, Y., Peng, Z., Lee, T.: Child speech disorder detection with siamese recurrent network using speech attribute features. In: INTERSPEECH, pp. 3885–3889 (2019)

11. Ng, S.-I., Ng, C.W.-Y., Lee, T.: A study on using duration and formant features in automatic detection of speech sound disorder in children. Age (Omaha) **3**(4), 5 (2023)
12. Geng, M., et al.: Investigation of data augmentation techniques for disordered speech recognition, arXiv Prepr. arXiv:2201.05562 (2022)
13. Sudro, P.N., Das, R.K., Sinha, R., Prasanna, S.R.M.: Significance of data augmentation for improving cleft lip and palate speech recognition. In: 2021 Asia-Pacific Signal and Information Processing Association Annual Summit and Conference (APSIPA ASC), pp. 484–490, IEEE (2021)
14. Serizel, R., Giuliani, D.: Deep-neural network approaches for speech recognition with heterogeneous groups of speakers including children. Nat. Lang. Eng. **23**(3), 325–350 (2017)
15. Cheng, J., Chen, X., Metallinou, A.: Deep neural network acoustic models for spoken assessment applications. Speech Commun. **73**, 14–27 (2015)
16. Evanini, Y.Q.X.W.K., Suendermann-Oeft, D.: Improving DNN-based automatic recognition of non-native children's speech with adult speech. In: 5th Workshop on Child Computer Interaction, pp. 40–44 (2016)
17. Dong, L., Xu, S., Xu, B.: Speech-transformer: a no-recurrence sequence-to-sequence model for speech recognition. In: 2018 IEEE International Conference on Acoustics, Speech and Signal Processing (ICASSP), pp. 5884–5888. IEEE (2018)
18. Karita, S., et al.: A comparative study on transformer vs RNN in speech applications. In: 2019 IEEE Automatic Speech Recognition and Understanding Workshop (ASRU), pp. 449–456. IEEE (2019)
19. Zhou, S., Dong, L., Xu, S., Xu, B.: Syllable-based sequence-to-sequence speech recognition with the transformer in mandarin Chinese, arXiv Prepr. arXiv:1804.10752 (2018)
20. Zhang, Q., et al.: Transformer transducer: a streamable speech recognition model with transformer encoders and RNN-T loss. In: ICASSP 2020–2020 IEEE International Conference on Acoustics, Speech and Signal Processing (ICASSP), pp. 7829–7833. IEEE (2020)
21. Gulati, A., et al.: Conformer: convolution-augmented transformer for speech recognition, arXiv Prepr. arXiv:2005.08100 (2020)
22. Salazar, J., Kirchhoff, K., Huang, Z.: Self-attention networks for connectionist temporal classification in speech recognition. In: ICASSP 2019–2019 IEEE International Conference on Acoustics, Speech and Signal Processing (ICASSP), pp. 7115–7119. IEEE (2019)
23. Wang, Y., et al.: Transformer-based acoustic modeling for hybrid speech recognition. In: ICASSP 2020–2020 IEEE International Conference on Acoustics, Speech and Signal Processing (ICASSP), pp. 6874–6878. IEEE (2020)
24. Baevski, A., Zhou, Y., Mohamed, A., Auli, M.: Wav2vec 2.0: a framework for self-supervised learning of speech representations. Adv. Neural. Inf. Process. Syst. **33**, 12449–12460 (2020)
25. Radford, A., Kim, J.W., Xu, T., Brockman, G., McLeavey, C., Sutskever, I.: Robust speech recognition via large-scale weak supervision. In: International Conference on Machine Learning, pp. 28492–28518. PMLR (2023)
26. Shi, B., Hsu, W.-N., Mohamed, A.L Robust self-supervised audio-visual speech recognition, arXiv Prepr. arXiv:2201.01763 (2022)
27. Getman, Y., et al.: Wav2vec2-based speech rating system for children with speech sound disorder. In: Interspeech, International Speech Communication Association (ISCA), pp. 3618–3622 (2022)
28. Javanmardi, F., Tirronen, S., Kodali, M., Kadiri, S.R., Alku, P.: Wav2vec-based detection and severity level classification of dysarthria from speech. In: ICASSP 2023–2023 IEEE International Conference on Acoustics, Speech and Signal Processing (ICASSP), pp. 1–5. IEEE (2023)
29. Schneider, S., Baevski, A., Collobert, R., Auli, M.: wav2vec: unsupervised pre-training for speech recognition, arXiv Prepr. arXiv:1904.05862 (2019)

30. Baevski, A., Schneider, S., Auli, M.: vq-wav2vec: self-supervised learning of discrete speech representations, arXiv Prepr. arXiv:1910.05453 (2019)
31. Jiang, D., et al.: Improving transformer-based speech recognition using unsupervised pre-training, arXiv Prepr. arXiv:1910.09932 (2019)
32. van den Oord, A., Li, Y., Vinyals, O.: Representation learning with contrastive predictive coding, arXiv Prepr. arXiv:1807.03748 (2018)
33. Conneau, A., Baevski, A., Collobert, R., Mohamed, A., Auli, M.: Unsupervised cross-lingual representation learning for speech recognition, arXiv Prepr. arXiv:2006.13979 (2020)
34. Mohiuddin, K., et al.: Retention is all you need. In: International Conference on Information and Knowledge Management Proceedings, no. Nips, pp. 4752–4758 (2023). https://doi.org/10.1145/3583780.3615497

Echoes of Concern: Security Challenges in Voice Assistant Systems

Rakesh Kumar Singh[1] and Charu Gupta[2(✉)]

[1] Department of IT, Indira Gandhi Delhi Technical University for Women, Delhi, India
rksingh@igdtuw.ac.in
[2] Department of Distance and Continuing Education, University of Delhi, Delhi, India
charu.gupta@sol.du.ac.in

Abstract. Voice Assistant systems like Alexa, Echo Dot, Siri, Google Assistants, and Cortana are widely used for the ease of being hands-free and being controlled through voice commands. Voice assistants utilize speech recognition, speech identification, and other machine learning algorithms to perform a task, connecting smart home devices, and smart vehicles, searching the web and even playing a game. The components of Voice assistants are exposed to attackers to gain unauthorized control through varying methods of injecting audio, speech, and inaudible voice commands. The attacks through the voice commands pose security and data privacy risks that need urgent attention. In this paper, different security challenges, and vulnerabilities in the Voice assistants are outlined. The study provides a brief overview of possible solutions to minimize the security and privacy risks associated with using Voice Assistants.

Keywords: Speech Recognition · Voice Assistants · Privacy · Security · Human-Computer Interaction

1 Introduction

The interaction of humans with computers and mobile devices has enormously evolved from typing to sending voice messages. Mobile and computers are nowadays equipped with sensors and software components that understand the human voice and execute a set of functions from switching on /off the smart home appliances, searching the nearest restaurant to helping in writing an exhaustive article. The ease, perfection, and accuracy of software components are further enhanced by implementing advanced speech recognition, Artificial Intelligence (AI), and Natural Language Processing (NLP). The sophisticated software applications embedded in computers and mobile devices that sense the human voice and process it to perform various tasks are called Voice Assistants [8]. The Voice Assistants are trained to execute a multitude of operations such as responding to queries, conversing like a human, setting reminders, controlling smart home devices, playing music, map navigation in smart automotive and entertainment. Popular Voice Assistants namely Amazon Alexa, Amazon Echo Dot, Google Assistant, Apple Siri, Microsoft Cortana, Samsung Bixby, and Hound are available in billions of

A. Sharma and R. Rani (Eds.): AIST 2024, CCIS 2389, pp. 346–357, 2025.
https://doi.org/10.1007/978-3-031-91331-0_27

mobile and computer devices. Over 8 billion people are using different Voice Assistants for their day-to-day activities [2]. More than 50% of the users use voice assistants while driving to navigate the route, approximate 73% of the people use voice assistants to listen music on their mobile or laptop, while 43% of the people use voice assistants to control smart home devices [2]. With the extensive use of Voice Assistants as shown in Fig. 1, challenges that deal with the security and privacy of sensitive information, user data, bypassing a locked screen, and device controls have also increased exponentially. Voice Assistants (VAs) provide internet services that include searching and browsing the web, writing and sending emails, and posting messages to social media sites. VAs also provide telephony services such as starting and ending a phone call, writing and sending text messages, and saving or searching contacts from the address book through voice commands. Another set of services provided by VAs on mobile and desktops are the local services such as setting up alarms, creating notes, typing in a document, setting reminders, launching games and applications, and even changing system settings [6].

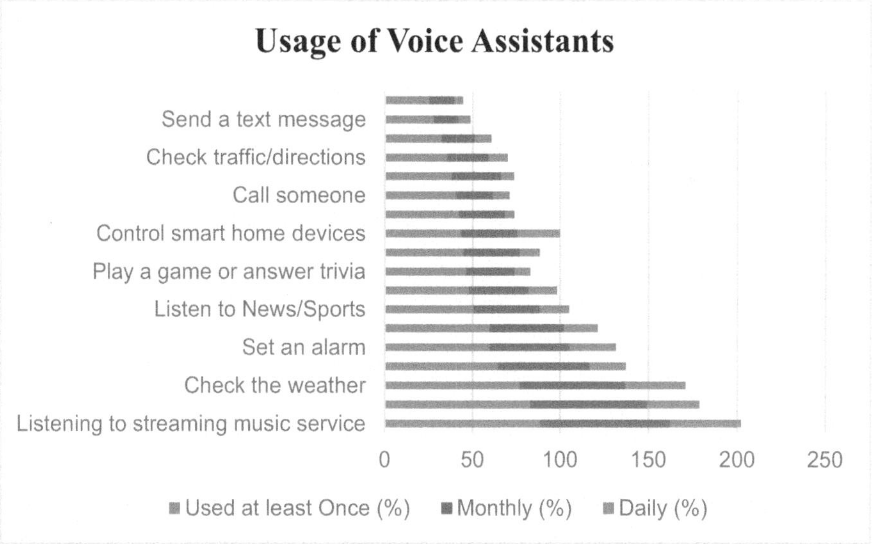

Fig. 1. Usage of Voice Assistants [32]

However, the interaction with computers and mobile apps using human voice commands has brought high-security concerns as shown in Fig. 2. Attackers have used inaudible ultrasound waves to gain unauthorized access through voice assistants [1]. Several vulnerabilities have been detected in Apple's Siri that allow an attacker to access sensitive user data, and private calendar information, gain access to call history, execute commands, send messages through the WhatsApp application, and even unlock the locked screen [1]. Attackers also exploited vulnerabilities in Amazon Echo Dot to pair malicious Bluetooth devices and erase all user data by starting a factory reset [1]. Attackers scan voice-recognition systems to find hidden vulnerabilities and use voice spoofing techniques to pretend to be an authorized user by mimicking a user's recorded voice to do unauthorized tasks or obtain sensitive information [5]. In addition, man-in-the-middle attacks are a risk in the transmission of data because they intercept and alter the voice data forwarded. There is a chance of leakage of data. More so, voice assistants are normally designed to be always listening, meaning the device would record private conversations on its own and store them sensitively without the user's consent, thus violating privacy. The risk associated with privacy is voice assistants, most of the time, listen for wake words like 'Hello Google' or 'Hey Siri' or 'Alexa' that inadvertently capture and store sensitive conversations [5]. Attackers have used frequency-modulated antenna to transmit radio waves and transform them to sound waves [5, 6]. Moreover, attackers find it easier to execute remote attack vectors to gain personally identifiable information through Voice Assistants [10].

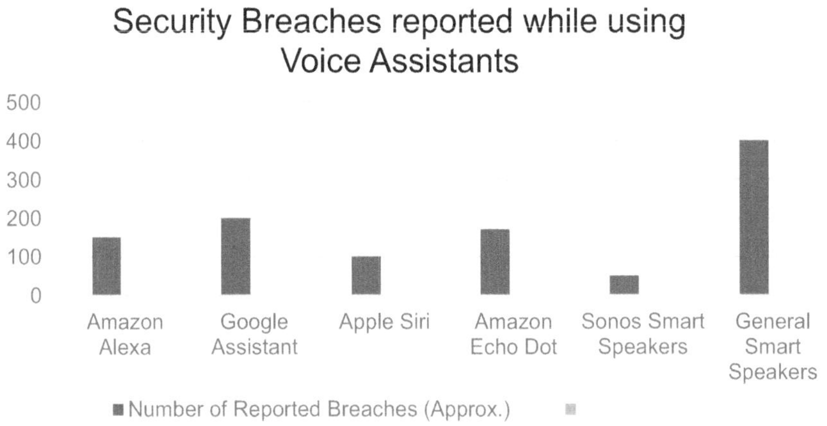

Fig. 2. Security Breaches reported while using Voice Assistants [2]

In addition, the inclusion of third-party applications will worsen security as vulnerabilities with such applications give way to attackers [11, 19, 20]. Users generally are uninformed of such risks and, therefore, seem to practice poor security measures such as a weak voice password or even weaker account protection. For user privacy and integrity, developers must ensure that proper security measures are built robustly with periodic updates and educating users on safety practices [18, 19]. Pal et al. [8] gave a taxonomy of privacy issues in Voice Assistants. Contextual privacy includes social privacy, location privacy, access control privacy, and visual Privacy. The other categories of privacy concerns in Voice Assistants are bystander privacy (speech privacy), Data Sharing privacy, and Environmental Privacy. The different attacks and vulnerabilities in VAs pose security and privacy concerns that require a legal and policy-based framework to minimize the risks. There is a need to address the security challenges in Voice Assistants as speech recognition technology evolves to ensure a secure and trustworthy user experience.

In this paper, the authors have identified various security challenges that are associated with the use of voice assistants and the possible mitigation strategies that are available in the literature.

2 Related Work

Alepis and Patsakis [5] used Android intents and created a set of interactive attacks on popular voice assistants namely, Google Assistant, S Voice, Cortana, Siri, and Alexa. In their work, they showed that the attack workflow can exploit the Android applications without requesting permission from the users or without the knowledge of the user. The attacks presented by [5] gained local privileges, executed advanced commands, and remote code execution, bypassed security measures, and leaked sensitive information.

Kasmi and Esteves [6] showed that the headphone jack which acts as an FM antenna, when connected to a computer and mobile is used to create an attack vector to inject remote voice commands. The voice command thus injected could gain local access, spying through recorded audio, sending undesired text messages, and installing malicious applications. Lei et al., [7] presented a threat model that could gain access to Alexa home devices using fake voice commands by connecting Bluetooth speakers, and smart TVs. The threat model could initiate a home burglary by instructing the command "Alexa, open the main door" and even placing a fake order using the Amazon e-commerce app.

Yen et al., [9] presented new threats that were triggered by inaudible ultrasound signals. The ultrasound signals were capable of propagating through solid media and launched attacks using Voice assistants in mobiles. The attack thus modeled by Yen et al., [9] is termed a surfing attack and gets access to passcodes received via SMS or even makes a fraud phone call without the user's knowledge.

Chen et al., [13] presented and summarized various attack methods on Voice assistants that exploit the hidden vulnerabilities via normal speech, voice spoofing, unintelligible speech, inaudible signal, skills, and adversarial examples.

Certain countermeasures and solutions to prevent attacks on VAs have also been proposed in the literature. One such solution, MegaMind a security extension for Amazon Alexa and Echo Dot Voice Assistants was proposed as a prototype by Talebi [11]. The security extension provides secure communication with third-party apps and is effective in maintaining security and privacy goals. In their survey, Cheng and Roedig [12] discussed the importance of securing voice authentication and preventing VAs from acoustic Denial of Service (DoS) attacks. Pathak et al., [14] performed a comprehensive security analysis on Amazon Echo dot devices and provided mitigation techniques for a wide range of software, hardware, and system vulnerabilities in the voice assistants. Jingjin Li et al., [15] in their exhaustive survey of security and privacy issues in popular Voice Assistants, gave a taxonomy of security attacks and defenses on the Automatic Speech Recognition (ASR) model and Speech Identification (SI) workflow. The security and privacy concerns in Voice Assistants are analyzed by Ren et al., [16] in the speaker anonymization and stuttering analysis in AI models of speech recognition.

3 Architecture of Voice Assistants

The architecture of voice assistants majorly consists of receiving an audio signal, processing it, and performing a task. The general overview of the architecture of Voice Assistant consists of the following components [15]:

1) Voice receiver: The audio receiver is a hardware device like a microphone embedded in the system or an external audio jack. The audio receiver takes the Voice commands as input and further sends it to the audio processing modules.
2) Voice Pre-Processing: The audio processing module includes speech pre-processing, converting sound to audio signals, audio to digital processing, vectorization, converting speech to text, and speech identification modules. The modules focus on improving the speech quality and reducing the noise.
3) Advanced Algorithms processing: The module or the software component is used for processing the voice-to-text, extracting features, and processing it using advanced algorithms of Speech Recognition, Speech identification, and Natural Language Processing. The automatic speech recognition applies template matching, stochastic and probabilistic modeling methods, and then follows speech identification workflow to identify and confirm that the voice received is of the authenticated user. The performance of speech recognition and identification models are evaluated using Word Error Rate, Sentence Error Rate, Recognition Rate, and other metrics related to training datasets such as training duration, size, and reaction time.
4) Voice Service Manager, Action execution and response generation: The Service manager processes the commands received and handles the context for interaction with various hardware and software applications, cloud service providers, and third-party apps. The response is generated based on the identified intent and entity. The services then call the system or mobile APIs to perform tasks (playing music, connecting with IoT, launching an app). The response is then delivered in the form of output tasks performed (music playing on the speaker, smart bulb switched on /off, or any other task as given by the voice command.

Figure 3 shows a typical model of the Amazon Alexa Voice service model, which utilizes its own Alexa devices, and cloud services. The Amazon Voice Assistants namely Alexa, Echo, and Echo Dot devices take voice as input through a microphone, and a speaker, and use the wake word 'Alexa' to start. Once the Voice Assistant is activated, the device records audio and transmits it into the Amazon cloud services for pre-processing for the audio information. The advanced computations for Automatic Speech Recognition and Natural Language Processing are also done at Amazon Alexa Cloud services [7, 10, 14]. Third-party IoT devices like Philips Hue, August Wi-Fi, and other companion apps of Amazon Alexa provide additional voice-controlled functionalities for smart home skill adapters. Third-party applications such as ride-sharing apps, and food ordering apps are also integrated and enrich the user experience [14].

Figure 4 shows the working of a Google Assistant, and its interaction with an Android app to use the voice command for ordering pizza. The user gives a voice command "Order pizza from an App". Upon receiving the voice command, Google Assistant processes it and selects the appropriate app through matching Android intents. The Android app executes the action and responds to the user through Google Assistant that the task of ordering pizza has been completed [21].

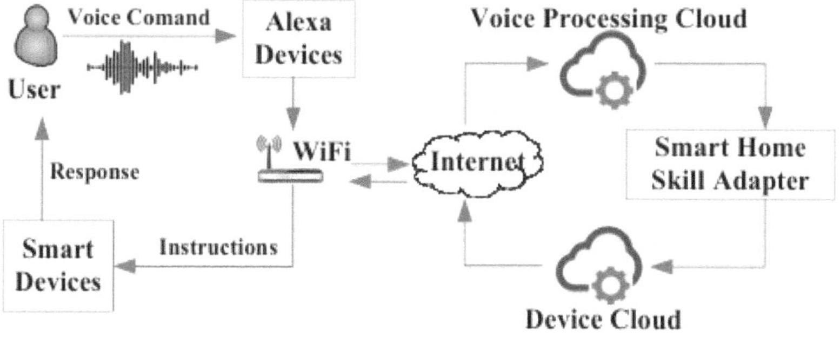

Fig. 3. Alexa Voice Service Model [7]

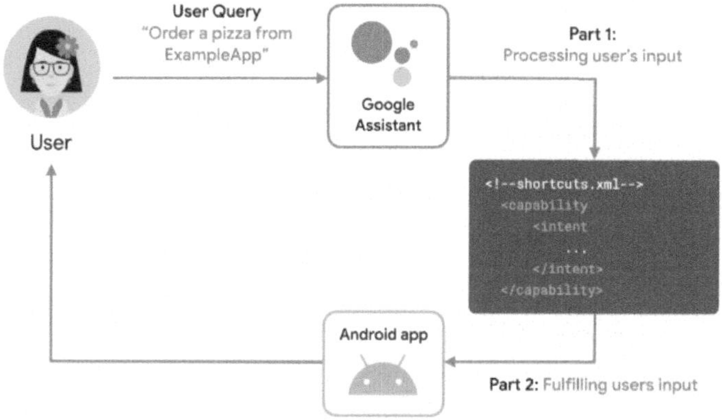

Fig. 4. The Google Voice Assistant App Action Model [21]

The Hey Siri, Voice Assistant workflow is shown in Fig. 5. Voice commands as audio input are captured through Core Audio and passed to the Voice Trigger Framework. Voice Trigger Framework pre-processes the audio input and sends it to Siri Server. The Siri Server checks up on the initial words of a voice command and may decide to drop the trigger. The Siri client is triggered by the wake-up word 'hey Siri' and executes tasks and sends the desired output.

The architecture and design of Voice Assistants may contain design flaws or hidden vulnerabilities. The vulnerabilities are then detected and exploited by the attackers causing security and privacy challenges. In the next section, common attacks and security challenges on Voice assistants are presented.

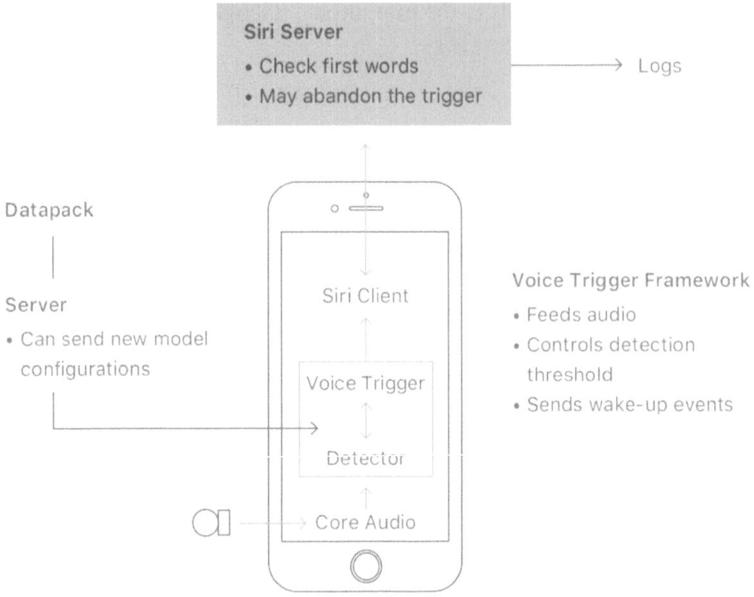

Fig. 5. The Hey Siri flow on iPhone [20]

4 Vulnerabilities and Security Challenges

The ease of being hands-free and using voice commands, advancements in processing of speech and audio signals, sophisticated methods of AI, NLP, and machine learning algorithms, and integration of IOT devices and third-party applications have made Voice Assistants an inevitable part of daily life [16]. The increasingly growing technology and development leave certain loopholes in the design and implementation of Voice Assistants, speech recognition models, and Android apps [23]. It has been reported that 20 million Amazon echo dot devices and Google Assistants are vulnerable to Bluetooth hack attacks [30]. Attackers have exploited such vulnerabilities and pose significant concerns regarding possible security breaches and privacy violations [17].

A) **Vulnerabilities in recognizing audio Signals:** The audio signals are recognized by Automated Speech Recognition (ASR) models that convert audio signals to text. However, attackers are capable of injecting inaudible ultrasound signals in the voice commands to Voice Assistants. The ultrasound signals are inaudible to human ears but can easily be interpreted by ASR systems and converted to text that triggers the Voice Assistant servers to respond to a task. When the inaudible signals are injected into pre-trained datasets, they lead to back door attacks in ASR systems of Voice Assistants [15]. The inaudible signals are also hidden inside music clips, and voice mail messages [15]. Examples of such attacks using ultrasonic waves to trigger voice commands in Automatic Speech recognition systems are backdoor attacks [15], adversarial attacks in recurrent neural networks, deep learning algorithms [14], Dolphin Attacks [9, 14], Surfing Attacks [9], Automatic Speech Recognition Errors

[14], Near Ultrasound Inaudible Trojan (NUIT) [1, 3–5, 31] attacks to control Voice Assistants (Apple Siri, Amazon Alexa, Google Assistant).

Voice Assistants are also susceptible to Electromagnetic Wave (EM) interference that uses FM waves and the FM antenna of the microphone in smartphones. The malicious voice commands were hidden and injected using EM signals via a microphone/headphone that acts as an FM antenna [6].

B) **Vulnerabilities in Authorisation Mechanisms:** Security attacks are executed because of vulnerabilities in Speech Identification algorithms by spoofing the voice of a user. Speech recognition derives 'what was spoken' whereas speech identification derives 'who was the speaker'. Voice Assistants comprise a component called speech identification or voice authentication [12, 15] to identify the speaker using acoustic and signal characteristics. The speech identification module in Voice Assistant is susceptible to voice spoofing [22], voice replay, impersonation, speech synthesis, voice conversion, and adversarial attacks [15]. The attacker injects spoofed voice or replays an already sent voice command to trigger the Voice Assistant. The voice commands can unlock a locked screen due to glitches detected in Siri and Cortana by using spoofed and replayed voice commands. Moreover, voice spoofing attacks can trigger the launch of other apps, send SMS, and voice messages, delete the data, and bypass the authentication mechanism. Voice masquerading attacks [14] occur due to the exploitation of a vulnerability by an attacker to switch or terminate the task and skills through voice impersonation. Voice Authentication mechanisms

C) **Vulnerabilities in Cloud Services:** Voice assistants, like Amazon Alexa, Google Assistant, and Siri, utilize the services of the cloud for voice pre-processing, storage, running NLP algorithms, and delivering the response. The use of cloud services brings vulnerabilities and attacks associated with them. The attacks due to cloud vulnerabilities are Man-in-the-middle attacks, data poisoning, data privacy risks, network traffic analysis, skill squatting attacks, insecure API, and third-party apps [14].

D) **Vulnerabilities in connecting other devices:** Voice Assistants (such as Alexa Echo dot) interpret malicious voice commands to connect with nearby Bluetooth devices [14]. The BlueBorne attack connects Bluetooth devices, smartphones, smart TVs, IoT devices, speakers, microphones, and smart devices to gain control and steal data, spread malware, or even trigger the task of switching on/off a smart home device. Other similar attacks are booting a device firmware, device pairing protocol attack, and REEVE attack. Remote Voice Control attack (REEVE) exploits devices like TVs, speakers, radios, smart home appliances, and smart vehicles to gain unauthorized access and even send multiple voice commands to trigger a denial-of-service (DOS), cross-site scripting (XSS) attack.

Voice assistants are prone to hidden vulnerabilities in speech recognition, speaker identification, cloud services, and authentication mechanisms. They are compromised through voice spoofing, adversarial attacks, man-in-the-middle-attack, network analysis, and gaining unauthorized access to data and devices triggering undesired tasks without the knowledge of the users.

5 Mitigation Approaches

In literature, different mitigation approaches to minimize the risk and security breaches while using the voice assistants have been proposed.

A) **Vulnerabilities in Authorization Mechanism:** Attacks on voice assistants due to weak authentication mechanism can be prevented by implementing two-factor authentication. REEVE attacks can be mitigated by implementing a voice authentication mechanism, two-factor authentication, and VSButton [7], biometric-based voice authentication [33] to ensure the physical presence of the user [14].

B) **Vulnerabilities in recognizing audio Signals:** Voice injection attacks in speech recognition and speech identification components can be minimized through the use of feature-based methods or acoustic features to improve speaker privacy [12, 16]. Privacy-preserving for Occupancy Estimation [26, 27] technique preserves speaker occupancy while remaining related to speaker identity. Another method, speaker anonymization [24, 25] removes the personal information from the speaker's speech while retaining other audio attributes. These methods ensure audio privacy and maintain the quality of the speech [16].

   Hidden voice commands can be identified by using learning algorithms that differentiate conventional and hidden voice instructions, ultrasonic, and other EM signals [15]. Such detection algorithms will extract temporal and frequency-based characteristics from acoustic signals. This will further help in identifying and analyzing audio signatures of spoken commands in the vibration domain. The vibrations detected by motion sensors are difficult to replicate and bypass the authentication mechanisms [28].

   Surfing and Dolphin attacks can be prevented by reducing or eliminating acoustic vibrations that fall in the range of ultrasonic waves. Another category of defense against Dolphin attacks is to improve the microphone's hardware that differentiates the frequency of attack and normal signals [15, 29].

C) **Vulnerabilities in Cloud Services, Third Party Integrations and Skill Intents:** Various mitigation approaches have been presented by the authors of [14] to prevent security breaches due to third party integration and skill intents. Skill Squatting attacks can be prevented by using a Skill Response checker, word-based techniques, and a User intention classifier.

D) **Vulnerabilities in connecting other devices:** Connecting other devices via Bluetooth also pose risk due to vulnerabilities in Bluetooth functionalities. The BlueBorn attack due to connecting with other Bluetooth devices can be preventing by updating the devices with security patch. Moreover, secure configuration, strong password, two-way authentication, avoiding auto-connect for the Bluetooth security prevent from connecting with insecure devices via Bluetooth.

Specialized defense measures that are easy to implement without affecting the performance and quality of Voice assistants include voiceprint verification to prevent normal speech attacks, signal distortion detection to prevent voice spoofing attacks, audio transformation for preventing adversarial voice commands, and strict skill certification to thwart malicious skill attacks [13]. The security attacks can also be minimized if users avoid high-risk applications such as banking apps, and unlocking homes using voice assistants [13].

6 Conclusion

This paper provides a comprehensive survey of security and privacy concerns of voice assistants along with the mitigation techniques. The general architecture overview of a voice assistant is provided in the paper. An overview of several types of attacks, voice spoofing, surfing attacks, adversarial examples, inaudible ultrasonic signals, BlueBorn attacks, REEVE attacks, and skill squatting, were categorized based on vulnerabilities in the component of Voice Assistant namely, speech recognition mechanisms, speech authentication mechanisms, vulnerabilities in cloud services and vulnerabilities in connecting devices. The mitigation approaches to prevent different voice injection commands are also presented. In the future, the authors intend to present a model that will improve voice authentication, speech recognition, speech identification, and detection of inaudible waves in Voice Assistants.

References

1. NVD - Home. https://nvd.nist.gov/. Accessed 26 Sept 2024
2. Rogers, P.: Voice Search Statistics 2024 (Usage & Emerging Trends) (2024). https://www.answeriq.com/voice-search-statistics/. Accessed 24 Sept 2024
3. Sophos News: Siri and Google assistant hacked in New Ultrasonic attack, Sophos News (2020). https://news.sophos.com/en-us/2020/03/02/siri-and-google-assistant-hacked-in-new-ultrasonic-attack/. Accessed 24 Sept 2024
4. CERT-IN: CERT-in issues advisory related to vulnerabilities in these Apple platforms, Business Standard (2024). https://www.business-standard.com/technology/tech-news/cert-in-issues-advisory-related-to-vulnerabilities-in-these-apple-platforms-124080500681_1.html. Accessed 24 Sept 2024
5. Alepis, E., Patsakis, C.: Monkey says monkey does: security and privacy on voice assistants. IEEE Access **5**, 17841–17851 (2017)
6. Kasmi, C., Esteves, J.L.: IEMI threats for information security: remote command injection on modern smartphones. IEEE Trans. Electromagn. Compat. **57**(6), 17521755 (2015)
7. Lei, X., Tu, G.H., Liu, A.X., Li, C.Y., Xie, T.: The insecurity of home digital voice assistants-vulnerabilities, attacks, and countermeasures. In: 2018 IEEE conference on communications and network security (CNS), pp. 1–9. IEEE (2018)
8. Pal, D., Arpnikanondt, C., Razzaque, M.A., Funilkul, S.: To trust or not trust: privacy issues with voice assistants. IT Prof. **22**(5), 46–53 (2020)
9. Yan, Q., Liu, K., Zhou, Q., Guo, H., Zhang, N.: Surfing attack: interactive hidden attack on voice assistants using ultrasonic guided waves. In: Network and Distributed Systems Security (NDSS) Symposium (2020)
10. Bolton, T., Dargahi, T., Belguith, S., Al-Rakhami, M.S., Sodhro, A.H.: On the security and privacy challenges of virtual assistants. Sensors **21**(7), 2312 (2021)
11. Talebi, S.M.S., Sani, A.A., Saroiu, S., Wolman, A.: MegaMind: a platform for security & privacy extensions for voice assistants. In: Proceedings of the 19th Annual International Conference on Mobile Systems, Applications, and Services, pp. 109–121 (2021)

12. Cheng, P., Roedig, U.: Personal voice assistant security and privacy—a survey. Proc. IEEE **110**(4), 476–507 (2022)
13. Yan, C., Ji, X., Wang, K., Jiang, Q., Jin, Z., Xu, W.: A survey on voice assistant security: attacks and countermeasures. ACM Comput. Surv.Comput. Surv. **55**(4), 1–36 (2022)
14. Pathak, S., Islam, S.A., Jiang, H., Xu, L., Tomai, E.: A survey on security analysis of Amazon Echo devices. High-Confidence Comput. **2**(4), 100087 (2022)
15. Li, J., Chen, C., Azghadi, M.R., Ghodosi, H., Pan, L., Zhang, J.: Security and privacy problems in voice assistant applications: a survey. Comput. Secur.. Secur. **134**, 103448 (2023)
16. Ren, Z., Qian, K., Schultz, T., Schuller, B.W.: An overview of the ICASSP special session on AI security and privacy in speech and audio processing. In: Proceedings of the 5th ACM International Conference on Multimedia in Asia Workshops, pp. 1–6 (2023)
17. Gupta, C., Singh, R.K., Mohapatra, A.K.: A formal approach for implementing security constraints in security patterns. In: 2021 9th International Conference on Reliability, Infocom Technologies and Optimization (Trends and Future Directions) (ICRITO), pp. 1–7. IEEE (2021)
18. Gupta, C., Singh, R.K., Mohapatra, A.K.: Securing web applications using security patterns. In: ICT for Competitive Strategies, pp. 485–494. CRC Press (2020)
19. Mishra, P., Gupta, C.: Cookies in cross-site scripting: type, utilization, detection, protection, and remediation. In: 2020 8th International Conference on Reliability, Infocom Technologies and Optimization (Trends and Future Directions) (ICRITO), pp. 1056–1059. IEEE (2020)
20. https://machinelearning.apple.com/research/hey-siri
21. https://developer.android.com/develop/devices/assistant/overview
22. Anniappa, D., Kim, Y.: Security and privacy issues with virtual private voice assistants. In: 2021 IEEE 11th Annual Computing and Communication Workshop and Conference (CCWC), pp. 0702–0708. IEEE (2021)
23. Gupta, C., Singh, R.K., Bhatia, S.K., Mohapatra, A.K.: DecaDroid classification and characterization of malicious behavior in Android applications. Int. J. Inf. Secur. Priv. (IJISP) **14**(4), 57–73 (2020)
24. Tomashenko, N., et al.: The Voice Privacy 2022 challenge evaluation plan. arXiv preprint arXiv:2203.12468, 20 p (2022)
25. Tomashenko, N., et al.: The voice privacy 2020 challenge: results and findings. Comput. Speech Lang.. Speech Lang. **74**(2022), 101362 (2022)
26. Williams, J., Yazdanpanah, V., Stein, S.: PrivacyPreserving occupancy estimation. In: Proceedings of ICASSP, Rhodes Island, Greece (2023)
27. Zen, H., et al.: LibriTTS: a corpus derived from LibriSpeech for text-to-speech. In: Proceedings of INTERSPEECH, Graz, Austria, pp. 1526–1530 (2019)
28. Wang, C., Anand, S.A., Liu, J., Walker, P., Chen, Y., Saxena, N.: Defeating hidden audio channel attacks on voice assistants via audio-induced surface vibrations. In: Proceedings of the 35th Annual Computer Security Applications Conference, pp. 42–56 (2019)
29. Zhang, G., Yan, C., Ji, X., Zhang, T., Zhang, T., Xu, W.: Dolphin attack: Inaudible voice commands. In: Proceedings of the 2017 ACM SIGSAC Conference on Computer and Communications Security, pp. 103–117 (2017)
30. The Hacker News: Bluetooth hack affects 20 million Amazon Echo and google home devices, The Hacker News (2017). https://thehackernews.com/2017/11/amazon-alexa-hacking-bluetooth.html. Accessed 24 Sept 2024
31. Robert Lemos, C.W.: Hey, Siri: Hackers can control smart devices using inaudible sounds, Hey, Siri: Hackers Can Control Smart Devices Using Inaudible Sounds (2023). https://www.darkreading.com/vulnerabilities-threats/siri-hackers-control-smart-devices-inaudible-sounds. Accessed 24 Sept 2024
32. Mishra, A.: Privacy of the People: Alexa, Google, Siri, we hear for you (2024). https://internetfreedom.in/privacy-of-the-people-voice-assistants/. Accessed 24 Sept 2024

33. Zhang, L., Tan, S., Yang, J.: Hearing your voice is not enough: an articulatory gesture based liveness detection for voice authentication. In: ACM CCS (2017)

Author Index

A. Sharma and R. Rani (Eds.): AIST 2024, CCIS 2389, pp. 359–361, 2025.
https://doi.org/10.1007/978-3-031-91331-0

The manufacturer's authorised representative in the EU is Springer Nature Customer Service Centre GmbH, Europaplatz 3, 69115 Heidelberg, Germany. If you have any concerns regarding our products, please contact ProductSafety@springernature.com

Printed and bound by CPI Group (UK) Ltd, Croydon, CR0 4YY
30/09/2026
02225560-0012